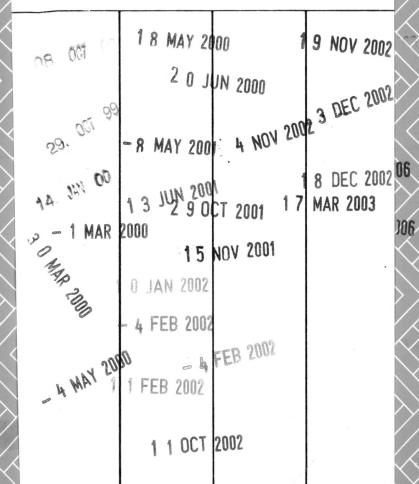

Adding Value

**Comparative and International Business Series:
Modern Histories**
Edited by Geoffrey Jones and Mira Wilkins

Banks as Multinationals
Edited by Geoffrey Jones

Industrial Training and Technological Innovation
Edited by Howard F. Gospel

The Rise and Fall of Mass Marketing
Edited by Richard S. Tedlow and Geoffrey Jones

The Precision Makers
Mari E. W. Williams

The Growth of Global Business
Edited by Howard Cox, Jeremy Clegg and Grazia Ietto-Gillies

Adding Value

Brands and Marketing in Food and Drink

Edited by Geoffrey Jones and Nicholas J. Morgan

London and New York

First published 1994
by Routledge
11 New Fetter Lane, London EC4P 4EE

Simultaneously published in the USA and Canada
by Routledge
29 West 35th Street, New York, NY 10001

© 1994 Geoffrey Jones and Nicholas J. Morgan

Typeset in English Times
by Pat and Anne Murphy, Highcliffe-on-Sea, Dorset
Printed and bound in Great Britain by
Mackays of Chatham PLC, Chatham, Kent

British Library Cataloguing in Publication Data
A catalogue record for this book is available from the
British Library
ISBN 0−415−09516−6

Library of Congress Cataloging in Publication Data
Adding Value: brands and marketing in food and drink/edited
by Geoffrey Jones and Nicholas J. Morgan.
    p.   cm. − (Comparative and international business)
Includes bibliographical references and index.
ISBN 0−415−09516−6
1. Food − Marketing − History.
2. Beverages − Marketing − History.
3. Alcoholic beverages − Marketing − History.
4. Brand name products − Marketing − History.
I. Morgan, Nicholas, 1955−   .   II. Series.
HD9000.5.M352   1994   93-26161
664'.0068'8−dc20   CIP

Contents

vi *Contents*

Figures

Tables

Contributors

V. N. Balasubramanyam is professor of development economics at Lancaster University. His main research interests are in international trade and international investment. His publications include *International Transfer of Technology to India* (1973), *The Economy of India* (1984) and *Multinational Enterprise in the Third World* (1980). He has also written on international trade in services and entrepreneurship in the British food and drink industries.

Mark Casson is professor of economics and head of the department of economics at the University of Reading. His recent publications include *Enterprise and Competitiveness* (1990) and *Economics of Business Culture* (1991).

E. J. T. Collins is director of the Rural History Centre at the University of Reading. He has published extensively in the fields of agricultural and food history. His food interests focus on food growing and the American influence on British diet. He is editor of the *Agrarian History of England and Wales, vol vii, 1850–1914*.

T. A. B. Corley has recently retired from the department of economics at the University of Reading. He has published extensively in the field of business history, most notably on the growth of multinational enterprise. His history of Huntley & Palmers was followed by a two-volume history of the Burmah Oil Company.

August W. Giebelhaus is professor and director of the School of History, Technology and Society at the Georgia Institute of Technology. Among his publications are *Business and Government in the Oil Industry: A Case Study of Sun Oil, 1876–1945* (1980); (ed. with Lewis Perelman and Michael Yokell) *Energy Transitions: Long-Term Perspectives* (1981); (with Robert C. McMath et al.) *Engineering the New South: Georgia Tech, 1885–1985* (1985); and (with Rodney

Carlisle) *Bartlesville Energy Center: The Federal Government in Petroleum Research, 1918–1983* (1985). He was formerly associate editor of *Technology and Culture* and remains on the editorial board of that journal.

Geoffrey Jones is professor of business history in the economics department of the University of Reading. He is the author or editor of fifteen books on the history of international business and marketing, including *The State and the Emergence of the British Oil Industry* (1981); *Banking and Empire in Iran* (1986): (ed.) *Banks as Multinationals* (1990); (ed. with Harm Schröter) *The Rise of Multinationals in Continental Europe* (1993); (ed. with R. S. Tedlow) *The Rise and Fall of Mass Marketing* (1993); and *British Multinational Banking 1830– 1990* (1993). He is co-editor of the journal *Business History*, and was president of the Association of Business Historians in 1992–3.

Hans Chr. Johansen is professor of economic history at the University of Odense in Denmark. He has published extensively in the fields of business history, historical demography, mercantilism, and the history of transport and communications. Among his books in Danish business history are histories of the Albany Breweries, the Danish cement industry, the insurance company Alm. Brand, and the Danfoss concern.

David Merrett is an associate professor in economic history at the University of Melbourne where he teaches Australian banking and business history. He has published extensively in the area of Australian economic history, concentrating on banking. His contributions to this field include *ANZ Bank* (1985). He is a past co-editor of the *Australian Economic History Review*.

Nicholas J. Morgan is archivist with United Distillers, the spirits company of Guinness plc, where he is involved with the marketing of spirits brands. Formerly a lecturer in Scottish history at Glasgow University, he has published widely on business and urban history.

Christopher Napier is senior lecturer in accounting at the London School of Economics and Ronald Leach Fellow of the Institute of Chartered Accountants in England and Wales. He has published extensively in the fields of corporate financial reporting and accounting history, and is currently researching into the emergence and development of British corporate accounting principles over the last 150 years.

M. A. Salisu is a lecturer in econometrics and development economics at the University of Maiduguri in Nigeria. He is currently on leave from the University of Maiduguri and is Guinness Teaching Fellow in the department of economics, Lancaster University. His doctoral dissertation completed at Lancaster University is on 'Oil and the Nigerian Economy'. His publications include articles and reviews on foreign direct investment. Currently he is working on foreign direct investment and trade aspects of the British food and drink industries.

Leigh Sparks is professor of retail studies at the Institute for Retail Studies and head of the department of marketing at the University of Stirling, Scotland. He has been researching retail and distribution topics for thirteen years and has published widely on his research results through both journal articles and book chapters. He obtained his PhD from the University of Wales for work on employment aspects of food superstores; his first degree is in geography from Cambridge University. He is co-editor of the *International Review of Retail, Distribution and Consumer Research*, which is published by Routledge.

Vernon Ward is head of the department of technology and consumer sciences at Roehampton Institute, London. Formerly an economist with the Government Economic Service, he has published on the economics of renewable energy resources, energy use within the food manufacturing industries and, while at Central Statistical Office, also published on the use of consumer confidence surveys for short-term forecasting of consumers' expenditure.

R. B. Weir is provost of Derwent College, University of York, and a member of the department of economics. He has published widely on the Scottish whisky industry and is currently writing a history of the Distillers Company.

Greg Whitwell is senior lecturer in economic history at the University of Melbourne. He is the author of *The Treasury Line* (1986), *Making the Market: The Rise of Consumer Society* (1989), and (with Diane Sydenham) *A Shared Harvest: The Australian Wheat Industry, 1939–89* (1991).

Mira Wilkins is professor of economics at Florida International University, Miami, Florida. Her many publications include *The Emergence of Multinational Enterprise: American Business Abroad from the Colonial Era to 1914* (1970), *The Maturing of Multinational Enterprise: American Business Abroad from 1914 to 1970* (1974), and

The History of Foreign Investment in the United States to 1914 (1989). Her article, 'The neglected intangible asset: the influence of the trade mark on the rise of the modern corporation', published in *Business History* (1992), received the 1993 Cass Prize for the best article of the prior year.

Bridget Williams is archivist and historian to the Sainsbury group, which includes the hypermarket subsidiary Savacentre, Homebase, a DIY chain which is jointly owned with GB-Inno-BM of Belgium, and the US supermarket company Shaw's Supermarket Inc. She was educated at Exeter and Leicester Universities and is a visiting fellow in business history at the University of Reading. She has lectured widely on the use of business archives as a marketing resource. She edited *And the Two Became One: An Informal History of Shaw's* (1992).

Richard G. Wilson is director of the Centre of East Anglian Studies at the University of East Anglia. He has written widely on the brewing industry, including *Greene King: A Business and Family History* (1983) and (with T. R. Gourvish) *The British Brewing Industry, 1830–1980* (1994).

Preface

This is the second book on the history of marketing to emanate from the business history group at the University of Reading. The first, Richard S. Tedlow and Geoffrey Jones (eds) *The Rise and Fall of Mass Marketing* (1993), examined the development of mass marketing in the United States and, later, elsewhere, and the subsequent challenge that it faced from the adaptable marketing systems which emerged in the late twentieth century. This volume retains the internationally comparative focus of its predecessor, but takes a more in-depth look at the evolution of marketing, and in particular the history of branding. We believe that this book represents a major and original addition to a still-sparse literature on this subject.

This volume grew out of a conference held at the University of Reading, UK, in April 1993. In addition to the contributors to the volume, Jonathan Brown, Frank H. H. King, Alan McKinlay, Peter Mathias, Michael Moss and Oliver Westall contributed to the success of the original meeting. The conference was generously sponsored by United Distillers. Michael Burkham and Clive Simms, former and present employees of United Distillers, made important contributions to the conference discussions, as did Gerry Landers, of Brands Positioning Services. Michael Burkham and Dr E. J. T. Collins, the director of the Rural History Centre at the University of Reading, played key roles in the initiative to hold a conference on this subject. Although the chapters in this book began their lives at the conference, they have been rewritten for publication, some of them extensively.

Lynn Cornell undertook most of the conference administration, and has played an indispensable role in getting the book ready for publication.

Geoffrey Jones
Nicholas J. Morgan
Reading and Edinburgh

1 Brands and marketing

Geoffrey Jones

Adding value, according to a recent book on corporate strategy, is 'both the proper motivation of corporate activity and the measure of its achievement' (Kay 1993: 19). Firms add value in many ways. This volume considers one of the most important: their marketing strategies. Marketing involves a complex range of issues, including logistics, pricing and positioning decisions, advertising, packaging and branding. All of them are considered here, but the discussion has been focused in order to allow a consideration of issues in-depth.

There is, first, a focus on branding. It is, perhaps, an exaggeration to claim that 'the primary capital of many businesses is their brand' (Kapferer 1992: 8), but in certain industries and products there is a great deal of truth in such a view. The following chapters explore a number of crucial questions about brands. What is their function? What is the difference between a product and a brand? What is the value of a brand? How were successful brands created? How have some national brands spread across borders to become global brands?

The second focus is on food and drink. There are considerable differences in marketing strategies between consumer and industrial goods, and between durable goods, non-durable goods and services. Branding is relevant only for a limited range of commodities, of which food and drink products are among the most prominent. However, it is believed that the material presented here is of relevance and use to a much wider range of industries than food and drink.

The concentration on food and drink helps to explain the otherwise obsessive preoccupation with the English-speaking world. The marketing stories explored here – Coca-Cola, Kellogg, Johnnie Walker, Foster's Lager, Sainsbury's – originate from the United States, the United Kingdom or Australia, though some non-Anglo-Saxon companies and products – such as Carlsberg – are considered. Food and drink are industries in which companies from the English-speaking countries have traditional – and continuing – strengths. By 1914 US entrepreneurs had developed a range of products and brands which were to dominate the world industry for the rest of the century: examples included Coca-Cola, Heinz, Campbell Soup and Quaker Oats (Chandler 1990: 149–57). British firms developed fewer global brands, but their influence in food and drink was almost as great. In the 1980s the internationally competitive position of Britain in consumer packaged goods remained a strong part of an otherwise mediocre economy (Porter 1990: 482–96). A volume on brands and marketing of cars and consumer electronics would draw on many Japanese examples. In food and drink, the Americans, British and Australians offer instructive cases.

The third focus is historical. Marketing practitioners and marketing academics have rarely displayed much interest in the history of marketing, but since the early 1980s this situation has changed and there has been 'a stunning growth' of research on the subject, at least in the United States (Hollander and Rassuli 1993: xv). The literature on the history of marketing elsewhere is less rich, although recently there has been a steady stream of publications on Britain (Corley 1987; Davenport-Hines 1986; Tedlow and Jones 1993). The very nature of a brand, whose identity is built over time and which can rest so fundamentally on its heritage, makes an historical approach particularly appropriate. Many of the following chapters draw on completely new research as they explore brands and marketing over time. Together, they represent an important addition to the literature on the history of marketing, and add an historical perspective to subjects of major strategic importance in contemporary business.

The chapters in this volume fall into four groups. Chapters 2 to 5 raise many of the key issues of this volume. In particular, they explore the nature and functions of brands, and their value – to firms, consumers and society as a whole. Wilkins provides the essential historical framework in her study of how and when brand names developed in the food and drink industries. She traces their origins back 4,000 years, but shows that in their modern form their growth can be more precisely correlated with the key changes in economic and business life in the late nineteenth century: the rise of the modern industrial enterprise, the development of national as opposed to local markets, changes in the technology of food and drink processing, and urbanization and rising personal incomes.

Wilkins takes us to the heart of brands. Brands guarantee quality and performance delivery. They are a haven of stability in an unstable, or unknown, world. They became important, Wilkins argues, when producers ceased to know consumers personally, as was the case from the late nineteenth century. Their essential and positive function was to convey information. Brands inform the consumer about a product, provide a guarantee of continuing standards of quality, and enhance consumer choice. The reduction of time in transactions lowers the costs of food and drink. There are equal benefits for producers. Brand names enabled firms to expand their markets, and thereby achieve economies of scale and scope, and to use intermediaries and develop modern means of distribution.

Casson, in Chapter 3, also addresses the function of brands, and their welfare consequences, but arrives at some different conclusions from Wilkins. Casson begins by disagreeing with views that branding automatically promotes economic efficiency by improving the quality of consumer information. Branding can suppress information to consumers, and there might in any case be other ways of improving consumer information of more value to society. Brands also do more than provide information – a point with which, incidentally, Wilkins readily agrees. They transmit various 'cultural' characteristics which manipulate consumer demand. They provide a badge of allegiance, and convey messages about status. Such attributes of brands are well established. The 'identity' of a brand consists of a great deal more than a physical description of a product and a guarantee of consistency. Brands develop personalities. They symbolize sets of values, including cultural values of one sort or another. A brand reflects a consumer's image – not necessarily who they are, but who they wish to be seen to be (Kapferer 1992: 30–45). This is an important reason why brands are so important for alcoholic drinks such as whisky or beer, which are often consumed in public places. It is these characteristics of brands which play such a decisive role in developing a consumer franchise that insulates a brand owner from price competition.

It is the consequences of these branding characteristics that most divides Wilkins and Casson. For Wilkins, consumers are given the choice of which 'image' they want to purchase. If the reality of the product does not please her or him, there will be no repeat purchase. For Casson, consumer preferences can be manipulated in ways which make their choice illusory. He points in particular to the fact that mass-produced branded products are often targeted on consumers in the lower social groups. This means that the premium prices charged for branded products are often borne by the poorer sections of society. From the point of view of society, Casson concludes, it might be better to improve reality than to sell dreams and fantasies.

Balasubramanyam and Salisu examine in Chapter 4 the different strands of the conventional economics literature on brands. They begin by considering the debates on the social costs of advertising, but, unlike Casson, incline to the view that advertising plays an important role in educating consumers, whatever manipulative features it may possess. Brands are part and parcel of modern affluent consumer societies, the authors argue. Ostentation and status seeking are features of the consumption patterns of such societies: by facilitating such consumer desires, brands and advertising perform a useful function for society as a whole. There is little evidence, they conclude from their examination of the alcoholic drinks industry, that the spirits distilling firms are able to significantly impact total consumer expenditure on alcohol, although they can shift spending between brands. Balasubramanyam and Salisu also explore the literature on the importance of product differentiation as a barrier to entry of new firms into an industry. It is evident that in young markets the first successful brand can benefit from pioneer advantages, although some would argue that such advantages are not great unless consumers are satisfied with the product. What brands can do is contribute to the exploitation of economies of scale and scope in production and distribution.

In Chapter 5, Napier approaches the role of brands in adding value from another direction: the value of brands on balance sheets. From the mid-1980s, as brands acquired almost a cult status in consumer industries, there was a growing debate on their actual accounting value. This raised in turn wider issues relating to the valuation of intangible assets which had been debated among accountants for decades. Different countries reacted differently to the problem. Germany and Japan were resistant to the concept of brand capitalization. In the United States, accounting conventions made it difficult to show intangibles as assets in company accounts, although there is now an emerging wider debate on the inclusion of 'soft' assets on US balance sheets. British companies were more radical in brand valuation, a development stimulated by the high level of corporate acquisition activity seen in the United Kingdom in the 1980s. A series of British companies in the 1980s capitalized the brands of acquired companies, and in 1988 one large firm went even further and capitalized its own home-grown brands, thereby considerably increasing the size of its balance sheet.

As Napier shows, the debate over brand valuation poses extreme difficulties. While few would now deny the role of brands in 'adding value', existing brand valuation techniques appear less than wholly reliable. Some of the problems were graphically illustrated by the Philip Morris decision in early 1993 to sharply reduce the price of its Marlboro cigarette. The Marlboro brand – the product of 'one of the most successful marketing campaigns in history' (Kay 1993: 258) – had been hailed as the world's most valuable brand in the early 1990s, but had suddenly experienced rapidly falling sales because of competition from cheaper alternatives. The Marlboro price cuts led, in the short term, to substantial reductions in the share prices of many of the world's leading branded goods businesses. The episode did not spell the 'end of brands', but it certainly illustrated why financial accountants still remained to be convinced about brand valuation techniques.

The issues raised in these opening chapters reappear throughout the rest of this volume, but a number of new themes are also introduced. The chapters which follow demonstrate how successful brands in food and drink were created, and show why some have survived and prospered over long periods. The authors also explore how some brands – outstandingly Coca-Cola – have spread across borders to become global. However, there are also studies of the demise of brands, or their relative decline in the face of new competition.

The four chapters in Part II are concerned specifically with aspects of the history of the marketing of alcoholic drinks. Wilson in Chapter 6 examines the marketing of beer in Victorian Britain. A central theme is the rise of large national brewers in Britain between 1830 and 1900, which included a small number of really big firms such as Bass and Guinness. The marketing strategies of these breweries were centred on networks of agents, which permitted them to break out of their local areas and reach wider markets. Brand names also appeared in this period, but the Victorian brewers maintained that their key competitive advantage lay in maintaining product quality and consistency. Brands have a voice and exist only through communication, but in this period before the extensive use of advertising by brewers, the voice was largely the spread of reputations by word-of-mouth.

Beer is also the subject matter of Chapter 7. Johansen explores the reasons why foreign beers have made such a minor impact on the Danish market, while Danish beers have been a notable international success, at least from the 1950s. The lack of import penetration was in part the result of consumer loyalty to Danish products, but also important were a long tradition of trade barriers and to other legislation which prescribed the use of cans and certain types of bottles. From the 1890s the Danish industry was dominated by two firms that eventually merged in 1970 to create Carlsberg; it proved hard for any other brewer to challenge the market leaders, at least until the advent of supermarket own brands. The success of Danish beer abroad was based on considerable technical expertise in beer making. In this case, as in the others considered here, it is evident that strong brands can be considered as the rewards earned by a company for the quality of its product. Equally, however, not all good products become strong brands. Carlsberg had a successful marketing strategy, which included the creation of an attractive image for Danish beer, and the adept use of licensing and foreign direct investment strategies to penetrate foreign markets.

In Chapter 8 attention moves from beer to whisky. Weir focuses on the Distillers Company which, following a large merger in 1925, marketed about 60 per cent of Scotch whisky. From the point of view of this book, Scotch whisky is particularly interesting because of its long history of market segmentation. It had developed a national and international market from the 1860s with the rise of bottled, blended and branded whiskies (Morgan and Moss 1993: 122–3). After 1925 Distillers owned five of the seven leading brands of Scotch whisky, including the renowned Johnnie Walker Scotch whisky. Building on a tradition going back to 1820, Red Label and Black Label (a deluxe blend) were launched as brands in 1909. Distillers itself was eventually taken over in 1986 by Guinness. Weir draws a comparison between the 1920s and the 1980s, both periods when Scotch whisky faced declining demand. Some of the economic theories considered earlier would have predicted that Distillers' brand portfolio would have served as an effective barrier to entry to the industry, but the actual result was the opposite in the 1980s. When Distillers' management responded slowly to a loss of market share, the firm became subject to rival take-over bids which led to its acquisition.

Subsequently, under the control of Guinness, the brands of United Distillers were repositioned with an emphasis on high value-added brands and margins. The revival of the Johnnie Walker brand, the repositioning of Red Label, whose image had gravely deteriorated, and the brand extension strategies to use the Johnnie Walker name to fill high-priced and profitable gaps in international markets, became instant case studies in successful brand management (Kapferer 1992: 131–3). Weir leaves open the question whether the strategy of 'squeezing added value from brands' (p. 159) will be sustainable in the long term. Almost certainly, the brand identity of Scotch whisky makes such a strategy more viable than for products such as Marlboro cigarettes.

Merrett and Whitwell in Chapter 9 explain the reasons for the success of Australian beer and wine in Britain over recent decades.

Branding played a very important part in the foreign marketing of Australian beer. By the early 1980s two national brewers had emerged in Australia, who used brands as a tool in their fierce competitive rivalry. Having developed national brands and considerable brand management skills, the Australian brewers looked abroad for new markets. Australian beer brands, notably Foster's Lager, entered Britain in the wake of the young Australian expatriates who settled there in the 1960s, but they took off only when the Australian beer began to be produced under licence in Britain. In the mid-1980s the Australians strengthened their position by acquiring British brewers. Foster's Lager and other beers were promoted using powerful brand images about Australia. The use of the Australian comedian Paul Hogan to advertise Foster's proved particularly effective. Foster's acquired a distinctive and very positive brand identity which made it a successful challenger to Carlsberg in the British market by the late 1980s.

The wine story was different, though also a considerable success story. A major part was played by the Australian government marketing agency, which strove to improve and promote the overall image of Australian wines. This work was considerably assisted in the 1980s by the fact that the Australian wine industry had become heavily concentrated in the hands of a few firms which could implement a high degree of quality control, as well as by the depreciation of the Australian dollar which made Australian wine very competitive in foreign markets. Australian wine prices in Britain were carefully positioned higher than the low-quality German wines which dominated the bulk end of the market, but lower than the upper-end price threshold held by certain French wines. Australian wine also drew on images of Australia, though rather more subtle ones of 'bottled sunshine' than that used in beer marketing. As in the case of Australian beers, however, the marketing strategies rested on high-quality products. By the 1980s Australian wine producers had developed advanced wine-making techniques which were applied to vineyards which had been planted with premium varieties. The result was wines beside which many French and German products were at a distinct disadvantage in quality.

Part III examines the marketing of non-alcoholic drinks and food products; it begins, appropriately, with Coca-Cola. The historical evolution of the marketing strategy of Coca-Cola and its fierce rival Pepsi-Cola have been extensively researched (Tedlow 1990: 22–111), but in Chapter 10 Giebelhaus introduces a new dimension in his study of Coca-Cola's marketing outside the United States. The result is a unique insight into how a truly global brand was created. As Giebelhaus writes, Coca-Cola's achievement 'in selling what amounts to flavoured sugar water around the world is a tribute to one of the most successful marketing stories in business history' (p. 211). How was it achieved? The answer lay in part in its franchising strategy. Coca-Cola abroad adopted its domestic practice of manufacturing its all-important concentrate, but franchising the bottling business to independent firms. At the same time, great effort went into the protection of its brand and in the promotion of its image. The company benefited enormously from supplying the US armed forces during the Second World War, by the end of which a large number of bottling plants and concentrate facilities were spread round the world, from North America to New Guinea. This provided the basis for the enormous international success story of the post-war world, which was only slightly marred by problems associated with Coca-Cola's identification with things American.

The strength and nature of the brand image of Coca-Cola continues to fascinate. During the course of the twentieth century Coca-Cola's advertising changed as it responded to changing consumer needs, but the inner identity of the brand – its value system – remained largely intact (Kapferer 1992: 73). It was changeless: hence the uproar when, in the mid-1980s, the advent of 'New Coke' threatened to violate its character.

In Chapter 11, Corley surveys the marketing of food and health drinks in Britain between 1930 and 1970. This is very much *terra incognita*, and Corley's contribution amounts to an important milestone in opening up this subject. While it seems evident that aspects of British marketing practices lagged behind developments in the United States in the early twentieth century, Corley uses neglected advertising and sales data to demonstrate that the extent and nature of any lag has probably been exaggerated. By the interwar years, market research techniques were being employed by certain British food companies. There was also some heavy advertising expenditure as well as other evidence of 'much marketing vigour' (p. 225) in the British industry during the 1930s. The rising real incomes of British consumers in this period, or at least the great majority of them which were in employment, seem to have provided a fertile ground for marketers of branded consumer products in the 1930s.

No British company appears to have benefited in the way that Coca-Cola did from the Second World War. On the contrary, wartime restrictions and rationing severely curtailed the potential for marketing innovations for a decade or more. Nevertheless, from the early 1950s there were again opportunities for developments in marketing. Corley shows that during the 1950s there were notably successful marketing strategies, including those of Beechams for its health drink products Lucozade and Ribena. Unilever emerges as a particularly active force at this stage. The firm transferred US marketing techniques to Britain, establishing its own market research division and engaging in extensive product development.

Corley sets the scene for the case studies of the marketing of breakfast cereals and malted milk products in Britain by Collins and Ward. Collins in Chapter 12 investigates the extraordinary penetration of the British market by the US breakfast cereal companies in the interwar years. Vigorous marketing campaigns were supported by the establishment of factories in Britain by some of the leading US firms, including Kellogg, Shredded Wheat and Quaker Oats. The British diet was transformed to a point where, in the early 1990s, British consumption per head of ready-cooked cereals was the second highest in the world after Ireland.

A striking aspect of this story was the long-term domination of the British market by a small group of companies and their key brands. Kellogg's sustained leadership position was particularly striking. It was achieved through a judicious mixture of advertising, product innovation and market segmentation. Kellogg's possessed pioneer advantages and advantages of incumbency, but it was evidently skilful brand extension and product development strategies which kept it as a market leader. Product quality was important too. As Collins notes, Kellogg's Corn Flakes continued to be favoured in blind tastings with competitor products, and this no doubt strengthened the use of Kellogg as an endorsing brand for its other products.

Ward in Chapter 13 offers a unique insight into British marketing history in the interwar years with his study of the malted milk drinks manufacturer, Horlicks. This was a virtually one-product company which utilized the advanced market research techniques of an American advertising agency. It was discovered that although originally targeted as a drink for the upper classes, Horlicks had unexpectedly developed a large working-class market. Out of this research came a well-designed marketing campaign, launched in 1933, aimed at promoting Horlicks as a drink that gave a sound sleep. The campaign introduced, and successfully exploited, the concept of 'night starvation', which Horlicks was claimed to successfully overcome. This study makes an important contribution to the early history of branding, for it shows in great detail how a successful brand identity was established by advertising and special promotions, which in turn enabled the company to charge consumers a premium rate. In the process, Ward's evidence lends credence to Casson's strictures about the regressive nature of branding.

In Part IV we turn our attention to retailing. As Wilkins notes in Chapter 2 (p. 30), there was a close link between the growth of modern brand names in food and drink products and changes in the nature of retailing. The development of supermarkets provided wide opportunities for the sellers of branded products. Retailers also introduced their own brands, which acquired their own identities and meanings. There is little doubt that the most serious threat to many manufacturers of branded products in recent years has come from these retailers' 'private-label' or 'own brands'. British retailers such as Marks and Spencer, Sainsbury's and Tesco were among the most aggressive developers of such own brands, although a number of other European retailers, notably the Swiss Migros group, have also made successful use of the strategy in recent decades.

In Chapter 14, Williams examines why 'own brands' have established an importance in total retail sales in Britain far above that in the United States. Williams provides a comparative study of two family-owned retailers, Sainsbury's and Shaw's, to explore this Anglo-American difference. Regulatory factors emerge as important. Anti-trust legislation in the United States focused competition primarily on price. In Britain, regulatory controls permitted retailers to establish their own brands as equal in quality to manufacturer's brands, as well as lower in price. The upshot was that the own brand of a firm such as Sainsbury's was able to acquire many of the characteristics of a proprietary brand. The retailer became the brand. The ability of the large British retailers to earn high profits from high-quality own-label ranges has challenged the profitability of branded food manufacturers, and since the early 1980s has attracted emulation from French and other European retailers.

Sparks in Chapter 15 addresses the critically important topic of distribution in retailing. Sparks begins by rehearsing the dramatic changes seen in British food retailing since the early 1960s, including the remarkable growth of own brands, before turning to the logistical changes that lay at their heart. The large British retailers have over time replaced manufacturers in controlling and organizing the supply chains. This development has been both encouraged and permitted by developments in electronic technology which have provided retailers with an enormous flow of information at outlets, which they have been able to use throughout the distribution channel. The proliferation of own brands provided one incentive for British retailers to seek greater control over distribution for a number of reasons, including the need to protect product quality and to ensure supply.

The distinguishing feature of this book is the rich historical experience which it assembles. There is no single 'message' and, indeed, there are conflicting views between authors on the function and consequences of brands.

Nevertheless, a number of points emerge from the individual chapters. Brands not only convey information, but also fulfil needs. They guarantee quality and consistency, and offer certainty, but they also deliver images and dreams. In their modern form, brands became of growing significance in many food and drink products from the late nineteenth century, though earlier in some products, such as Scotch whisky. Their growth was related to the appearance of national markets, and to urbanization. Casson would point also to the decline in religion in the western world, and to a corresponding search for new symbols and fantasies, though it was in the deeply religious United States that branding strategies were at their most vigorous. Whatever their causation, the ability of brands to 'add value' in modern business is evident from the case studies presented here, even though the precise measurement of that added value remains elusive.

What made a successful brand? The importance of market research and of advertising is evident. A basic purpose of a brand is to segment a market, and a 'brand' is valueless unless it communicates with potential purchasers. The pioneer advantages of being a first-mover are evident also in several chapters, though such advantages are shown to have depended on the continual upgrading of products, as well as of the brand identity. However, the chapters in this book also stress that brands must be treated within a wider context. Brands can convey dreams, but they do not have it in their power to convert a foul drink or inedible processed food into a world-class consumer good. Successful brands rest on quality products, supported by effective distribution and other arrangements. Coca-Cola built a global brand not only by building such a powerful and brand identity, but also through a distinctive franchising strategy which enabled the rapid penetration of foreign markets. Brands have enormous power to add value. At times they seem to have a life of their own, but in reality their strength rests on the wider corporate structures which sustain them, and which permit them to fulfil the desires and dreams of their consumers.

12   *Adding Value: brands and marketing*

REFERENCES

Chandler, A. D. (1990) *Scale and Scope: The Dynamics of Industrial Capitalism*, Cambridge, Mass: Harvard University Press.

Corley, T. A. B. (1987) 'Consumer marketing in Britain 1914–60', *Business History* 29(4): 65–83.

Davenport-Hines, R. P. T. (ed.) (1986) *Markets and Bagmen*, Aldershot: Gower.

Hollander, S. C. and Rassuli, K. M. (1993) *Marketing*, vol. 1, Aldershot: Edward Elgar.

Kapferer, J. N. (1992) *Strategic Brand Management*, London: Kogan Page.

Kay, J. (1993) *Foundations of Corporate Success*, Oxford: Oxford University Press.

Morgan, N. and Moss, M. (1993) 'The marketing of Scotch whisky: an historical perspective', in R. S. Tedlow and G. Jones (eds) *The Rise and Fall of Mass Marketing*, London: Routledge.

Porter, M. E. (1990) *The Competitive Advantage of Nations*, London: Macmillan.

Tedlow, R. S. (1990) *New and Improved: The Story of Mass Marketing in America*, London: Heinemann.

Tedlow, R. S. and Jones, G. (eds) (1993) *The Rise and Fall of Mass Marketing*, London: Routledge.

Part I
Concepts and debates

2 When and why brand names in food and drink?

Mira Wilkins

Food and beverages – what we eat and drink – are essential to daily life. The point has been made by the great French historian Fernand Braudel and by many others. Nourishment is basic to our very survival. Braudel, writing on 'civilization and capitalism' in the fifteenth to eighteenth centuries, studied the material life and diets. Yet, as I read his work, I searched in vain for any discussion of brand names, trade marks or trade names (Braudel 1981): I shall use these terms interchangeably (as in Wilkins 1992).

Commodities, such as wheat, were very early in history traded over substantial distances. They were labelled by locale, 'Russian wheat', for example, but not by brand. Of the trinity – grain, flour and bread – by the end of the eighteenth century, none seems to have been trade-marked in Europe, although, as I shall show, this had not always been the case with bread and, with the latter that was traded locally, there may have remained, in some instances, brands in certain European countries (there were marks on bread in the newly independent United States, in New York City) through the eighteenth and even into the early nineteenth century. In the United States, by the end of the nineteenth century flour was often trademarked, and in the twentieth century bread was also trademarked, but with an entirely different intent from the earlier marks.

Rice moved internationally in the fifteenth to the eighteenth centuries, yet no trade names were involved. By the second half of the twentieth century, in the United States rice was usually trademarked. In beverages, coffee and tea were traded as undifferentiated 'commodities', yet by the 1920s coffee was frequently sold to the consumer by brand and before then, Lipton's Tea and other trademarked teas were available to households. What caused the change from commodity to typically differentiated product? How universal was the change? If we go beyond these items to other foods and beverages, what conclusions can we draw on the when and why of branding? When did trade marks become common in the food and drink industry and why did they become common?

As urban dwellers in the 1990s, the food and drink that we consume is rarely obtained directly from the primary producer; it is bought through a distributor – be it a restaurant or a shop. At restaurants, the establishment itself usually provides the brand name, as it vouches for what it serves. The principal exception is in bottled beverages, where there are standardized products, where no change is made in the drink at the restaurant (that is, there is no preparation aside from opening the bottle), and where there is 'shelf-life' (that is, the product can be stored). At home, the fresh foods that we consume are usually not branded.[1] Packaged or bottled items, by contrast, are branded. The brands may be local (or regional) ones, store brands, or national (and international) ones.

A brand can be sustained over time only if consumers buy (and continue to buy) the particular differentiated branded food or beverage. Consumers make choices based on price and on a range of different considerations: curiosity, experimentation, convenience, general perceptions (including product image and status), and most important, experience. Only the positive reinforcement emerging from the last rationale can ultimately maintain a trade mark. If consumers have had bad experience with a brand (from unpleasant taste to negative associations to boredom), the trade mark becomes debased and product sales fall. Alternatively, if consumers find a superior product, a brand may fade away.

WHAT TRADE MARKS DO

Before I explore the whens and whys of the transition from commodity to brand in the food and drink industries, it is worthwhile to consider the function of trade marks in general. As noted at the start of this chapter, I am using the terms brand name, trade mark, trade name and also company name (when attached to a product) as synonymous; I am using the word 'commodity' to deal with a broad category of an undifferentiated product. Indeed, first and foremost, a trade mark acts to identify, to distinguish a product; it differentiates one good from others. This has been true, going back 4,000 years, when potters put their marks on their work.

In the Middle Ages, laws of municipalities and regulations by guilds required craftsmen to place marks on their output, so that bad workmanship could be singled out and the products linked with their delinquent makers. Trade mark historian Frank I. Schechter (1925) writes that

> The most typical regulatory mark of the Middle Ages and the one which, through the nature of the goods upon which it was imposed, always remained a regulatory or liability mark was that of the baker. The regulation of baking, the maintenance of standards of bread and the prevention of extortionate prices for bread have always constituted a source of anxiety of those who seek the welfare or the taxes of the people.
>
> (Schechter 1925: 48–9)

Schechter found the first statutory requirement on baker's marks was in 1266, during the reign of Henry III.

In colonial and early America, municipalities imposed weight and price controls on bread. As late as the start of the nineteenth century, inspectors in New York City checked for underweight loaves and identified erring bakers by their 'mark'. The mark was a 'liability mark', to snare the baker who was overcharging. It was for purposes of regulation. Interestingly, as in prior times (and so in later ones), the trade mark had assumed the function of protecting the consumer.[2]

Over the years, the trade mark shifted from being a 'liability mark', designed to single out bad quality or price gouging, to becoming an asset of the producer. People bought goods that had a distinctive mark or stamp, aware that the brand attested to the quality, and now the good quality, of the product. Producers desired to identify their own work (Schechter 1925; Wilkins 1992). The principal use of marks no longer was by outsiders for regulatory purposes. Instead, firms employed them to demonstrate the goodwill inherent in their output.[3] Once again, the consumer benefited.

Meanwhile, in colonial America, flour and pork, when shipped or before sale, were expected to be marked in some manner. In these circumstances the marking was not to link the producer and consumer; rather it was an attempt to try to grade, to ascertain overall quality, and to demonstrate that there was some form of general 'quality control' (Wilkins 1992: 72).

Commodities of all kinds were (and continue to be) identified not only by locale, but also by grade. When these commodities moved over distance, the individual producer was not known (or important) to the buyer. There were many producers, and the purchaser would have no expectation of ever returning to a single grower. Since within a specified locale (and subject to grade), products were homogeneous, there was no reason to have a trade mark. The brand – which identified the potter or baker of earlier years – had no similar role in relation to the individual grower, either in nearby or long-distance trade. Yet there was a common feature, which was the signifying of standards and quality. This persists through the years. The mark was identified by the buyer with defined expectations; however, grading and locale designations of commodities were not trade marks or brands of the *individual* primary producer.[4]

Throughout much of history, food was sold fresh. The consumer went to the farmer and more frequently, the market (or the store) and picked what was freshest, what smelled right, what looked good. In rural areas, farmers might go directly to a nearby mill and buy flour (or exchange produce for the flour). When staples – flour, rice and sugar – were purchased at a store, the shopkeeper would fill a bag from a large container; there was no pre-packaging and no need by the customer to know where the flour, rice and sugar came from. The flour, rice and sugar were out in the open and for sale. With milk, often the seller would ladle the milk from a big container. In none of these situations was there any reason for either the producer or the consumer to require a trade mark, much less one legally defined in the courts. Likewise, when local bakers made bread fresh, the bakers themselves came to be known to the consumer; when shops bought from bakers, the shop served as 'guarantor' of the freshness of the bread. If there were no price controls and no need to identify who was cheating, there was no regulatory need to trade mark.

In the late nineteenth and early twentieth centuries, changes in industrial structures altered the role of the trade mark dramatically and made it for the first time in history a particularly valuable intangible asset for the producer and a reducer of transaction costs to the consumer. The late nineteenth century saw major advances in technology and the rise of the modern corporation. For producers (processors) who sold their output in quantity *over distance to consumers who did not know them personally*, there had to be a means of getting the end-product buyer to identify the good with the individual maker. For a producer, who was not a price taker in the market place but large enough to have influence over price, to attract customers to its *own* output, there had to be a way of telling the consumer to purchase that maker's particular products and not those of competitors. In times past, the buyer knew the producer directly (or alternatively did not care who was the producer). Now, the buyer did not know the producer directly and the producer had a motive for seeking to identify the firm's output. The trade mark informed the consumer about the product; it differentiated the product from alternatives. Early trade-

A unique form will help to prevent "passing off."

mark litigation against imitators was won by companies on the basis that the trade mark rewarded the 'skill and industry' of the specific producer.[5] The reward was that the producer could tell the customer that this was *his* business's output and not that of a counterfeiter (Wilkins 1992: 70). The producer had controlled the quality of the inputs and the process of transforming them into the end-product. This activity was based on the producer's skill and industry.

Company advertising and brand marks went in tandem. Advertising did not make sense if there were not differentiated products – goods with trade names. If the consumer was to buy the advertised product, the consumer had to be able to distinguish that good. The brand – the trade mark – performed that service. Just as advertising carried information, so did the trade mark itself. It was what directed the purchaser to a designated product.

With the rise of the modern corporation, in many industries there were economies of scale or scope; to achieve these economies (lower unit cost with larger volume), the producer had to have a sizeable output. With modern products, the producer cannot assume that the output will sell automatically at the price that the producer wishes to sell it. The maker to obtain the volume (and the lower unit costs) had to be sure that buyers purchased the product of the particular producer. The trade mark made that possible, allowing economies of scale and scope in production and distribution (Wilkins 1992).

The brand name gave the producer the possibility of using intermediaries and developing modern means of distribution. Satellite firms – such as bottlers, wholesalers and retailers – not owned by the producer, could be authorized to use the trade mark to bring the firm's products to additional consumers. Such extended use of the trade mark reduced governance costs of internal organization, while at the same time assuring a broader market for the firm's output and lower costs to the consumer.

On the other side of the transaction, the trade mark also aided the purchaser in numerous manners. Foremost, it provided the buyer with reduced costs of production and distribution (because of the producer's achievement of economies of scale and scope in both functions). It told the consumer about the product – and other products with the same trade name. It defined what was being purchased. Because in modern society, buyers often do not have a personal relationship with the producer of the goods, they do not know directly whether a good is desirable. If buyers can touch, feel or smell the good, they may be able to make the decision on the product's desirability. If the good is bottled, packaged, or if its attributes are not readily apparent for other reasons, how then does the consumer obtain information? The brand name informs the consumer. Consumers who buy a trademarked product know that if they like the product, then they can make a repeat purchase and obtain a standardized, expected quality.

For the consumer, the existence of trade marks saves time and thus reduces the economic cost (including opportunity cost) of the item purchased. The consumer does not have to wait for the shop assistant to wrap or weigh a good, nor does the pre-packaged good have to be unwrapped for observation. Trade marks allow for efficient modern packaging. So, too, a bottled drink with a name does not have to be opened and tasted before purchase. It can be bought on the assumption that the qualities of the product are the same as similar branded beverages purchased on earlier occasions.

This time-saving is especially important with so-called 'convenience goods' (Porter 1976).[6] In modern societies convenience goods are purchased without 'shopping', that is, shopping around. They are contrasted with 'shopping goods', where the buyer often visits several retailers before making a decision on which product to buy. With convenience goods, which include the range of food and drink products – meat, dairy products, canned and frozen foods, grain mill products, bakery products, sugar confectionaries, vegetable and animal oils, beer, wine, brandy, whiskies and soft drinks – the buyer is highly responsive to advertising. With convenience goods repeat purchases are more frequent than with shopping goods; the trade mark tells the consumer whether to buy or not to buy a particular brand, according to the consumer's prior experience.[7]

Modern packaging, canning and bottling (and later freezing) improve the efficiencies of distribution and thus provide for lower cost products; such efficiencies would be impossible without the trade mark. If what was under the wrappings, inside the can or within the bottle was a surprise, consumer choices would be impeded. The trade mark eliminates the mystery. Uncertainties have costs; the trade mark reduces the search costs.

The trade mark has another major advantage to the consumer. Inherent in the trade mark is a built-in incentive for the producer to uphold quality standards. As Armen Alchian and William Allen (quoted in Wilkins 1992: 85) have put it, 'Reputations [of producers] are built and maintained on past reliable performance'. To obtain repeat purchases, each good must have the predictable, established quality. If producers or their agents (satellite firms) debase the quality, the producers will lose repeat sales. The consumer benefits from this maintenance of standards; with convenience goods, characterized by numerous repeat purchases by the same consumer, this becomes of crucial significance.

It has been argued that the trade mark provides its owner with monopoly rents and that the mark creates false images and deflects the consumer from lower-price substitutes of equal or higher quality, allowing the giant enterprise to seduce (to fool) the buyer. I (and public policy measures that protect the trade mark) reject this view of the 'whys' of trade marks. Indeed, the trade mark is held by price makers (not price takers); it does reward the producer. Yet the profits made are – I would suggest – based on the efficiencies created (through economies of scale and scope and managerial co-ordination) rather than a 'monopoly' achieved through the trade mark. Trademarked goods compete with other such goods, trademarked and generic ones. The view of the deceived consumer insults intelligence. Consumers may be deceived once, but particularly with convenience goods, rarely does a buyer repeat the mistake twice – or more than twice. Instead of deception and deflection, the consumer is informed and has added choices owing to the existence of the trade mark. In my view, and that behind the body of trade mark legislation and the court decisions upholding the trade mark, the consumer is rewarded (rather than harmed) by the presence of trade names.

It has similarly been argued that brand names standardize consumption, pushing out local varieties and substituting a pernicious homogeneity in consumption (Clairmonte and Cavanagh 1988: 13–14). Unquestionably, established brand names standardize consumption; what is behind the brand name is an expected quality (this is fundamental to the purpose of branding goods). Yet, to suggest a welfare-loss is to misunderstand the function of trade marks and, once more, to assume that consumers have no judgement – that they cannot make rational choices. In point of fact, consumers select branded products because they like that particular product, and also, instead of creating homogeneity in consumption, the existence of brand names has provided consumers on a global scale with more choices than ever in history.

A third assault on trade marks sees them as 'ruses', imposing a regressive tax on poorer, aspiring customers (see Casson, Chapter 3 in this volume). Because producers target particular customers, some buyers identify certain products with their own place or role in society, or perhaps with their own fantasies. Producers can use brands to convey images, identities or dreams. None the less, consumers make their own choices, based on *personal* preferences and taking into account experience. Should consumers perceive status (or engage in conspicuous consumption) through the purchase of brands, this is their *choice*. Buyers select to satisfy their desires – and the provision of satisfaction can usually be accepted as an improvement in well-being.[8] Consumers who pay extra for a premium whisky because they believe that displaying it at home or drinking it in a restaurant enhances their stature are making rational personal choices.

Indeed, because the trade mark serves producers and consumers alike (creating the economic – and social welfare – efficiencies described earlier), most modern societies provide legal protection for this intangible and valuable asset. The trade mark in its assistance to the consumer is very different from that other important intangible asset, the patent, which rewards the inventor (and the producer), but only indirectly, by encouraging innovation, the consumer. Brand names, by contrast, provide direct benefits to the consumer.

The legal protection that the law and the courts have given the trade mark is against those firms that seek to free-ride on the value created. The user of the trade mark is protected against the infringer, while the consumer is protected against the confusion created by the illegitimate use of the mark. However, not until the late nineteenth century did legal protection become imperative, since not until then did the producer require such protection and the consumer actually gain benefits from the legally supported trade mark. The efficiencies created by the use of the trade mark and brand name did not become widespread until the rise of the modern business enterprise. If the buyer on his or her own could verify directly (face-to-face) the work of the producer, there was no need for a legal regime to defend the mark. Only when there was distance between the producer and consumer, and the producer was large enough to attract the consumer to the particular product, did the mark become absolutely imperative and did it have to be maintained as a property right. The efficiencies that the legally protected mark offered were intimately associated with the industrial and marketing organizational structures new to the late nineteenth and twentieth centuries. Indeed, there was a coincidence of public policies furnishing legal protection of this property right with the development of the modern business enterprise (Wilkins 1992).

In short, there have been trade marks going back 4,000 years; the trade mark as such is not new. Brands in the Middle Ages and subsequently have served a regulatory role. More important, in early years and more recently, they have been a source of pride for the producer. The local shop (or market) stood in as the trade mark for centuries. In the late nineteenth and early twentieth century, however, for the first time, the trade mark became an essential intangible asset for the new modern industrial enterprises – and for modern industrial societies. When this occurred, trade marks required legal protection. Modern trade marks, which are legally protected, thus fill requirements far beyond those of previous times.

ABSTRACTIONS APPLIED

How do these abstractions apply in more detail to food and beverages? Clearly, industrial structures matter: by industrial structures I am referring to the organization of primary production, processing and distribution – wholesale and retail. How long is the chain from the producer to consumer? Where does 'production' (processing) occur? How perishable is the good? In the introduction to this chapter, I noted that the modern urban consumer seldom bought from the primary producer and that there was a difference in the use of food and beverage brands in restaurants and stores. There is also a difference between stores.

Certain products are branded at one distribution outlet and not at a second. Perishability seems to make a difference. Milk is not ordered by brand in restaurants. It is branded (and packaged) in stores. Ice cream is usually bought not-branded in restaurants and branded in most stores. Portions may make a difference. If the restaurant or the shopkeeper creates the portions, it becomes the 'producer' and its reputation stands in for the trade mark (Maria Willumsen, personal communication, 1993).

We order cookies in a restaurant, usually not by brand. In some shops (bakeries), we buy unbranded cookies. Why? We choose the restaurant and trust it 'to make' our dessert and to provide a cookie to our liking (just as we trusted it to serve fresh milk, knowing that if the milk were sour we would simply reject it; this would be inconvenient at the shop but easy at the restaurant). In the bakery the cookie is freshly made; the nearby producer becomes our proxy for the brand. Yet at a supermarket, all kinds of packaged, branded cookies are available; these products are *made* somewhere else, far away from the retail store where the consumer is deciding to buy or not to buy. The customer now requires a brand name on the product to distinguish one cookie from another and to select. Moreover, the packaging keeps the cookie fresh (consumers do not see the actual product that they are purchasing).

With candies, many of us can recall the small confectionery shop that made its own chocolates. These chocolates did not have brand names. Most of the candies we eat today are wrapped and branded; often we buy according to known names; we have no idea where the candy is produced (unless we look at the package and even that may not tell us the locale). As with the cookie, the packaging keeps the candy fresh (and out of sight).

Similarly, coffee and tea *made* in restaurants are not ordered by brand. (The prepared product must be freshly brewed.) In the specialty store we might buy coffee beans that are labelled 'Colombian' or 'Jamaican Blue Mountain'. In this instance, we trust the shopkeeper to have ordered the bean. Yet typically, the consumer buys branded, proprietary coffee and tea in shops; the shop is solely the distributor; the processing (the production) is done somewhere far away. The vacuum-packed coffee and the packaged tea are processed upstream. The name on the can or the box assures the buyer that care has been taken in providing this product and that if the customer has found it to be satisfactory in the past, it will be satisfactory now. We may buy shops' own brands: when we do, we are relying on the shop to make the selection. Chain stores often have their own brands; they are vouching for the coffee – or any other products so branded.

Bottled water, nationally (and internationally) branded soft drinks, beer and other alcoholic beverages are not 'made' in the restaurant or shop; they are on the shelf. They do not get stale – at least not for some time. The restaurant keeps inventories as does the shop. We buy these beverages by name in both restaurant and shop. Bottling takes place away from the site of exchange.

When we consider food and beverages and try to answer the question when and why brand names, what becomes evident in our discussion of modern times is the importance of packaging, bottling and canning. If a product is fresh or made nearby (French bread), it is generally not branded, either at the restaurant or the shop. If it is made (processed) somewhere else, and is packaged, bottled or canned, then it will be branded when offered for sale in a shop. Especially on matters of taste, where consumers apparently have different responses to the identical 'taste', it is impossible to describe adequately what each consumer's palate will taste. A standardized brand name tells the individual what he or she has tasted before – and liked or disliked (Michael Burkham, personal communication, 1993). That certain branded foods and beverages confer perceived status to buyers may be their rationale for the purchase.

Distance between the producer and consumer, along with modern packaging, requires the identification of the standards with the trade name. Most consumers do not want to buy the generic canned string beans or non-branded bourbon or scotch. Periodically in the United States, there have been arguments made on 'monopoly rents', that branding raises price; then attempts have been made to bypass these costs and provide the consumer with a canned or bottled generic food or beverage. The offerings in general have been short lived. Consumers do not trust the generic that will sometimes be satisfactory but other times not. The trade mark assures an anticipated standard. In cases where status purchases are made, the generic has proven to be totally unsatisfactory.

In food and beverages, particularly, individual consumers repeat purchases frequently. Brands allow consumers to make choices of predictable, standardized articles, meeting their preferences. Modern distribution systems give consumers options. Consumers can decide which of several similar (but not identical) products they want. Brand names offer the opportunity for informed choices in food and beverage selection. Moreover, since food and beverages are consumed, buyers want assurances of a hygienic processing procedure, that they will not get ill; the known brand name provides that 'guarantee'. In developed nations, governments set inspection standards; consumers, however, may have doubts about the government's ability to hold to the standards and the trade mark provides a further reliable guarantee.

Processed foods and beverages are convenience goods (as defined earlier), ones where there are numerous brands and choices, where there is daily consumption (in the broad category of food and drink), and where the trade mark serves to lower search costs. With modern distribution, the consumer can buy and rebuy branded packaged, bottled, canned foods and beverages – quickly. The brand 'signals' the choice, sharply reducing transaction costs. Many, but not all, branded foods and beverages save the consumer time not only in the market-place, but also in the kitchen. Flour and yeast were branded from the late nineteenth century onward; when the housewife spent time cooking, shop-bought yeast certainly saved time in the kitchen. So, too, branded biscuits replaced the home-made variety, as have numerous other prepared foods. In a restaurant or small neighbourhood shop, however, the consumer often continues to leave the selection to the restaurant owner or the shopkeeper, who act as proxies for the brand. This is no different from pre-modern times.

SOME HISTORY

Historically, most trade in food and drink was local; products were raised locally and consumed nearby. There was no need for a legally protected trade mark, owing to the intimacy between producer and consumer. Yet, there was, as noted, very early in certain commodities a long distance trade. With these commodities, there were usually many primary producers and the farmer had no power over price. The grower of the staples typically sold to a trader. At this point, the price of the commodity could be determined by supply and demand or by oligopsony (or occasionally monopsony) conditions.

More often than not supply and demand has determined the prices of agricultural commodities (frequently prompting government policies to safeguard the agricultural sector). Trade marks of the growers (primary producers) were not the ones found on the food and beverages when the latter were sold to the consumer, *unless* the grower was also trader and processor.[9] Thus, Castle & Cooke (now Dole Foods) owned pineapple plantations, canned pineapples, and sold this canned fruit under its Dole brand. Lipton owned tea plantations, packed tea, and marketed it under its trade name. Likewise, the British Brooke Bond, which sold trademarked products, developed extensive tea plantations in India and Kenya (Clairmonte and Cavanagh 1988: 37, 50). In each instance, the backward integration helped control the quality of the final product, by the monitoring of inputs.

The trade mark in food and beverages typically rewarded the skill and industry of the processor or distributor. It is at that level that the product became differentiated. It is, moreover, at that stage that the business can become large enough to have power to attract customers to its output and to have the need to do so.

In the nineteenth century, major changes took place in the technology of food and beverage processing and in the physical distribution network. Railways lowered transportation costs; refrigerated containers made it possible to move perishable goods over distances. The steamship did for water routes what railways did over land. The new transportation systems enabled processed goods to be transferred rapidly over substantial geographical areas. Innovations in canning and then in continuous processing revolutionized the United States' food industries – and to a lesser extent the food industries world wide. The earliest machine-made fancy biscuits came in Britain in 1846 (see Corley, Chapter 11 in this volume). What is remarkable is how most of the food and beverage enterprises affected by the new technologies quickly came to sell branded products.[10]

During the American Civil War there had been a new demand for canned goods. Gail Borden, who had been experimenting in condensing and canning milk, opened his first factory in 1861, two

months after the war began; from the start his cans of milk h
name (Clarke 1929: II, 33; Morgan 1986: 107). Early canners
using glass containers rather than cans) put their names on
products. The trade name Townsend Brothers Selected America
Oysters was registered at the US District Court in New York in 1867,
while in 1868 William Underwood's sons began to can devilled ham
and in 1870 registered their name and design under the first American
federal Trade Mark Act. Libby, McNeill & Libby in 1868 began to
produce corned beef in Chicago to sell in eastern markets; the company canned this beef in a specially designed tin container and after
1876 advertised this trademarked product extensively (Morgan 1986:
104–5, 108).

These developments of the 1860s and 1870s were dwarfed in the
next decades as innovations in food processing multiplied. High-
volume processing of flour in Minneapolis, begun in the 1870s, raised
output in the 1880s so much that many millers branded (and advertised) their products to attract distant customers to the particular flour
producer. How else could they sell their large-scale production? In
1883, Edwin and O. W. Norton introduced the first 'automatic line'
canning factory. It was now possible to solder the cans mechanically.
Campbell Soup, H. J. Heinz, Borden's Milk, and Libby McNeill &
Libby were among those adopting the new technology. All sold trademarked goods (Chandler 1977: 250–3, 295; Morgan 1986: 106).
Breakfast-food makers developed and produced in volume new
products; these too were sold under brand names. There were new
technologies in brewing, in distilling alcoholic spirits, and in sugar
refining; once again in these industries trademarked bottled and
packaged goods became the norm. The meat-packers, able to take
advantage of scale economies and able to ship with refrigerated containers, faced competition in distant markets and they too trademarked their output (Chandler 1977: 253, 256–7, 294, 299–302;
Mary Yeager, personal communication, 1990). The firms with the new
technologies all advertised and with advertisements brand names were
imperative. The trade marks gave these companies the opportunities
to achieve volume production and lower unit costs.

Milton S. Hershey devised a chocolate-moulding machine that
allowed his company to mass produce a high-quality chocolate bar at
a low price. Unlike most of the innovators of the late nineteenth and
early twentieth century, Hershey did not spend money to advertise.
However, his firm formed strong relationships with distributors
and employed a large sales staff; most significant, Hershey had a
brand name that consumers recognized when they saw his product

yed on confectionery counters (Horst 1974:

od processors became multinational enterprises
ld War and continued as major international
4; Wilkins 1970; 1974). Their trade marks were
ess at home and abroad. Each of the companies
more attention to the marketing of its products
than to the manufacturing (Horst 1974: 4). The trademarked goods
were those that could be packaged, canned or bottled – *and* sold outside the immediate vicinity of production. The trade marks obtained
legal protection in US legislation and in the courts – protection against
infringers, who fraudulently sought to capture the trade of those who
had invested in providing the specified goods (Wilkins 1992). Over
distance, the name could not be maintained merely by personal
contacts.

In the United States, the firm Lamont, Corliss & Co – co-operating
with J. Walter Thompson of New York and London (as of 1899) –
represented manufacturers of 'high-class food products'. Lamont,
Corliss specialized 'in the work of establishing trademarked food
products' in the United States. J. Walter Thompson handled the
advertising of many trademarked US food products, at home and
abroad (Wilkins 1989: 333–7, 799–800).

There were Canadian, British, continental European and Japanese
food and drink producers that also adopted trade marks in the late
nineteenth and early twentieth century, with very much the same goals
as their US counterparts: they too wished to distinguish their products
from those of their rivals. Once more, the packaged, canned and
bottled goods sold outside the immediate locale were those that
needed to be branded, to be identified: outstanding were firms such as
Hiram Walker, with Canadian Club; the British biscuit makers;
Liebig's Extract of Beef; Nestlé & Anglo-Swiss with canned milk,
baby food, and chocolates; Fabrique de Produits Maggi, SA, a Zurich
company; the Dutch margarine makers; the Dutch cocoa packers;
Lipton Tea; the British distillers; the French wine bottlers; and the
Japanese soy sauce producers.[11]

There were numerous German businesses in the late nineteenth and
early twentieth century with branded products: for example, a
Strassbourg firm, Ungemach, AG sold Loriot peppermints; the
Cologne company Gebrueder Stollwercke, offered a branded chocolate as did the Berlin chocolate maker 'Sarotti' Chokladen & Cacao-
Industrie, AG; a Ludwigsburg enterprise, Heinrich Franck Sohne,
sold 'Franck's Feinster Cichorien-Extract', while a Bremen company,

Kaffee Handels, AG, which owned 50 per cent of a US business, Kaffee Hag Corporation (formed in 1914), marketed in the United States a caffeine-free coffee (developed by the German firm), which its US subsidiary sold under the brand name DeKofa; many years later the same product would be sold as Sanka. And then, of course, there were the German breweries that had begun to sell branded beer (Chandler 1990: 431, 433–4, 697; Wilkins 1989: 801 n. 241, 335–7).

In Britain, sometimes the trade name was associated with the distribution network rather than the packaging per se. Thus Lipton had retail shops. So, too, many British pubs were 'tied houses', selling the beer of a particular brewer. Store brands were developed in the United States and Britain, with the A & P one most prominent in the United States and Sainsbury's in Britain. Lipton Tea was sold in retail stores not owned by Lipton (as well as those owned by Lipton); beers came to be bottled and sold not only through pubs. A & P brand, and other store brands in the United States as well as Sainsbury's in Britain, by contrast, never assumed a life apart from the retailer; in those situations, the distributor (the retailer) verified the quality and standard behind the brand name (see Williams, Chapter 14 in this volume).

One early US trade mark case involved a Hungarian shipper of mineral water to the United States. In order to sell such a product over distance, the producer had to guarantee its purity and its quality. Its trade name, its novel style of bottles and its peculiar label, was essential to its success; the suit – which eventually reached the US Supreme Court – was against a defendant who sought to appropriate these valuable intangible assets (*Saxlehner* v *Eisner & Mendelson Co* 1900, 179 US 19). For soft drinks, trade marks were necessary, if marketing was to extend beyond the immediate community. It is no accident that Coca-Cola was founded in the late nineteenth century and able to take advantage of the use of the trade mark as a valuable intangible asset (see Giebelhaus, Chapter 10 in this volume).

Coca-Cola was sold bottled; however, from its earliest days it was more frequently a drink at the local drugstore. Coca-Cola, unlike the British breweries, did not create an *owned* retail chain. Yet when its trade mark was defended in the court, the brand name was upheld not on the basis of the bottled product but rather that 'the name . . . characterizes a beverage to be had at almost any soda fountain' (Tedlow 1990: 53–5). Does this constitute an exception to the rule that modern packaging, canning and bottling was vital to the trade mark use in food and beverages? Perhaps modern distribution and advertisement must be added to the equation, which would cover Coca-Cola. (There was no absence of advertising Coca-Cola *at the soda fountain*: there were signs, glasses with the Coca-Cola name, and other items that employed the trade name to identify the product.)

Indeed, modern brand names in food and drink products seem closely linked with the nature of retailing. As the retailer carried many packaged, canned or bottled items and as retail chains developed (with shop brands), the shops themselves became associated with trademarked or non-trademarked products. The developments in retailing seem to help explain the 'whens' of trade marks in food and beverages. As modern chain stores emerged, they introduced their own brands – standing in for the quality of the good.

Another significant aspect of the explanation relates to disposable income of consumers. Coincident with the lower costs of production and distribution of processed foods and beverages came the rise, albeit slowly, of real personal incomes. Until the consumer had 'spending power', the purchase of a variety of products was impossible. With greater urbanization, with cash income, choices for the average consumer in food and beverages (and other products) became feasible.

THE INTERWAR YEARS

By the interwar period, there was a general recognition by producers of packaged, canned, or bottled foods and drinks – and those highly advertised and widely distributed through established marketing channels – that the trade mark, which included not only the name but also the package (or bottle) shape as well as the logo and the illustration on the label, was a valuable asset to be legally defended. As one author has put it, 'The commercial symbols became the public faces, or personalities of the products and companies they represented. . . . If the public reaction to the symbols was positive, manufacturers could count on a reliable base of business' (Morgan 1986: 11).

In 1913 an automatic bread-wrapping machine was invented; wrapped bread became more common and in the 1920s brand names in bread became an important factor, at least in the United States (Morgan 1986: 153). In December 1920, in a landmark case, the US Supreme Court upheld the Coca-Cola trade mark (Tedlow 1990: 54–5). By the 1920s it was accepted that trade marks in the United States had become a significant factor in trade (Wilkins 1992: 70). They were a property right, an asset, that had a public policy purpose and could be defended in court and the defence supported by a body of law and tradition.

In the 1920s packaged, canned and bottled foods and beverages were now almost always trademarked.[12] Consumer incomes were typically high enough to afford these goods. In the United States branded foods included dairy products, packaged bread, baking goods (such as flour, yeast, baking soda and baking powder, cooking chocolates, sugar and salt), baby food, breakfast cereals, soups, jams and jellies, sauces, condiments, pastas, biscuits, candies and soft drinks. With prohibition in the United States, distillers even continued old brands: 'Old Grand-Dad' whiskey, 'Unexcelled for Medicinal Purposes' (see 1925 label in Morgan 1986: 97). A number of former alcoholic beverage producers took steps to preserve their names – until better times. Many of the established pre-Prohibition brands resurfaced after Prohibition ended.

In 1922–30, in the US food processing industries, there were a number of major mergers (Horst 1974: 25–31). Merged enterprises kept and continued to maintain the brand names of their predecessors. Companies in the food and beverage industries enlarged their penetration of domestic and foreign markets – using established trade marks. Increasingly, the brand name adhered to the product rather than to the producer (to the firm) per se. Thus, while Kellogg's Corn Flakes used the persisting company's name, as did Coca-Cola, Wheaties was one of many products of General Mills. As companies moved from being single-line, single-brand firms, ever more often the trade name of the product took precedence in the market place over the manufacturer. General Foods made and distributed a wide range of trademarked goods, including Jello, Swans Down cake flour, Baker's chocolates, and Maxwell House coffee. So, too, Standard Brands – which by its very name emphasized the importance of brands – had a group of trade names from Royal Baking Powder to Chase & Sanborn coffee (Horst 1974: 28–9). In Britain, Distillers Company Ltd in 1925 acquired Buchanan-Dewar Ltd and John Walker & Sons – extending its collection of brands (see Weir, Chapter 8 in this volume).

The food and drink products that were branded – for national and international distribution – were those that could be shipped to distant markets, those where the producing company expected the consumer to make repeat purchases of *its* output, those where the producer established distribution channels to see to it that stores carried its products, and those where through modern packaging, bottling, or canning, the shelf-life of the product could be prolonged. There were also local and regional brands for products with shorter shelf-life (such as fresh dairy products).

In 1929 General Foods purchased Clarence Birdseye's patents for the quick-freezing process. Birds Eye Frosted Food became a registered trade mark used as early 1930 (Horst 1974: 28; Morgan 1986:

109). After the Second World War, when Americans began to have space in freezers for frozen foods, varieties of frozen foods became trademarked – with Birds Eye at least originally in the lead. A single trade mark came to be extended to a collection of goods, and not for the first time by any means (Heinz, after all, before the First World War had '57 Varieties', while Campbell Soup was the trade mark for many different types of soup).

In the 1930s, with the end of Prohibition in the United States, a wide range of alcoholic beverages – all trademarked – were aggressively marketed in the United States. The trade marks gave consumers extensive choices between similar but far from identical products. Producers actively trademarked their beverages. The trade mark protected the consumer from 'poisoning'. There came to be brand name segmentation, and premium brands targeted at high-income groups; 'status branding', while not new, took on more importance.

In the interwar period more than in previous years, in many processed food and beverage products, firms developed multi-plant operations.[13] This was true of national as well as multinational corporations; under such circumstances, once more, brands became identified increasingly with the products rather than the locale of production. According to A. M. McGahan (1991: 243), in 1936 the Falstaff Brewery of St Louis was the first US brewery to attach the same brand name to beer brewed in two geographically separate facilities. Until then, most brewers believed that water quality and other differences would mean the taste of the beer would vary by place of production and that using the identical trade mark for beer brewed in separate locations would destroy a brand's reputation. New technology allowed for controls. Falstaff's strategy was successful. Other brewers followed its lead.

In short, not only would a single company have multiple brands and brands stretched to cover product line extensions (different soups, premium labels), but also a single firm with multiple production sites could utilize an existing advertised, promoted brand to cover the marketing of a product made (processed or packed) in different locations. Multi-plant production involved modern managerial methods of control; products with the same name had to meet the same expectations, lest the product name be debased.

THE 1990s IN CONTEXT: THE ANSWERS

By the end of the interwar period through to the 1990s, there has been little change in the answer to the question, 'when and why trade marks in food and drink?' The answers that I have given in an historical context apply more broadly in recent times, to more companies in more countries. There were, and are, many more trademarked products – from frozen dinners, to frozen pizza, to freeze-dried coffee, to aerosol cans of whipped cream. More often, they represent convenience to the consumer in preparing meals. To a large extent, the brand proliferation reflects shifts in consumption patterns, based on, for example, more women in the workforce (with less time to make meals) and household technology (more consumers own freezers and microwave ovens). Higher incomes – more disposable incomes – mean that consumers buy greater quantities of trademarked processed foods in ever wider varieties. Higher incomes offer more possibilities of choice in consumption. Consumers are ready to sample more items; they are open to more different 'taste experiences'. The spread of information and travel tempt consumers to try new types of ethnic dishes. Higher incomes mean more flexibility and experimentation, more 'risk-taking' in food consumption. Marketing channels have altered as supermarkets came in the United States, in particular, and then elsewhere, to outsell the local grocery shops.[14] The opportunities to stock more trademarked goods, for the chain supermarket to buy in quantity a vast array of products, opened wide the possibilities for producers and distributors of branded goods. At the same time, new advertising methods, including the use of television, meant a broader spread of consumer knowledge about trademarked products.

There was not only increased brand proliferation, but also more product-line extensions. The Coca-Cola name was applied to the Coca-Cola 'Classic', and to other Coca-Cola beverages. Unilever's US subsidiary, Thomas J. Lipton, Inc., sold not only tea, with which it had long been identified, but also such goods as a 'Cup-a-Soup' line that carried the Lipton brand name. Similarly, a well-known brand often represented products processed or bottled at a number of locations. Brewers learned how to standardize output, so the quality of beer brewed at different sites could have the identical brand name; many other trademarked food and beverages were processed at many separate geographically dispersed locales. It was typical for multinational corporations to produce the same products in different locations using a single brand name.

Mergers and acquisitions, divestments, and corporate reorganizations of recent years have resulted in the transfer of brands from one corporate owner to another with an unprecedented alacrity. The story of Campbell Soup Company is simple. It was a soup company (with a range of different soups); it had acquired a small pasta business in the

1920s and the V-8 Vegetable Juice Company in 1948. Then it grew, taking over Pepperidge Farm, with its large line of branded frozen foods. In addition, it bought a number of other specialty food companies. Through acquisitions, it became a multibrand company (Stopford 1992: I, 254–61).

More complex was the progression of mergers and divestments involving companies such as R J R Nabisco, for example. At one time, this enterprise produced, among its panoply of products, Inglenook Wines, Canada Dry Ginger Ale, Chase & Sanborn Coffee, Nabisco Biscuits, all the Del Monte branded goods, A-1 Steak Sauce, Patio Mexican Foods, and Chun King Foods. Over time, however, it divested many of these goods, selling the plant facilities and also the rights to the brand name to other food and beverage conglomerates (Burrough and Helyar 1990; Clairmonte and Cavanagh 1988: 100–7).

In 1969–70 Philip Morris purchased Miller Brewing Company, the fourth largest brewer in the United States; in 1985, the tobacco company bought General Foods – already a giant multibrand firm – and in 1988, it took over the huge Kraft Inc. In the interim (and subsequently) it has acquired other food and beverage companies. Philip Morris in 1986 had 50 per cent of its sales in tobacco products and 50 per cent in food and beer. Four years later (in 1990) this enterprise had only 41 per cent of its sales in tobacco, and 58 per cent in a broad variety of branded food and beverage products (Elzinga 1977: 232; Stopford 1992: II, 1,024–6).

Notwithstanding all these recent and dramatic changes, including the rise of the multiproduct, multibrand multinational food and beverage conglomerates, the basic when and why answers to the question in my title seem an echo of the past: trade marks are needed when a producer or distributor wants to distinguish a product. If a producer or distributor desires to draw repeat customers to its product(s), there must be identification, which comes from the mark. Advertising of a particular product is impossible without a trade name. In modern times, as companies extend themselves over space, moving their offerings through added outlets, as the consumer, no longer knows the producer personally, a legally protected identification mark becomes essential, lest others capture the advantages of maker.

Whereas when the trade mark initially became an asset, it adhered to the 'skill and industry' of the producer of the good, over time it has increasingly been attached to the product itself. The consumer now has no idea about the producer of the product (owner of the plant and ultimate owner of the brand name) and could not care less. The name adheres to the food or beverage – and here the consumer does care, for the trade mark directs the consumers' choices. Companies can extend the brand name to other goods; a product can be produced in different locations; companies can be acquired, merged and divested; yet, the intangible asset, the established brand name, can continue to be maintained, having the desired effect of attracting consumers to the product. If what was behind the name was not upheld by the newly branded product (covered by the extended mark), by the production in alternative locales, or by a new owner, if the product was debased (inferior to consumer expectations), then there would not be repeat purchases and the value of this intangible asset would be sacrificed. There was every incentive for the producer to retain and to maintain the reputation, the standardized known quality and special identity, since that was what made the brand an asset.

As in earlier years (with Heinz's '57 Varieties' for example), so in the post-war years, an established trade name in food and beverages could be stretched. As in past times, production could be in multiple locales. As in former decades, companies could be merged and the consumer would not know the owner of the brand name. The brand name's link with the product rather than the corporate owner was a process well established before the wave of corporate changes that characterized the 1970s and particularly the 1980s. Multibrand companies – based on mergers – are not new to recent times; what is new is the extent of product as well as brand proliferation within a single giant enterprise.

Now, as ever more frequently food and drink companies merged and became objects of acquisitions – and this was true not only in the United States but also on a global scale – the trade name became ever more frequently identified with the good per se. This was the case as more and more, large food and beverage companies, principally because of such mergers and acquisitions, became multibrand firms. This is evident as one looks at the brands offered, for example, by the French BSN, the American CPC International, Campbell Soup Company, and Philip Morris, the British/Dutch Unilever, the British Grand Metropolitan PLC, Guinness PLC, and Cadbury Schweppes PLC, the Swiss Nestlé, and the Canadian Seagrams Company Ltd (Stopford 1992).

The food and beverages that are packaged, bottled, canned and frozen are the ones that are branded. The exceptions to this (such as 'Chiquita' on bananas, trademarked fresh chickens, and advertised draught beer) are still few and far between. In these instances the owner of the brand name had *control* over the inputs, over the characteristics of the trademarked good. Thus here too, the trade mark assures the buyer of an expected, anticipated standardized quality – essential in convenience goods with repeat purchases. This saves the buyer search costs.

The commodities shipped from countries in both the First World and the Third World remain untrademarked (unless owned by the processor). When I embarked on writing my article, 'The neglected intangible asset' (Wilkins 1992), I was struck by the presence of companies with national and international trade marks headquartered in the industrial world and not in less developed nations. This seems true in food and beverages, and our historical chronology would seem to explain it. My sole puzzle relates to Germany (particularly the former West Germany). Every other major industrial country has important food and beverage enterprises with national and international brands. Germany had such 'international' marks, as I would expect, in the period before the First World War; German beer brands are internationally known, but few other marks. More research seems necessary on the German food and beverage industries. Clearly, however, in Germany in the 1990s, trademarked products in the shops are the norm.[15]

The answer to this chapter's 'when-and-why' questions seems to lie both in the needs of the producer and of the consumer. Trade marks have a long history. They identify the product. For centuries, however, most producers of food and beverages did *not* brand their products. On the other hand, in modern times, trade marks have had an expanded and extended use in the food and drink industries. What is new to the late nineteenth and twentieth centuries are regionally, nationally and internationally established trade marks in numerous products, including food and beverages. Trademarked food and drink products multiply as incomes rise. Buyers purchase not only basics, but also extras. They buy not only to meet needs of survival, but also to satisfy other social and emotional needs. Trademarking has become vital for the consumer in our present-day modern, urbanized society. For the buyer, time has cost, opportunity cost. Information is scarce and expensive: the trade mark carries information. The reduction of time in transactions lowers the cost of the food and beverages that are fundamental in daily life, and at the same time adds the possibilities of a vast array of new varieties and a proliferation of choices. The trade mark makes possible the existence of modern distribution systems. The brand name reduces search costs. Time is saved not only in the transaction but also in the kitchen. That the trade mark is a legally protected asset gives this intangible property added value for its owner and for the consumer. This defined 'property right' is necessary when the customer cannot personally, directly and quickly, verify a product's genuineness. To be sustained, existing trade marks must be backed by a defined quality of goods and by a high standard. The consumer benefits.

Broadly speaking, in food and beverages, the answer to the when question is: when societies developed large-scale modern enterprises, with modern distribution systems, and with consumers able to expand their purchasing beyond a basic diet. The answer to the why question for modern times is: the trade mark was used (and legally protected) because it introduced efficiencies in production, distribution and also in the nexus between supply and demand, the transaction itself; in addition, it provided the consumer with savings in time in the preparing of meals, with greater choices, and with more possibilities for satisfaction.

ACKNOWLEDGEMENTS

I am indebted to Geoffrey Jones for his invitation to participate in this conference and his stimulating comments. My thanks go to George B. Simmons, my husband, for many walks and talks on this topic. Howard Rock was extremely helpful, as were Ann Witte, David Cook, Yasuo Homma, Maria Willumsen, Panos Liossatos and Mark Casson. My reading of the materials of Wayne Broehl on the wheat trade was invaluable. Steven Topik got me thinking about coffee. Many of my first (and subsequent) insights on trade marks and their importance came from correspondence and discussions with Tony Corley. Gus Giebelhaus kindly opened some doors for me when I was initially thinking about writing on this subject; Mary Yeager and Ken Sokoloff had ideas for my 1992 article that were very helpful on this one. All the participants in the food and drink conference were wonderful in pushing me to clarify my argument and in shaping my views; Hans Christian Johansen, Michael Burkham and Peter Mathias deserve special thanks.

NOTES

1 There are exceptions. Fresh celery in my Florida supermarket is wrapped and has a brand name, 'Crisplicart'. In the 1990s chicken is often wrapped and labelled. Likewise, Chiquita Brands International (the 1990 successor to United Brands, which in turn was the successor to United Fruit) now puts a label, 'Chiquita Banana', on the bananas it sells (and, to emphasize its brand, it changed its corporate name to coincide).

2 I am deeply indebted to Howard Rock, an expert on artisans in early America, for insights on this subject. He kindly searched his files for inspectors' reports and found a Report of the Inspector of Bread (4 April 1803), in which the inspector criticized a baker for not having more than two 'marking irons' to identify his loaves and also took another baker to task for having mislaid his iron and who was caught distributing unmarked bread. See also Clark (1929: I, 6) on inspections and their purpose.

3 The use of a mark for regulatory purposes did not, however, entirely disappear; it reappears in the twentieth century with, for example, meat inspectors' stamps.

4 In the late nineteenth and twentieth centuries, the 'grading' of a traded commodity might be verified, however, by the *trader's* reputation. The mark did not go back to the primary producer, unless trader and primary producer were one and the same.

5 The recurrent phrase 'skill and industry' appears in one of the earliest – if not the earliest – trade mark manuals (Upton 1860).

6 Elsewhere in this volume, the phrase 'convenience foods' is used, connotating *convenience in the kitchen*. Following Porter (1976), I am using the phrase 'convenience goods' to connotate *convenience in the transaction*.

7 I did not introduce the distinction between convenience and shopping goods in Wilkins (1992), since for some shopping goods such as motor cars it seems to me that there is more consumer responsiveness to advertising than for certain trademarked foods. In my view, it is not so much advertising that is associated with the difference between convenience and shopping goods, but the way the consumer shops, that is the number of transactions per year between seller and buyer in the particular product (with convenience goods, the potential for numerous repeat purchases by the individual consumer is far greater and sequencing of repeat purchases more frequent than with shopping goods).

8 Clearly, 'the provision of satisfaction' is *not* universally favourable to well-being, for example in the abuse of drugs.

9 Cattle was 'branded', and the brand was an asset to the livestock raiser. The purpose of the brand here was – like other brands in their original usages – to establish the identity of the owner. The cattle brand was a 'property right'. It separated one owner from another and provided information to the processor (the buyer). The eater of the meat – the final consumer – however, is never aware of the cattle brand (i.e. the owner of primary raw material). The cattle brand was not, in short, passed on through the processing to the final consumer.

10 I use the word 'remarkable' out of sheer delight at how the paradigm that I put forth in Wilkins (1992) fits the food and drink industry so perfectly.

11 See the wonderful material in Fruin (1983: 96ff) on brands in Japan. Kikkoman registered its trade mark in California in 1879 and in Germany in 1886 (Kinugasa 1984: 54).

12 I am, of course, referring to pre-packaged and pre-bottled goods, not those packaged or bottled in a retail shop or market.

13 On the economies of multi-plant operations and the impact of branding, see Scherer et al. (1975: 239ff). The only food and drink product dealt with in Scherer's volume is beer, but the generalizations are appropriate in

a far wider context. Wilkins (1970; 1974) and Horst (1974), as well as numerous histories of food and beverage companies have shown that by the interwar period and even earlier, multinational corporations in food and beverage industries were multi-plant operations.

14 By the early 1970s, supermarkets accounted for roughly 70 per cent of US grocery turnover, a percentage that remained unchanged in the 1980s. By contrast, in Europe, there were dramatic changes in the 1970s and 1980s: in Britain supermarkets had 53 per cent of grocery turnover in 1974, 68 per cent in 1980, and over 80 per cent by the mid-1980s; in West Germany, the figures went from 58 per cent in 1974 to 67 per cent in the mid-1980s; in Holland from 44 to 60 per cent in the same period. In Japan, with the persistence of small retailers, by the mid-1980s the figure was 43 per cent (Clairmonte and Cavanagh 1988: 175n.2). The use of the automobile in shopping, particularly in the United States, also made a difference.

15 In Stopford (1992) there are no large German food and beverage companies with branded goods. Alfred Chandler (1990: 402, 430–4) would explain that Stollwerck had been an exceptional German firm in the early years and he would include the other pre-First World War German branded food enterprises as equally exceptional; the German forte was elsewhere. Clairmonte and Cavanagh (1990) list and discuss the fifty largest beverage companies (with beverage sales in excess of $500 million). All had branded products. Of these fifty, sixteen had headquarters in the United States, eleven in the United Kingdom, seven in Japan, and five in France. None was German. The authors note two German breweries and two German fruit juice makers (Tchibo and Oetker) that were excluded because the writers could not get sales information. Clairmonte and Cavanagh (1990) also describe Tchibo as one of the big four coffee roasters in Germany. See also Clairmonte and Cavanagh (1988: 96–8, 129). It is perhaps noteworthy that at our conference on food and beverages, there was no paper dealing specifically with Germany, albeit one participant remarked on a German yogurt brand at our British breakfast table. The privately owned Bavarian dairy company, Molkerei Alois Muller, had in three years (1988–92) raised from 4.3 to 17.8 per cent its share of the British yogurt market (*Financial Times*, 22 April 1993). Note also that a number of indigenous German food brands (Knorr, for example) have been acquired by foreign multinationals.

REFERENCES

Braudel, F. (1981) *The Structures of Everyday Life*, New York: Harper & Row.
Burrough, B. and Helyar, J. (1990) *Barbarians at the Gate: The Fall of R J R Nabisco*, New York: Harper & Row.
Chandler, A. D. (1977) *The Visible Hand*, Cambridge, Mass: Harvard University Press.
—— (1990) *Scale and Scope: The Dynamics of Industrial Capitalism*, Cambridge, Mass: Harvard University Press.
Clairmonte, F. and Cavanagh, J. (1988) *Merchants of Drink: Transnational Control over World Beverages*, Penang, Malaysia: Third World Network.

40   Adding Value: brands and marketing

—— (1990) 'TNCs and the global beverage industry', *The CTC Reporter* **30**, Autumn: 27–33.

Clark, V. S. (1929) *History of Manufacturers in the United States*, 3 vols, New York: Carnegie Institution.

Elzinga, K. G. (1977) 'The beer industry', in W. Adams (ed.) *The Structure of American Industry*, New York: Macmillan.

Fruin, W. M. (1983) *Kikkoman*, Cambridge, Mass: Harvard University Press.

Horst, T. (1974) *At Home Abroad: A Study of the Domestic and Foreign Operations of the American Food-Processing Industry*, Cambridge, Mass: Ballinger.

Kinugasa, Y. (1984) 'Japanese firms' foreign direct investment in the US', in A. Okochi and T. Inoue (eds) *Overseas Business Activities*, Tokyo: University of Tokyo Press.

McGahan, A. M. (1991) 'The emergence of the national brewing oligopoly: Competition in the American market, 1933–1958', *Business History Review* **65**, Summer: 229–84.

Morgan, H. (1986) *Symbols of America*, New York: Penguin.

Porter, M. E. (1976) *Interbrand Choice, Strategy, and Bilateral Market Power*, Cambridge, Mass: Harvard University Press.

Report of the Inspector of Bread (4 April 1803), New York City Common Council Papers; the original is in the New York City Municipal Archives; I used a copy in the files of Howard Rock, Florida International University.

Schechter, F. I. (1925) *The Historical Foundations of the Law Relating to Trade-Marks*, New York: Colombia University Press.

Scherer, F. M., Beckenstein, A., Kaufer, E., Murphy, R. D. and Bougeon-Maassen, F. (1975) *The Economics of Multi-Plant Operations*, Cambridge, Mass: Harvard University Press.

Stopford, J. (1992) *Directory of Multinationals*, 2 vols, New York: Stockton Press.

Tedlow, R. S. (1990) *New and Improved*, New York: Basic Books.

Upton, F. H. (1860) *A Treatise on the Law of Trade Marks with a Digest and Review of the English and American Authorities*, Albany, NY: Weare C. Little.

Wilkins, M. (1970) *The Emergence of Multinational Enterprise: American Business Abroad from the Colonial Era to 1914*, Cambridge, Mass: Harvard University Press.

—— (1974) *The Maturing of Multinational Enterprise: American Business Abroad from 1914 to 1970*, Cambridge, Mass: Harvard University Press.

—— (1989) *The History of Foreign Investment in the United States to 1914*, Cambridge, Mass: Harvard University Press.

—— (1992) 'The neglected intangible asset: The influence of the trade mark on the rise of the modern corporation', *Business History* **34**, January: 66–99.

3 Brands

Economic ideology and consumer society

Mark Casson

This chapter is concerned with the implications of branding from the standpoint of society as a whole. It is not primarily concerned with the profitability of branding from the company's point of view, but whether what is profitable for the company is also beneficial for society. Contemporary economic analysis of this issue tends to argue that branding is socially beneficial. It sees a harmony between the private interests of the firm and the goals of society. If a brand adds value to the company, it adds value to society as a whole, it is said.

This view is oversimplified – so oversimplified, in fact, that it is seriously misleading. It is a product, not so much of rigorous economic analysis, as of contemporary social values. These values reflect the dominant ideology of the market system, which is based on an atomistic and consumer-oriented culture. Contemporary culture is atomistic in the sense that it perceives society as a collection of rational and autonomous individuals rather than as an organic entity that transcends these individuals and moulds their preferences. It is consumer-oriented in the sense that individuals are assumed to derive their principal satisfactions from the private consumption of goods rather than from their work or from participation in communal activity.

This emphasis on the value of private consumption highlights the potential role of branding in ensuring that the experience of consumption matches its expectations. Rational consumers cannot be misled by branding, it is said, and will buy branded products (particularly for a second time) only if it is in their interests to do so. These individual interests are sovereign because of the atomistic nature of society. Thus the very fact that consumers choose branded products in preference to others shows that branding makes people better off, and so society, as a simple aggregate of individuals, must be better off as well.

This view of human nature is not, however, shared by those responsible for the actual marketing of products. To put it simply, an evening spent watching TV advertising does not suggest that the typical viewer is believed to be a rational and autonomous individual. Advertisers derive their professional expertise not from economic models but from psychological theories of cognition and motivation. They attempt to exploit factors, such as hidden needs, of which consumers themselves may not be fully aware.

Since TV advertising involves large sums of money spent by some of the most successful firms, it is reasonable to suppose that the advertisers know what they are doing. This chapter accepts the advertisers' point of view, and reconsiders the implications of branding in this light. With a rather different view of human nature, these implications are a good deal more ambiguous than contemporary opinion suggests. This chapter also relates branding to a number of other issues. These include whether branding facilitates the exploitation of economies of scale, and whether brands are a separable asset in the firm's portfolio. There is also the question of whether the premium price of branded goods constitutes a regressive tax on poorer consumers, who are the major purchasers of certain types of branded goods. Finally, the chapter attempts to relate the historical growth of branding to long-term economic and cultural change.

BRAND REPUTATION AS MARKET INFORMATION: A CRITIQUE

This section considers whether the economic theory of markets gives the kind of support to branding that is often claimed. It argues that the most familiar supporting arguments do not, in fact, refer to brands at all (see Balasubramanyam and Salisu, Chapter 4 in this volume). They relate instead to product differentiation, quality control and producer reputation. Most arguments for branding assume that in the absence of branding these factors would be undersupplied, so that there is a market failure which branding helps to correct. But even in the absence of branding there could be too much of some of these factors, notably product differentiation. Even if there were too little, it does not follow that branding will necessarily provide more. Branding will normally improve the situation only if it enhances the quality of consumer information. Branding can certainly do this, but it can also be used to suppress information instead. Most significantly, however, there are other ways of improving consumer information, and some of these tackle the issue more directly than does the use of brands. Thus brands are not necessarily the most effective way of doing the things that it is claimed that they do.

Product differentiation

According to Lancaster (1979) each product may be regarded as a bundle of characteristics. The relevant characteristics of a motor car might be acceleration, fuel economy, passenger capacity, and so on. Consumers demand characteristics, not products. The demand for products is a derived demand, the intensity of demand for a given product reflecting the desirability of the particular mix of characteristics it offers.

A differentiated product does not have to be branded because it is always possible to order it by its specification. This is exactly what happens when customized products are made up to individual order. When just a small number of standard varieties are offered then each variety can be ordered either by specification or by a reference number of some kind. When only one variety is available then the generic name can, of course, be used. Thus a brand name is not necessary to signify the product under any circumstances. In this context the advantage of a brand name lies only in the economy of communication. The longer the string of distinguishing characteristics that must be enumerated, and the more subjective and qualitative these characteristics are, the greater is the advantage of using a brand name instead.

The learning of a brand name, and its mental association with particular characteristics, involves a set-up cost for the consumer, however. This is in addition to the cost to the producer of devising and publicizing the name. It follows immediately that a brand name is most useful in two circumstances.

The first is repeat trading. Customers learn the name the first time they buy the product. This investment is paid back in subsequent transactions when only the name needs to be specified. The simpler and shorter the name, the easier it is to specify.

The second case is where the product is advertised away from the point of sale. Customers then need to remember what they want from the time they read the advertisement until the time they make their purchase. Customers also need to remember it from one purchase to the next, of course, so that memory is relevant to repeat trading too, but since it is easier to remember a product that has already been purchased than one that has not, memory may not be quite so significant in this case.

Learning costs can be reduced if the brand name resonates with the characteristics claimed for the product. The consumer's demand is a demand for the characteristics, as noted above, and the translation of this into product demand is facilitated by association of ideas. A brand name should not only be succinct and memorable, therefore, but also be imbued with relevant associations.

The link between branding and repeat-purchase indicated above works well in the food industry. Because of their bulk and perishability most food items are purchased repeatedly and this may explain why many foods, although their characteristics are relatively simple, are heavily branded. The subjectivity of the key characteristic – taste – is also likely to be important. Within the food sector branded goods purchased in single small transactions – confectionery and snack bars distributed through newsagents and drugstores, for example – are particularly prominent. Perhaps this is because the typical consumer of these products is in great haste and so places economy of communication at a premium.

Quality control

The essence of product differentiation is that products are different by design and not by accident. Each variety is unique, but each unit of a given variety is the same. Customers dislike variability between units because this creates uncertainty about the characteristics of any particular purchase. Their concern is typically asymmetric, however: they dislike too little of a good characteristic, but are not averse to too much of it. Quality control is therefore normally concerned with assuring minimum standards. The probability that a unit is below the minimum standard defines the defect rate.

To a certain extent the defect rate is just another characteristic of the product; it does not require a brand name to indicate that the defect rate is low. Producers are, however, remarkably coy about publishing their defect rates. Even the top producers prefer to cultivate a general quality image rather than publicize low defect rates. For example, a top-quality car rental firm does not advertise that 'Only 3 per cent of our customers say they are dissatisfied', even though internally managers may be quite proud of the fact. This indicates one of the ways in which branding can suppress information. Inter-brand competition focused on defect rates would impair valuable subjective characteristics with which the generic product is imbued (see p. 50) and thereby damage producer interests in the industry as a whole. The suppression of defect information is therefore a rational collusive response by producers to the fact that consumers really do not want to know about the risks of a product. Although on average consumers' welfare may be improved by withholding unwanted information, such collusion may damage their welfare when, in an emergency, serious hazards remain concealed.

Another special feature of the defect rate is that it provides a particularly strong incentive for the producer to cheat by claiming that the defect rate is lower than it really is. This is because a lower defect rate is always much better for the consumer than a higher defect rate, but to achieve a lower defect rate is very costly. With natural variability in production inputs, a lower defect rate normally implies a higher rejection rate, and hence more waste of output (Duncan 1974). To lower the defect rate without raising the rejection rate it is necessary either to purchase higher quality materials, or to improve the sorting or filtering process so that fewer good items are wrongly rejected along with the bad ones. Both of these strategies involve extra costs. Advocates of branding argue that it overcomes this incentive problem by allowing producers with low defect rates to gain a reputation for good quality. This is true – but only up to a point. Branding is neither a necessary nor sufficient condition for this to occur.

The key issue is the nature of the sanctions against a cheat. The most obvious sanctions are fines and imprisonment effected by the state. The state can either respond to complaints made by consumers, or make its own investigations. The state brings to bear on the issue its monopoly of force and its reputation for impartiality, as reflected in its legal procedures; it also has access to expert opinion. The main limitation of the state is its requirements for evidence. Evidence is difficult to obtain when key characteristics are subjective or qualitative or where the evidence is liable to be destroyed in the act of consumption – both of which apply to food and drink. The collection and weighing of evidence constitutes a fixed cost, so that legal procedures are prohibitively expensive where small-value transactions are concerned – which again applies to food and drink.

In some cases the role of the state can be delegated to a producers' association. Like the state, a producers' association has access to expert opinion but, unlike the state, it is not weighed down with onerous rules of evidence. Fellow producers have an incentive to punish cheats provided that they feel that the industry as a whole is in danger of being brought into disrepute. They may even be able to share the revenue generated by a fine levied on the cheat. If the producers' association has a statutory monopoly then it has a powerful sanction to extract a fine, since it can force the cheat who does not pay up to leave the industry. In the absence of statutory monopoly, however, some other exclusion mechanism may be required. The existence of an industry-wide public good – such as a co-operative distribution system – may be required for this purpose. The main disadvantage is that a producers' association can maintain prices at monopoly levels, discourage innovations that would disturb market-sharing agreements, and so on. The prices maintained by a producers' association are therefore likely to reflect not merely a quality premium, but a monopolistic mark-up too.

Producer reputation

Both of these approaches are, in essence, collective ones. Advocates of branding argue that punishment should be delegated to the consumer. The consumer's sanction is to withhold a repeat purchase, normally by switching future patronage to a different brand instead. The more quickly that information on defects diffuses through the market, the more the producer's reputation is 'on the line'. Branding is valuable because by reducing communication costs (see p. 43) it strengthens reputation effects. The advantage of this approach is that it relies upon competition between firms rather than on the monopolistic powers of a producers' association or the state. It has a number of weaknesses, however, related to this reliance on reputation effects.

To begin with, it is driven by the consumer's own evaluation of defects, rather than on expert opinion. The 'defects' may arise because the consumer is misusing the product without realizing it. If there is no feedback of information to an expert – for example, because no warranty claim is made – then the consumer as well as the producer may lose out.

More significantly, the reputation effect relies on consumers collecting sufficient information on defective items that they can appraise the relative defect rates of different varieties. They need to combine this information with data on other characteristics in order to make an informed choice. Because it is relative defect rates that matter, consumers need information about defects in the products they do not buy as well as in those that they do. Since it is the defect rate, and not just the incidence of a single defect that is relevant, consumers also need information from a number of different units taken from different batches of each product. These information requirements constitute a very 'tall order' indeed.

It is not sufficient to say that a satisfied consumer should repeat-buy the product because this does not provide information on the other products as well. Consumers need to learn from each other wherever possible. This does not mean, though, that every instance of a defect should attract maximum publicity, as some sections of the contemporary media seem to believe. The objective is not to expel from the industry every producer that supplies defective items, because the optimal defect rate is not normally zero. The requirement is rather that consumers should share their experiences, both good and bad, and learn as much as possible from each other before deciding on future purchases.

Finally, the sanction of loss of future custom is far more serious for some firms than others. A firm that is optimistic about market growth, or which has a low cost of capital (and hence discounts future profits relatively little) will attach more weight than others to a loss of future revenue. More significantly, a firm that has sunk a large amount of non-recoverable capital into the product is far more vulnerable to loss of custom than a 'hit and run' entrant with versatile equipment and negligible sunk costs. This is one reason for long-lived firms enjoying a reputation for quality and integrity that start-up firms do not.

The problem of the 'hit and run' entrant does not arise with state regulation because the penalty in that case is a fine, although a 'hit and run' entrant might attempt to evade the fine by strategically filing for bankruptcy. The problem could arise with a producers' association if the entrant preferred to leave the industry instead of paying the fine – but then the association may well have the power to keep the entrant out unless the entrant is willing to commit sunk costs at the outset.

It has been argued that the problem of insufficient sunk cost is not a problem where brands are concerned because the building of a brand reputation is precisely a sunk cost of this kind (Klein and Leffler 1981). The difficulty with this argument is that it does not explain why the firm wants a brand name in the first place. It explains why, given that the brand is valuable, the irreversible nature of the investment in the brand will discourage cheating. Investing in a brand name that has no independent value does not increase the penalty of cheating, however, since a loss is incurred as soon as the expenditure is made, and no further loss is involved if and when cheating occurs.

Thus it is a mistake to suggest that, say, celebrity endorsements build up brand reputation just because well-publicized celebrity fees assure consumers that the firm has much to lose from poor quality. For if the consumers really believed that no one is influenced by these endorsements then they would consider that the endorsements were a waste of money anyway, and they would suppose that the firm had already written off its investment whatever its product quality turned out to be. Only if the consumers believed that the managers believed (wrongly) that they (the consumers) were influenced in this way would the consumers expect product quality to be signalled by endorsement fees.

Further observations

In practice both collective and competitive incentive systems can be used together. Where defects are potentially hazardous and difficult to detect by inspecting the product, statutory regulation of production is the norm. A uniform standard is set by professional experts reporting to the state. Hygiene regulation in the food industry is an obvious case in point. Consumers do not rely on brands to avoid food-poisoning. Because food-poisoning is so hazardous to health, and bacteria are so difficult to detect, inspectors are given statutory powers of entry at the point of production. It is the quality of taste, and not the purity of the product, that is assured by the brand.

In some less developed countries, however, state regulation is weak or unreliable, and here brands have a significant role in assuring basic levels of quality. Reduced incidence of salmonella could be a real selling point in this case. More generally, the higher that cultural standards of quality are relative to regulatory standards, the greater is the scope for brands in assuring quality.

Historically, self-regulating producer associations have been an important alternative to the state. Like the state, they have concentrated on setting a uniform industry-wide standard of quality. Allowing producers to set their own standards, and be judged on their own individual claims, is a more recent innovation associated with the growth of brands. Thus the trade marks favoured by medieval guilds were not intended to build brand reputations but were an aid to detecting those suppliers of substandard items who were putting the reputation of the group at risk.

Fears that associations introduced to raise quality may eventually turn to rent-seeking activities are supported by the experience of medieval guilds (and of many craft trade unions too). The guilds' concern with quality gradually gave way to price-fixing and to lobbying for protection of the local market. This probably explains why the state rather than the producers' association seems to have gradually become the dominant authority in collective quality control. It is the combination of state control of basic quality and brand incentives governing premium quality that is characteristic of the modern market economy.

Policy implications

The common thread that runs through the preceding analysis is that brands promote efficiency if and when they improve the quality of consumer information; but there are many other ways of improving consumer information instead. One of the problems with brand loyalty is that customers are far better informed of the characteristics of the product they do consume than of the products they do not. This problem can be overcome if firms offer free samples to loyal consumers of rival products. Consumers can then check whether or not their loyalty is misplaced. Producers can also offer ordinary customers tours of their factory, thereby disseminating information which might otherwise remain locked into the official factory inspectorate. Producers can also submit to independent quality audit by reputable organizations who apply standards above the statutory minimum. Specialized media, such as magazines for enthusiasts and connoisseurs, play an important role in this, although there is a potential conflict of interest because of the dependence of the media on advertising revenue from the producers.

Producers can further reassure customers by offering generous warranties and readily enforceable money-back guarantees which avoid the need to make small claims in the courts. They can also sink costs in relevant activities, such as automated quality control. Such investments are doubly useful: not only are they directly relevant to quality but also they demonstrably penalize poor quality because the firm is so dependent on future sales to pay the investment back.

Producers can also take action to strengthen reputation effects by encouraging consumers to socialize with each other. By organizing their own enthusiasts' clubs they not only promote interest in the product but also provide a mechanism for disseminating information about the defect rate.

None of these mechanisms is directly linked to branding, in the sense that they can be employed for unbranded products too. One of the general insights of economic theory is that most incentive problems should be tackled at source wherever possible. Indirect solutions are only second-best. In the present context this means that incentive problems caused by imperfect information should be tackled by measures that directly improve information flow. Branding sometimes complements these measures but is not a direct measure of itself.

BRANDING AND CULTURAL CHARACTERISTICS

The most important motivation for branding, it is suggested here, is that it imbues products with cultural characteristics. Giving the product a name makes it possible to think of a 'personality' that goes with that name; the characteristics can then be linked to the personality of the product. Unlike the physical characteristics of a product, cultural characteristics are not objectively measureable. They are economically relevant, however, because they are characteristics for which consumers are willing to pay. It is not irrational for consumers to determine their purchasing behaviour from given preferences. Preferences establish a priority ordering and rationality translates this ordering into appropriate behaviour under scarcity constraints. Economists do not say that one set of preferences is more rational than another, however peculiar some people's preferences may appear to be. Preferences are said to be irrational only if no consistent ordering prevails.

Consumer preferences for cultural characteristics are taken as given. This means that when the cultural characteristics of a product are modified by branding, preferences with respect to products will change. Thus by imbuing products with new cultural characteristics, branding manipulates consumer demand.

Four main types of cultural characteristics may be identified. The first simply makes the consumer feel good in a purely private sense. It is the emotional analogue to the material satisfaction gained from private consumption. The emotion may be related to a private fantasy: when sipping Australian wine I may be mentally transported to the Australian bush (see Merrett and Whitwell, Chapter 9 in this volume). The fantasy may activate pleasant memories, or simply compensate for the fact that I will not be able to go there (or go back there again). A variant on the fantasy is the dream. The economic significance of dreaming is slightly different. Dreams may well come true, and the realization of a dream is often a focus for ambition, and hence a motivator for work (Schumpeter 1934). Indeed, a product imbued with dream-like qualities may offer more emotional rewards before it is consumed than when it is consumed because the reality lacks the dream-like quality of the image on which expectations were focused. A camping holiday in the Australian bush might come into this category. Another kind of private satisfaction is the sense of virtue in consuming a product which is morally good. Moral and religious systems are widely used (often for good reasons) to promote certain kinds of fantasies and dreams and to censor others. A morally acceptable fantasy therefore provides more emotional benefit than an unacceptable one, which will be impaired by feelings of guilt. A consumer's morality is therefore an important determinant of his or her preferences for cultural characteristics. Thus a Protestant fundamentalist might condemn the consumption of an organic wine for its intoxicating effect, while an ardent environmentalist might approve on the grounds that it is ecologically sound. This moral dimension is considered further (on pp. 55–7).

The second main type of cultural characteristic is the badge of allegiance. It has social rather than private significance. Blue jeans, VW Beetles and Renault 2CVs can all be used to make a personal statement of values to other people. The economic significance of a badge of allegiance is that it facilitates the operation of social groups. People with shared values can recognize each other through their conspicuous consumption of symbolic products. Since social groups can reduce transaction costs between their members (Casson 1991), badges of allegiance may serve to promote efficiency. There is, however, an important difference between badges that unify hitherto disparate individuals and those that segment hitherto homogeneous groups into rival factions. While the former reduces transaction costs, the latter raises them. Thus while blue jeans may promote economic interactions among the young, they may reinforce a generation gap which inhibits economic interactions between young and old. The net contribution to efficiency depends upon which of these interactions is the most important. In the case of blue jeans it could be argued that because so many young people are employed by older people, the cost of widening the generation gap is greater than the benefit of promoting social solidarity among young people.

The third type of characteristic is related to status. Status is a social phenomenon, like allegiance, but is concerned with the differences and not the similarities between people. Reinforcing status-related characteristics through branding is economically wasteful. To appreciate this, consider a group divided into two factions: the 'haves' and the 'have-nots'. The haves possess the status good and the have-nots do not (Hirsch 1977). When two haves, or two have-nots, meet each other, the encounter is emotionally neutral (any positive effect would fall under allegiance, as described above). But when a have meets a have-not, the have feels good and the have-not feels bad. This creates a strong incentive to have the good. If you meet a have, you avoid feeling inferior, while if you meet a have-not you feel superior, so that whoever you meet you feel better off. If the good is reasonably priced, and the emotional benefits are strong, then everyone may buy the good. Since no one is then inferior, no emotional benefits are obtained.

But everyone needs the good because they would feel inferior to everyone else if they were the only people without it. Actually, no one is better off emotionally than if no one had the good at all. Yet everyone buys the good, and so is actually worse off by an amount equal to the purchase price. Individually it is rational to buy the good because of the fear of feeling inferior, but collectively it is stupid because when everyone buys the good there is no one to feel superior to.

If status is so inefficient, it may be asked, why are status systems so important and why have they lasted so long? Historically status has been an important form of occupational reward and, indeed, a good deal of status is still related to occupation today. Status rewards can compensate for missing pecuniary rewards in activities where the social benefits are difficult for the producer to appropriate. Thus doctors may enjoy high status to compensate for the fact that they cannot charge their poorest and sickest patients much for their skills. This is not the only way of rationalizing status, of course, but even in this context, allowing people to buy status tends to diminish efficiency. If people who can appropriate rewards can acquire through consumption the same status as those who cannot, then status will eventually be devalued and recruitment to important occupations will be impaired. Other mechanisms – such as a state subsidy – will have to substitute for the weakened status mechanism.

The final type of characteristic is one that makes the product suitable as a gift. It is important to remember that trade itself appears to have originated in gift-giving, and that many gifts are still given in the expectation of receiving some unspecified future benefit in return. This reflects the fact that gift-giving continues to support a wide range of non-market economic activity, for example, the production of household services within the family. The difference between early and modern societies is simply that in modern societies the market sector has expanded and been formalized, and that most gifts used in the non-market sector are now procured through this market sector instead of being produced by the donors themselves.

A product does not make a suitable gift simply because it is useful to the recipient. There are many utilitarian items that are quite inappropriate as gifts. Indeed, if mutual convenience were the dominant criterion then most gifts would consist of money. A gift is rather an expression of the esteem in which the recipient is held. Gifts contain information to recipients because they are unsure of exactly how their reputation stands. A gift is therefore a symbolic statement of the reputation of the recipient, as interpreted by the donor. Because gifts are such an important co-ordination mechanism in the non-market economy, the inculcation of relevant attributes through branding is potentially very valuable. By allowing the donor to pick off the shelf a highly distinctive and apparently exclusive product, the costs of finding suitable gifts are dramatically reduced.

Comparing the four types of characteristics discussed suggests that the branding of products as status symbols is very inefficient (from the social point of view) compared with branding them as badges of allegiance. In terms of emotional rewards, status is typically a zero-sum game, because in every encounter the superior feeling of one party is offset by the inferior feeling of the other. When played out with branded products, however, it becomes a negative sum game because of the waste associated with the production of the product.

Badges of allegiance have an ambiguous effect because they can either unify people into a group or fragment an existing group into factions. Because badges of allegiance are mainly of significance to adolescents, few of whom are engaged in significant economic activity, the impact of badges on economic performance is probably fairly slight in any case.

Gift-related characteristics can be generally commended because of the continuing importance of gift-giving in organizing economic activity within the household, and in clubs, societies and other small not-for-profit organizations.

FURTHER IMPLICATIONS

Because of its wide-ranging nature the preceding analysis has implications for a number of other issues that are commonly raised in connection with brands. It confirms the view that brands can be an important form of barrier to entry. It has already been noted that a long-lived incumbent firm demonstrates by its continued presence in the market that it is not a 'hit and run' entrant seeking to profit from poor quality. Consumers are also likely to believe that long-lived firms have accumulated more production experience than others, and that they are therefore more competent in assuring quality than their newer rivals.

Incumbent firms also have an opportunity to imbue their products with cultural attributes that are difficult to imitate. Foods and drinks containing mysterious ingredients or made to secret family recipes appear to consumers as inherently difficult to copy, so that any entrant must be under suspicion if it claims to offer an identical product. Of course, if the ingredients or the recipes are not particularly tasty then new firms can enter with their own secrets and mysteries. Marginal customers will be attracted away from incumbent firms until profits in the industry are reduced to normal levels.

The analysis also confirms the view that advertising persuades as well as informs. Advertising does not persuade by argument so much as by stimulus of the imagination. This explains why so many advertisements are important cultural artefacts, even if they fall slightly short of being major works of art. It is advertising that typically imbues the branded product with its cultural characteristics, although celebrity endorsements, sponsorship of sport events and other marketing ploys also have a role in this.

The fact that advertising is not really intended to inform is emphasized by the fact that so much relevant information is left out of advertisements – most notably the product price. Even where products are advertised as being good value for money, price information is often withheld. Many advertisements also fail to mention at which shops the product can be found, which is another vital piece of practical information.

An important debate in accountancy concerns whether the capitalized value of a brand should appear on the firm's balance sheet, and this is reduced to the question of whether brands are separable from the firm's other assets (Barwise 1990; see also Napier, Chapter 5 in this volume). In so far as brands are linked to quality control, a reasonable case can be made that the brand is inseparable from the firm because quality assurance depends on the training of the personnel and the management procedures used, which customers would believe to be different if ownership were to change. If, on the other hand, a brand is no more than a distinctive combination of cultural characteristics, then it is much more independent of the firm. Note, however, that while these characteristics may be independent of the ownership of production, they often depend on the location of production – an obvious point in the case of, say, whisky brands. Firms that acquire brands therefore need to be careful about the subsequent rationalization of production locations.

It is sometimes suggested that brands are socially beneficial because they facilitate the exploitation of economies of scale. This may be true historically in the case of the transition from customized production to mass production, or the integration of regional into national markets. In these cases branding provides the boost in sales that is needed to get a new large plant fully utilized. In other cases, however, such as petroleum refining, an integrated market for a generic product may be segmented by branding into smaller markets with a consequent loss of some economies of scale. In general there is no particular reason to associate branding with either economies or diseconomies of scale.

Mass produced branded products are often targeted on consumers in the lower socio-economic groups (see Ward, Chapter 13 in this volume). One reason for this is simply that they are the most numerous. On the other hand, they are certainly not the wealthiest, nor are they likely to be the groups most concerned with intrinsic product quality. The most probable explanation is that these consumers are the ones most likely to value the cultural characteristics with which advertisers associate their branded products. This sensitivity to cultural characteristics may in turn reflect the consumers' underlying concerns about their social status which they believe that branded products can help alleviate. It may also reflect the poorer urban environment in which these consumers live, which places a large premium on the fantasy element in the consumption of branded goods.

Two things follow if this interpretation is correct. The first is that the premium prices charged for branded products are borne by mainly poorer people, so that the pricing structure is regressive: wealthy shareholders extract rents from poor consumers, in other words. This is not to deny that the consumers benefit; they would not buy the products if they did not appreciate the fantasy and feel that their status had been enhanced. It does mean, however, that there may be better ways of improving welfare than selling branded products as compensation for low social status and a depressing environment. Given that status-seeking is at best a zero-sum game, tackling status problems head-on might be a better approach. The same goes for the quality of the environment: creating new fantasies may be second-best to improving reality, at least up to a point. The second consequence is therefore that intensive demand for branded products is not necessarily a tribute to the success of the market system – it may actually be a compensating reaction to some of the failures of the system instead.

IDEOLOGY AND BRANDS

The emphasis in this chapter on the cultural significance of brands suggests a reappraisal of the standard historical interpretation of the growth of brands (see Wilkins, Chapter 2 in this volume). Conventional wisdom relates the growth of branding to a combination of rising incomes, improved transportation and mass production technology which has widened the market area over which consumer goods are distributed. Particular emphasis is placed on the role of packaging in maintaining the quality of the product between factory and consumer and in permitting colour and design to enhance point-of-sale display. Packaging also enhances the subjective degree of product differentiation, so that consumers perceive a greater variety of choice as well.

The arguments above are broadly consistent with this story, but they add a further dimension, namely the link between the growth of brands and cultural change. Cultural historians (for example, Williams 1982) have shown that one of the consequences of commercial growth and industrialization has been the erosion of the monopoly power of traditional religion and the emergence of a moral pluralism sustained by mutual toleration. The promotion of brands through advertising taps into this moral pluralism by linking products to appropriate consumer lifestyles (Earl 1983). Morality – particularly in its puritan manifestations – no longer provides such a tight constraint on consumerism. Morality becomes more permissive, and the choice between different moralities may even degenerate into just another aspect of consumerism itself.

The moral system which has achieved the greatest advance in its influence since the early 1970s is the one centred on the ideology of the market. It is this system of thought which justifies making individual autonomy supreme and subordinating traditional moralities to the status of taboos which people may respect as they wish. As noted at the outset, it is from this point of view that most of the conventional analysis of brands is written. This analysis purports to show that brands are beneficial because branding is a product of the market system. Brands are good because this system is essentially good. It is admitted that the system is not perfect, but it is claimed to be better than any feasible alternative. Indeed, the recent downfall of socialist economies is cited in support of this.

The evidence on the growth of brands suggests a rather different interpretation, however. The major role claimed for branding – namely quality control – is in fact performed by statutory authorities in most developed countries. It is, ironically, only in developing countries that branding demonstrably performs a quality assurance role. The evidence suggests that the major role of branding is to imbue products with cultural characteristics – characteristics increasingly linked to the major lifestyle options of a pluralistic society.

The view of human nature indicated by this evidence is rather different from that of the calculating materialistic consumer promoted by market ideology. It suggests a rather imaginative and even romantically inclined individual searching for objects with the kind of meaning and significance that the symbols of the great religions once had. It is an individual preoccupied with his acceptance by society and his status within it, who uses products as part of a strategy for social advancement. This individual prefers not to be informed about some of the risks he runs – thus information about defect rates is usually not desired, as explained above. To indulge his fantasies he needs to sustain a degree of self-esteem which objective self-appraisal might undermine. The individual therefore prefers to be rewarded by flattering gifts rather than by money payments which would indicate objectively his market value. Brands 'add value' for this individual mainly because they support his fantasies, rather than because they reduce his anxieties about defect rates. But just as there are alternatives to brands in assuring product quality, so there are also alternatives to brands in generating emotional satisfactions too.

In her study of French intellectual attitudes to consumerism, Williams (1982: 152) notes that religious dogmatism is one answer to the needs of the individual who is 'determined to rise above the banality of mass merchandising'. In pre-industrial society religious observance certainly seems to have afforded many of the emotional satisfactions which in a secular society are generated by lifestyle experiments supported by branded goods. Market ideology encourages individuals to satisfy their emotional needs through consumption, but it seems possible that, for some individuals at least, these needs might be better met in a more traditional way. This suggests, therefore, that branding is neither an essential quality assurance mechanism, nor an indispensable source of emotional satisfaction, as market ideology seems to suggest.

REFERENCES

Barwise, P., with Higson, C., Likerman, A. and Marsh, P. (1990) 'Brands as "separable assets" ', *Business Strategy Review* Summer: 43–59.
Casson, M. C. (1991) *Economics of Business Culture: Game Theory, Transaction Costs and Economic Performance*, Oxford: Clarendon Press.
Duncan, A. J. (1974) *Quality Control and Industrial Statistics*, Homewood, Ill: Richard D. Irwin.
Earl, P. E. (1986) *Lifestyle Economics: Consumer Behaviour in a Turbulent World*, Brighton: Wheatsheaf.
Hirsch, P. E. (1977) *Social Limits to Growth*, London: Routledge & Kegan Paul.
Klein, B. and Leffler, K. (1981) 'The role of market forces in assuring contractual performance', *Journal of Political Economy* 89: 615–41.
Lancaster, K. (1979) *Variety, Equity and Efficiency*, Oxford: Basil Blackwell.
Schumpeter, J. A. (1934) *The Theory of Economic Development* (trans.

R. Opie) Cambridge, Mass: Harvard University Press.

Williams, R. H. (1982) *Dream Worlds: Mass Consumption in Late Nineteenth-Century France*, Berkeley, Calif: University of California Press.

4 Brands and the alcoholic drinks industry

V. N. Balasubramanyam and M. A. Salisu

Marketing experts understandably wax eloquent on the role of brands in modern business. One expert avers that 'the concept of a brand is probably the most powerful idea in the commercial world . . . the way in which it provides a means of explaining the phenomena of business life, is in some ways analogous to the impact of Newton's theories on the physical sciences' (Cowley 1991). Although economists may not be persuaded that the concept of brands provides the key to unlocking the mysteries of modern business, brands have not entirely escaped their attention. The controversy on advertising in the early 1960s was essentially a debate on the role of brands, with Galbraith condemning the wastefulness of advertising in creating new wants in an opulent society and Harry Johnson advocating the view that advertising played a role in educating the consumer. The recent revival of interest in brands has all to do with competitive strategy – in their role in preventing entry into oligopolistic industries, in the optimal timing of new brands and in the role of brand management in promoting efficiency in production and distribution. Brands or more specifically differentiated products have also figured prominently in the theoretical literature on international trade and investment grounded in models of imperfect competition. Another development, which we owe to business historians, is the analysis of the role of brands in particular and distribution in general in the internationalization process of several British and US business firms.

This chapter has the modest objective of analysing the role of brands in the alcoholic drinks industry. Among other things it examines the relevance of the various strands of the literature on brands to the marketing and distribution strategy of alcoholic drinks producing firms. For the most part the discussion is confined to the spirits distilling firms as opposed to firms in brewing.

SOCIAL COSTS AND BENEFITS OF BRANDS

The literature on brands in economics can be grouped into three broad categories. The first of these relates to the social costs of brands and advertising, the second to the role of brands and advertising in the competitive strategy of firms and industries and the third, which is intimately related to the second, discusses the role of brands and more generally differentiated products in promoting productive efficiency and growth of firms. These categories do overlap but such a classification aids discussion.

The lineage of the debate on social costs of advertising, brands, trade marks can be traced to the seminal work on imperfect competition and monopolistic competition by Joan Robinson (1963) and Edward Chamberlain (1933). Their work in the 1930s has spawned a vast literature on the role of non-price factors such as advertising and brands on the structure, conduct and performance of firms and industries. But their interest in advertising, especially that of Robinson, was confined to its influence on product choice by consumers. As Robinson puts it 'the customer will be influenced by advertisement, which plays upon his mind with studied skill, and makes him prefer the good of one producer to those of another because they are brought to his notice in a more pleasing or more forceful manner'. But on the issue of whether or not advertising was a good thing Joan Robinson preferred the safe ground of agnosticism in the belief that it is impossible to separate advertising from other forms of aggressive selling or to separate aggressive selling from the economic system of which it is a part (Robinson 1951).

It is this agnosticism of economists concerning the social costs of advertising which surprises Galbraith and he attributes it to the inability of economists to accommodate advertising in their conventional models of consumer behaviour which assumes that wants are independently determined. Economists have stuck to the assumption of independently determined wants because 'it is far better and much safer to have a firm anchor in nonsense than to put out on the troubled seas of thought'. When he himself ventures on the troubled seas of thought Galbraith is persuaded that 'the fact that wants can be synthesised by advertising, catalysed by salesmanship, and shaped by the discreet manipulations of the persuaders shows that they are not urgent' (Galbraith 1987: 131). Needless to say the resources spent on creating these wants are a social waste. His condemnation of the waste of resources involved in advertising is even more trenchant when he argues that while the forty-two million dollars worth of skill, art and paper spent in 1949 for cigarette advertising and the twenty-nine million dollars devoted to alcoholic drinks served no urgent social purpose the same is true of the cigarettes and the liquor. It is not clear that the community would be better off if those now engaged in selling tobacco and liquor were employed instead in the production of more and cheaper cigarettes and whisky.

(Galbraith 1961: 97)

Galbraith's strictures on advertising should be considered in the context of his main thesis. It is that affluence is the main reason for the existence of advertising. It is only those who are far from physical want, those who do not know what they want, who can be effectively persuaded by advertising. But should not those who do not know what they want be informed and educated? This, in fact, is the basis of Harry Johnson's (1962) case for advertising. In an affluent society the standard of wants has to be raised, one's taste needs to be educated and refined. Advertising can perform these functions and in cases where it results in the exploitation of the helpless consumer there are social and government processes which can be set to work. Galbraith's premise is that advertising is a product of opulence and it creates new wants which may not be urgent. While Johnson accepts the premise that advertising is a product of opulence he draws from it the conclusion that in an opulent society advertising has an essential role to play; that of educating the opulent consumer and refining his wants. In sum consumer learning is as important as producer learning and advertising plays an essential role in educating the consumer.

While the early literature was concerned with the social costs of advertising the more recent literature is largely devoted to a discussion of the role of advertising and brands in the competitive strategy of firms and industries; or what Galbraith refers to as the efforts of firms to shift the demand curve at the expense of others or change its shape through product differentiation. Efforts of incumbent firms at preventing entry of new firms into a profitable industry forms a part of the competitive strategy of firms. Joe Bain was the first to recognize the importance of product differentiation along with scale economies and absolute cost advantages as a method of preventing entry (Bain 1956). His finding that both profits and concentration tend to be relatively high in industries characterized by entry barriers has been confirmed by other studies. Significant in this context is the importance of product differentiation in consumer goods industries (Comanor and Wilson 1967). It is also argued that, given certain assumptions, brand proliferation could be successful in preventing entry (Schmalensee 1978). The assumptions underlying the proposition are increasing returns to scale in the production of each of the existing brands, localized rivalry between brands and relative immobility of brands in economic space. The assumption of localized rivalry suggests that although there may be many brands of a product on the market, price competition is confined to brands which are close substitutes for one another. In other words small changes in price of a particular brand will have a noticeable impact on the demand for only a small number of rival brands. The assumption of relative immobility of brands implies that repositioning of existing brands in economic space involves substantial repositioning costs and such repositioning is rarely undertaken. On the basis of these assumptions Schmalensee argues that brand proliferation by existing producers is a much more effective entry deterrent than either price cutting or advertising. Although the hypothesis rests on several assumptions, Schmalensee argues that it fits the case of the US ready-to-eat breakfast cereals industry during the period 1950–72, when the existing six leading producers of cereals introduced over eighty brands and there was no significant entry into the industry.

The order of entry of brands into a market is also shown to influence market shares. Brands which enter a market early enjoy a higher market share than those which follow. This is because consumers who are convinced of the performance of the first brand may be reluctant to invest the time and effort in learning about new brands. In other words brands provide information on product quality and the acquisition of information is costly in terms of time and effort. This sort of a pioneer brand advantage is supposed to be large in the case of convenience goods for which retailers do not provide much information (Schmalensee 1982; Urban et al. 1984).

These propositions concerning the role of brands in preventing entry and the advantages they confer on the pioneers are not entirely free of controversy. The so-called Chicago school of industrial organization, for instance, argues that dominant firms in an industry owe their position to superior performance, not to strategic behaviour or the history of entry into the industry, and profits are simply the rents that accrue to superior technology (Gilbert 1989). While the Chicago school does not deny the role of barriers to entry in preserving profits, it is treated as secondary to the incumbent firms ability to satisfy consumers better than prospective entrants. The Chicago school thesis is a weak version of the recent contestable market thesis in which both entry to and exit from an industry are costless and the very threat of entry can enforce good conduct on incumbents.

However, could the possession of reputable brands bestow advantages in production and distribution on incumbent firms? Is it likely that brands and trade marks may be a significant factor in the technology firms possess? The role of trade marks in promoting productive efficiency is cogently argued by Mira Wilkins (1992; see also Chapter 2 in this volume). The reputation of brands and trade marks can pull customers to the products produced by the firm and enable it to increase the volume of production and reap economies of scale, the possession of reputable brands may enable firms to borrow capital much more cheaply than its rivals in capital markets, skilled labour may be attracted to the firm because of the reputation of its brands, possession of reputable brands may provide the resources required for reaping economies of scale and scope in research and development and trade marks also enable the firm to push the demand curve outward for its products continually over time and paves the way for further economies of scale.

It is this ability of the firm to reap economies of scale and scope not only in production but also in distribution which enable it to grow and maintain its competitive position in both domestic and international markets. Well known in this context is Chandler's (1990) explanation of the rise and growth of the modern corporation, with its emphasis on the role of economies of scale and scope. Economies of scale is a familiar concept in industrial economics but the concept of economies of scope is of recent vintage. Economies of scale are said to exist if total costs rise less proportionately than output. Economies of scope are said to exist if the cost of producing a number of products jointly is less than the total cost of separate production of each of the products. Such economies of scope arise if factor inputs are imperfectly divisible and the production of a limited set of goods results in excess capacity. They can also arise if inputs are in the nature of a public good and the utilization of such inputs for one purpose does not preclude their use for the purposes. An example of the latter would be technology and know how including marketing know how. If firms are to survive and grow in the face of ever-changing markets and technologies they have to continually reduce costs, achieve functional efficiency in production and distribution, innovate new products and processes and seek efficient methods of resource allocation. All this the modern corporation has achieved through the exploitation of economies of scale and scope in production and distribution and by reducing transaction costs. Mira Wilkins's analysis underscores the contribution of brands and trade marks to the exploitation of economies of scale and scope in production and distribution.

Business historians have graphically described the advent and growth of British and US firms specializing in the production of branded and packaged products in the international markets during the late nineteenth and early twentieth centuries (Jones 1984; 1983; Wilkins 1988). The growth of these firms abroad was primarily based on the organizational abilities that they had developed in marketing and distribution rather than in production. Brands and differentiated products have figured prominently in the international economics literature in recent years with the observed growth in intra-industry trade or trade in differentiated products. Such trade has increased because of convergence in taste patterns across countries. The starting-point of the story is that consumers demand variety or differing attributes in products and production of differentiated products are subject to economies of scale. Because of the presence of economies of scale no one firm can produce all the known varieties of a product. Indeed no one country can produce all the varieties because of the presence of economies of scale in production and the size of the domestic market limits the number of varieties that can be produced in any one country. Now if tastes overlap between countries trade in differentiated products takes place. Empirical tests of the theory suffer from ambiguities surrounding the definition of a product and product differentiation. Nevertheless several tests have attributed the observed growth in intra-industry trade between developed countries in several consumer and producer goods to the presence of scale economies in the production of differentiated products and over-lapping taste patterns (Greenaway and Milner 1986). It is of significance that economies of scale which figures centrally in Mira Wilkins's (1992) analysis of the importance of trade marks in promoting productive efficiency also provides an explanation for the growth of intra-industry trade. It is worth noting that economies of scope may also enable firms to produce a number of varieties of products and engage in intra-industry trade.

BRANDS AND MARKETS FOR ALCOHOLIC DRINKS

The alcoholic drinks industry provides an eminent case study of the various propositions concerning brands, trade marks and advertising in its literature. It is an industry dominated by a few large firms. In the case of the UK, for instance, the five firm concentration ratio in the brewing sector exceeds 50 per cent and in the case of the spirits distilling industry the ratio is around 64 per cent. More than 56 per cent of the total sales of spirits in the world market in the year 1990 was on account of ten firms, of which three were British (see Table 4.1).

Table 4.1 World's top ten spirits companies, 1990

	Nine litre cases (million)	World market share (%)	Rank	Country of origin
International Distillers and Vintners (IDV)	57.3	10.6	1	US
United Distillers (UD)	53.5	9.9	2	Britain
Seagram	41.2	7.6	3	Canada
Hiram Walker	28.3	5.2	4	Britain
American Brands	26.7	4.9	5	US
Bacardi	26.5	4.7	6	Barbados
Suntory	22.6	4.2	7	Japan
Pernod Ricard	20.2	3.7	8	France
Pedro Domeck	17.9	3.3	9	Spain
Brown-Forman	13.9	2.6	10	US
Subtotal	308.1	56.7		
Total world	540.0	100.0		

Source: Unpublished data provided to the authors by Impact Databank

The alcoholic drinks industry has a major presence in the UK manufacturing sector. It accounts for around 2.6 per cent of the net output of the manufacturing sector, 1.6 per cent of manufacturing employment and 2.6 per cent of the country's total of manufactured exports. It is also one of the three industry groups in the food and drinks sector along with chocolate and chocolate preparations and sugar confectionery which enjoys a revealed comparative advantage in export markets. The UK accounts for a substantial proportion of total world exports of spirits. In the year 1984 the UK's share of total value of world exports of spirits accounted for 43 per cent; this figure increased to around 48 per cent in the year 1990. The industry also acounts for a substantial proportion of the total foreign direct investment of the UK manufacturing sector. In the year 1989, the most recent year for which data are available, overseas production of the leading UK spirits distilling companies accounted for 6 per cent of the total £101 billion of such production by seventy-five major UK manufacturing companies, and 24 per cent of the production of all UK food and drink companies. Such overseas production consists of a diversified range of alcoholic drinks including beer and food products in the case of some of the firms such as Allied Lyons and Grand Metropolitan.

The success of alcoholic drink firms in international markets is grounded in the ownership advantages that they possess. Such owner-ship advantages or rent-yielding assets that they possess principally consist of an ability to identify market niches, engage in product development and product differentiation and their expertise in distribution in general. Statistical analysis of the determinants of foreign sales of the UK food and drink firms suggests that it is heavily influenced by their human capital endowment and their ability to diversify and differentiate their products (Balasubramanyam 1993).

The firms in the industry are market driven, distribution and marketing rather than production technology being the main driving force for these firms much more so than for firms in most other industries because of the nature of the products they produce. Brand names, product differentiation and innovations in packaging all play a major role in the survival growth of these firms. The leading firms in the spirits distilling industry can boast of a varied number of brands they produce, although in recent years some firms have followed a policy of consolidation and concentrated on a selected number of reputable brands. Brand positioning, brand management and innovative organizational changes in distribution are characteristic features of the competitive strategies of the firms in the alcoholic drinks industry. Another feature of the alcoholic drinks industry which has attracted much attention is its expenditures on advertising. It ranks high among the leading advertisers within the food and drinks category (see Table 4.2). This should be of little surprise given the importance of distribution and marketing in the industry.

The industry though is an obvious target for not only those concerned with problems of alcohol abuse but also the critics of advertising in general. As stated earlier, Galbraith (1961), for instance, singles out the whisky and cigarette producers in his attack on advertising. The theoretical case against advertising in general, however, is not matched by empirical evidence in support of it. Schmalensee's (1972) detailed survey of the evidence led him to conclude 'there is barely a molehill of hard evidence behind the mountain of prose on the subject of advertising'. Statistical studies on the demand for alcoholic drinks in the UK also conclude that 'the influences of advertising on total drink demand and upon its distribution between types of drink (if these influences exist at all) are very small indeed in both an absolute sense and in comparison with the effect of income and to a lesser extent prices' (Duffy 1987). Estimated elasticities with respect to advertising for beer and spirits are as low as 0.1 and 0.2 respectively.

These and other studies appear to lend little support to Galbraith's

Table 4.2 Advertising expenditure on major consumer goods in the UK, 1989

	Sales (£million)	Advertising (£million)	Advertising as % of sales
Beer	10,677	102.41	0.96
Lager	5,285	64.50	1.22
Other beers	5,392	37.91	0.70
Spirits	5,311	45.69	0.86
Whisky	2,202	15.70	0.71
Vodka	836	0.92	0.11
Rum	517	1.68	0.32
Liqueurs	409	11.25	2.75
Gin	570	2.96	0.52
Brandy	444	5.62	1.27
Vermouth/aperitifs	246	6.18	2.51
Port	87	1.38	1.58
Wine	3,173	7.04	0.54
Champagne	515	1.19	0.23
Sparkling	122	2.08	1.71
Biscuits	961	14.36	1.49
Bread	1,933	7.43	0.38
Ready-to-eat cereal	510	61.04	11.97
Sugar confectionery	931	15.12	1.62
Chocolate confectionery	2,528	82.43	3.26
Ice cream (take home)	387	6.18	1.60
Fresh vegetables	2,170	0.98	0.05
Frozen vegetables	544	5.65	1.04
Household textiles	746	0.68	0.09

Source: Advertising Association 1989

view that advertisers manipulate consumer demand and exert a power-ful influence on the manner in which they allocate their expenditures between products. Why then do drink firms advertise? They may do so for a number of reasons including the need to maintain and pro-mote their share of the market by providing information on the brands they produce, to prevent the entry of new firms and to avoid price competition. But in all this do they educate consumers and refine their tastes? Talk about educating the consumer of alcoholic drinks would no doubt seem strange to the anti-alcohol lobby. The only education they would advocate is one which eliminates the demand for such drinks, but the less dogmatic and less puritanical consumers who accord a place for alcoholic drinks in their pursuit of pleasure, relaxa-tion and entertainment may see some merit in advertising. As has been repeatedly stated, advertising and brands save consumers valuable time and effort in their search for quality and chosen attributes in a product. Beyond that differentiated products and advertising may serve to improve the quality of the product and inform the consumer of the quality enhancement achieved by the producers. In this context two features of the demand for alcoholic drinks are of relevance. First, they are a product of the affluent society; they are luxury goods. Estimated income elasticities of demand for spirits and wine in the UK are of the order of 1.8 and 2.5 respectively (Duffy 1987; Selvanathan 1988). Both wine and spirits are luxury goods in most other developed countries also. Second, there is some evidence in support of the view that although total demand for alcoholic drinks in general and spirits in particular may not be buoyant in recent years the demand for superior quality or relatively high-priced brands may be increasing. As Sir Anthony Tennant, the former chief executive of Guinness, puts it, 'the modern European consumer may be drinking slightly less but he, or she, is certainly drinking better'. Also revealing is his comment that this is a situation which places a major value on strong brands with developed international reputations for quality and *prestige imagery*.

If advertising and brands are successful in persuading affluent consumers, who do not know their wants, to drink less but better, they can claim to have had some success in educating the consumer. The prestige imagery which Sir Tennant refers to may also be of importance to the consumer in an affluent society. Consumption of whisky or wine is not only a matter of quenching one's thirst or satisfying one's taste buds but also a sign of affluence and one's status. Status and affluence have to be signalled by drinking the most prestigious and high-priced brands. In the jargon of economics there are externalities in consumption.

Thorstein Veblen (1963) may have been the first to identify this trait, which he labels the ceremonial differentiation of the diet of the leisure class; a trait according to Veblen best seen in the use of intoxicating beverages and drugs. As he puts it, if these articles of consumption are costly, they are felt to be noble and honorific. They are honorific because the consumption of these more excellent goods is an evidence of wealth. This search for qualitative excellence in eating and drinking affects not only the manner of life but also the training and intellectual activity of the gentleman of leisure; in order to avoid stultification he must also cultivate his tastes, for it now becomes incumbent on him to discriminate with some nicety between the noble and the ignoble in consumable goods. Indeed, Veblen appears to have foreshadowed Harry Johnson when he wrote

this cultivation of the aesthetic faculty requires time and application, and the demands made upon the gentleman in this direction
therefore tend to change his life of leisure into a more or less
arduous application to the business of learning how to live a life of
ostensible leisure in a becoming way.

(Veblen 1963: 64)

Although Veblen may not have approved of the leisure class his
narration of the arduous efforts and time required to distinguish
between the noble and ignoble in consumables is prescient. In short
hedonism and ostentation, whether or not one approves, are marks of
affluence, signs of refined tastes; if advertising and brands assist consumers in their search for such refinement and saves them time and
effort, they have a place in the affluent society. To the extent that the
alcoholic drinks industry caters to these needs of the consumer through
its efforts not only at improving the quality of whiskies and wines but
also in providing prestigious goods with the right image, it can claim
to serve consumers in their search for quality and prestige. Promoting
the right image of a product is no easy task. The image of a product
depends on not only the intrinsic quality of the product but also the
manner in which it is packaged, its brand name and its price.

It is worth noting that the major spirits distilling companies in the
UK all feature a range of prestigious high-priced brands which they
have nurtured over time through advertising and other methods of
promotion in international markets. Examples of such deluxe brands
include Old Parr, Johnnie Walker Black Label and Dimple brands of
whiskies produced by United Distillers (UD), and Chivas Regal and
Glenlivet produced by Seagrams. It is the possession of these brands
which enabled these firms to penetrate international markets for
spirits characterized by a demand for high-status, image-conferring
brands. As a report on the operations of UD puts it, 'while buying for
simple consumption is moving more and more towards commodity in
developed markets (and remains dominated by local products), the
international market is increasingly concerned with high status, image
conferring brands which are bought as much for their social halo as
for their satisfaction in consumption' (James Capel 1988). Also
notable is the growing convergence in taste patterns in the European
markets for alcoholic drinks in general, with the traditional beer and
spirits-drinking Northern European countries displaying a growing
taste for wine, and the traditional wine-drinking Southern European
countries displaying a taste for spirits and beer. This tendency towards
convergence of taste patterns is a reflection of the demand for variety

and emulation of the taste patterns of one's neighbours. Such over-lapping taste patterns result in increased intra-industry trade. The estimated index of intra-industry trade for the alcoholic drinks group as a whole for the UK in recent years is as high as 74 per cent.

These observed trends in taste patterns for variety and prestigious brands and products in the alcoholic drinks industry underscore the importance of brand management and distribution in international markets. Survival and growth in these markets demand growth in efficiency and innovation not only in production but much more so in distribution. The alcoholic drinks industry in the UK has displayed considerable vigour in promoting productive efficiency. Readily available evidence shows that labour productivity in the drinks industry increased at an annual average rate of 7.6 per cent per year during the period 1979–86; which was substantially higher than the productivity growth of 3.6 per cent achieved by the manufacturing sector as a whole during this period. Much of this growth in productivity was achieved through shedding of labour, increased investment and improvements in management (Balasubramanyam and Nguyen 1991).

One of the developments in the industry which has attracted much attention, however, is its attempts at streamlining the distribution end of the business. Equally well known are the acquisitions of foreign-owned firms and the various sorts of alliances that British-owned firms have entered into with foreign firms in the drinks sector. One of the motives underlying these alliances is the desire to promote efficiency in distribution in international markets on the part of British firms. Three main aspects of the interrelationship between the alliances that British firms have forged with foreign firms on the one hand and efficiency in distribution on the other are noteworthy. These are exploitation of scale and scope economies in distribution, internalization of distribution and economies in transaction costs, and prevention of entry of new firms.

While there is a considerable volume of theoretical literature and a few empirical studies on economies of scale and scope in production there are very few detailed studies on economies of scope and scale in distribution. The one exception is the discussion of economies of scope and scale in distribution in the context of the rise and growth of the modern corporation provided by Chandler (1990). The question posed by Chandler is why do firms integrate forward into distribution and when does it become profitable for them to eliminate the intermediaries and take over distribution. In the initial stages it pays to operate through intermediaries specializing in distribution. These intermediaries reap economies of scale and scope by acting as distributors for a number of manufacturers. But when the volume of production of individual manufacturers increase and they are able to reduce the cost of transportation, storing and distribution to the level of the intermediaries, the latter lose their cost advantage. And when the products of the individual manufacturers increasingly demand specialized facilities and skills in marketing, the intermediaries lose economies of scope also. Thus with the growth in volume and differentiation of products it pays the firm to integrate forward and reap economies of scale and scope in distribution.

An illustration of forward integration into distribution in recent years is provided by the decision of United Distillers, one of the leading firms in the UK spirits distilling industry, to terminate more than 700 distribution agreements with its agents abroad and either take control of its own distribution or form joint ventures with other drink companies in overseas markets. Such rationalization of distribution is reported to have provided UD with control over 75 per cent of its distribution, compared with 25 per cent in 1987. This development appears to have paralleled the growth in exports of the company from £377 million (11 per cent of total turnover) in 1986 to £641 million (23 per cent of turnover) in 1988 (see Table 4.3). Both the growth in overseas sales of the company and the policy of concentrating on specialized premium and deluxe brands appears to have motivated its assumption of increased control over distribution. Such assumption of control over distribution or internalization is likely to have resulted in considerable savings in costs of transactions.

The joint ventures with overseas producers which the leading UK firms have entered into in recent years also illustrate their desire to exploit scope and scale economies in distribution. Allied Lyons, the food and drink conglomerate, for instance, has entered into a total number of forty-seven joint ventures of varying sizes across the world. Another example of an innovative and novel alliance between international firms is the one between Guinness, of which UD is an integral part, and Moët Hennessy (LVMH) of France. The fourteen joint ventures around the world that the two companies have forged allow Guinness a 24 per cent equity share in LVMH and LVMH a 24 per cent share in Guinness. The British company has also entered into a number of other joint ventures with producers in Spain, Germany and Greece, besides acquiring Schenley, a key distributor in the United States. Several features of such joint ventures are worth noting. These joint ventures enable UD to market its famous brands of alcoholic drinks such as Johnnie Walker whisky and Tanquary gin alongside the equally well-known Hennessy cognac without incurring the hefty costs

72 *Adding Value: brands and marketing*

Table 4.3 Export performance of top four spirits companies, 1986–91

	1986	1987	1988	1989	1990	1991
Guinness: exports (£million)	377.4	580.3	641.3	718.0	817.0	849.0
Exports as % of sales	11.6	20.6	23.1	23.3	23.3	20.9
Allied-Lyons: exports (£million)	139.5	221.1	236.0	273.0	352.0	358.0
Exports as % of sales	4.2	6.1	5.6	6.1	7.4	7.0
Grand Met: exports (£million)	160.6	183.2	197.4	228.3	259.2	289.0
Exports as % of sales	3.0	3.2	3.3	2.5	2.8	3.3
Seagram: exports (£million)	149.2	172.4	189.7	213.1	224.5	243.2
Exports as % of sales	9.1	10.1	8.6	7.8	8.0	7.7

Sources: Financial Times 1988; 1990; 1991; 1992; *Annual Reports and Accounts; Hoover's Directory of World Business* 1992

of total acquisition of the foreign firm. The press and company reports frequently refer to the economies of scale in distribution that such arrangements confer on the partners to the joint ventures. It is, however, likely that these advantages are more in the nature of economies of scope rather than economies of scale. The latter are attained with the growth in sales of a particular variety of a product or growth in sales of related varieties. But arrangements such as the Guinness and LVMH joint venture bring together producers of products which are somewhat distant substitutes for each other in consumption – Scotch and gin brands of UD and Hennessey cognac and Moët et Chandon champagnes of LVMH. The arrangement allows both companies to bring together their expertise in distribution of premium products. Thus Moët Hennessey may be able to utilize UD's expertise in distributing spirits to sell its products in the UK and UD has access to the expertise of LVMH in selling champagnes to promote its products in international markets. In other words joint distribution of champagnes and spirits may be much less expensive than the distribution of each of the products separately. The expertise in distribution both companies possess is in the nature of an indivisibility and the joint venture enables both companies to make optimal use of such expertise and reduce costs of distribution. It enables them to fully utilize the infrastructure and facilities already in place and reduce costs of distribution. As business economists have noted, production-related advantages based on costs of production including low labour costs may be less durable than brand and distribution advantages. It may be much more difficult for competitors to penetrate the markets of a firm which has built up scope and scale economies in distribution than the markets of a firm acquired solely on the basis of production cost advantages. This would be especially so in the case of industries, such as the alcoholic drinks industry, which are heavily distibution oriented. Joint ventures may be an ideal method of building up extensive distribution networks world-wide.

Yet another feature of the joint ventures the leading firms have contracted is the prestige it confers on both partners: a tie up between a producer of some of the leading brands of Scotch whisky and a producer of reputable cognac and champagne is likely to further promote the image of the two companies in the market-place and enhance the market for the premium brands they sell. It is also possible that such joint distribution arrangements pose problems of entry for new firms. Faced with incumbents who not only possess a range of premium brands in each of the major drink categories but also a portfolio of drinks; prospective entrants into international markets may find the costs of setting up distribution facilities anew steep if not prohibitive. The only feasible option for them would be to enter into distribution contracts with the incumbents. In other words it is the prestige and scope economies that incumbents enjoy which pose a barrier to entry rather than brand proliferation recognized as an entry barrier in the literature.

CONCLUSION

This chapter has reviewed some of the main propositions on brands and advertising in the economics literature and examined their relevance to the alcoholic drinks industry. A frequent criticism of advertising in general and advertising by the alcoholic drinks industry in particular is that it distorts consumer preferences, creates new and unnecessary wants, and results in a social waste of resources. There seems to be very little empirical evidence in support of these propositions, especially so in the context of advertising by the alcoholic drinks industry in the UK. Such advertising appears to have had little impact on consumer expenditures on alcohol. We have argued that, contrary to popular opinion, advertising may promote consumer learning and assist the consumer in search of product quality. It should be added that in reaching this conclusion we do not in any sense condone alcoholism or alcohol abuse but accept the fact that consumption of alcoholic drinks in pursuit of pleasure, relaxation and entertainment is a feature of consumption in the affluent society. We also argue that ostentation, prestige and status seeking are all features of consumption in an affluent society and are an integral part of the utility function of the affluent consumer. And to the extent that brands, advertising and product differentiation cater to these attributes sought by consumers they do perform a useful function. Product differentiation, brand image, brand management and distribution all figure prominently in the industry, much more so than in the case of several other industry groups producing consumer goods. In recent years consumer demand for alcoholic drinks in general and spirits in particular in the UK has been none too buoyant. The industry, however, has not only survived but also recorded considerable growth in sales in international markets. These achievements are due not only to growth in productive efficiency of the industry but also to efficiency in distribution. Indeed, the expertise in distribution that the UK firms possess, much more so than their productive efficiency, may be a key factor in their success in international markets. They have acquired this expertise in distribution not only through development and management of brands but also through the innovative alliances they have forged with overseas producers. These alliances appear to have served the firms well in exploring scale economies and more importantly scope economies in distribution. These propositions, however, await empirical verification.

ACKNOWLEDGEMENTS

We are grateful to Geoffrey Jones and to Christopher Davidson of Guinness plc for their comments.

REFERENCES

Advertising Association (1989) *Advertising Statistics Yearbook*, Henley-on-Thames: NTC Publications.

Bain, J. (1956) *Barriers to New Competition*, Cambridge, Mass: Harvard University Press.

Balasubramanyam, V. N. (1993) 'Entrepreneurship and the growth of the firm: the case of the British food and drink industries in the 1980s', in J. Brown and M. B. Rose (eds) *Entrepreneurship, Networks and Modern Business*, Manchester: Manchester University Press.

Balasubramanyam, V. N. and Nguyen, T. (1991) 'Structure and performance of the UK food and drink industries', *Journal of Agricultural Economics* 42: 56–65.

Chamberlain, E. (1933) *The Theory of Monopolistic Competition*, Cambridge, Mass: Harvard University Press.

Chandler, A. D. (1990) *Scale and Scope: The Dynamics of Industrial Capitalism*, Cambridge, Mass: Harvard University Press.

Comanor, W. S. and Wilson, T. (1967) 'Advertising, market structure and performance', *Review of Economic Studies* **53**: 423–40.

Cowley, D. (ed.) (1991) *Understanding Brands*, London: Kogan Page.

Duffy, M. H. (1987) 'Advertising and the inter-product distribution of demand: a Rotterdam Model approach', *European Economic Review* **31**: 1051–70.

Financial Times (1988) 'Top 100 UK exporters – 1987', 13 September: 6.

—— (1990) 'Britain's top 100 exporters – 1989', 28 September: 8.

—— (1991) 'Britain's top 100 exporters – 1990', 1 October: 6.

—— (1992) 'Financial Times top 100 UK exporters', 28 October: 4.

Galbraith, J. K. (1961) *American Capitalism: The Concept of Countervailing Power*, London: Hamish Hamilton (first published 1957).

—— (1987) *The Affluent Society*, London: Pelican (first published 1958).

Gilber, R. J. (1989) 'The role of potential competition in industrial organization', *Journal of Economic Perspectives* **3**(3): 107–27.

Greenaway, D. and Milner, C. (1986) *The Economics of Intra-Industry Trade*, Oxford: Basil Blackwell.

Hoover's Directory of World Business (1992) Austin, Tex: Reference Press.

James Capel & Co. Ltd (1988) *United Distillers Group (UDG)*, London: Libra Press.

Johnson, H. (1962) 'The political economy of opulence', in H. G. Johnson (ed.) *Money, Trade and Economic Growth*, London: Allen & Unwin.

Jones, G. (1984) 'Multinational chocolate: Cadbury overseas 1918–1939', *Business History* **26**: 59–76.

—— (1993) 'Transnational corporations – a historical perspective', in G. Jones (ed.) *Transnational Corporations: A Historical Perspective*, vol. 2, London: Routledge, for the United Nations Library of Transnational Corporations.

Robinson, J. (1951) 'The economic effects of advertising', in J. Robinson *Collected Economic Papers*, London: Basil Blackwell.

—— (1963) *The Economics of Imperfect Competition*, London: Macmillan.

Schmalensee, R. (1972) *The Economics of Advertising*, Amsterdam: North-Holland.

—— (1978) 'Entry deterrence in the ready-to-eat breakfast cereal industry', *Bell Journal of Economics* **9**: 305–27.

—— (1982) 'Product differentiation advantages of pioneering brands', *American Economic Review* **72**: 349–65.

Selvanathan, E. A. (1988) 'Alcohol consumption in the UK, 1955–85: a system-wide analysis', *Applied Economics* **20**: 1,071–86.

Urban, G., Gaskin, S., Carter, T. and Mucha, Z. (1984) 'Market share reward to pioneering brands', *Management Science* **32**: 645–59.

Veblen, T. (1963) *The Theory of the Leisure Class*, New York (first published 1899).

Wilkins, M. (1988) 'European and North American multinationals, 1870–1914: comparisons and contrasts', *Business History* **30**: 8–45.

—— (1992) 'The neglected intangible asset: the influence of the trade mark on the rise of the modern corporation', *Business History* **34**: 66–95.

5   Brand accounting in the United Kingdom

Christopher Napier

If this business were to be split up, I would be glad to take the brands, trade marks and goodwill, and you could have all the bricks and mortar – and I would fare better than you.[1]

Brands have long been regarded as important sources of value to companies in the food, drink and consumer goods industries. It is therefore strange at first sight that the debate over whether brands should be included as assets in the balance sheet should appear to be one of recent and local origin. In the United Kingdom, the stimulus for the brands debate was the move by the large food company Ranks Hovis McDougall to include 'home-grown' brands as assets on its 1988 balance sheet. Yet treating brands as accounting assets – 'brand capitalization' – is a phenomenon that has its roots not in Britain but rather in Australia, where a decade of corporate take-over and merger activity in the 1980s (particularly in the food and drink and the media industries) provided a climate in which the most aggressive companies boosted their balance sheets by capitalizing on such diverse 'intangible' assets as newspaper titles, licences to operate television stations and brands of beer (Goodwin and Harris 1991).

In Europe, brand capitalization is spreading: increasing numbers of French, Italian and Spanish companies are including brands on their balance sheet (FEE 1992: 236). Many of these are in the food and drink industries: in France, for example, drink company Pernod Ricard and food producer BSN have reflected brands on the balance sheet, the latter (ironically for a French company) capitalizing such traditional British brands as 'Lea & Perrins Worcestershire Sauce' (Alexander and Archer 1992: 173). However, those countries with a rigid tradition of conservatism in accounting, such as Germany and Japan, have so far resisted brand capitalization. The most anomalous situation is in the United States, where rigid accounting rules make it very difficult for intangibles to be shown as assets in company accounts, even though they often count as assets for tax purposes.

If the brands debate in the UK had simply been a reaction to a single company's innovative accounting policy, then brand accounting might be regarded as one of those ephemeral issues that trouble a profession for a short time and then disappear from the agenda. Accounting for brands is, however, only the most recent manifestation of fundamental conflicts in the nature and purpose of corporate accounts. In attempting to resolve the brands issue, accountants must come closer to answering questions as to the essential nature of assets, the relative status of cost and value, and, at a professional level, how far accountants are able to assert a monopoly over the form and content of company accounts.

As intangibles, brands fall into a class of potential assets that have created quandaries for accountants throughout the last 150 years, the whole period of corporate financial reporting. In the first section of this chapter, the accounting issues raised by brands and other intangibles are considered. The second section examines how intangibles in general, and those precursors of brands as objects of accounting, trade marks, were accounted for up to the late 1970s. The third section reviews the brands debate, and the final section concludes with some thoughts on how brand accounting is likely to resolve itself in the future.

THE ACCOUNTING PROBLEMS OF INTANGIBLES

The central financial statements that make up a company's annual accounts are the balance sheet and the profit and loss account. These statements derive from the method of double-entry bookkeeping, which emerged in Italy around 1300 and over the next 500 years became accepted as the predominant mode of commercial record-keeping. The profit and loss account is an integral part of the double-entry system, functioning as the account in which all items of revenue and expense are ultimately recorded, the annual balance of this account representing the profit or loss for the year. The balance sheet, however, stands outside the double-entry, being a summary of the balances on those accounts which are left open at the end of the year. These are the accounts relating to resources of the business (assets) or claims against the business (liabilities) which are considered to provide benefits, or require settlement, after the balance sheet date, or accounts representing the interest of the owners of the business (equity).

Assets include such items as cash, money owed to the business (debtors), goods held by the business for resale (stocks), property held by the business in order to earn rent, interest and dividends (investments), and machines and equipment used by the business in processing the goods it sells or carrying out the services it provides. These assets would be stated in the balance sheet at amounts derived from the double-entry records. These amounts themselves would be based on what was paid for each asset, as the double-entry system's fundamental notion is that activities are accounted for in terms of the exchange of resources.

Balance sheets derived from double-entry would by that very fact be based on *cost*; but what was to stop businesses simply putting down for any asset an amount different from cost? Here the ambivalent nature of the balance sheet first shows itself. A mere bookkeeping statement of balances drawn from the accounting records in itself makes no assertions about the 'state of affairs' of the business. However, the balance sheet has the potential to do more than this: it appears able to give us an insight into the financial position of the business. This is possible only if the amounts attributed to the assets and liabilities shown in the balance sheet are entered on some rational basis, and the central problem of financial accounting is to decide how to attribute amounts to assets and liabilities.

When this problem was first addressed systematically in the later years of the nineteenth century, the influence of double-entry was strong, and cost-based approaches were the norm. This period saw the emergence of the accountancy profession. The early professional accountants had worked mainly in bankruptcy and corporate insolvency (Napier and Noke 1992), and not surprisingly were biased towards 'prudent' accounting practices (Yamey 1960). Where the 'value' of an asset was less than cost, it was considered appropriate to reduce the amount at which the asset stood in the accounts. This was straightforward for assets such as debtors (where provision could be made for bad and doubtful debts) and stocks (where provision could be made for goods that could be sold only at amounts less than cost), but was less easy to apply to those assets expected to provide benefits over a longer period – 'fixed assets'. An extensive literature emerged in the professional accountancy press in the late nineteenth century on how such assets should be accounted for (Brief 1976).

The ultimate consensus was as follows.

1 Assets should be included in the balance sheet only if they were recorded in the underlying books of account, and thus had a

recorded cost (although it was permissible *not* to show particular assets on the balance sheet, even if they were recorded in the books; this was one way of creating a 'secret reserve' – Edwards 1989: 137).

2 The amount at which an asset was included in the balance sheet should not exceed cost (except in highly restricted circumstances), and should be written down below cost where this was appropriate.

3 For long-lived assets, it was acceptable to write down their cost on a systematic basis over the expected lives of the assets, even if the resulting net book values did not correspond to any external measure of value such as resale price. In a 'going concern' it is assumed that such assets will be held for their useful lives rather than being resold. Thus current market values of such assets are normally irrelevant.

These principles, which later generations were to label the 'historical cost convention', are still fundamental to financial accounting in the UK, although they have come under increasing challenge in recent years. The principles seem to work well if we simply regard the balance sheet as a statement of resources and claims (to which amounts are attributed), but when we try to use the balance sheet as an estimate of the value of a business, we run into the predicament that the business as a whole is usually more than the mere sum of its parts.

This was well recognized by the accountants and business people of the nineteenth century, who had a ready explanation for the phenomenon:

We see, for instance, in the business world a man – A. – starting a fresh business (for our present purpose let us say the manufacture of some article), either under his own name or under some name assumed for trade reasons. He works hard, pushes his business judiciously, advertises widely, and after some years his name becomes a household word, and the articles he manufactures are very widely known. We feel at once that beyond his works, his machinery, and his stock-in-trade, A. has something else, much more intangible, but none the less valuable, which for the moment we may describe as the reputation of his name and goods, or more succinctly as 'his business', using that term as it is familiarly used as denoting something more than the material assets. We examine A.'s books, but we find no entry to correspond with this intangible property. There will come a time when our business man himself, or his executors after his death, will want to sell his business, and he or they will want to realise this intangible property along with the works, stock-in-trade, and other visible and tangible assets. What he can pass on to another of this intangible property is commonly known as 'Goodwill'.

(Dicksee and Tillyard 1906: 1–2)

A business as a whole is worth more than the sum of the assets and liabilities of the business, and this difference is known commercially as *goodwill*. Yet the goodwill that a business develops over a period of years is not recorded as an asset in the business accounts. This is because no identifiable expenditure is incurred on buying such goodwill, unlike the cash spent on buying buildings, machines and trading stocks. Following the principles of historical cost, such goodwill is thus not reflected on the balance sheet.

Yet goodwill *was* accounted for in the nineteenth century when one business bought another as a going concern. Goodwill would be recorded in the purchaser's books of account at whatever amount was attributed to it in the purchase agreement, or as the residual left after specific values for the separately identified assets less liabilities being acquired were deducted from the total purchase consideration. Thus *purchased* goodwill would be accounted for when internally generated or *inherent* goodwill was not.

Once goodwill was included in the accounting records, there were three approaches to its treatment in subsequent balance sheets. First, it could be eliminated altogether as quickly as possible. This treatment was popular with accountants either because it would produce consistency of accounting for both purchased and inherent goodwill or, more radically, because goodwill was not a 'proper' asset, and therefore had no place in the accounts. Second, the goodwill could be carried forward as an asset at the amount originally attributed to it or this amount could be reduced *unsystematically* in years of abnormally high profits. Third, goodwill could be depreciated *systematically* in the same way as machines and other long-lived assets with finite lives. In practice, most companies preferred the second of these options (Dicksee 1892: 127).

This haphazard approach to accounting for goodwill persisted until the 1970s, but with one significant complication. The occasion of this was the introduction in 1948 of a requirement that each 'parent company' should present, in addition to its own financial statements, a 'group' balance sheet representing the state of affairs of itself and the companies that it controlled, its subsidiaries, as if they were a single entity. The most common method of preparing group accounts, the 'acquisition' method of consolidation, operated with the premise that the parent company, by acquiring a controlling interest in the shares of a subsidiary, 'purchased' the underlying assets and assumed the underlying liabilities of the subsidiary. When the consideration given to acquire the shares in the subsidiary exceeded the value of the assets less liabilities deemed to be acquired, the difference was labelled 'goodwill'. Unlike the case of the purchase of a business, however, the goodwill was not as such recorded in the books of the parent company or its subsidiary: it appeared only in the group accounts. This in itself led some commentators (for example, Chambers 1966: 218) to question whether 'goodwill arising on consolidation' was an asset at all.

As the accounting notion of goodwill became formalized, two different approaches to conceptualizing it developed (Gynther 1969). One approach was to attempt to identify goodwill in terms of its attributes: a *qualitative* view. The other was to envisage goodwill in terms of its method of calculation: a *quantitative* view. Often, accountancy textbooks shifted unreflectively between approaches. For example, Rowland (1934: 115–17) noted that goodwill was represented by such factors as the situation of the business person's premises, the personal reputation of the individual business person, and 'the reputation of the good sold, arising from the high standard of quality of the goods themselves, e.g., a well-advertised brand of proprietary goods'. He went on to consider how goodwill arises on the purchase of a business, but most of his discussion was devoted to a description of the 'super-profit' method of valuing goodwill:

> If the average profits of a business are greater than those normally earned in similar businesses, the excess is deemed to be due to goodwill, which is thus taken as the capitalised value of profits in excess of the investment yield on the net capital actually employed.
>
> (Rowland 1934: 116)

The key words in the above passage are 'deemed to be'. According to Rowland, goodwill cannot be measured independently of the business to which it adheres, because it is impossible to envisage goodwill being sold separately from a business, even though the other assets can be sold and liabilities settled on an individual basis. So goodwill in itself does not have an observable market value: any attempt to attribute a value indirectly, such as through the 'super-profit' method, always begs the question as to whether what is being calculated is actually the value of goodwill (or indeed any other asset) at all.

Accountants were thus unsure whether or not goodwill is an asset; whether or not it should be written off immediately, carried indefinitely or depreciated systematically; how it could be measured; and whether the measurement methods used in practice actually measured what they claimed. If the goodwill problem could not be solved, however, it could be evaded. One approach was to minimize the amount attributed to goodwill on the purchase of a business. The subsidiary's recorded assets could be taken in at 'fair' values rather than book values, but this might not be enough to eradicate goodwill. Accountants thus tried to identify other resources that had not been accounted for, but could be included as assets in determining the residual amount attributed to goodwill. Such resources were almost always intangible ones, and they included items described by companies as trade marks, patents, licences, copyrights, titles and brands. From simply being *attributes* of goodwill, these intangible resources began to be viewed as assets in their own right. How this came about, and why it did not happen sooner, will be considered in the next section.

CREATING INTANGIBLES AS ASSETS

The emergence of a wide range of intangibles as assets recognized in financial statements has generally relied on two interdependent preconditions: the ability to define something as an intangible distinct from goodwill, and an incentive to make this distinction. Until the late 1970s, in countries such as Australia as much as in Britain, the incentive was lacking, so there was little concern to separate intangibles off from goodwill. This is not to say that the accounting literature failed to recognize that rights such as trade marks and patents could constitute separate assets. But until the notion that trade marks could be registered and defended in court emerged through the Trade Marks Registration Act 1875 (the legal protection of patents has a much longer history), there was little likelihood that accountants would recognize them as assets. Indeed, even when patents and trade marks were firmly defined legally, they would rarely be accounted for separately. The cost of obtaining these rights was normally very small in relation to the general revenues of a business; accountants therefore encouraged businesses to write them off out of revenue (Pixley 1924: 412). Until the law changed in 1938, trade marks could not be sold separately from goodwill, while patent rights were rarely sold for large sums.[2]

When companies were floated on the Stock Exchange to acquire existing businesses, however, it was quite likely that a valuation would be placed on the intangible assets. This would often be reported in a prospectus issued by the company, and from 1900 the amount attributed to goodwill in such an acquisition had to be disclosed (Companies Act 1900, s. 10(1)(g)). Even before then, companies were likely to disclose the goodwill figure, and this could represent a substantial proportion of the purchase consideration.[3] This was particularly the case with some of the large brewers which converted themselves into limited companies in the 1880s. Goodwill represented at least half of the £6 million valuation placed on Arthur Guinness & Co. when it went public in October 1886, while it amounted to about 40 per cent of the £3.3 million valuation attributed to Samuel Allsopp & Sons in February 1887.[4] The high proportion of goodwill in the Allsopp flotation led to adverse press comment, although it did not prevent the issue being a great success:

> It would be rash and hazardous, therefore, to let the million and a quarter or so, which apparently is to be given for goodwill, stand as a permanent asset in the accounts. Prudence requires that it be written down from year to year out of profits. . . . There is, so far as we know, no parallel for such immense amounts as have been paid for the goodwill of such concerns as Guinness & Co. and Allsopp being retained as assets in the books of joint-stock trading companies, and the question of how they are rightly to be dealt with has as yet been too little considered, for it may be fraught with very serious consequences to shareholders in the future.
>
> (*The Economist* 5 February 1887: 168)

Both the Guinness and Allsopp flotations involved the issue of fixed interest securities (debentures and preference shares) as well as ordinary shares. The fixed interest securities tended to be represented by tangible assets, leaving the ordinary shares represented by intangible assets. This was also the case in the flotation of Lever Brothers Limited, whose prospectus (25 June 1894) notes the price being paid by the new company for the soap business of William Hesketh Lever as £1,389,559, made up of £639,559 for Lever's Port Sunlight Works, stocks and debtors, and £750,000 for trade marks and goodwill (quoted in Hodgkins 1979). Lever retained £750,000 of ordinary shares, while the public acquired preference shares equating to tangible assets.

Other pre-1900 prospectuses put a relatively high value on goodwill: for example, in the prospectus for tea company Brooke Bond (14 June 1892), goodwill represents £100,000 out of a total purchase price of £150,000. Some prospectuses are more coy, but explicitly refer to goodwill and its components. Two examples must suffice. The prospectus for soap manufacturers A. & F. Pears Limited (31 May 1892) notes: 'The value of the goodwill has been largely enhanced by advertising in all parts of the world. During the last seven years alone this expenditure has amounted to upwards of £609,000.' Net profits after advertising for the same period were reported as £375,000. The prospectus for the Earl of Dudley's Round Oak Iron and Steel Works Limited (23 April 1891) not only states that 'the Company has been formed for the purpose of taking over, as a going concern, . . . the Earl of Dudley's well-known Round Oak Iron Works . . . including the very valuable Goodwill, and the well-known Brands, Trade Marks, &c.', but actually includes reproductions of the 'brands'.[5]

After 1900, the requirement to show goodwill separately in prospectuses might have encouraged companies to report relatively low amounts under this heading. Thus, the jewellery firm Mappin & Webb's prospectus (14 December 1908) ascribes a value of £50,000 to its trade marks (cutlery patterns) and £121,811 to goodwill, out of a total consideration of £650,000. On the other hand, the prospectus of the manufacturers of 'Wright's Coal Tar Soap' (21 June 1909) values trade marks and registered designs at £10,000 and goodwill at £66,864 out of a total of £135,000. These examples illustrate how goodwill was becoming the name given to the residual in the valuation of a business: in both cases the business being acquired was valued at a round sum and specific valuations for other assets deducted to get the goodwill amount. A final prospectus from this period makes prominent reference to brands – the Ardath Tobacco Company (20 February 1912) notes: 'Among the many valuable trade marks and registered brands which are being acquired by the Company are: "Ardath", "Quo Vadis", "State Express", "Splendo", "Winfred" '. Goodwill represents £120,000 out of a total consideration of £245,000, but no specific valuation for the brands is mentioned.

The highly variable nature of intangible valuation is illustrated in the creation of sugar giant Tate and Lyle. In 1918, the precursor business Abram Lyle & Sons was converted into a limited company. Goodwill and trade marks that had previously not been reflected in the accounts of the business were valued at £355,955, the residue of the total valuation of the business of £2.25 million after tangible assets were specifically valued. Three years later, the goodwill and trade marks were valued at just under £1 million when Lyle's company combined with that of the Tate family to form Tate and Lyle (Chalmin 1983: 137–9).

These examples show that, by the early years of the twentieth century, business people and accountants saw little problem in including goodwill on the balance sheet when a business changed hands (especially when it was converted into a company for the purpose of flotation), and were indifferent between including trade marks and similar rights as part of goodwill or accounting for them separately. The notion of a 'brand' was beginning to emerge, but it seems to have been assimilated by accountants to that of a trade mark or a business name.

Especially after the First World War, when a tendency arose for companies to combine different classes of assets on their balance sheet into a small number (in some cases only one) total (Kitchen 1972), it became increasingly difficult for outsiders to track the goodwill figure after a company was floated. Indeed, as it became more common for businesses to be organized from the beginning as limited companies, rather than converting to this status when going public, company owners could ensure that goodwill was eliminated as much as practicable before flotation. By the end of the 1920s, it became fashionable to declare that no part of the funds raised in a new issue of securities would be attributed to goodwill (Thomas 1978: 31, quoting *Statist* 10 December 1927: 1,078). This growing suspicion of goodwill in the late 1920s had an influence on the legislators. The Greene Committee on Company Law Amendment (Board of Trade 1926: 35) recommended that companies should be obliged to disclose any goodwill in their accounts not only at the time of flotation but also annually. This was enacted in the Companies Act 1929 (s. 124(2)(c)), which also required disclosure of trade marks and patents.

The change in the law led to an immediate disclosure of substantial items for goodwill and intangibles,[6] but in the longer run it encouraged companies to write such intangibles off. Companies which underwent reorganization in the 1930s readily wrote intangibles out of their accounts when they reduced their capital. The use of parent company structures also facilitated the suppression of intangibles. Subsidiaries could be operated as private companies, whose accounts were not published. In the parent company's balance sheet, only the cost of investment in the subsidiary would be disclosed. For example, throughout the 1930s, British American Tobacco (BAT) showed in its balance sheet a mere £200,000 for goodwill and trade marks, while 'shares in associated companies' represented about £30 million (Cox and Smith 1990: Appendix 2). Much of this would have represented intangibles such as BAT's valuable cigarette and tobacco brands.

This suppression of intangibles was to come to an end in 1948, with the requirement to publish group accounts. As noted above, the normal method of preparing group accounts (consolidation) involved replacing the single asset in the parent company's balance sheet representing the investment in a subsidiary with that subsidiary's individual assets and liabilities. The difference between the amount at which the investment was stated and the amounts attributed to the subsidiary's assets and liabilities was usually positive, and was deemed to be 'goodwill'. Early writers on consolidation were confused as to whether this difference represented a 'hidden' asset of the subsidiary, or the premium that the parent company was willing to pay in order to gain control over the subsidiary's assets (the 'cost of control') or some combination of these (Bogie 1949: 50). They were, however, agreed that there was no need to write such consolidation goodwill down unless at some time in the future the subsidiary started to make losses (Bigg and Wilson 1945: 303). On the other hand, British accountants could see no reason to criticize companies that decided to write off consolidation goodwill against group reserves at the time of acquisition of a subsidiary.

In the United States, however, the years after the Second World War saw considerable official interest in accounting for intangibles. The American Institute of Accountants issued in 1953 *Accounting Research Bulletin No. 43* (ARB 43), which defined purchased goodwill as the difference between the amount paid for a business and the fair value of the net *tangible* assets of that business. This provision implied that intangibles such as trade marks were part of goodwill. ARB 43 prohibited the immediate write-off of purchased goodwill, and distinguished between that part of goodwill that had a limited useful economic life – this should be amortized – and the residue that had no effective limitation on its useful life – this could be carried indefinitely at its original value but written down in the event of significant adverse changes in circumstances (Committee on Accounting Procedure 1953: ch. 5). By 1970, official opinion in the United States had hardened: it was no longer acceptable to carry goodwill indefinitely in the balance sheet. However, goodwill could be written off over a period not exceeding forty years (Accounting Principles Board 1970), and in practice this maximum was generally adopted as the period for write-offs (Andrews 1981). In the United States, therefore, despite the 'marketing culture' associated with that country, brands have not emerged as an accounting issue. The assimilation of all intangibles under goodwill, the requirement to amortize this over a potentially very long period, and the prohibition of revaluations of assets above their historical cost combine together to take brands off the accounting agenda.

So why did brands and other intangibles come to occupy such a high place on the accounting agenda in Britain? Several factors interacted in the 1970s and increasingly in the 1980s to bring brands to the fore. On the business side, there was increasing awareness of the role played by brands not just as a convenient marketing concept but more significantly as the focus of the value added by the whole business. As capital markets expanded and grew in sophistication, the numbers shown in financial statements came to be regarded by company directors as crucial signals of corporate performance and well-being (and indeed as determinants of their own personal income and wealth). The take-over waves of the 1980s raised many problems of how acquisitions and mergers should be accounted for. On the accounting side, the standardization programme which began in 1970 inevitably regarded goodwill as a target for attention.[7] But accounting standards came increasingly to be drawn up in the shadow of national and European company law, while the movement towards constructing 'conceptual frameworks' for financial accounting also overshadowed the deliberations of accountants. How brand accounting emerged from these intersections will be considered in the next section.

THE BRANDS DEBATE

Brand accounting emerged as a by-product of the attempts by the British accountancy profession (which are still not finally resolved) to standardize the accounting treatment of goodwill. This twenty-year process (summarized by Holgate 1990) culminated in a Statement of Standard Accounting Practice, SSAP 22 *Accounting for Goodwill* (ASC 1984), that permitted two radically different accounting treatments. Companies could either write off goodwill against reserves at the time of acquisition or treat it as an asset and amortize it over its useful economic life. Goodwill could not, however, be carried indefinitely on the balance sheet. The standard defined goodwill as 'the difference between the value of a business as a whole and the aggregate of fair values of its *separable* net assets' (ASC 1984: para. 21, emphasis added).

At first sight, this definition of goodwill is the same as that used in the United States, but the key word 'separable' made it possible to envisage the attribution of fair values to intangibles.[8] As SSAP 22 said:

> Separable net assets may include identifiable intangibles such as those specifically mentioned in the balance sheet formats in the Companies Act 1981 [now the Companies Act 1985], i.e. 'concessions, patents, licences, trade marks and similar rights and assets'; other examples include publishing titles, franchise rights and customer lists. (This list of examples is not intended to be comprehensive.)
>
> (ASC 1984: para. 13)

Note that brands were not mentioned, but neither were they ruled out. However, as separable net assets were defined as 'those assets (and liabilities) which can be identified and sold (or discharged) separately without necessarily disposing of the business as a whole' (ASC 1984: para. 22), the stage was set for one of the crucial points at issue in the brand accounting debate: do brands constitute separable assets?

In the background to the deliberations of the Accounting Standards Committee was the incorporation into British law of the European Community's Fourth Directive on Company Law. This endeavoured to harmonize corporate reporting practice throughout the EC, and imposed on British companies a more regulated and codified body of accounting law. As currently enacted in the Companies Act 1985, the law requires companies to draw up their balance sheets in accordance with specified formats. The balance sheet formats include several categories for intangible assets, of which the most important are 'goodwill' and 'concessions, etc.' Goodwill is heavily restricted: it can be included only if it was 'acquired for valuable consideration', so inherent goodwill cannot be shown on the balance sheet; its valuation on the balance sheet must be based on its historical cost; and it must be written off over a period not exceeding its useful economic life. These provisions do not prevent goodwill from being written off in full immediately. However, the rules for other intangible assets are more flexible: they may be included at their 'current cost' rather than their original historical cost, and they need be depreciated only if they have a 'limited useful economic life'.

Acquisitive companies therefore had a potential method of reducing the amount attributable to goodwill arising on a take-over. To understand why they saw this as desirable, we must note the consequences for a company's accounts of following the permitted alternatives for goodwill. Either companies would have to take a charge in their profit and loss accounts over a period of years, thus reducing reported earnings per share, or they would have to write down the equity interest shown on the balance sheet. The latter could have the paradoxical effect of showing rapidly *declining* (even negative) equity in group accounts for a business which was growing through acquisition. Directors whose rewards were a function of asset and earnings growth were, not surprisingly, reluctant to adopt accounting methods that reduced both of these.

It would be an exaggeration to claim that SSAP 22 on its own was the cause of the creative accounting boom of the 1980s (Griffiths 1986; Smith 1992). But many of the issues that trouble the accountancy profession can be traced back to problems with accounting for business combinations. The 1980s were a period in which corporate take-overs and mergers in Britain reached unprecedented heights: in four of the decade's years, annual merger and acquisition activity exceeded the *total* for the 1970s (Smith 1992: 16–17). Moreover, no company was safe from a bid, and directors looked for ways to bolster their defences against possible predators.

An early example of a company specifically identifying intangible assets on an acquisition was food and household products manufacturer Reckitt & Colman. In 1985, it acquired Airwick from the Swiss concern Ciba-Geigy. Out of a total consideration of £165 million, Reckitt & Colman assigned £55.8 million to trade marks (Buchan and Brown 1989: 83). Note the choice of words: 'trade marks' are specifically mentioned as intangible assets in the Companies Act and SSAP 22. Reckitt & Colman repeated this practice in 1986, when it acquired the Durkee Corporation for £185 million. After deducting the net tangible assets of £67 million, Reckitt & Colman divided the remaining £118 million between trade marks and goodwill (Rutteman 1990: 60). Similarly, in the mid-1980s, the restructuring of the newspaper and book industries led to many companies including amounts for titles, copyrights and other publishing rights that they acquired through take-over (Norton 1992).

However, the historical cost convention was still seen as a stumbling block to the inclusion of home-grown intangibles such as brands. This was a particular point at issue in the contested take-over of the chocolate and confectionery producer Rowntree in 1988. Rowntree was a long-established company whose main brands dated back to the 1930s. These brands were particularly attractive to a rival in the confectionery industry, and the Swiss chocolate company Nestlé ended up paying substantially over the book value of Rowntree to acquire the company. After the bid succeeded, it was argued that Rowntree might have avoided take-over had it been able to reflect the value of its brands on its balance sheet (Bourke 1989: 98; Smith 1992: 117).

The Rowntree affair helped to encourage several companies to bring brands on to the balance sheet. In some cases this involved writing back goodwill that had previously been written off on acquisitions and reclassifying it as brands; home-grown brands were not recognized as assets. Thus Grand Metropolitan retrospectively capitalized the brands of the North American drinks business Heublein and Almaden Vineyards (acquired earlier in the 1980s), and its enhanced balance sheet strength made it easier to finance the take-over of food manufacturer and retailer Pillsbury in 1988. Guinness capitalized

£1,375 million, mainly in respect of its spirit brands acquired when it took over Bells and Distillers (the very valuable 'Guinness' name was not capitalized). Indeed, the Guinness 1988 annual report repeatedly stressed the role of brands as the main source of value to the concern; a marked contrast to the 1986 annual report (the year in which Guinness acquired Distillers), where the word 'brand' scarcely appears. The accounting policy adopted by Guinness emphasized separability:

> Acquired brands are only recognized where title is clear, brand earnings are separately identifiable, the brand could be sold separately from the rest of the business and where the brand achieves earnings in excess of those achieved by unbranded products.
>
> (Quoted in Rutteman 1990: 61)

However, the case that gained greatest notoriety was that of Ranks Hovis McDougall (RHM). In 1988, this company faced a bid from the Australian food group Goodman Fielder Wattie. Its defence document emphasized the contribution made by RHM's brands, and RHM procured an independent valuation of these by the specialist company Interbrand. The valuation showed RHM's brands at about £680 million, against its net tangible book value of only £300 million. The valuation was accepted by RHM's auditors, and incorporated into the 1988 balance sheet.

All these accounting treatments were endorsed by the auditors of the respective companies, indeed, all of the 'big six' international accountancy firms have accepted that brand capitalization gives a 'true and fair view' of the state of affairs of at least one of their clients. Yet the initial *official* reaction of the accounting profession was to assert that 'the balance sheet does not purport to be a statement of corporate value, and the amounts at which assets are stated in the balance sheet do not in themselves determine a company's market value' (ASC 1989a: para. 1). Companies were discouraged from incorporating revaluations of intangibles such as brands in the balance sheet, as the ASC considered that the bases of calculation and the figures derived were unreliable. If companies did include brands on the balance sheet, the presumption was that these had a limited useful economic life, which would require them to be depreciated.

Over the next year, the terms of the brands debate became clearer. A meeting at the London Business School on 10 January 1989 was attended by representatives of the accountancy profession, the investing community, companies which had incorporated brands in their balance sheet, and brand valuers. No consensus emerged from this meeting, with the brand valuers and their clients convinced that they were applying appropriate methods to value genuine assets, while the accountants argued that the methods were dubious or at the least untried, that they did not measure what they claimed, and that brands were simply an aspect of goodwill. The meeting was chaired by Professor Andrew Likierman, who later in 1989 brought out a report (Barwise et al. 1989) strongly critical of the whole notion of including brands on the balance sheet. The 'LBS Report' concluded that the separability of brands could not in general be established, so valuation methods were fatally flawed. Even if brands were separate assets that could in principle be valued, the heavy use of estimates about the future in such valuations made them irredeemably subjective. The LBS Report declard 'that the present flexible position, far from being neutral, is potentially corrosive to the whole basis of financial reporting and that to allow brands – whether acquired or home-grown – to continue to be included in the balance sheet would be highly unwise' (Barwise et al. 1989: 79).

Although the writing of the LBS Report was financially supported by the Institute of Chartered Accountants in England and Wales (ICAEW), its conclusions were reached independently, and its very hard line came as a surprise to many observers. However, the report must have stiffened the backbone of the Accounting Standards Committee, which issued Exposure Draft 52 *Accounting for Intangible Fixed Assets* (ASC 1990) in May 1990. This seems to have been written with the express intention of making it as difficult as possible for companies to continue to carry intangibles on the balance sheet, and it proposed conditions on the recognition of such assets going some way beyond the restrictions of company law.

The main provisions of ED 52 were as follows.

1 Intangibles could be recognized if and only if (a) they either had a known historical cost or such cost could be shown to be readily ascertainable; (b) they were clearly distinguishable from goodwill and other assets; and (c) their cost could be measured independently of goodwill, of other assets, and of the earnings of the relevant business or business segment.
2 Revaluations above historical cost were permitted only on the basis of depreciated replacement cost, and allowed only when this figure could be measured with reasonable certainty.[9]
3 Intangibles should be depreciated over their useful economic life, which was considered finite, and not normally exceeding twenty years (as an absolute maximum, a forty-year period might be adopted in special circumstances).

4 It might be appropriate to disclose the identity and book value of major individual intangibles.

The Accounting Standards Committee was replaced by the Accounting Standards Board in July 1990, and the new body has not yet issued a Financial Reporting Standard specifically relating to brands. Any pronouncement is likely to reflect the general approach to determining accounting standards implicit in ED 52. This is a 'top down', concepts-based approach, in accordance with which standard setters endeavour to resolve accounting issues by reference to statements of generally applicable principles ('conceptual frameworks') rather than emerging practice. ED 52's reiteration of notions of 'cost', 'finite useful life', 'separability' and so on seems simply irrelevant to those organizations in the vanguard of brand valuation and accounting.

The attitude of accounting standard setters to brands raises the question of why they set themselves to oppose rather than channel emerging brand accounting practices. There are probably two main factors involved here. First, accountants fear that public criticism arising from accounting 'failure' will lead to the government constraining their activities as auditors. Corporate collapses of companies which had included very high amounts for intangibles on their balance sheets with no demur from the auditors, such as Maxwell Communications Corporation[10] and Polly Peck, could be used as ammunition against the accountancy establishment.

At the same time, accountants were coming under challenge from commercial brand valuers such as Interbrand. The relationship of an auditor to the external valuer of an asset is a complex one (Napier and Power 1992: 92). The auditor must rely on the credibility of the valuer, yet by doing so may actually end up *conferring* such credibility on a potential business rival. Accountancy firms have increasingly entered the valuation market themselves, but auditors cannot independently audit their own valuations. The ICAEW has recently amended its *Guide to Professional Ethics* to make it clear that a firm should not audit a client's financial statements which include the product of a specialist valuation that it has carried out, and have specifically included the valuation of brands and other intangibles within this provision (*Accountancy*, January 1993: 101). The result may be that accountancy firms will have to 'take in each other's washing' by valuing the intangibles of their competitors' clients.

The political dimension of the brands debate (Napier and Power 1992; Power 1992) is as significant as the discussion of accounting methods, and it may be that the prospect of having to pass work on

to their competitors will make the big accountancy firms more willing
to support accounting standards that hinder brand accounting. But it
cannot be denied that brand valuation is becoming better established
in the UK. As brands become created as separate marketable assets, it
is more difficult for accountants to resist including them in the
balance sheet. Theoretical support for inclusion has been provided by
Arnold et al. (1992), in a report for the ICAEW. The writers of this
report recommend that 'intangibles . . . should be permitted to be
treated as assets provided that their existence and amount can be satisfactorily justified. . . . Internally created intangibles may be dealt with
in the same way as purchased ones' (Arnold et al. 1992: x). The
authors are relaxed about revaluation of intangibles, although they
propose a 'ceiling test' that the amount at which intangibles are stated
is no more than their recoverable amount. Similarly, they do not
rigidly insist on systematic depreciation of intangibles, as this is better
dealt with through periodic revaluation. The only recommendation of
ED 52 that Arnold et al. endorse is for greater disclosure of the nature
and amount of important individual intangibles. In the context of the
last recommendation, it should be observed that many of the companies capitalizing brands have disclosed simply an aggregate figure,
with virtually no information as to how this has been arrived at. Few
companies even go so far as to emulate the 1991 annual report of
Guinness, which at least lists the principal brands included in the
valuation.

THE WAY FORWARD

The Arnold et al. (1992) proposals could well provide a basis for
compromise on the brands issue, but they still leave many problems
unresolved. It is becoming increasingly hard for accountants to assert
that brands do not exist as accounting assets, when they are valued,
bought and sold, maintained, enhanced and scrapped, and are
increasingly accepted as the focus of corporate management in many
industries (Guilding and Pike 1990). Yet many of the valuation
methods advocated by brand valuers seem almost designed to play
into the hands of those who claim that they do not measure brand
value at all, but something else (such as goodwill). Thus, many of the
methods proposed in the recent report *The Valuation of Intangible
Assets* (Arthur Andersen & Co. 1992) determine the brand value by
'separa[t]ing the earnings of the intangible asset to be valued from the
earnings of all other assets' (Arthur Andersen & Co. 1992: 55). As
Napier and Power (1992) observe:

The whole family of brand contribution methods stands or falls on the issue of whether the use of such residual approaches can in fact dichotomise the economic benefits attributable to a business, business segment or product into those attributable to the intangible and those attributable to other assets or to a baseline unbranded product. The critic will regard this strategy as begging the crucial question whereas the supporter will simply accept the separability assumptions inherent in this method.

(Napier and Power 1992: 89)

Brand valuation methods are likely to prove more acceptable to accountants to the extent that they do not mimic the calculation of goodwill by determining a residual. Thus methods to isolate the brand from the other resources involved in generating profits and to measure the value of the brand directly will have to be developed (or accountants will have to be convinced that existing methods achieve this already).

A suggestion made by many accounting standard setters is that those companies which wish to disclose brand valuations should simply give this information by way of a note to the accounts (Tweedie and Whittington 1990: 91) or an unaudited supplementary 'economic' balance sheet (Wild and Everitt 1989: 68). However, this seems to be an abdication of responsibility on the part of accountants, especially as most companies that have capitalized brands have done so precisely because of the impact on the balance sheet. Including brands on the balance sheet has consequences for key company ratios, such as the debt/equity ratio, which is often used as the basis of restrictions on borrowing in company Articles of Association and loan agreements. It also becomes less likely that the Stock Exchange's asset tests for issuing Class 1 Circulars and obtaining shareholder consent for acquisitions are triggered.[11] So brand accounting is not just a matter of showing a 'more accurate' picture of the company through the balance sheet. Indeed, in an investigation into share price reaction to decisions taken to capitalize brands, Mather and Peasnell (1991) found little support for the argument that brand accounting provided useful new information to the stock market, and suggested that the motives for brand accounting were not a desire to inform but a wish to give the balance sheet a cosmetic face lift.

The Chairman of the Accounting Standards Board, David Tweedie, sees brand capitalization as merely an aspect of 'creative accounting', and talks about 'stripping away all the flim-flam from accounting and getting down to the economic reality' (quoted in Bruce 1993: 10). But what accountants mean by 'economic reality' and what managers of brand-rich companies mean may be very different. The conceptual approach adopted by accounting standard setters focuses attention on the 'ontological' question of whether brands are assets. The issue of whether brands can be *made* assets (in the accounting sense) through appropriate methods of valuation goes by default.

Unfortunately, the 'proprietorial' nature of brand valuation militates against the education of accountants. General descriptions of brand valuation techniques lend themselves to easy (and perhaps unfair) criticism.[12] Yet brand valuers may believe that wider and more detailed knowledge of their preferred valuation techniques would afford opportunities to competitors rather than inform accountants. Publications such as *The Valuation of Intangible Assets* (Arthur Andersen & Co. 1992) are intended as much to market a particular firm's services and to lobby accounting standard setters as to inform and educate (Napier and Power 1992). They do not help the case for brand accounting.

A further issue is that the accountants have tended to concentrate on the valuation of well-established brands. Yet within brand-focused organizations, there is a perception that present accounting practices prejudice *emerging* brands. The costs of creating and establishing a new brand are regarded as overheads rather than as investments. Brand development must pay off very rapidly if brand managers are to be allowed to maintain and cultivate new brands. To some commentators, this short-termism is highly regrettable:

> Investments in brand-building strategies are explained, not in terms of what can be justified on the basis of expected returns, but in terms of what can be afforded on the basis of reported profits. . . . Marketing investment, consequently, is thought of as an appropriation of forecast profits. Strong established brands can afford to invest more than weak young brands.
>
> (Allen 1990: 2)

In Britain, companies are permitted to capitalize the costs of developing new products and processes (ASC 1989b). Although market research is explicitly excluded from the definition of development costs, there are clear parallels between product development and brand establishment (indeed, in consumer goods industries, the distinction between these is artificial). Brand-oriented companies might wish to design their internal management accounting systems in order to identify the costs of establishing and developing new brands, with a view to using the ASC's own logic in the case of product development costs as a justification for capitalizing the costs of creating and establishing new brands.

While the notion of managing brand value may have become self-evident to the marketing industry (Aaker 1991), and may be penetrating management accounting, financial accountants remain sceptical about putting brands on the balance sheet. The situation in property valuation, where fundamental principles and detailed techniques are widely accepted and known both inside and outside the valuation industry, is one to which brand valuation must aspire, if it is to become credible not only to auditors but also to external users. Ultimately, marketing experts will have to apply their skills to selling the propriety of brand accounting to accounting standard setters. They will succeed not by emphasizing the images that particular brands are expected to create in the minds of potential customers – accountants will instinctively recoil from being asked to include on the balance sheet such qualities as 'care', 'harmony' and 'security' – but by showing that brand valuations are reliable and that brand capitalization provides useful information.

NOTES

1   John Stuart, president and son of the founder of the Quaker Oats Company, to a colleague in the 1920s, quoted by Marquette (1967: 265).
2   Exceptionally, the pneumatic tyre patents acquired from John Boyd Dunlop and others by the Pneumatic Tyre Company were shown as an asset valued at £60,000 when that company was reorganized as the Dunlop Pneumatic Tyre Company in 1896 (McMillan 1989: 11).
3   The claim by a leading brand valuer (Murphy 1989b: xi) that 'In the nineteenth century most of a company's assets were "tangible" – property, plant, stock, investments, cash, etc.' is simply incorrect.
4   My thanks to Richard Wilson for these examples.
5   These were the marks stamped on the iron made at the Works before this was shipped out. Such marks were a common practice in the iron and steel industry and were seen by contemporaries as valuable. In the law case *re Barrow Haematite Steel* ([1900] 2 Ch. 846), for example, the judge commented: 'I think . . . that a company of this magnitude, whose goods are known all over the world by their particular *brand*, must have a Goodwill of considerable value' (emphasis added).
6   For example, in the 1928 accounts of meat extract manufacturer Bovril, £3 million of assets was covered by an omnibus description 'goodwill, trade marks, freehold and leasehold properties and interest in associated companies, government stock, etc.' The 1929 accounts revealed that £2.4 million of this total represented goodwill and trade marks (Edwards 1989: 134).
7   In 1973–4 a survey of 300 companies showed that about one-third wrote goodwill off immediately at the time of acquisition, a further third carried

it indefinitely at cost, and the rest wrote it down, not necessarily according to any systematic method (quoted in Holgate 1990: 10).

8 The impetus towards brand accounting in Australia was exactly the same: the issue of an accounting standard for goodwill in 1984 encouraged the inclusion of identifiable intangibles at fair value on the balance sheet (Goodwin and Harris 1991).

9 In practice, depreciated replacement cost is a virtually meaningless number for highly specific assets such as brands, and most valuation approaches attempt to estimate an 'economic value' by discounting expected future cash flows or profits.

10 Maxwell Communications Corporation included over £2 billion of 'publishing rights, titles and benefits' on its last balance sheet before its collapse in 1991. These mainly arose from Robert Maxwell's acquisition campaign in North America, including the purchase of Official Airlines Guide and the US Macmillan business. According to the former Maxwell financial director, Reg Mogg, the valuation of these intangibles was 'a very professional operation' (quoted in Bower 1991: 506). If this was so, it was a remarkable coincidence that the value of the intangibles precisely equalled the difference between the cost of the companies and their tangible net assets.

11 The asset tests are based on published balance sheet figures. In general, an acquisition representing more than 25 per cent of a company's net assets requires shareholder consent. RHM probably capitalized its brands in 1988 because take-over bidder Goodman Fielder Wattie controlled about 30 per cent of its shares, and thus could threaten to block any acquisitions that required shareholder approval. The RHM board had an incentive to minimize the need for a Class 1 Circular, as they wished to bid for various European businesses being sold by US food giant Nabisco, itself a take-over target (Burrough and Helyar 1990).

12 Thus the generally adverse comments on brand accounting made by Smith (1992: ch. 11) were met with a stern rebuttal in a press release from Interbrand (20 August 1992), which concluded: 'We are disappointed that a procedure which attempts separately to identify and value the overwhelmingly most potent and valuable assets of very many companies should be singled out for such attack'.

REFERENCES

Aaker, D. A. (1991) *Managing Brand Equity: Capitalizing on the Value of a Brand Name*, New York: Free Press.
Accounting Principles Board (1970) *Intangible Assets*, Accounting Principles Board Opinion no. 17, New York: American Institute of Certified Public Accountants (AICPA).
Accounting Standards Committee (ASC) (1984) *Accounting for Goodwill*, Statement of Standard Accounting Practice 22, London: ASC.
—— (1989a) *The Accounting Standards Committee's Provisional Views on Accounting for Intangible Assets with Special Reference to Brands*, Technical Release 738, London: ASC.
—— (1989b) *Accounting for Research and Development*, Statement of Standard Accounting Practice 13 (revised), London: ASC.

—— (1990) *Accounting for Intangible Fixed Assets*, Exposure Draft 52, London: ASC.

Alexander, D. and Archer, S. (1992) *The European Accounting Guide*, London: Academic Press.

Allen, D. (1990) *Creating Value: The Financial Management of Brands*, London: Chartered Institute of Management Accountants (CIMA).

Andrews, W. T. (1981) 'The evolution of APB Opinion No. 17 *Accounting for Intangible Assets:* a study of the US position on accounting for goodwill', *Accounting Historians Journal* Spring: 37–49.

Arnold, J., Egginton, D., Kirkham, L., Macve, R. and Peasnell, K. (1992) *Goodwill and Other Intangibles: Theoretical Considerations and Policy Issues*, London: Institute of Chartered Accountants in England and Wales.

Arthur Andersen & Co. (1992) *The Valuation of Intangible Assets*, London: The Economist Intelligence Unit.

Barwise, P., Higson, C., Likierman, A. and Marsh, P. (1989) *Accounting for Brands*, London: Institute of Chartered Accountants in England and Wales.

Bigg, W. W. and Wilson, H. A. R. J. (1945) *Spicer & Pegler's Bookkeeping and Accounts* (11th edn), London: HFL Publishers.

Board of Trade (1926) *Report of the Company Law Amendment Committee*, Chairman: W. Greene, Cmd 2657, London: HMSO.

Bogie, D. J. (1949) *Group Accounts: A Complete Manual on Consolidated Accounts*, London: Jordan & Sons.

Bourke, M. (1989) 'Brand valuation and the investor', in J. Murphy (ed.) *Brand Valuation: Establishing a True and Fair View*, London: Hutchinson.

Bower, T. (1991) *Maxwell the Outsider* (revised and updated edn), London: Mandarin.

Brief, R. C. (ed.) (1976) *The Late Nineteenth Century Debate over Depreciation, Capital and Income*, New York: Arno.

Bruce, R. (1993) 'Tweedie vents fury at directors and auditors', *Accountancy Age*, 4 February: 10.

Buchan, E. and Brown, A. (1989) 'Mergers and acquisitions', in J. Murphy (ed.) *Brand Valuation: Establishing a True and Fair View*, London: Hutchinson.

Burrough, B. and Helyar, J. (1990) *Barbarians at the Gate*, London: Arrow.

Chalmin, P. (1983) *Tate and Lyle: Géant du Sucre*, Paris: Editions Economica.

Chambers, R. J. (1966) *Accounting, Evaluation and Economic Behavior*, Englewood Cliffs, NJ: Prentice-Hall.

Committee on Accounting Procedure (1953) *Restatement and Revision of Accounting Research Bulletins* no. 43, New York: American Institute of Accountants.

Cox, H. and Smith, R. (1990) 'An assessment of BAT Co.'s profitability between the wars', Paper presented at the Accounting, Business and Financial History Conference, Cardiff, September.

Dicksee, L. R. (1892) *Auditing: A Practical Manual for Auditors*, London: Gee & Co. (reprinted New York: Arno, 1976).

Dicksee, L. R. and Tillyard, F. (1906) *Goodwill and its Treatment in Accounts*, London: Gee & Co. (reprinted New York: Arno, 1976).

Edwards, J. R. (1989) *A History of Financial Accounting*, London: Routledge.

Fédèration des Experts Comptables Européens (1992) *FEE Analysis of European Accounting and Disclosure Practices*, London: Routledge.

Goodwin, J. and Harris, K. (1991) 'The intangibles debate: some empirical evidence', *Australian Accounting Review* November: 19–29.

Griffiths, I. (1986) *Creative Accounting: How to Make your Profits What you Want them to Be*, London: Firethorn.

Guilding, C. and Pike, R. (1990) 'Intangible marketing assets: a managerial accounting perspective', *Accounting and Business Research* Winter: 41–9.

Gynther, R. S. (1969) 'Some "conceptualizing" on goodwill', *Accounting Review* April: 247–55.

Hodgkins, P. (1979) 'Unilever: the first 21 years', in T. A. Lee and R. H. Parker (eds) *The Evolution of Corporate Financial Reporting*, Sunbury-on-Thames: Thomas Nelson.

Holgate, P. (1990) 'The history and regulation of goodwill accounting', in M. Power (ed.) *Brand and Goodwill Accounting Strategies*, Cambridge: Woodhead-Faulkner.

Kitchen, J. (1972) 'The accounts of British holding company groups: development and attitudes to disclosure in the early years', *Accounting and Business Research* Spring: 114–36.

McMillan, J. (1989) *The Dunlop Story: The Life, Death and Re-birth of a Multinational*, London: Weidenfeld & Nicolson.

Marquette, A. F. (1967) *Brands, Trademarks and Good Will: The Story of the Quaker Oats Company*, New York: McGraw-Hill.

Mather, P. R. and Peasnell, K. V. (1991) 'An examination of the economic circumstances surrounding decisions to capitalise brands', *British Journal of Management* 2(3): 151–64.

Murphy, J. (ed.) (1989a) *Brand Valuation: Establishing a True and Fair View*, London: Hutchinson.

—— (1989b) 'Foreword', in J. Murphy (ed.) *Brand Valuation: Establishing a True and Fair View*, London: Hutchinson.

Napier, C. and Noke, C. (1992) 'Accounting and law: an historical overview of an uneasy relationship', in M. Bromwich and A. Hopwood (eds) *Accounting and the Law*, Hemel Hempstead: Prentice-Hall.

Napier, C. and Power, M. (1992) 'Professional research, lobbying and intangibles: a review essay', *Accounting and Business Research* Winter: 85–95.

Norton, J. (1992) 'Accounting for publishing rights and titles: the regulatory framework and the choices made', Working Paper, Department of Economics, University of Reading.

Pixley, F. W. (1924) *The Accountant's Dictionary*, London: Waverley.

Power, M. (ed.) (1990) *Brand and Goodwill Accounting Strategies*, Cambridge: Woodhead-Faulkner.

—— (1992) 'The politics of brand accounting in the United Kingdom', *European Accounting Review* May: 39–68.

Rowland, S. W. (1934) *Principles of Accounting*, London: Gregg.

Rutteman, P. (1990) 'Accounting for brands and separability', in M. Power (ed.) *Brand and Goodwill Accounting Strategies*, Cambridge: Woodhead-Faulkner.

Smith, T. (1992) *Accounting for Growth: Stripping the Camouflage from Company Accounts*, London: Century.

Thomas, W. A. (1978) *The Finance of British Industry 1918–1976*, London: Methuen.
Tweedie, D. and Whittington, G. (1990) 'Financial reporting: current problems and their implications for systematic reform', *Accounting and Business Research* Winter: 87–102.
Wild, K. and Everitt, H. (1989) 'The accountancy perspective in the UK', in J. Murphy (ed.) *Brand Valuation: Establishing a True and Fair View*, London: Hutchinson.
Yamey, B. S. (1960) 'The development of company accounting conventions', *Three Banks Review* September: 3–18.

Part II
Alcoholic drinks

6 Selling beer in Victorian Britain

Richard G. Wilson

This chapter looks at the marketing of beer in Victorian Britain. At first sight the task, at least measured by success, seems an easy enough operation. Output in the United Kingdom doubled between 1831 and 1873; some breweries grew greatly in size; no industry generated larger fortunes for its business leaders. Bass, Allsopp and Guinness had become by the 1870s perhaps the greatest – certainly the best-known – names in British industry. On closer inspection, however, a study of beer reveals that marketing arrangements were complex and unusual: complex in that beer was a varied and fragile product relying at point of sale upon tens of thousands of publicans only indirectly controlled by the brewers themselves; unusual among Britain's major industries in that the export market was, except for a handful of firms, unimportant (never more than around 3 per cent of output found its way overseas). The retailing of beer therefore embraces a large number of primarily domestic outlets. What were successful strategies in this big industry under constant government and temperance surveillance in the nineteenth century? Again on the surface, no industry appeared to retain its traditions better. The 'Beer and Britannia' image of Sydney Smith was preserved, its close links with British agriculture continued, its conservative business leaders appeared to eschew the march of science, so that the production of beer seemed much the same in 1900 as it had done seventy years earlier. Yet it did not remain detached from the progress of industrialization and urbanization transforming Victorian Britain. Therefore at the outset it is necessary to outline the major changes encompassing the beer market in these years.

BEER CONSUMPTION

On the demand side, the *consumption* of beer expanded rapidly during the mid-Victorian period. Actually, the figures that every

Table 6.1 Consumption of beer for the UK and England and Wales, 1800–1913[a]

	United Kingdom	England and Wales
1800–04	—	33.9
1805–09	—	32.8
1810–14	—	30.2
1815–19	—	28.0
1820–24	—	29.0
1825–29	—	28.4
1830–34	21.7	33.8
1835–39	22.9	35.4
1840–44	19.5	30.5
1845–49	19.4	29.2
1850–54	21.1	29.5
1855–59	22.0	29.3
1860–64	24.7	31.6
1865–69	28.8	35.9
1870–74	31.1	38.2
1875–79	33.2	40.5
1880–84	29.1	33.6
1885–89	28.3	32.5
1890–94	29.7	33.4
1895–99	31.2	34.5
1900–04	30.2	34.3
1905–09	27.3	30.9
1910–13	26.9	29.4

Source: G. B. Wilson 1941: 331–3, 369–70; Mitchell & Deane 1962: 8–10

Note: [a] Annual averages in gallons per head, based on total population.

historian has used from G. B. Wilson's well-known compilation of statistics, *Alcohol and the Nation* (1941), are a *production* series, ingeniously compiled by Wilson from the quantities of malt (and sugar) used in brewing (see Table 6.1). Since, however, exports were relatively unimportant and private brewing declined sharply between 1830 and 1870, calculations about *consumption* made from them are reasonably plausible, except in that after 1830 his series is compiled for the *United Kingdom*. Subsequently, historians have used them to discuss working-class living standards especially since they showed (his figures for 1800–29 were for *England and Wales* only) a steady decline in beer consumption from 1800 to 1850 (G. B. Wilson 1941: 332–3). In fact, Wilson's post-1830 UK data seriously understate beer consumption in England and Wales – the beer-drinking heart of the United Kingdom. For production of beer in Ireland and Scotland was small in relation to their population (especially Ireland's). The English series, easily worked out after 1830 from the malt figures and population statistics, are set out in Table 6.1. The salient point is that in England and Wales per capita consumption, already high in the 1830s, steadied in the 1840s and 1850s, and then surged by some 38 per cent in the next twenty years.

Table 6.2 Beer production in the UK, 1831–1914

	England and Wales	*Scotland*	*Ireland*	*UK*
1831–34	13,486	518	846	14,850
1835–39	14,908	574	941	16,423
1840–44	13,824	449	540	14,813
1845–49	14,059	469	647	15,175
1850–54	15,222	560	633	16,416
1855–59	16,150	612	932	17,694
1860–64	18,382	852	1,176	20,411
1865–69	22,154	1,166	1,485	24,805
1870–74	25,087	1,284	1,736	28,107
1875–79	28,217	1,149	2,061	31,427
1880–84	25,002	1,138	2,083	28,223
1885–89	25,532	1,453	2,355	29,340
1890–94	27,735	1,749	2,609	32,093
1895–99	30,290	2,052	2,864	35,206
1900–04	30,577	1,981	3,244	35,802
1905–09	28,692	1,778	3,382	33,852
1910–14	28,863	1,856	4,022	34,741

Source and note: G. B. Wilson 1941: 369–70

Note:
The figures from 1831–80 are based on the quantities of malt (and sugar) used in brewing. From 1881 to 1889 the 'standard' barrel had an original gravity of 1057°, not 1055°; the quantities have been calculated on the basis of 1055° to preserve 'uniformity'.

See Prest (1954: 76, 85) where Wilson's standard barrelages after 1870 are converted into bulk barrels.

Figures are in thousands of standard (1055° gravity) barrels (annual averages).

The sharp rise is explained by a marked advance in money wages (especially pronounced between 1860 and 1874): the working classes spent a good deal of their increased earnings upon alcohol. A. E. Dingle (1974) explained the latter phenomenon: 'it is likely that the peak of drink consumption in the 1870s was a response to a situation in which purchasing power had temporarily outstripped the supply of consumer goods available, once basic needs had been satisfied' (Dingle

1974: 608–22). In other words, at least for the skilled, higher-income, wage-earners, the pub provided opportunities both for leisure and for a less restrictive and dreary diet. In these circumstances, the 1860s and 1870s were wonderful years for those commercial or common brewers beginning to improve their range of beers and extend their tied-house holding.

The surge in mid-Victorian drinking was largely an urban phenomenon. Philip Snowden, the Labour Politician (writing in 1908) thought that 'the drink question in our country resolves itself into grappling with the traffic as a town problem'. Indeed, he believed, 'the temperance agitation arose with the growth of modern towns' (Snowden 1908: 123). Snowden's view was reinforced by the statistics of drunkenness proceedings in Britain which revealed a pronounced urban and industrial dimension (G. B. Wilson 1941: 437–8).[1] Moreover, there was a growing acknowledgement that urbanization created the conditions that encouraged heavy drinking. For the brewer, therefore, sales strategy was to target this rapid urban-based growth in beer consumption.

After 1880 beer consumption per capita declined so that by the 1900s it had returned to the levels of the early Victorian and pre-Beer Act periods. As is well known, the living standards of the *entire* working classes rose, at least to 1900; for the first time, however, they did not expend this increase upon alcohol. The role of temperance propaganda was important: discussion about local veto, a whole series of government inquiries into the trade, and hostile legislation after 1900 kept the drink question constantly before the public between the 1870s and the First World War. More important, however, were shifts in drinking habits. The upper and middle classes led the way; by a demonstration process a decline in the consumption of alcohol spread to the skilled working class. The heavy drinking binges which had been such a feature of labourers' lives was diminishing. There was greater sobriety at work. Above all, the shift in drink consumption patterns was determined by changes in the supply of consumer goods. A whole range of cheaper articles, often imported, was made available by improved retailing and distribution methods – mass-produced clothing and shoes, machine-produced furniture and packaged foodstuffs. Moreover, the price of beer remained essentially unchanged. In comparison with foodstuffs – whose prices sharply declined in the 1880s and 1890s – it became relatively expensive. This was significant in a period when money wages were not increasing. Large discounts to publicans and off-licences in the free trade and the 'long pull' did not disguise the fact that beer prices remained essentially the same for the drinker. Because working-class consumption patterns shifted, the proportion of their incomes spent on drink declined appreciably – from around 15 per cent in the mid-1870s to around 9 per cent by the 1900s.

The decline in consumption between 1880 and 1914 should not be exaggerated, however: not only did it revive in the late-1890s boom and briefly again in 1912–13, but also the lower levels of the 1880s and early 1890s was simply a return to those of half-a-century earlier – never represented as ones of modest consumption. Drinkers had not turned away from the national beverage in 1914. The reversal in trend around 1880, however, was sufficiently pronounced – given the beginning of licensing restrictions – to convince many brewers that the only way forward was the wholesale acquisition of tied outlets and the absorption of smaller rivals.

THE BEER PRODUCER

On the supply side the significant feature is that in these demand conditions – a rapidly rising, urban-based consumption to the late 1870s – the *commercial* brewer triumphed. Mathias in his classic study, *The Brewing Industry in England* (1959), depicted the increasingly dominant role of the great London porter brewers in the metropolitan area during the late eighteenth and early nineteenth centuries. But the scale of their operations was to be found nowhere else in Britain, even by 1830. Brewing in the England of the Beer Act (1830) was one of contrasts. In the south and east of England, the position of the London breweries was in some degree replicated. Here there were breweries which tied their trade by running scores of public houses (in London the tie was maintained by loans) and which enjoyed trades of tens of thousands of barrels each, although these sales were a far cry from those of Barclay Perkins, Whitbread, Truman and Meux-Reid (Mathias 1959: 552).[2] For example, Steward and Patteson in Norwich; with its totally untypical estate of around 250 public houses in 1837, probably had an output of around 40,000 barrels by the mid-1840s; Lacon's, a Great Yarmouth brewery with a big London market, had average sales of 36,352 barrels of strong beer in the 1840s; but Georges, the great Bristol brewery, did not produce more than 30,000 a year until the late 1850s.[3] These country breweries were market leaders in their regions. Most thriving breweries in the south and east, the prime malt-producing areas, owning and leasing dozens of public houses in the early Victorian period, had outputs of no more than 10,000–20,000 barrels per year. Elsewhere in Britain, public house ownership by brewers was rarer. In some areas, particularly in the south-west, in the West Midlands, in and around Birmingham, Leeds and Manchester, the common brewer had made little headway by the 1830s. Here the publican brewers flourished, making the distinctive beers of their region. Moreover, private brewing was still extensive. Wilson reckoned as much as one-fifth of the beer consumed in England in 1830 was brewed by gentry, farmers, institutions, and even the agricultural labourer (G. B. Wilson 1941: 55–6). Most brewed in October and March, the larger establishments with the aid of an itinerant brewer, but the repeal of the beer duties in 1830 effectively killed off private brewing in Britain. It survived in rural pockets, such as Suffolk and Wales where malt could be obtained in small parcels, and traditions died hard. Elsewhere by the 1870s it was to all intents and purposes a dying art (Wilson believed that production had contracted to 3 per cent by 1870). In 1830, when the sole tax on beer was raised on malt, the private brewer was placed on an equal footing with the common brewer (previously the former had escaped the beer duty levied on brewers for sale). Private brewers could not compete in terms of quality, of extract rates from their malt and, sometimes, of price. It became simpler for them to obtain their beer from the local brewery and sell or scrap their brewing utensils.[4] Many a Victorian brewery flourished on the 'family' trade of the gentry, clergy and middle classes, the majority of whom would not have dreamt of entering a public house.

The demise of the private brewer was followed by that of the publican brewer, whose position in 1830 was a strong one. The figures for the proportions of malt made into beer by common brewers, licensed victuallers and beer-house keepers in England and Wales and Scotland between 1830 and 1900 provide a unique statistical view of an industry in transition from a point at which commercial and domestic production was roughly equal, to one in which large-scale output predominated (see Table 6.3). The figures for a variety of reasons are not without their problems but they underline a broad trend. Setting private brewing aside, common brewers in England and Wales produced around 55 per cent of beers output on Queen Victoria's accession, the licensed victualler just under 33 per cent, and the beer-house keeper – the new, free-trade entrant to the industry in 1830 – around 12.5 per cent. At the end of her reign (1901), the first produced 95 per cent, the other two categories together a diminutive 5 per cent (in Scotland this pattern of concentration had been already achieved by 1830). The key decades in the transition to commercial brewing are the 1870s and the 1880s. In the year ending September 1870, 20,095 victuallers and 9,735 beer-house keepers still produced

Table 6.3 Numbers of and quantities of malt brewed by common brewers, victuallers and beer-house keepers in England and Wales, and Scotland, 1832–1900

Year ending	Common brewers (CB)		Licensed victuallers (LV)				Persons licensed to sell beer (PLB)[a]				% brewed by		
	No.	Bushels brewed (million)	Total	No. brewing	As %	Bushels brewed (million)	Total	No. brewing	As %	Bushels brewed (million)	CB	LV	PLB
5. 1.1832 England and Wales	1,654	14.26	50,547	23,889	47.3	9.01	31,937	13,446	42.1	2.99	54	34	11
Scotland	221	0.83	17,861	318	1.8	0.09	–	–	–	–	90	10	–
5. 1.1841 England and Wales	2,258	17.69	57,379	26,880	46.8	8.55	42,613	16,376	38.9	3.37	60	29	11
Scotland	197	0.09	16,015	245	1.5	0.10	–	–	–	–	90	10	–
30.10.1850 England and Wales	2,281	17.80	59,676	25,851	43.4	7.15	39,158	13,448	34.3	3.23	63	25	11
Scotland	151	0.83	14,971	178	1.2	0.12	–	–	–	–	88	12	–
30.10.1860 England and Wales	2,326	26.02	64,455	24,578	38.1	7.33	44,504	12,283	27.6	3.34	71	20	9
Scotland	105	1.41	12,040	126	1.0	0.22	–	–	–	–	87	13	–
30. 9.1870 England and Wales	2,512	33.94	69,903	20,093	28.7	7.03	47,568	9,735	20.5	3.27	77	16	7
Scotland	79	1.73	12,644	123	1.0	0.30	–	–	–	–	85	15	–
30. 9.1880 England and Wales	2,507	41.93	69,761	12,336	17.7	5.00	49,404	6,157	12.5	2.71	84	10	5
Scotland	88	1.87	12,259	81	0.7	0.38	–	–	–	–	83	17	–
30. 9.1890 England and Wales	2,175	42.70	73,016	6,312	8.6	2.92	44,296	3,319	7.5	1.70	90	6	4
Scotland	115	3.90	11,767	37	0.3	0.25	–	–	–	–	92	8	–
30. 9.1900 England and Wales	1,711	45.45	73,271	2,884	3.9	1.50	41,579	1,582	3.8	0.88	95	3	2
Scotland	125	3.65	11,208	3	0.03	0.01	–	–	–	–	100	–	0.04

Source: British Parliamentary Papers (PP) 1831–2 XXXIV parts one and two; PP 1841 XXXVI parts one and two; PP 1851 LIII parts one and two; PP 1861 LVIII parts one and two; PP 1870 LXII parts one and two; PP 1881 LXXX iii parts one and two; PP 1890–1 LXXVII; PP 1901 LXIX

[a]These are almost all beer-house keepers, although from 1841 the figures do not distinguish between those brewing 'to be drunk on premises' and 'not to be drunk on premises'. Totals of both categories are given.

Table 6.4 Number of common brewers paying for licences in the UK, 1834–1914[a]

Barrels	1834	1851	1861	1871	1881	1891	1901[b]	1911[b]	1914[b]
1,000–9,999	1,302	1,654	1,614	1,810	1,677	1,370	911	716	580
10,000–19,999	89	151	160	216	275	284	263	202	197
20,000–199,999	45	121	103	154	197	279	326	310	310
200,000–499,000			10	8	10	13	11	11	16
500,000–999,999				4	2	2	6	5	5
1,000,000–1,999,999					1	2	2	1	2
2,000,000 +							1	1	1
Total	1,436	1,926	1,887	2,192	2,162	1,950	1,520	1,246	1,111

Source: 1834 XXIV, p. 173 Fourth Report of the Committee appointed to inquire into the Department of Excise, and into the Management and Collection of the Excise Revenue throughout the UK Survey of Brewers Accounts and Papers, 1852–3 XCIX. 1861 LXVII, p. 101. 1872 LIV, p. 4. 1882 LXXXIII, p. 82. 1892 XCIII, p. 80. 1902 XCIII, p. 101. 1912–13 (38) LXVIII, p. 644. 1914–16 LIV, p. 414

Notes:

[a] The definition of a common brewer is one who produced more than 1,000 barrels a year. In 1834 around 200 of those who produced less nevertheless considered themselves common brewers. At the margin, the distinction in size between common and publican brewers is not clear cut. But very few of the latter can have produced more than 1,000 barrels, and increasingly a 1,000 barrels output was a minimum scale of operation for a common brewer.

[b] Persons or firms licensed.

some 23 per cent of total output. By 1890 their numbers had fallen by more than two-thirds. Ten years later they were on the endangered species list of domestic producers. Why did the publican brewer and beer-house keeper retreat from the Victorian brewing scene? First, they could not match the range or quality of the common brewers' beers – or at least the better examples of the species, pale ale particularly. Second, their efforts became inextricably intertwined with their chief creditors, the maltster and brewer. Many folded under the burden of debt, selling their pubs willingly to brewers when prices for tied property rose sharply after 1870. Charles Barclay, the great London brewer and Member of Parliament, had talked of 'power-loom' brewing in 1830; in Victorian Britain it spread everywhere.

In an environment of strong market growth especially from the late 1850s to the late 1870s, and with the private and publican brewers placed at an increasing disadvantage, the more energetic and competent common brewers flourished as never before. Selling around 7 million barrels in 1830, having eliminated their private and publican competitors, their annual sales had reached almost 35 millions in the years before 1914. It was a fivefold growth which signalled expansion even for the most hesitant brewer and opened an El Dorado for those of vision and enterprise. The chief feature of Victorian brewing is therefore the emergence of large firms across Britain (see Table 6.4).

Once largely confined to London, the big common brewery had spread everywhere, even in the heartland of publican brewing (Birmingham), to dominate regional production by 1900. The lead was given by brewers in Burton, Dublin, Edinburgh and the Liverpool area. Bass, Allsopp and Guinness, with barrelages touching and exceeding 1 million by the 1870s, were in a class of their own. But by the 1890s brewers producing 100,000 plus barrels – unknown outside London two generations earlier – were quite common.

THE CHANGING TASTE OF VICTORIAN BEERS

Two further items, essential in a discussion of the Victorian beer market have been ignored to this point: the changing nature of the product and the number of outlets through which it was sold. Both require a moment's attention. It is difficult to recreate the exact taste of Victorian beers, although brewing enthusiasts are attempting to unravel the secrets head brewers entered in their brewing books 100–150 years ago. In general, early Victorian beer was strong, dark and matured. It varied considerably in price from the cheapest milds and porters retailed at around 4*d*. a quart to the finest Burton and

Scottish ales which sold at up to twice that amount. What contemporaries stressed, however, was the differences between beers in the regions. W. L. Tizard wrote in the mid-1840s:

> Who is there in Britain that cannot discover a difference of flavour and gust between the London and Dublin porter? Who that has travelled would expect to find the London taste in Newcastle ale, or either of these in the ales prepared at Liverpool, Lincoln, Nottingham, Sheffield, Birmingham, Derby, the Staffordshire potteries, Maidstone, Dorchester, Davenport, Alton or North or South Wales? . . . Each respective article in any of these places if of good quality, is preferred by the local consumers 'of the cheer' generally, to every other that in their opinion can be brewed.
>
> (Tizard 1846: 133)

There were, however, two significant developments in the nineteenth century. The first is well known. In the 1840s the Burton brewers began to retail nationally a beer – IPA (India Pale Ale) – they had begun to produce twenty years earlier for the Indian market. It was pale, light and heavily hopped. Expensive, often bottled and looking far better than a murky porter in the new, mass-produced glass drinking vessels, it captured the better end of the Victorian beer market, becoming the status drink of the middle and skilled working classes. It was a beer every London and country brewer came to imitate after the 1860s. Seldom, except at Tadcaster, Alton and Newark-upon-Trent, which possessed similar hard waters, did other brewers capture the special qualities of Burton ales – at least to the 1870s when brewing liquor (water) could be 'Burtonized' by chemical means. The second trend is equally important, although contemporary brewing writers, who enthused about pale ale and Burton – the extraordinary, mushroom-growth capital of British brewing – tended to ignore it. This was the production of a cheap, sweet, mild ale, which increasingly replaced porter and the old strong vatted beers (although not stout) in working-class drinking habits. A visitor to Cobbs' Margate Brewery in 1875 wrote: 'It is strange how the taste of these days [the French Wars, 1793–1815] for old stale beer has turned to the opposite extreme in the liking for new and sweet by the present generation.'[5] When Alfred Barnard visited the great East End brewers, Mann, Crossman and Paulin, he commented 'the fickle public has got tired of vinous flavoured vatted porter and transformed its affections to the new and luscious mild ale' (Barnard 1889–91: I, 378). In London, no brewer matched Mann's mild. At the turn of the century they were selling close on 500,000 barrels. By the 1880s drinkers were demanding 'fresh' beers, often 'October' ales brewed from the new season's malt. Since these mild or 'running ales' were less heavily hopped and never brewed to store, they were not easy to produce in summer. Brewers, after Gladstone's replacement of the malt tax by beer duty in 1880, began to experiment with portions of sugar, maize and rice to achieve lightness and stability in their beers. By 1914 these beers were appreciably weaker than those generally consumed fifty years earlier. A Birmingham brewer wrote in 1907:

> Since the brewers have had more control over the houses, beers have undergone a great improvement, for with the aid of Scientific knowledge, hygienic breweries and suitable appliances, they have succeeded in producing beers containing 25 per cent less of alcohol than the beers formerly retailed in Birmingham public-houses.
>
> (Pratt 1907: 297–8)

E. A. Pratt, noting in the same year a decline in the strength of mild ale (which he put at 15–20 per cent since the early 1880s) concluded 'we have the important fact that the British working-man's beer of today is already practically a temperance beverage' (Pratt 1907: 229–30, 241). Beneath the exaggeration, Pratt was making an important point about consumer taste and lighter beers.

BEER HOUSES, THE FREE AND TIED TRADES

In 1830 the Beer Act had controversially attempted to revolutionize the retailing of beer. It created a fourth class of drinking establishment – the beer house. Any householders who were ratepayers might apply for a two guinea excise licence to sell beer – and brew it when they could manage to – on their premises. Within a mere eight years almost 46,000 of these beer houses were added to the stock of some 51,000 licensed premises. In fact although the number of beer houses grew so rapidly (see Table 6.5), the promised free trade revolution in beer never took off. First, the brewers from the outset, by a variety of tying arrangements, controlled the sale of beer through many beer houses. Only in the centres of publican brewing did they find an independent niche. Second, those beer-house brewers who were meant to open up competition and lower beer prices never produced more than 13.4 per cent of the national beer output at their peak in 1836. The reasons were clear from the outset. They were incapable of producing a reliable beer; they had difficulties in finding capital to buy a decent set of brewing utensils; they often relied upon the common brewer for credit. Always vulnerable to local complaint, the better beer houses were an easy prey for common brewers when they acquired tied property more vigorously after 1870.[6]

Table 6.5 Number of beer houses licensed in England and Wales, 1831–1914

	'On' licences	'Off' licences		'On' licences	'Off' licences
1831	30,978		1875	39,267	4,211
1836	39,104	5,030	1880	37,639	11,765
1840	36,871	5,742	1885	32,960	12,609
1845	32,624	3,687	1890	31,766	12,497
1850	36,080	3,343	1895	30,496	12,376
1855	39,877	2,911	1900	29,394	12,331
1860	41,094	2,947	1905	28,522	12,082
1865	46,637	2,853	1910	24,891	11,653
1870	44,501	3,078	1914	26,517	17,929

Source: G. B. Wilson 1941: 395–8

In the previous year, after forty years of constant clamour to curtail them, the beer houses were brought under the control of the magistracy and, in a well-known movement, all licences were eventually brought under stricter supervision and numbers marginally reduced until the 1904 Act provided compensation – from a fund levied upon the brewers – for surrendered licences. Then the number of licences declined more appreciably, although never at the rate that the government had prophesied in 1904. Nevertheless, the result was that the number of persons per on-licence increased from 223 to 1 in 1873 to 324 to 1 in 1906. The pivotal points for the common brewer were the Beer Act, the threatened restriction of licences after 1870 (more real after *Sharp* v *Wakefield* in 1891), the compensation scheme of 1904, and the wholesale attack upon the trade by Lloyd George in 1908–9. In general, free trade survived to 1870; after 1885, when the larger breweries took company status and raised loan capital very easily during the next fifteen years, brewers acquired tied property at an unprecedented rate.

THE AGENCY NETWORK FOR RETAILING BEER

The real key to market strategy by brewers at least to the 1880s was not a wholesale reliance upon tied houses whereby they could easily retail beers and concentrate upon providing a first-class product which could stand comparison with their local competitors. To the 1880s the agenda in a primarily free trade was more difficult. It was set by the Burton brewers and Guinness in the 1840s. Those brewers throughout Britain who sought to expand sales beyond their immediate locality to secure growth essentially followed their lead.

Of course, there had always been at least from the seventeenth century a wider trade in beer. London drinkers enjoyed the products of famed brewing centres such as Dorchester, Derby, Nottingham, Burton and the estuarine towns of Kent; country drinkers were by the late eighteenth century supplied with porter by the leading London brewers. Nevertheless the trade was relatively small: beer did not travel well; its bulk, low value and the ease with which its casks could be broached in transit militated against it being moved more than a few miles except by waterborne transport.[7] Essentially, it was the rail- ways which opened up the Victorian beer trade, reducing freight charges and slashing journey times.[8] Bass's home trade quadrupled within four years of the railway coming to Burton (1839). When the Burton breweries were at the height of their fame in the 1870s, com- mentators waxed lyrical about the benefit of the railways in Burton itself and in the transit of beer throughout Britain. Already Bass was the largest railway customer in the world.

The railways allowed the creation of agencies and stores which became the lifeblood of the Burton breweries and the free trade after 1840. Indeed, they were the most significant feature of the distribution of beer in Victorian Britain, for the more enterprising breweries every- where followed the lead of Bass, Allsopp and Guinness in creating them. Historians of the industry have tended to ignore them, yet an outline of the agency system is the key to marketing strategies and the remarkable growth of the leading breweries following the completion of a national rail network.

In fact, a reconstruction of any brewery's agency network and the logic behind its construction is not easy, for records seldom survive for the pre-1880s period. Nevertheless it is certain that the lead in their creation was given by the Burton brewers. Bass and Allsopp were the key firms, although the system had its origins in the arrangements, usual in the eighteenth century, whereby a trader on the spot could look after the interests of a distant merchant or manufacturer. Trumans, the big London porter brewers, had attempted in the 1790s to rationalize their numerous country customers through the accounts of half-a-dozen merchants. Agencies were therefore a response to the problems of opening up distant markets more profitably. When M. T. Bass succeeded his father he devised an agency network to expand the sales of his beer in England as well as abroad. In the 1830s he had established agents in London, Liverpool, Stoke-on-Trent and Birmingham, even before the railway came to Burton in 1839. Within four years a further three had been added.[9]

Worthington's brewery provides a good example of the setting-up and development of an agency network.[10] Before the early 1860s their business centred upon the local trade and a London store opened in 1854. Then in the mid-1860s they quickly expanded their agency business. Its construction in 1863–4 was a rapid, ramshackle affair. Some two dozen names were mentioned, the firm giving a 12.5 per cent commission on cash sales and requiring security, usually of £200 with the agent being made responsible for a quarter of his bad debts. The initiative did not invariably come from Worthingtons, but sometimes from the agent himself. Some like those in Glasgow, Derby, Manchester, Lancashire, West Yorkshire had potential; those in rural areas like Anglesea and Spilsby (Lincs) did not. Worthington's output grew rapidly after the 1860s – a growth fuelled by their agency network. In 1875 the firm advertised in the *Licensed Victuallers Gazette* that it had twenty-six agencies – six in the Midlands, ten in the north, four in the south of England, three in Wales, one in Scotland, and two in Ireland.[11] Like all the major Burton breweries, Worthington's most important stores were in London. As early as 1875 it had two: one at St Pancras serving the Midland Railway connection, a second at Moorfields for the north-western route. Together they were capable of storing 3,000–4,000 barrels. Fifteen years later they had moved to Broad Street, poised to deliver 1,000 barrels a week (a quarter of their sales). The firm, which had vigorously acquired pubs after 1886, was still relying on its agencies to retain its sizeable free-trade market (58.5 per cent of sales in 1910).[12]

If Worthington's records provide a rare case study of the agency system, it was the example of Bass's model network that provided the inspiration for every aspiring Victorian brewer.[13] As early as 1846 53.6 per cent of its total sales were made from its agencies with no less than 35.7 per cent being sustained from its London store. Some of the firm's export trade found its way into the London figures, but London and Liverpool held a key place in Bass's home trade. Its vast store in the lower floor of the Midland Railway's great St Pancras station after 1867 housed 120,000 barrels and employed 150 men. Eventually in all the major cities of the four countries in the United Kingdom, smaller versions of the London store were set up by Bass; altogether there were twenty-two in 1890 and a peak of twenty-five in 1900. In the latter year the London agency did a trade of £840,950; Newcastle almost £300,000; Liverpool, Manchester and Glasgow with just over £200,000 apiece and five others had sales in excess of £100,000 – the turnover of any one would have satisfied most provincial breweries.

Behind these statistics the agent had a key role in Bass's affairs. It was his vigour that created sales, his character that advertised Bass's presence in any of these two dozen centres. He was the firm's eyes and ears. Not only did he endlessly report upon the quality and condition of their beers, and manage the travellers, storemen and draymen in the store but also he eventually came to play a key role in Bass's policy of supplying loans to tie a fast-declining free trade after 1886. The agents were also essential links in reporting back to Bass about the incursions and strategies which other breweries were employing in the industry's trade wars after the 1890s. As discounts (the chief competitive weapon) soared, it was the agents and travellers who appraised the firm of the acute problems that all brewers faced in the free trade after the 1890s.

Few breweries besides Guinness maintained as extensive an agency system as that erected by the big Burton breweries, and none on the scale of Bass, Allsopp and Ind Coope. Yet it was the Bass model that clearly provided the example for all those breweries who aimed to expand beyond their own district by incursions into the free trade. The more enterprising Scottish breweries grew exactly in this way. Donnachie (1979), generalizing from the example of McEwans, represented the typical, big Edinburgh and Glasgow brewery around 1880 making half its sales locally, a quarter in the country trade, and the rest split between the English and export trades (Donnachie 1979: 215–17). William Younger, the most prominent Scottish brewery, had erected a network of fourteen agents by 1873 to achieve these ends.[14] Smaller firms like Ballinghall's of Dundee and James Calder of Alloa had stores in Newcastle and Liverpool, as well as in Glasgow; the Edinburgh and Leith Brewery Company reputedly sold its beers principally in England (Barnard 1889–91: III, 142–66; IV 384, 386–94). In England, John Smith's of Tadcaster similarly expanded by creating an agency network. It possessed sixteen offices and stores and twenty-two agencies in the 1880s, although its competitors maintained that a good deal of its success was due to the discounts of 20 per cent or more which they found difficult to match. But the earliest surviving evidence of a firm which copied Bass's route to prominence comes from Tetley's of Leeds. It witnessed a rapid growth in output from 36,000 barrels in 1859 to 166,740 in 1876 (its pre-1906 peak).[15] Part of this surge was due to its endeavour to set up a national distribution centre in six cities – London, Dublin, Liverpool, Birmingham, Manchester and York. By 1859 its agency system was impressive,

although, unlike the Burton brewers, this early promise was not maintained. In the 1880s it was effectively squeezed from the London and
Manchester markets.

On the other hand some large breweries made no attempt to open
agencies and stores: they simply used travellers, working from the
brewery office, to service their tied trade and open up the free and
private trades in their vicinity. Invariably these breweries were in the
largest conurbations, growing fast in the post-1860 expansion – Peter
Walker of Warrington, William Butler in Wolverhampton, Henry
Mitchell in Birmingham, John Barras in Newcastle upon Tyne, Vaux
in Sunderland, Brain's in Cardiff, Georges in Bristol, Groves and
Whitnall in Manchester, the Nottingham Brewery, the five leading
Sheffield breweries, the Vale Brewery in Darwin and Lees of Middle-
ton, both in Lancashire.[16] All notably expanded by securing the ample
markets on their own doorsteps. Georges of Bristol was perhaps the
most extraordinary. It flourished without recourse to agencies or a
London store. The only mention in the company's minutes of an
agency (South Wales) comes as late as 1909. Its long-held reputation
as one of the soundest breweries in England was based upon its strong
position in Bristol. By 1893 it had already tied eight-ninths of its
business. In 1905 its travellers did little besides visit the firm's 440
houses and few private customers.[17]

A more usual distribution pattern was for brewers to use a mixture
of agencies and stores to achieve local and regional aspirations. Firms
like Eldridge Pope, Greene King, Cobbold of Ipswich, Steward and
Patteson in Norwich, Simond's of Reading, Garton & Co of Bristol,
Hudson's of Pampisford (Cambs), Robin's of Brighton, the Pheonix
Brewery of Dover, the Lion Brewery of Ashford and Warwicks and
Richardsons of Newark all followed a similar route to regional
dominance, each utilizing a mixture of agencies and stores to serve
their tied and extend their free trades.[18] Some achieved growth by
developing one big-extra regional interest. The north Kent breweries
capitalized their access by sea to London as did Lacons in Yarmouth;
Joules of Stone concentrated upon the Liverpool market as well as
their own 158 public houses in Staffordshire; the trade of Bentleys of
Woodlesford (Leeds) was local except for their Manchester connection; Benskins of Watford ran a big London depot.[19] On the other
hand there were breweries that employed scores of agents on a commission basis. These agents, often wine and spirit merchants, or
grocers, were already numerous by the 1830s. Even rural areas were
well supplied with them. Therefore it was not difficult to find an agent
everwhere in Britain to retail beer. Some breweries relied on whole

armies of agents, presumably not very profitably. Arrangements with them must have been poles apart from those enjoyed by Bass. Rogers of Bristol employed 80 besides a London store; Watkins of Hereford had over 100 scattered across southern England; the Anglo-Bavarian Brewery in Shepton Mallet had 250 selling agents (Barnard 1889–91: II, 329–30; III, 513–22). Their average sales must have been very small. Clearly, there was a variety of experiences: in Burton, in the big industrial cities, and in rural centres. No brewery therefore was quite typical in its distribution pattern. A great deal depended upon local conditions and the drive of the brewery partnership.

Surviving brewery records are only rarely sufficiently complete to reconstruct the precise arrangements between brewer and agent. Lists of agencies and columns of barrelages unfold neither decisions nor strategies. It is only with the survival of so unique a record as the partners' diaries of the Tadcaster Tower Brewery that the detailed picture emerges.[20] This section concludes with a brief survey of the way that this brewery built up a network of agencies, stores and travellers to ease the tight margins imposed by the purchase of an overpriced business in the late 1870s.

The Tower brewery had its origins in a York brewery – Hotham's. It was sold with ninety tied houses – about one-third of the city's pubs – for £36,000 in 1875. Six months later the new partners acquired a further dozen houses; in 1879, fifty more, again almost all in York, at the inflated price of £63,000. From that moment on the partnership was frequently in dire financial straits. Their brewery in George Street was a poor one, most of their tied houses were in an appalling state of repair, attracting an appalling class of tenant. In 1882, as if deliberately to distance themselves from this morass, the firm built a new brewery on the latest tower principle nine miles away in the Yorkshire brewing centre of Tadcaster. Managerially, it was something of a nightmare for the partners, who continued to operate the business from their York office. Transport by rail to York cost 3*s*. 6*d*. a ton, control of a succession of head brewers was difficult. For years they seemed incapable of brewing and racking bright 'running' beers. Even worse was the brewery's financial plight. Mortgages, although easily raised among the partners' grand acquaintances, were numerous and after 1880 trade in York declined sharply. As evidence the manager quoted the turnover of fifty-four of their pubs that had declined from £15,660 in 1877 to £11,923 in 1885. Only fifteen of their houses had shown an increase.

The firm's only way to ease its tight margins was by exploiting the free trade. In November 1885 the manager made his policy clear:

To increase therefore, with a falling trade at Home in their Tied Houses, we must 'look-a-field', the Firm wants to see 20,000 Blls. sold this year against 18,600 last! The question is where to go to?? What to do?? If a [rail freight] rate could be obtained suitable and a really good Buying Agent in London found who would give real security, here might be a centre?! we have written for quotations etc. And Liverpool has during the past fortnight come much under notice.

(Tadcaster Tower Brewery, Partners' Diary)

In fact their options were severely limited. With prohibitive carriage rates of 23s. 4d. a ton to London, and the realization that the only trade in Liverpool would be with beer houses, nothing was done. Moreover, although the firm was fortunate in that its well-connected partners could bring in the business of the military hospital, the prison and, above all, the army canteens at the new barracks at Strensall, five miles north of York, they could not afford to improve and rationalize their pubs in York, nor acquire additional tied property elsewhere except on a minimal scale. Even in the free trade their room for manoeuvre was circumscribed by the competition of John Smith and Joshua Tetley. Smith's offered 20 per cent plus discounts; Tetley's brewed a much better product in Leeds, the obvious market for Tadcaster beers. Yet within these constraints the manager pursued a clear strategy which was adventurous in seeking out new opportunities. First, he set up a number of agents on a part-salaried, part-commission basis in a number of Yorkshire and north-east towns with travellers working from four stores. Second, he acquired three small, run-down breweries in areas where he could envisage expansion: Castleford, Wakefield and Grimsby. The spartan pubs in and around Castleford, dependent upon workers from the potteries and mines, drove a brisk trade. Grimsby provided new opportunities, 'a nice sea-port fishing Town: good streets, good houses, and mostly all new within the past 20 years'.

Eventually, as trade generally picked up in the late 1880s and the firm's beers improved, the travellers working from Castleford, Wakefield, Grimsby, Darlington, Stockton and, eventually, Newcastle did turn round the fortunes of the brewery by their endeavours in the free trade. A total barrelage of 14,264 in the year ending 30 September 1884 had almost doubled to 27,549 in 1887–8. The manager assured his workforce that he could allay any fears about the growth of the tied trade generally. It was a curious viewpoint to defend in 1888, but it demonstrated the success of the firm's free-trade strategy in difficult years.

There were other factors: an improvement in their beers and a growing army canteen trade. But the company's survival rested upon their expansion of the free trade, encouraged by increasing discounts and a concentration upon four distinct areas: Castleford–Wakefield; Grimsby; the string of Cleveland towns from Darlington to Saltburn-on-Sea; and Newcastle upon Tyne.

CONCLUSION

There were then two ways forward for Victorian common brewers to achieve increased sales: they could attempt to achieve growth by acquiring public houses locally (usually within a fifteen–twenty miles radius) *and* by securing free trade in the district by turning out consistently good beers at competitive discount rates. Of course all brewers operated from this type of base – although their ownership and tying of property varied considerably before the late 1880s – but some notably extended their sales by the use of agencies and stores. The railways allowed national networks to be built up after the 1840s. From rail-connected depots, agents and travellers, with varying degrees of success, pushed their beers by assiduity, discounts and reputation into the neighbourhood. Market brands were clearly important for these brewers aspiring to national reputation – Bass, Allsopps and Guinness and, later, Whitbread and Worthington, who matched them in notable bottling ventures in the 1890–1914 period.

Specific brands appear to have come in with bottling and labelling. Casks went virtually unmarked except for identification purposes; they were hidden in cellars anyway. Previously drinkers appreciated generic types of beer: London porter and the best regional ales; strong Scotch (from Edinburgh), Dorchester, Burton and Derby ales, stouts from Dublin and Cork. All – except London porters – were premium beers. But drinkers saw no brand identification; they sampled by taste, swearing by a particular brewer's product until his brew varied – a regular occurrence to the 1900s. Bottling with clear labelling – looking attractive on mirrored bar shelves – guaranteed identification nationally; and it is clear that bottling was earlier than once thought. The majority of larger brewers began to bottle in the 1890s as the technology improved (in part borrowed from the United States). In fact, especially in the export trade, which briefly took off in the 1850s, the Burton brewers, the Scottish exporters from Edinburgh and Alloa, and Guinness in Dublin pioneered bottling. They did not necessarily carry out the task directly, for big independent bottling firms (about which we know very little) in London and the major cities – often operating through sole agreements with Bass, Allsopp and Guinness – were involved from the outset. To identify and protect their product sold via the bottlers the brewers had to introduce trade marks. Bass was using one in London in the late 1830s; its famous red triangle was first registered in 1855. Other brewers followed as legislation aided the patentee in the 1860s and 1870s. In reality, beer trade marks were difficult to protect at home and almost impossible to do so overseas. Litigation was complex and continuous, for beer was easy to imitate and adulterate. Chemical analysis made the task easier from the 1870s, yet the brewery traveller had to be constantly vigilant for infringements. The trade mark offered little to the consumer by way of direct guarantee: it indicated no strength, it simply meant that they could order the beer of their choice backed by the reputation of the brewer.

Oddly, this reputation was reinforced by little direct advertising before 1914. Most pubs, unfettered by any planning legislation, were externally littered with show-boards and their counters with show-cards; otherwise there was little emphasis on promotional *advertisement*. Most breweries put their sales efforts into their agencies and tied houses where everything depended upon good managers, good travellers, good tenants and, in the free trade, good discounts. Only after the 1890s did a market leader like Whitbread expend more than a few hundred pounds on advertising. Reputation was encouraged by more nebulous features in the nineteenth century: a careful promotion of the brewer and his brewery in the local press, reports about involvement in politics and in charitable effort and, above all, the growth of the brewery sketched in those statistical terms that the Victorians demanded.

In this situation, it is unsurprising therefore that the Victorian brewers concentrated upon production, not marketing. Given the lack of direct advertisement, it was absolutely essential for brewers to turn out good beer whether they were selling it locally or nationally. The consumer was knowledgeable about beer in the nineteenth century; there is evidence that any marked drop in gravities and quality drove away customers in hordes. Brewers were obsessed with obtaining consistency in their beer; marketing and advertising came a poor second. The origins of the latter are to be traced in this period, although little was spent by brewers and discussion about it in directors' minutes or the brewing journals is minimal. There was no market research about the overall beer market and its growth, none about consumers, and none about demand for particular types of beer. Allsopps attempted in 1899 to launch a substantial investment in lager brewing without either market research or advertising (R. G. Wilson 1993). Their approach was typical of all brewers: get the beer right and success would inevitably follow. The sale of beer before the First World War was largely achieved by thousands of well-paid travellers and agents – the unsung heroes of Victorian business life. Their use of brands, trade marks and advertising was in its pioneering stage before 1914.

ACKNOWLEDGEMENT

The author is grateful for the research assistance of Dr Fiona Wood of the Brewers' Society.

NOTES

1 See Harrison (1971: 315) for a discussion about the care with which these figures should be interpreted.
2 In 1829 the four London breweries produced 175,600; 163,300; 211,500; 165,300 barrels each respectively.
3 Gourvish (1987: 13–48); Whitbread Archives 193/239; Courage Archives (Bristol) LM/A/1.
4 For example in 1883 Lord Wenlock sold his brewing plant at Escrick Hall (Yorkshire) valued at £147.50 for its fifty-one casks, two sets of unions, and some vats, to the Tadcaster Tower Brewery. Thereafter, he obtained his beer from them (Bass North, Leeds, Tadcaster Tower Brewery, Partners' Diaries, Dec. 1882, Feb. 1883). Barnard (1889–91) cites several breweries relying upon a good private trade. 'The principal trade of the Lion Brewery [Ashford], he noted, 'is with private families and the nobility and gentry of the district' (vol. 4, p. 204).
5 *Licensed Victuallers' Gazette* 4 December 1875.
6 However, Gutzke (1989) has argued that brewers acquired their tied property estates earlier than historians have assumed. Certainly, country brewers in the south and east owned a sizeable number by the early Victorian period. But in London, the Midlands and the north, the movement gained real momentum only in the mid-1880s, although brewers a decade earlier were aware of the need to acquire first-class public houses whose licences were less likely to be forfeited.
7 The firm of John Day and Sons of St Neots was typical. By the early 1830s the firm was producing around 3,000 barrels of beer a year (they owned thirty-four pubs in 1814) which was distributed by road to customers in villages within an eighteen-mile radius of St Neots. The ideal market for a low-value bulk product like beer was under ten miles.
8 However, water carriage remained important along the east coast, especially the Edinburgh–London route, in the Thames Estuary and, of course, from Dublin.
9 See Owen (1992: 55, 64) for an account of Bass's early agency system.
10 Bass Museum, Burton-on-Trent (A 179) Worthington's 'Board' Meetings, 1862–71.

11 *Licensed Victuallers' Gazette* 2 June 1875. Salt and Co. (Burton) had six-
    teen agencies in 1874, the Burton Brewing Company twenty-one in 1873.
12 Bass Museum, Worthington & Co. Agencies, F/15/1.
13 This section is based upon Bass's agency records, and the Secretary's
    'Private Box' and Bass's volumes of scrapbooks, Bass Museum, A 135,
    558.
14 *Licensed Victuallers' Gazette* 4 January 1873.
15 Courage Archives (Tadcaster), JA/M/6; T. R. Gourvish and R. G. Wilson
    (1994: 158–9).
16 The list is compiled from Barnard (1889–91) which includes (or in these
    cases ignores) lists of agencies and stores.
17 Courage Archives (Bristol), 35740 BG9(c).
18 Seekings (1988); R. G. Wilson (1983); *Licensed Victuallers' Gazette* 14
    August 1875 (Cobbolds); Corley (1975–6; 1980); Gourvish (1987); for the
    rest see their entries in Barnard (1889–91).
19 Whitbread Archive, 197/239; Barnard (1889–9 III, 83–106; 247–53; IV,
    29–52).
20 This section is based upon the Partners' Diaries of the Tadcaster Tower
    Brewery: see note 4.

REFERENCES

Barnard, A. (1889–91) *The Noted Breweries of Great Britain*, 4 vols, London:
    Sir Joseph Causton and Sons.
Corley, T. A. B. (1975–6) 'Simonds' Brewery at Reading, 1760–1960',
    Berkshire Archaeological Journal **68**: 77–88.
—— (1980) *The Road to Worton Grange: Simonds and Courage Brewery at
    Reading 1785–1980*, Reading: Courage (Central) Ltd.
Dingle, A. E. (1974) 'Drink and working class living standards in Britain,
    1870–1914', *Economic History Review* **25**(4): 608–22.
Donnachie, I. (1979) *A History of the Brewing Industry in Scotland*, Edin-
    burgh: John Donaldson.
Gourvish, T. (1987) *Norfolk Beers from English Barley: A History of Steward
    and Patteson*, Norwich: Centre of East Anglian Studies.
Gourvish, T. R. and Wilson, R. G. (1994) *The Bristol Brewing Industry,
    1830–1980*, Cambridge: Cambridge University Press.
Gutzke, D. (1989) *Protecting the Pub: Brewers and Publicans against Temper-
    ance*, Woodbridge: Boydell Press for the Royal Historical Society.
Harrison, B. (1971) *Drink and the Victorians*, London: Faber & Faber.
Mathias, P. (1959) *The Brewing Industry in England, 1700–1830*, Cambridge:
    Cambridge University Press.
Mitchell & Deane (1962) *Abstracts of British Historical Statistics*, Cambridge:
    Cambridge University Press.
Owen, C. C. (1992) ' "The Greatest Brewery in the World": a history of Bass
    Ratcliffe & Gretton', *Derbyshire Record Society* **XIX**.
Pratt, E. A. (1907) *The Licensed Trade: An Independent Survey*, London:
    John Murray.
Prest, A. R. (1954) *Consumers' Expenditure in the United Kingdom 1900–
    1919*, London: Cambridge University Press.

Seekings, J. (1988) *Thomas Hardy's Brewer: The Story of Eldridge Pope & Co.*, Wimborne: Dovecote Press.

Snowden, P. (1908) *Socialism and the Drink Question*, London: Independent Labour Party.

Tizard, W. L. (1846) *The Theory and Practice of Brewing Illustrated*, London: Gilbert & Rivington.

Wilson, G. B. (1941) *Alcohol and the Nation*, London: Nicholson & Watson.

Wilson, R. G. (1983) *Greene King: A Business and Family History*, London: Bodley Head/Jonathan Cape.

Wilson, R. G. (1993) 'The introduction of lager in late-Victorian England', in T. Riis (ed.) *A Special Brew: Essays in Honour of Kristof Glamann*, Odense: Odense University Press.

7 Marketing and competition in Danish brewing

Hans. Chr. Johansen

The Danish beer brands of Carlsberg and Tuborg have dominated the Danish market for about a century and gained a world-wide reputation after 1945. In contrast, foreign breweries have had little success in penetrating the Danish market, and even other Danish breweries have in most cases limited their sales to local areas close to where production takes place. This situation, reinforced by agreements among the producers, and a special Danish distribution system, created a domestic market situation which was neither pure oligopoly, monopoly or price leadership, but one which found its own logic, and which has been only marginally opposed by the Danish government until recently.

In foreign markets, Danish exports have met with strong competition. Over the years various strategies have been used in order to gain a firm foothold in markets of much larger size than that of a small country with about 5 million inhabitants, not all of whom were beer consumers.

THE STRUCTURE OF THE DANISH INDUSTRY

Before the middle of the nineteenth century there were few large firms in Danish brewing. Most beer brands belonged at that time to the top-fermented types where there were few scale effects in production. This situation changed when bottom fermentation was introduced, and several large breweries were founded using Bavarian methods. Among them were the Carlsberg brewery from 1847, and the Svanholm brewery from 1853, both in the Copenhagen area. Also the first provincial breweries, Ceres in Århus and Albani in Odense, date from this period, being founded in 1856 and 1859 respectively.

From the 1880s there was a process of concentration followed by cartelization. The 1880s saw fierce competition between the breweries in Copenhagen which stopped only when a series of mergers and agreements had been implemented. The first step was a merger in 1891 of Svanholm and ten other breweries into the United Breweries. From 1894 this also included the Tuborg brewery, and the whole enterprise came to be often just called Tuborg because this was used as the name of the principal beer brand. As a result of these mergers, Carlsberg and Tuborg produced nearly two-thirds of the total Danish beer of the lager type (Johansen 1988: 59–63, 103–6). The next step was a cartel agreement in 1895 between these companies about the rules of competition and the sharing of profits. Later supplements, signed in 1903 and 1912, included joint investment financing, although within the given set of competition rules there remained room for individual efforts to conquer market shares.

The agreement of 1903 covered the period until the year 2000, that is for nearly one hundred years, but in the 1960s there were growing tensions between the two companies because of disagreements about export policy as well as an imbalance in the economic advantages from the surplus sharing. Prolonged discussions and negotiations ended in 1970 with a formal merger which created the Carlsberg and Tuborg Breweries, the United Breweries Ltd. From December 1987 the simpler name of Carlsberg Ltd was used. Carlsberg had been owned by a foundation belonging to the Royal Danish Academy of Sciences and Letters, whereas Tuborg had been a limited company with a large group of stockholders. Under the terms of the merger approval granted by the Danish Ministry of Justice, the Carlsberg Foundation was required to retain 51 per cent of the share capital (Glamann 1976; Hjejle 1982). The merger produced sweeping rationalizations and automatization of the company plants. As a result, their production is now much larger, but their employment in Denmark has been reduced by two-thirds. Overall, throughout the twentieth century the combined production of Carlsberg and Tuborg has varied between 70 and 80 per cent of total Danish production, and apart from some years in the 1950s, Carlsberg has had a larger share than Tuborg (Thomsen 1973).

There have been in the twentieth century only two attempts from other Danish breweries to build up a nationwide distribution system on a large scale. The first was undertaken by the brewery Stjernen, founded in 1902 by the Copenhagen Federation of Trade Unions. In the interwar period production reached 10 per cent of the national total, but after the Second World War sales declined. The brewery ran into economic difficulties and production stopped in 1964. The second attempt was by the provincial Faxe Brewery which in the 1970s increased its sales to about 10 per cent of the national market by means of aggressive advertising and new types of bottles. The success was short-lived. In 1989, after several years of economic difficulties, Faxe merged with another provincial brewery which was supported by Carlsberg money.

The dominance of Carlsberg and Tuborg did not leave much room for other breweries. Most of the provincial firms founded in the late nineteenth or early twentieth centuries were closed after the Second World War; as a result only a handful of independent provincial breweries remained in the 1990s. Some of them possessed a strong market position in their local areas, but even the largest covered less than 10 per cent of national consumption (Boje and Johansen 1989).

THE BREWERS' ASSOCIATION

Limitation of domestic competition has also been carried out in other forms. The Danish Brewers' Association, formed in 1894, tried from an early date to regulate competition among its members. In 1911 breweries representing about 90 per cent of national production agreed about minimum prices on all important types of beer, and over the years a whole set of rules and practices were established which regulated competition among the members of the association.

An important part of these rules concerned the distribution system. Until very recently nearly all distribution had to take place either by direct deliveries to retailers and restaurants, or by means of what was called beer depots, that is local wholesalers who were allowed to trade only the brands of a single brewery, and their activities and rights were clearly defined by the brewery. The larger breweries would have a net of depots each covering a well-defined area. From the brewery or the depot, lorries called at the retailers regularly, and sales took place on the spot with immediate delivery from the lorry. Sales promotion was in this way limited to visits done by sales agents from the breweries, and to the quality of the services of the lorry drivers. The retailer who was not in competition was excluded both directly and indirectly, since the rules of the association did not allow discounts and other ways of bypassing the minimum prices which in principle became fixed prices used by all breweries. There were also limitations on certain forms of advertising, use of the same types of bottles on all breweries, a ban on loans and other economy ties to retailers, and regular distribution of statistics making it possible for each member to follow its share of sales in various parts of Denmark.

When these rules were introduced it could be done free of any public intervention, as the first restrictive practices legislation was not enacted until 1937. After that year the Registrar of Restrictive Trade Practices had to be notified on the agreements within the Brewers' Association, and price changes were negotiated with the Registrar before they could be enforced. The convention was that permissions for changes were only given if it could be proved that they were caused by cost rises from external sources (Betænkning 1960; Simonsen 1974).

THE ABSENCE OF FOREIGN COMPETITION

After the Second World War domestic consumption of beer increased until the early 1980s, and, as demonstrated in Table 7.1, the Danish breweries have been able to maintain their dominance of the market. Only in two years, which saw prolonged strikes at the breweries – 1965 and 1985 – were imports of any significance.

Table 7.1 Danish production and consumption of dutiable beer, 1950–91[a]

	Production (1,000 hl)	Imports (1,000 hl)	Exports (1,000 hl)	Consumption (1,000 hl)
1950–54	2,764	—	306	2,458
1955–59	3,224	—	596	2,628
1960–64	4,188	2	730	3,460
1965–69	5,301	22	1,126	4,197
1970–74	7,688	30	2,041	5,677
1975–79	8,009	17	1,762	6,264
1980–84	8,782	2	1,404	7,380
1985–89	8,625	57	1,830	6,852
1990–91	9,314	22	2,428	6,908

Sources: Statistisike Meddelser; Statistisk Tabelværk

Note: [a]Border trade is excluded; figures are annual averages

There were several reasons for the very limited sales of foreign products. On the demand side, most Danish consumers were very faithful to their favourite brand, or at least to Danish products, as many local beer brands disappeared. Regular beer drinkers came to not just ask for 'beer' in the bar or when they go shopping, but would order a Tuborg, a 'Hof' (the popular term for the ordinary Carlsberg brand), or perhaps a Faxe or a local favourite. This loyalty is very surprising, taking into account that the various brands are very equal in taste and appearance. However, the upshot of this brand loyalty was very real, for it meant that retailers had limited possibilities of influencing the distribution of their sales on various brands, but had to market all brands which were in demand in their trading area. This brand loyalty has had as a result that comprehensive advertising campaigns undertaken by Danish breweries until the last few years have met with limited success. A foreign producer attempting to market an unknown brand met inevitably with still larger difficulties in gaining a foothold on the Danish market. This strong brand loyalty is a peculiarly Danish phenomenon, and is also witnessed in several types of food. Danish marketing researchers normally ascribe it to a certain conservatism in consumer habits, but in the case of beer it may also be the result of the limited number of brands which have been available on the market for nearly a century.

However, it might also have been market restrictions rather than consumer attitudes which provide the more plausible explanation for the low import penetration. Danish beer was over a long period protected by high tariffs and narrow import quotas. Around 1960 the tariff rate was between 60 and 130 per cent of the price ex-works and before duties. Beer was given area treatment under the European Free Trade Area (EFTA) agreement, and this opened the market for potential suppliers from other member countries. Few foreign breweries tried, however, their luck and no one succeeded in penetrating the Danish market. The former protection had, thus, no real significance. Within the European Community (EC) there are no tariff restrictions on beer, but Table 7.1 shows that not even the removal of barriers towards the continental countries was sufficient to make the Danish market attractive for foreign producers.

Another factor in explaining the low import penetration was Danish legislation which, since the early 1870s, has banned the use of cans and special types of bottles, and also prescribed the recycling of bottles, making it necessary for a foreign brewery to establish a bottlery adapted to Danish standards. This legislation was passed for environmental purposes and has had very beneficial effects to that end, but it has also been claimed that it was a non-tariff barrier. In 1986 the Danish government was sued at the European Court for violating Article 30 of the Treaty of Rome. The case ended, however, with a verdict of not guilty.

A final factor explaining the lack of important penetration in the market may be the lack of a group of wholesalers with experience in marketing beer (Boje and Johansen 1989: 245–6; Johansen 1988: 218–21; 287–9).

NEW DEVELOPMENTS IN THE 1970s

The marketing system described above was nearly universal until the opening years of the 1970s, but has subsequently been somewhat modified. The direct reason was that some smaller breweries which remained outside the association made contracts with supermarket chains about delivering beer with special labels at prices well below the established minimum prices – so-called 'trade brands'. Although their sales were at first insignificant compared to the total market, this was felt as a threat to the dominance of the association's agreements. In December 1977, and in an extended form two years later, the association decided that its members should be given the same opportunity, but the discount given should be equal to the savings obtained by selling large quantities at a time instead of using the normal delivery system.

The result was increased price competition, and even members of the association lowered their prices considerably and most likely more than the stipulated savings. Occasionally the wholesale prices for trade brands were about 20 per cent lower than those of traditional brands. Overall, in the 1980s, about 10 per cent of Danish consumption was of trade brands.

The discipline among the association's members was further weakened when the Registrar of Restrictive Trade Practices in the mid-1980s decided to undertake an investigation of the brewing industry. In a comprehensive report in 1987, the marketing and competition practices in the beer trade were spelled out and it was concluded that there was no direct link between prices and cost differences on individual breweries. It was also claimed that the distribution system was detrimental to efficiency. Shortly afterwards, negotiations began with the association in order to encourage competition (Monopoltilsynet 1987). Many of the association's rules were abolished in 1988, opening possibilities for free price competition among all breweries and the fixing of wholesale prices according to actual delivery costs. New ways of distributing beer were also introduced. The depots have either been integrated totally into the breweries' sales organization, or have become more independent in their sales promotion, and a group of new beer wholesalers marketing brands from several breweries have come into existence.

The years since 1988 have seen an increased price competition in Denmark both among wholesalers and retailers, more advertising – although within certain 'ethical' limits agreed upon by the breweries – and also a certain redistribution of market shares at Carlsberg's expense. The long-term effects on the structure of the trade remain unclear.

DANISH BEER ON FOREIGN MARKETS

As early as before the First World War Carlsberg and Tuborg had started a modest export business. Even in the interwar period growth was moderate, and it was not until the 1950s that foreign markets became of major interest for the Danish breweries (cf. Table 7.1). The smaller breweries also tried to export their products in this period, but as a whole they had little success, either both in direct exports, or in licensing technical know-how to foreign breweries.

Marketing beer abroad has been a very different business from the domestic market for the Danish breweries. Competition has been much stronger on foreign markets, which were often supplied by large multinationals. Furthermore, tastes have often been different, and local legislation and protection have posed many new challenges.

Marketing has taken various forms at different times and in different markets as the two large breweries and, from 1970, the United Breweries tried to adapt their strategies to what was most profitable in a given situation. The simplest strategy was to use agents with a good knowledge of the local market, in many cases local breweries. This was often the first step into a new country, but the drawback was that it gave the Danish company little control of the trade. A more developed strategy was to establish sales offices and local stores in various foreign countries from which wholesalers could be supplied. This has been used in relatively few cases, however, probably because detailed knowledge of local practices was an essential precondition for success.

A special problem in trading beer is that neither beer in casks nor bottled beer is easy to transport over long distances without harming taste and quality – among other things, because it is difficult to ensure that a correct handling takes place by the transporting agent. An obvious answer to this problem was to produce on the spot, either by granting licences to use the brewery's form of production, or else by establishing breweries abroad through foreign direct investment. This could, however, be done only in markets large enough to obtain the necessary scale effects, or in developing countries with little or no previous experience with brewing and high tariff protection. In the latter group of countries, it proved possible in some cases to build breweries as development projects which were integrated into national industrialization plans. This in turn, helped in obtaining the necessary local authorizations.

The first step from exporting Danish produced beer to production in foreign countries was taken in 1968, and from 1974 foreign production was larger than exports (see Table 7.2). This reorientation resulted in a temporary decline in exports, but in the late 1980s progress in sales at nearby markets has once again been rising. The combined effect of exports and foreign production are now so important that they play a much larger role for Carlsberg than the Danish market.

Table 7.2 Domestic and foreign sales of Carlsberg and Tuborg beer, 1967–83[a]

	Sold in Denmark (1,000 hl)	Exported from Denmark (1,000 hl)	Produced abroad[b] (1,000 hl)
1967/68	3,625	1,282	—
1968/69	3,882	1,355	74
1969/70	4,122	1,578	236
1970/71	4,346	1,933	351
1971/72	4,648	2,219	473
1972/73	4,949	2,468	1,118
1973/74	4,947	1,999	2,225
1974/75	4,934	1,949	2,855
1975/76	5,234	2,004	3,630
1976/77	4,859	1,555	4,832
1977/78	4,972	1,293	5,420
1978/79	4,910	1,215	5,735
1979/80	5,022	1,118	6,009
1980/81	5,076	1,057	6,509
1981/82	5,177	1,110	6,582
1982/83	5,349	1,142	6,964

Sources: Annual reports of the breweries

Notes: [a] Accounting year 1 October–31 September

[b] This excludes production under licence

It has involved a major effort in international marketing to represent Danish beer as a type of an especially high quality, and one which is consumed by people with an especially good taste. In advertising the company has been described as 'The Danish Master Brewer', and it is claimed that 'for generations Tuborg has been part of the noble art of beer drinking in all European countries'. Having succeeded in creating this image, it has been possible to sell Carlsberg brands in most markets at higher prices than local beer. Since early in the century, brand names have used only the names Carlsberg and Tuborg, although some particular types of strong beer have also carried an additional name, such as the Carlsberg 'Elephant beer'.

The reputation for quality has not been based solely on the careful generation of an image by means of advertising. As early as 1875, the Carlsberg Laboratory was founded. This became one of the leading research centres in the world for the study of the use of enzymes and yeast in the brewing industry (Glamann 1976: 107–16).

The marketing of Carlsberg and Tuborg products still varies from one market to another, but a few examples may illustrate different practices used. As a first approach, the importance of individual countries as importers of Danish beer is shown in Table 7.3. More than 100 countries have been importers, but with very different degrees of importance. During the total post-war period markets in western Europe have dominated, but from an early stage there were also significant exports to countries and territories as far away as Nigeria, Hong Kong, Malaysia and Singapore. However, other markets, especially in eastern Europe, have been until recently almost impossible to penetrate.

Table 7.3 demonstrates the dominance of the British market in the early years, accounting for nearly 40 per cent of total exports in 1960. Carlsberg, and to a lesser extent Tuborg, beer penetrated the British market in the 'pre-lager' period because they had a niche position in the restaurant and club trade. For a long time the Danes relied on exports to Britain. In 1937 Carlsberg and Tuborg discussed plans for building a brewery in London, but this was given up; it was not until 1974 that a large modern Carlsberg brewery was inaugurated in Northampton, which began as a joint venture with the British brewer Watney Mann. After 1972 Tuborg beer was also produced under licence at Truman Hanbury Buxton & Co. in London. The results of the shift from exports to local production in Britain is clearly demonstrated in Table 7.3. The combined sales of Danish and British-produced beer still made the British market the most important one for the Carlsberg concern. The main reason for the success in Britain after Carlsberg became a domestic brewer in the early 1970s was the distribution arrangements, and especially the Danish firm's link with the British hotels and pubs conglomerate, Grand Metropolitan. Grand Metropolitan had acquired a 49 per cent shareholding in Carlsberg by 1972, but this was sold in 1974. When Grand Metropolitan and Watney Mann merged in 1975, the Northampton joint venture was sold entirely to the Danes. However, the distribution arrangements continued, and Carlsberg was able to distribute its products through

Table 7.3 Danish exports of beer by countries of destination, 1960–90

	1960	1970	1980	1990
		(million Danish Kroner)		
Individual countries				
Sweden	3	53	57	60
UK	33	67	11	33
Belgium	3	23	98	49
Germany	7	6	99	465
Italy	2	6	16	264
US	7	17	12	30
Regions				
EFTA	37	130	86	110
EC	16	48	253	893
Other W. Europe	2	11	12	13
E. Europe	—	3	9	36
The Americas[a]	9	25	72	74
Africa	8	6	7	31
Asia	13	21	32	22
Oceania	—	1	1	7

Source: Statistiske Efterretninger; Statistisk Tabelværk

Note: [a]Including Greenland

Grand Metropolitan's substantial retailing estate. The most recent development in Britain has been a close co-operation between Carlsberg and some of the largest local brewery groupings in a new company called Carlsberg-Tetley.

EFTA membership gave easier access to several markets, but it was especially in Sweden that new opportunities emerged. This was not only because of the EFTA tariff reductions which took place in the 1960s; Sweden had a long tradition of state intervention in trade in beer, and of restrictions on types of beer being permitted in the market, but in 1965 beer of the Danish lager type was allowed access to the Swedish market. The Danish breweries established subsidiary companies for the distribution of their products. As a result, Sweden emerged as the second largest export market in the early 1970s.

In 1975 an agreement was made with the largest Swedish brewery, AB Pripps Bryggerier, about starting brewing Carlsberg and Tuborg beer on their plants under licence. Pripps also took over marketing of part of the beer imported directly from Denmark. Among the reasons for the agreement was that Sweden was introducing a new bottling system and a maximum on alcoholic strength lower than that of ordinary Danish beer. As a consequence direct exports to Sweden have stagnated, but production under licence by Pripps and, more recently, by Falcon AB also plays an important role on the Swedish market.

The common external tariff of the EC has an *ad valorem* duty of 24 per cent on beer to which should be added several national non-tariff barriers, such as the German so-called *Reinheitsgebot* which prevented imports of beer using raw materials other than barley, yeast and hops. Although the EC area included several countries with a large consumption of beer it was consequently difficult for the Danish breweries to export to these countries until Denmark was admitted to the Community in 1973. The only EC country of some importance before 1973 was Belgium – the country with the highest per capita consumption of beer in the world. Marketing took place by means of local agents (Brasserie Haelterman and Cavenor SA) who worked in a very competitive environment where active advertising and service was a necessity. In spite of this Danish beers were, in many years, the most popular foreign brands, and in the mid- and late-1970s Belgium was the most important market for exports of beer from Denmark. Developments in the 1980s have been less satisfactory due to increased competition. Carlsberg's main trading partner in Belgium is now Interbrew SA.

Instead sales in Germany expanded rapidly after 1973 when tariff protection over a transition period of five years was removed, and when the *Reinheitsgebot* in 1988 was declared in conflict with the competition rules of the EC. Tuborg established a trading subsidiary in Kiel in 1975 which achieved good results in northern Germany. Later a close co-operation developed with Deutsche Brau GmbH, which became the major agent for Tuborg. Carlsberg followed suit with a trading subsidiary in 1979, and in the late 1980s Hannen Brauerei GmbH in Mönchengladbach was taken over. Italy also became an important export market in the 1980s, with Danish beer being brewed under licence by Industrie Poretti SpA.

Outside Europe, the United States has in most years been an important market. Carlsberg brands are imported from Denmark, and since the mid-1980s marketed by the world's largest brewery-group, Anheuser-Busch, Inc., whereas Tuborg brands for some years were produced locally under licence.

Apart from the Northampton plant in Britain, production abroad was mainly planned in countries located a long way from Denmark. Foreign production was first started by Carlsberg in Malawi. A brewery in Blantyre was inaugurated in 1968. Tuborg's first foreign undertaking was in Turkey, where a brewery in Izmir was inaugurated in 1969. Later developments have mostly been concentrated in the Far East.

It is not possible in the present context to describe market and supply developments in the more than 150 countries where Carlsberg products can now be bought, but a short survey of the present overall conditions may give an impression of how varied a business the Danish contemporary beer trade is. Out of the total production of Carlsberg and Tuborg brands between half and two-thirds are now brewed abroad, either in own breweries or under licence, and domestic consumption is only one-fourth of total production. Foreign production takes place in nearly thirty countries, mostly under licence, whereas Carlsberg has got capital interests in the producing firms listed in Table 7.4. A brewery in Thailand is at present under construction. Among the breweries listed in the table, the British is by far the largest.

Table 7.4 Carlsberg's foreign subsidiary companies and associated firms with beer production, 1992

	Turnover	*Equity*	*Carlsberg's share*
	(million)	*(million)*	*(%)*
Carlsberg Brewery Ltd, UK (£)	232	42	100
Hannen Brauerei GmbH, Germany (DM)	148	39	100
Carlsberg Brewery, Malaysia (M$)	374	174	26
Carlsberg Malawi Brewery Ltd (K)	173	63	49
Carlsberg Brewery Hongkong (HK$)	484	179	50
	(billion)	*(billion)*	
Industrie Poretti SpA, Italien (L)	192	26	50
Unicer-Uniâo Cervejeira, Portugal (Esc)	41	19	31
La Cruz del Campo SA, Spanien (Pta)	53	41	10

Source: Carlsberg, *Annual Report* 1991/2

In addition, marketing takes place in around 100 countries, sometimes through subsidiary trading companies, but mostly by using local agents (Carlsberg, *Annual Reports*, 1970–92).

CONCLUSION

The marketing results of Carlsberg have so far been a success story. The dominance of the brands Tuborg and Hof on the Danish market was secured nearly a hundred years ago, and has never been seriously challenged. The company still displays great activity in advertising and other forms of marketing on the Danish market, but it is doubtful how much effect this has on market shares. Only the recently developed market for trade brands seems to be one in which there is real competition among Danish breweries, but in that market Carlsberg has probably a somewhat lower share than in the traditional way of selling beer in Denmark.

In international markets Carlsberg has in the post-war period developed into a substantial multinational, and has been an active partner in the centralization process which has characterized the world brewing industry in recent years. This has been achieved by means of a high-quality product strategy and intense marketing efforts all over the world – always adapted to the local circumstances. The firm's dominant position in its home market has no doubt been a considerable competitive advantage. The result is perhaps best described by the fact that, in several years over recent decades, Denmark has been the largest beer exporting country in the world.

ACKNOWLEDGEMENTS

I am most grateful to Terry Gourvish and the editors for their helpful comments on earlier drafts of this chapter.

REFERENCES

Betænkning nr. 246 (1960) *Bryggeribranchen*, Copenhagen: Schultz.
Boje, P. and Johansen, H. C. (1989) *Altid på vej* . . . , Odense: Odense University Press.
Carlsberg Breweries (1970–92) *Annual Reports*, Copenhagen: Carlsberg Breweries.
Glamann, K. (1976) *Carlsbergfondet*, Copenhagen: Rhodos.
Hjejle, B. (1982) *Hof eller Tuborg*, Copenhagen: Nyt Nordisk Forlag.
Johansen, H. C. (1988) *Industriens vækst og vilkår 1870–1973*, Odense: Odense University Press.
Monopoltilsynet (1987) *Bryggeribranchen*, Copenhagen: Monopoltilsynet.
Simonsen, J. (1974) 'Bryggeriforeningen 1899 – 6. september – 1974', *Brygmesteren* **9**: 219–88.
Statistiske Efterretninger (1960–90), Copenhagen: Danmarks Statistik.
Statistiske Meddelelser (1950–91) *Industriel produktionsstatistik*, Copenhagen: Danmarks Statistik.
Statistisk Tabelværk (1950–91) *Danmarks Vareindførsel-udførsel*, Copenhagen: Danmarks Statistik.
Thomsen, B. N. (1973) *Tuborg 1873 – 13, maj – 1973*, Copenhagen: De forenede Bryggerier.

8 Managing decline
Brands and marketing in two mergers, 'The Big Amalgamation' 1925 and Guinness–DCL 1986

R. B. Weir

This chapter compares the role of brands and marketing in two mergers, 'The Big Amalgamation' of 1925, when the Distillers Company (DCL) acquired Buchanan-Dewar Ltd and John Walker & Sons Ltd, and the acquisition of DCL by Guinness in 1986. Although the two events occurred in different institutional circumstances, with large financial institutions playing a key role in 1986 and private shareholders predominant in 1925, the trading environment was similar in so far as both mergers were preceded by declining spirit consumption. Between 1920 and 1925 the home market (61 per cent of total demand) was contracting at 7.5 per cent per year and exports by 1 per cent. Between 1980 and 1985 home demand (16 per cent of total whisky consumption) was falling by 2.2 per cent a year and exports by 2.8 per cent. In both periods changes in the distribution of consumer expenditure were evident, resulting in overproduction of whisky and surplus stocks. Managing decline placed brands and marketing in a strategic position.

The chapter begins with the background to 'The Big Amalgamation' of 1925. It then considers marketing in the newly formed DCL Group. Both parts utilize the internal documents of the participating firms. The third section looks at the way the parties to the contested acquisition of 1986 – DCL, the Argyll Group and Guinness – presented their marketing capabilities to shareholders. The fourth section deals with Guinness's reorganization of the brands acquired from DCL through its spirit division, United Distillers. These sections rely on sources in the public domain, including bid documentation and statements by senior executives.

'THE BIG AMALGAMATION' (1925)

By 1930 the Scotch whisky market was dominated by seven leading brands of which five – Buchanan's, Dewar's, Walker's, Haig's and White Horse – were owned by the DCL Group. Quite why this happened has never been satisfactorily explained. It was not a feature of the whisky trade in 1870 nor even in 1900 when Scotch had become well established in England and overseas. Combined sales of 'The Big Three' blenders – Buchanan, Dewar and Walker – were 3.9 million proof gallons (mpg) in 1909, less than 12 per cent of the market for home produced spirits. Just before the amalgamation of 1925 they accounted for 46 per cent of Scotch whisky sales and, with DCL's sales, the new Group marketed about 60 per cent of Scotch whisky.

This concentration and The Big Amalgamation originated in the early months of 1909 when the principals of The Big Three invited Edwin Waterhouse to prepare a scheme of amalgamation. What prompted this was concern about the cost of selling branded whisky, particularly advertising and discounts. Waterhouse found that both had risen sharply between 1900 and 1909. As total sales for The Big Three were still expanding the point had not been reached where these firms were redistributing a fixed volume of sales among themselves though, with declining consumption, that point had been reached for the whisky industry as a whole. Competitive advertising was a potential rather than an actual threat to profitability, a situation exacerbated by discounting after the large increase in spirit tax in Lloyd George's 'People's Budget'. As Tommy Dewar read the situation:

> I feel that we are drifting into more aggressive and costly competition and making allowances involving large sums which could be saved by immediate agreement.

(DCL/1)

James Buchanan viewed amalgamation as highly desirable because of

> the manifest advantages which would accrue to all three companies by the cessation of aggressive and costly competition, and the further benefits to be derived from a united policy of action in home and foreign markets.

(DCL/2)

The costs of competition were mainly incurred in the home market. Exports remained highly profitable. In 1912 Dewar's net profit margin on export sales was 52 per cent compared to 14 per cent at home; Buchanan's figures were not much different: 52 per cent and

9.6 per cent. Merger talks began in earnest in June 1910, when a committee was appointed 'to draw up a scheme of amalgamation (Financial and Administrative) with or without the DCL' (DCL/3). DCL's involvement was a new element, and DCL was anxious to participate, but immediately the amalgamation assumed a much larger form: what W. H. Ross, its managing-director, had in mind was a radical restructuring of the entire whisky trade with DCL as the holding company. This was opposed by Walkers, who doubted

> the wisdom of . . . brands being identified in the public mind with grain whisky and plain spirit – in short the public might be taught that they could get whisky for their stomach or spirit for their motor car out of the same concern.

(DCL/4)

Walkers feared that DCL's involvement with industrial alcohol might prompt an unfavourable reaction from whisky consumers and that DCL would emerge as the dominant firm. Yet restructuring had its attraction: there was a precedent in another consumer goods industry characterized by a multiplicity of competing brands, each of which had retained its individuality:

> The Imperial Tobacco Co. Ltd. has always been in my mind as a guide in this – tobacco and whisky go together don't they? I have always conceived of 'The Scotch Whisky Co. Ltd.' as the title for the combine. The labels on the bottles are the same, price lists etc. except that like Imperial you print in minute letters at the bottom – 'The Scotch Whisky Co. Ltd.' And like the Imperial you are always open to take in lesser rivals as they appear.

(DCL/4)

Tobacco and whisky had much in common: the emphasis on brands, high levels of promotional expenditure, the shift of responsibility for marketing from the retailer to the producer, and the high capital requirements of exciseable commodities. As it turned out, whisky and tobacco did not go together because the whisky industry did not face an external threat similar to that posed to British tobacco manufacturers by the American Tobacco Company. Lloyd George's budget has some-times been seen as such a threat but it only temporarily halted the expansion of profits. By 1911 they had resumed their upward trend and, as a participant in the merger talks somewhat wearily remarked, 'the Principals are all too well off to sit down for days and months, if need be, to work out a merger' (DCL/4). This was in the aftermath of the budget, and it was even more so once profits recovered. The pressures on the industry before 1914 were insufficient to sustain a restructuring along the lines adopted by the tobacco industry. This was no bad thing. Imperial Tobacco's corporate structure was scarcely an ideal model (Alford 1977). With the multiplicity of family interests which 'The Scotch Whisky Company' would have had to accommodate it had great potential for being an organizational nightmare.

Merger discussions began with the premise that sales costs could be curtailed and that there were additional economies from centralized buying, financing and pricing. What advocates of amalgamation were unable to explain was how individuality and uniqueness, the whole point of branded goods, could be protected and sustained in an amalgamation. This anxiety looks ridiculous to modern eyes when brands are freely traded and portfolios of brands collected. It was, none the less, a real worry and one reason why The Big Amalgamation took sixteen years to achieve. The principals of The Big Three had devoted their lives to creating proprietary brands and found it inconceivable that a single firm could market Dewar's whisky at the same time as Walker's or Buchanan's. What ultimately emerged from these discussions was not a solution to 'the big question' of relations between the blenders and DCL, nor a grand restructuring, nor even a merger of The Big Three but a holding company, Scotch Whisky Brands Ltd, formed in 1915 by Dewars and Buchanans. This involved no change in marketing: 'the two Brands and the two Houses would remain quite apart' (DCL/5). For its creators the advantages lay in scrutinizing the comparative expenses of branch offices, agencies, and malt distilleries. Why marketing was not closely fused again had much to do with the fear that the public and the trade would react unfavourably. Nevertheless, with a capital of £6 million, Scotch Whisky Brands was three times the size of DCL. By 1919, when it was renamed Buchanan-Dewar Ltd, it was the thirty-third largest British manufacturing company; the trade's view was that Buchanan-Dewar rather than DCL would be the basis for The Big Amalgamation.

Ironically, at the very moment that Scotch Whisky Brands was formed, wartime anti-drink policy was limiting competition much more effectively than the blenders ever could. This was especially true of the Immature Spirits (Restrictions) Act 1915 which introduced compulsory bonding. Traders lacking mature stock were forced into the market to buy it; those who possessed stock found the value greatly enhanced. In explaining why a few proprietary brands became predominant, historians have generally referred to their better quality and to blenders' marketing skills. An alternative explanation – acknowledged by the brand owners – is the Immature Spirits Act. It gave 'the proprietary brands . . . a fillip' (DCL/6). James Buchanan thought that the Act

> is all in our favour. I know for a fact that it puts out of the market from 8 to 10 million gallons of cheap raw whisky, which has been sold from the Tap by publicans all over the country.
>
> (DCL/7)

Such certainty was misleading, for neither the trade nor the government had sufficient information to judge the true stock position, but what mattered was that traders behaved as if there was a stock shortage.

Proprietary brands competed not only against each other but also with brands produced by the brewers and with 'tap' whisky, that is unbranded whisky supplied in bulk and sold from the tap in public houses. 'Tap' whisky gave consumers no guarantee they were purchasing good quality, well-matured spirit. Proprietary brands claimed to be, so the competitive situation was between a commodity with a known reputation and higher price, and one of uncertain quality and lower price. Between 1915 and 1916 an intense debate occurred among The Big Three and the Brands Association about whether to raise prices and reap the profit from mature stock or to leave prices unchanged while 'tap' whisky, not backed by mature stocks, was increased and came closer to the price of proprietary brands. It was an argument about maximizing either profits or market share. Walker wanted to go for market share, Buchanan-Dewar to maximize profits. Walkers won the argument, but what all parties recognized was that so long as Walkers stood outside the combine, The Big Three could not control the market.

External pressures on the whisky industry mounted alarmingly during 1916. In grain distilling, government orders were gradually squeezing out potable customers; by the end of the year all output had to be allocated for munitions. Malt distilling was reduced and by June 1917 prohibited. Life was no easier in blending where the Central Control Board, formed in May 1915 to regulate the drink trade, imposed restrictions on wholesalers and retailers, including a reduction in the strength at which whisky could be sold. With raw material prices rising rapidly even Walkers reluctantly dropped the market share argument:

> Mr Stevenson, whilst arguing against (a price rise) from the point of view of beating the brewer and wiping out the small whisky houses

... left me with the impression that Kilmarnock was very desirous for a 3/- per case rise.

(DCL/8)

Exports were free from control but with home customers rationed retailers were demanding that exports be curtailed. Blenders were unwilling to concede this and had the power to resist:

If the wholesale trade cares to put their heads together the retailer can be made to pipe any tune they may care to call. The stock is in their possession, and that fact is the key to the situation. We could never think of agreeing to any restrictions on exports.

(DCL/9)

Ownership of stocks was the key to the whole industry, a fact that Ross seized on to bind DCL and The Big Three closer together.

These difficulties made many wholesale firms consider whether it was worth continuing. The prospect of Excess Profits Duty increased the attraction of getting out while stocks could still be sold without handing the proceeds to the taxman. One of the first firms to go into voluntary liquidation was Robertson, Sanderson & Co. The trustees expected a high price as blenders competed for the stocks. Ross thought differently:

Ross thinks we should do or say nothing between now and the issue of the lists, and proposes then that one or two of the leading firms should meet and come to an arrangement.

(DCL/10)

Nothing quite signalled the blenders' new relationship with DCL as their response. Collusion was welcomed. DCL and The Big Three would jointly value the stock, one firm would bid, and the stocks would be divided between the participants. As more firms left – Ross estimated over fifty distributors departed – joint purchasing became a regular practice. In January 1918, when it became known that the Ministry of Food was going to control spirit prices, it was imperative that stock values were not bidded up and the arrangement was formalized through a Buying Committee. This reduced risk. Nobody knew if mature whisky prices had reached their peak. The extraordinary position created by the three-year age limitation and the cessation of potable production could not be permanent, but nor could post-war consumption levels be forecast accurately.

Joint action also occurred over distilleries. In 1918 one of the three remaining independent grain distilling firms, Yoker Distillery Ltd, was purchased by Ross in the interests of 'the proposed combine', while the blenders agreed not to negotiate with James Calder & Co. Ltd for Bo'ness or Gartloch distilleries without DCL's consent (DCL/11). There was no guarantee that such wartime co-operation would endure. DCL, Buchanan-Dewar and Walker remained separate companies and the creation of a single firm was to take another seven years. There were two preliminary requirements before 'the big question' could be resolved: the blenders should be sufficiently large to absorb the majority of DCL's output and DCL should control all, or nearly all, the grain distilleries in the UK.

Before 1914 The Big Three accounted for only about 20 per cent of DCL's grain whisky fillings and hostility to a combine might result in orders being switched to other grain distilling firms or, worse still, the foundation of a new grain distillery. This had originally persuaded Ross that a large-scale restructuring was vital, for only if the combine embraced most of the grain distillers – DCL, North British and Calder – and the large blending houses – The Big Three, Mackie, Usher, Robertson & Baxter, and Watson – could it curb competition.

Anti-drink legislation fulfilled the first condition by creating an environment suitable for the consolidation of blending. Stock shortages removed the blending houses that had dealt in new whisky and the cessation of distilling made replenishment impossible. The main beneficiaries were the owners of proprietary brands who were well stocked. Their market share increased, as did their market power. Price cutting and discounting, once the bane of proprietary blending, had disappeared by 1918. Sales of bulk blended whisky declined, blenders preferring to retain stocks and market bottled goods on which profit margins were higher. Whether these changes consoled blenders is another matter, for the market as a whole was much diminished. Demand had averaged 34.8 mpg between 1909 and 1914; by 1918 it was 14.3 mpg.

DCL had also altered as a result of the war. It had strengthened its position in blending by acquiring two export houses in 1916 – John Hopkins & Co. Ltd and John Begg Ltd – and was now selling blended whisky in the home market. According to Ross, this was an unanticipated development which arose from the purchase of J. & G. Stewart, a blending firm, in December 1917. DCL's intention was 'to get the stocks' – some 800,000 gallons – 'take any export business there was and drop the home trade', but after the deal had been completed DCL found that government regulations forced it to continue supplying Stewart's home trade customers. Thus, 'it came about that, against its own inclinations, the Company was forced to enter into the home business for blended whisky' (Ross 1926). Whether DCL was an unwilling entrant may be doubted, for the disappearance of so many customers gave it a strong incentive. Once in, DCL liked what it found and further acquisitions followed: John Haig & Co. Ltd in March 1919, Andrew Usher & Co. Ltd in October 1919, James Gray & Son Ltd in March 1920 and J. G. Thomson & Co. Ltd in April 1921.

Circumstances had changed but was the time right for the big combine? A plan for one was vetoed by DCL on the grounds that DCL would have to further strengthen its position in patent still distilling. This was achieved by June 1922 with the acquisition of Calder's distilleries and the Irish grain distilling group, United Distillers Ltd. Both had important implications for distribution because they increased DCL's blending subsidiaries from five to eleven, giving it an even greater presence in this part of the trade. As a result, the continuing discussions about amalgamation began to display less concern about production and more about marketing, in particular the interrelated problem of the shortage of mature whisky and the number of brands the market could support.

So long as joint purchases were designed to enable DCL and The Big Three to acquire stocks for use in their own brands, they raised no fundamental issues about the number of brands or the competitive relationship between them. This situation changed between November 1922 and October 1923 when three firms owning substantial stocks and successful brands were offered for sale: Robertson & Baxter ('Haig & Haig'), James Watson & Co. ('No. 10') and Peter Mackie & Co. ('White Horse'). Each brand was popular with consumers, each competed with brands marketed by DCL and The Big Three, each posed the question whether the brand should continue and thus raised the fundamental issue of whether the loose alliance could cope with marketing disputes.

Robertson & Baxter owned over 2 million gallons of stock and among its many brands was Haig & Haig. Before prohibition this brand was becoming popular in the US; now the United States was dry it enjoyed a thriving bootlegging trade. The stocks were a major attraction for The Big Three and also interested DCL, but DCL was even keener to acquire Haig & Haig as its removal would benefit DCL's recently purchased subsidiary, John Haig & Co. Ltd. DCL had turned Haig's into a highly profitable brand and there was a major advertising commitment. A joint bid in December 1922 secured the stocks and the brand, and it was agreed to liquidate Haig & Haig. In February 1923 a new complication arose when the owners of Haig's Millburn distillery in Inverness proposed to market a brand under the name Haig & Haig. If DCL and The Big Three were not using the brand, the proposed registration might succeed.

Before this could be resolved James Watson & Co. was offered for sale. Holding 5.5 million gallons, it was among the best stocked firms and had been able 'to continue to market blends of pre-war reputation and quality', but the quantity was too large for DCL to handle alone, so Ross invited The Big Three to participate. They were keen to acquire the stocks but wanted the 'No. 10' brand withdrawn. DCL thought this would be a mistake, for it was a high-quality brand, well established in Australia, and amply backed by stocks and a modern bottling line. Ross proposed that Watson should be carried on jointly 'until the proposed big blending proposition comes along' but The Big Three rejected this, wanting the stock for their own brands. DCL withdrew, forfeiting its share of the stock, much to Ross's annoyance (DCL/12).

It was improbable that the firms could agree a coherent marketing strategy while they retained their independence, but before this could be discussed the third blending firm, Peter Mackie & Co., approached Buchanan-Dewar. Sir Peter Mackie had planned for his son to succeed him but his son was killed in 1917. By 1923, aged 68, Sir Peter was looking for another firm to join, with a preference for Dewar's 'as we have always worked so harmoniously together' (DCL/13). It was not past harmony that pushed Mackie into the arms of Buchanan-Dewar but lack of capital for stocks. Buchanan-Dewar wanted 'White Horse' off the market, something Sir Peter was against:

> I feel that in the interest of the Trade it would be a mistake to wipe out the 'White Horse' Brand, as public opinion is at present strong on this point.
>
> (DCL/14)

It proved impossible to agree a financial basis for a merger or even for the purchase of the stocks. By the autumn of 1923 there were the first signs of a break in the mature whisky market and Mackie could not find a buyer. The failure of the merger was a mixed blessing: an opportunity to increase market share had been lost but Mackie's recruitment to The Big Three would have added another interest to be taken into account in The Big Amalgamation.

When it looked as if a competing Haig & Haig brand would be launched, Alex Walker suggested that this could be prevented by an earlier joint acquisition, Dailuaine-Talisker Distilleries, marketing a small quantity of Haig & Haig to keep the brand alive and deny its use by competitors. Ross took exception to this:

My objection to this plan all along has been that it is mixing up the Dailuaine Company . . . with a matter in which they are not concerned & for reasons which would alone benefit certain of their biggest shareholders. The alternative suggested is to form a small new Company to take over the brand which would carry on the sale to a greater or less extent. Is this the proposal now put forward from London? If so I am equally against this alternative on the ground that it is merely to play with the matter in order to prevent others appropriating the brand, it is incurring needless expense, and if to carry out an intensive sale of the brand it would be creating opposition to the brands of all four firms interested.

But why this anxiety to perpetuate a brand which has now been off the market for nearly two years? It seems utterly at variance with the attitude of Messrs B-D & W when the Watson's brand was offered for sale. I then pleaded strongly for that mark being retained as a live brand but was left in a hopeless minority and sacrificed my right to a share of the stock in consequence.

Later when the suggestion was made that the 'King George IV' brand should be put upon the Home Market and I claimed freedom of action without committing myself either way I was told that there was not room for another brand and your object in buying up recent businesses was to reduce the number of brands.

There must be some other reason therefore – hitherto undisclosed – for being so concerned in restoring the Haig & Haig brand, and I think it is due to me that you and the others should tell me candidly what is at the back of your minds. It may then be possible to meet the situation or at all events would enable me to say clearly what our attitude is to be. When that time arrives I suggest we have a special meeting.

(DCL/15)

At that meeting, on 6 November 1924, The Big Three objected to Ross's statement that Watsons had been acquired to eliminate the No. 10 brand. Ross conceded that stocks had been the incentive but stated that DCL would consider the revival of Haig & Haig as 'an unfriendly act'. It then emerged that The Big Three wished to restore the brand for the bootlegging trade, building on the brand's strength before prohibition:

it was foolish not to make use of this brand now that it was our joint property, rather than spend money to advertise a new name. Also the large sum previously spent in advertising the Haig & Haig brand was still of value, and should be utilised.

(DCL/16)

This was not an argument about the intangibility of property rights in brands – Haig & Haig was 'a great asset acquired and paid for' – the problem was that the partners' interests were opposed: three of the four firms wanted to use the brand, whereas the fourth derived large benefits from a brand which clashed with Haig & Haig. No decision was reached and a further meeting was arranged for 17 November. Between meetings the blenders considered three options. One was to sell the brand to DCL and let DCL decide its future. A second was to buy out DCL's share and work the brand jointly. The final option was for Buchanan-Dewar to acquire the brand and market it through W. P. Lowrie. The first option, which in effect meant withdrawing the brand, was ruled out on the grounds that

> when we took over Robertson & Baxter's stocks we were told by them that we would lose a golden opportunity if we did not continue the Brand, as it was getting such a favourite in the American markets.
>
> (DCL/17)

For obvious reasons the third option did not appeal to Walkers, so The Big Three agreed to buy out DCL's interest and market Haig & Haig as a premium brand. The spirit of the decision was quite explicit:

> we must not be influenced against our own interests by D.C.L. regarding carrying on as an unfriendly act.
>
> (DCL/17)

The brand's future had the potential to rupture relations between The Big Three and DCL.

That the meeting on 17 November had an entirely different outcome was due to James Stevenson of Walkers, who proposed that the Haig & Haig problem could be solved if the larger question of amalgamation was finally tackled. A single firm would find it easier to decide which brands to promote and which to withdraw. Marketing was thus the dominant consideration. Although all agreed amalgamation was the ideal solution, two issues were fiercely contested: the choice (and location) of the holding company and the valuation of the firms. For marketing reasons Dewars opposed DCL as the holding company: 'it would certainly look bad . . . to the public [and] would really do our brands a lot of harm' (DCL/18). Ross, and the DCL Board, were determined that DCL should be the holding company and Scottish registered. For DCL it was inconceivable that the premier firm in the Scotch whisky industry should be registered in England, though this was what Buchanan-Dewar's financial adviser, Sir Gilbert Garnsey, argued in a highly tendentious document which asserted that 'London was the centre of the business world' and dismissed such virtues as Edinburgh might possess with a rhetorical question: 'it may be asked what advantages a Company situated in Edinburgh offers over one whose Headquarters are in London' (DCL/19).

Garnsey's document was offensive to any nationalistically minded Scot, and DCL's Board was not short of these, for whom the drift southwards was symptomatic of much that was wrong with post-war Scotland. It smacked too much of the City dictating to industry. Unfortunately, it was also a realistic assessment of the attitude of City institutions, though this became evident only much later. What resolved the issue was DCL's hitherto concealed financial strength:

> Ross' figures were certainly amazing. His profit for last year was £1,569,000, while his published statement showed about half a million. . . . The Company is certainly in a most prosperous position, and a very desirable one for us to amalgamate with.
>
> (DCL/20)

Between 1909 and 1925 the desire to restrain competition remained a constant theme, but the environment changed beyond recognition. In 1909 it was possible to believe that the whisky trade had a long-term future; by 1925 few whisky men subscribed to that proposition. All would have been content to maintain the market they held; few believed it would be possible to do so. Further contraction seemed inevitable and for many the key question was how to get out of the trade with some capital intact. The Big Amalgamation created exactly the kind of institution to which they could turn.

It was not only falling demand that caused this shift in entre-preneurial outlook, but also the feeling that government and public were hostile to the trade. Most whisky people held the wartime anti-drink campaign responsible; only a minority recognized that a more sophisticated explanation, involving changes in social habits, was needed to account for the fact that falling consumption predated the war. New leisure activities and consumer goods were pushing Scotch down the league table of consumer expenditure: in 1900 alcoholic drink accounted for 18 per cent of total consumer expenditure; by 1930 it would be just under 7 per cent. Only rarely did this crucial long-term change surface in the amalgamation discussions. Because it was seldom recognized, the amalgamation was not regarded as a means of halting and reversing the decline, but rather as an instrument for preserving the profitability of such trade as remained. Ross saw it as a means of shielding smaller firms from the chill wind of competition. The blenders saw it as a financial transaction rather than a change in their status and operating policies. As Sir Alexander Walker assured his shareholders:

> the change . . . in . . . ownership . . . will make no difference to the conduct of the business. We shall continue to carry on the old firm on the traditions and policy of the past.

> (DCL/21)

The implications did not escape financial commentators who pointed out that, as each company would retain its separate identity, it would prevent the realization of any great economies. Attachment to the status quo reflected the blenders' belief that they were not being swallowed by a predator but participating in a treaty between the Great Powers of the whisky world. Ross propagated this view and quite specifically, and approvingly, used the analogy. Yet Ross also knew that it would be necessary to rationalize the blending subsidiaries. Hard decisions had already been taken to deal with excess distilling capacity. Was there any reason to spare blending? The blenders had a ready answer: brand loyalty. Rationalization of distribution proved contentious, eluding even Ross's powers of persuasion. When it came to marketing, the new DCL would be less the result of a treaty between the Great Powers than a modus vivendi for an Emperor and his War Lords.

MARKETING IN THE DCL GROUP 1925–39

The new DCL Group maintained two strategies already in place before the merger, rationalization and diversification. Diversification into industrial alcohol, chemicals and pharmaceuticals was forced by the need to find new outlets for alcohol and to spread risk. It contrasts sharply with drink companies in the 1980s, including Guinness, where concentration on core activity has been the dominant strategy (Weir 1990).

DCL's organizational structure after 1925 has been the subject of unfavourable comment by business historians. Chandler regards DCL as ineffective in building a managerial organization with the result that it remained

> essentially a federation of whiskey makers [in which] top level decisions as to strategy and allocation of resources continued to be made from the personal perspective of a small number of whiskey producers.

> (Chandler 1990)

DCL's organization was also criticized in the contested bid in 1986 but, as far as the interwar period is concerned, Chandler's view is based on a misinterpretation of the decision to formalize the management committee in 1935. In fact DCL operated tight controls over its subsidiaries and resource allocation was not a reflection of whisky interests. The composition of the Board, designed to reflect the amount of capital contributed by each of the parties to the amalgamation, gave it a federal appearance but this altered with the changing balance of trading activities. Brand marketing was supervised by the malt distilling and blended whisky sales committee. Strategic issues were settled by the management committee and reported to the Board. Two marketing issues proved particularly controversial.

The first was advertising expenditure. Given the background to the merger it was scarcely surprising that this should be a target for economies. In practice they proved difficult to achieve for commercial reasons. Until June 1927, when White Horse Distillers was acquired, it could be argued that a reduction in advertising would cause loss of market share. With White Horse in the Group 'the opportunity should at once be seized' to economize (DCL/22). What impeded cuts was a demand from brewers and wholesalers for a larger margin on proprietary whiskies. DCL was not prepared to concede this and regarded more intensive advertising as a way of preventing it by securing consumer loyalty. By 1931 the advertising budget was £1.2 million and fell under the scrutiny of the Economy Committee. This reduced it to £750,000 by 1933, a sum that proved insufficient after the repeal of prohibition when advertising was essential to re-establishing brands. By 1937 advertising costs had stabilized at £1.3 million excluding a £70,000 'Fighting Fund' to meet exceptional competition.

The second controversy was sparked off by Ross's frustration with the limited progress in cutting sales costs. He wanted sales centralized and argued that

> if the Economy Committee studied the history of the DCL it would be seen that while the production end had been fully rationalized there had been little change in the method of blending and marketing of the Group Brands of whisky for the last forty years. Unless we got on some other lines we would not get the benefit of the Group amalgamation.

> (DCL/23)

An experiment with a single distributing company for all the Group's brands was tried in Australia in 1930. It was scrapped in 1934 when the company proposed to handle Australian whisky as well as Scotch, something the blenders strongly opposed because of the risk that the two products would be identified as one by consumers. Centralization also increased paperwork and lengthened the lines of communication between the blenders and their customers. Rationalization of distribution remained contentious, opposed by those who believed it would destroy the mystique of blending and blend individuality. The blenders' thinking has been described in the following way:

> As you know there can be forty different whiskies in a blend and each Company had its secret formulae, so to speak, and they felt if the whiskies went into a central place people would say 'Och it's all the same whisky: it's just a different label'.
>
> (Weir 1990)

Had centralization been tried in the home market, which was where Ross wanted to start, it might have met with more success but it was here where the retention of individual marketing arrangements was strongest. The amalgamation stopped price competition, but subsidiaries competed to have the best marketing organization and thus the biggest market share. Such rivalry was not regarded as unhealthy, but rather the essence of the DCL Group. It was less evident in the export trade mainly because changes in commercial conditions – the imposition of tariffs, the relaxing or tightening of anti-drink measures, the repeal of prohibition – required major strategic decisions. Such changes were invariably preceded by the visit of a Board delegation and followed by a central decision in which major distributors were appointed to handle the Group's brands. That some of these, for example Seagram in Canada and Schenley in the United States, subsequently prospered handsomely has been held to be a fault of this procedure; this can equally be read as the exercise of extremely good judgement. That point becomes evident when distributors' contracts are examined. As had long been common in the whisky trade they were highly detailed, specifying sales targets, prices, credit, advertising allowances, labelling and so on (Morgan and Moss 1993). In no sense could it be said, as it was in 1989,

> that when Distillers were in charge they just didn't think about marketing. A consignment of Scotch would be loaded on to a ship at Southampton and Distillers just waved it goodbye.
>
> (*Guardian* 30 November 1989)

Segmentation was employed, frequently with brands that would have been unknown to the home consumer. What was true of the 1930s was that in a world market fractured by trade blocs and currency regimes marketing sometimes took a back seat to trading, or the exchange of whisky for whatever commodity a buyer wished to offload, but given the circumstances DCL displayed admirable flexibility (Weir 1984).

A final point concerns personnel. Sales people were expected to acquire considerable experience of one brand. They might move around the Group but accumulated expertise was valued. Trade contacts were what was wanted rather than a short spell marketing chocolates or patent medicines or tobacco. Marketing skills were not seen as transferable across 'fast moving consumer goods'.

THE CONTESTED BID OF 1986

In contrast to the sixteen years of discussion that preceded The Big Amalgamation, the take-over battle between the Argyll Group and Guinness was quickly resolved; DCL lost its independence in four and a half months. Long the dominant firm in the whisky industry, DCL had been regarded as immune from predation because of its size and brands portfolio. This view was consistent with the belief that brands, as a form of product differentiation, constitute an entry barrier to new competitors (Devine et al. 1985). Indeed, brands have been regarded as more significant than scale economies or absolute cost advantages because of the cost of altering consumer preferences. Such protection from competition may be limited in that it depends on a firm's performance being acceptable to the public in terms of quality and service (Penrose 1963). This is usually expressed in terms of consumer willingness to pay a 'premium' price for a brand but, in the context of the 1980s, it may be more appropriate to consider a firm's ability to maintain its reputation with financial institutions. Since the 1960s DCL had been losing market share, particularly in the home trade, as the Scotch whisky market moved from a situation of 'constrained supply' to one of rapid geographical expansion (Simms 1993). This loss owed more to the expansion of hitherto relatively small producers such as Bell's and Teacher's, the entry of large brewing companies into distilling to produce whisky for sale in their own outlets and lower profit margins in the home trade than any obvious disenchantment on the part of consumers with DCL's brands. It was institutional dissatisfaction with DCL's slow response to the decline in exports after 1978, the first prolonged downturn in export demand since 1946 (see Table 8.1), that eventually enabled Gulliver's Argyll Group, hitherto a very minor player in the drinks business, to obtain sufficient institutional backing to launch its bid for DCL. Possession of brands did not limit competition; on the contrary, what financial institutions saw as the unexploited potential of DCL's brands became the main justification for competing bids. Economic theories which neglect this aspect of brands remain incomplete (see e.g. Bowbrick 1992).

Table 8.1 Exports of Scotch whisky and Northern Irish whiskey, 1946, 1978 and 1985

	Volume (MLPA)[a]	Rate (%)[b]	Value[c] (£million)	Rate (%)[b]	Value[d] (£million)	Rate (%)[b]
1946	15.261	—	10.60	—	96.4	—
1978	274.073	9.4	661.22	13.8	849.9	7.0
1985	227.988	−2.7	1000.80	6.1	741.6	−1.9

Source: Scotch Whisky Association (1986) *Statistical Report*, London

Notes: [a] Million litres pure alcohol
  [b] Compound rates of growth 1946–78 and 1978–85
  [c] Nominal value
  [d] Real value deflated by RPI (1980 = 100)

When the simmering discontent about DCL's performance was galvanized by James Gulliver into the contested bid between his Argyll Group and Guinness, brands and marketing played a key role in the battle for the support of institutional shareholders. Gulliver's opening salvo was a catalogue of DCL's managerial failings. DCL's share of the home market, 75 per cent in the early 1960s, had fallen to a mere 15 per cent by 1984. DCL had failed abroad where its share of the world Scotch whisky market had fallen from 45 per cent (or 31 million out of 68 million cases) in 1977 to 35 per cent in 1984 (or 23 million out of 65 million cases). DCL had failed to develop new whisky products except for Claymore, a heavily discounted brand. Gulliver blamed DCL's loosely co-ordinated federal structure. Top management was inbred and slow to respond to changing market conditions. This was also evident in brand marketing, where a long-established network of distributors did not give full control of marketing. DCL's business was international drinks marketing but the directors had failed to exploit their inheritance, 'a unique portfolio of brands bequeathed them by an earlier generation of management'. Nothing symbolized the wastefulness of the federal structure more (and, of course, the potential for cost-saving) than 'the seven prestigious offices in the West End' (Argyll Group/1).

DCL's initial response was to reassure shareholders that organizational change was already underway. This effectively conceded part of Gulliver's case, not least because it put production first and marketing

second. On assuming the chairmanship of DCL in September 1983
J. M. Connell had

> identified a number of areas in which change was needed in the
> management and organisation of the Group. . . . The first was the
> production of Scotch whisky . . . to reduce the level of stocks of
> maturing whisky whilst at the same time ensuring sufficient stocks
> of single whiskies to protect the quality of our brands.
>
> (DCL/24)

Only subsequently had marketing been reformed by establishing the
Home Trade Division to handle all brands in the UK. It was exactly
this order of priorities which DCL's critics disliked for, as one unidentified Guinness executive commented:

> This is all about brands and marketing and not about production.
> The days are gone when ownership of production could influence
> the market.
>
> (*Scotsman*, 2 February 1986)

With the recruitment of Bill Spengler, a US marketing expert, DCL
became more aggressive and sought to undermine the belief that a
grocer from Campbeltown had the skills necessary to run an international drinks company:

> Jimmy [Gulliver] deals in potatoes and canned beans. We are not
> selling brown water in cheap bottles. We are selling Scotch and that
> requires international marketing expertise.
>
> (*Scotsman*, 3 December 1985)

What this left unanswered was whether in a global market with
stagnant consumption, new trends in consumer behaviour – a move
from brown spirits towards wine and alternative drinks that were
perceived as healthier – and structural changes in retailing, DCL was
large enough to compete even with a restructured organization. A
turnover of at least 10 million cases was regarded as the minimum
necessary to support a worldwide network of distributors (*Financial
Times*, 4 July 1987). While DCL's sales were larger than that, the key
point was that the global drinks market was becoming dominated by a
relatively small league of multinational firms (this aspect is discussed
by Balasubramanyam and Salisu, Chapter 4 in this volume). The
rationale for combining Distillers and Guinness was that it would

> create a British drinks group with a range of international brands
> unique in the drinks industry. It will have financial, marketing and

product strength to compete with the largest and most efficient drinks companies.

(Guinness/1)

Guinness saw DCL's brand portfolio as the main asset thus making the crucial issue the respective abilities of different marketing teams to improve sales and profitability in international markets. The marriage was to be 'more than just a merger the creation of a truly exciting new British enterprise, an international consumer brands company' (Guinness/2).

Responsibility for unlocking DCL's potential fell not to Ernest Saunders, removed from office and deprived of his chance to fulfil his claim that the merger was 'probably the most exciting development in international brand names since the creation of the Beecham Group twenty-five years ago', but to Anthony Tennant, another marketing man (*Scotsman*, 2 February 1986). Tennant's later analysis of DCL's weaknesses might have been penned by Gulliver: it was 'in need of radical overhaul', it had been 'badly managed for years, with an archaic distribution system and almost non-existent marketing', it had 'some good brands . . . but production had been allowed to run out of control', ' "spirit lakes" were compounded by the chaos of the marketing side, where brands were allowed to compete against each other in the same market', and DCL had little control over its international agency network (*Independent*, 27 February 1989). What were the results of this analysis between 1987 and 1993?

UNITED DISTILLERS

If office buildings reveal the soul of a company, the contrast between Torphichen Street, DCL's Edinburgh headquarters for over a century, and Landmark House, the London office of United Distillers, Guinness's spirits division, said much about a new corporate marketing culture. Heavily varnished wood panelling, dark linoleum flooring and the omnipresent Corps of Commissionaires were out; the plate glass tower block, light marble reception lounge (with brands prominently displayed) and contract security were in. But what internal reorganization occurred after the merger?

Guinness's annual report, a document whose design was as different from DCL's as chalk from cheese, explained the reorganization in 1988 (Guinness/3). United Distillers owned 200 spirit brands but was concentrating on those with the greatest potential. United Distillers was to be marketing led with resources concentrated on leading brands. Yet the first stage of restructuring would not have been unfamiliar to DCL's managers in 1925, for it was the rationalization of distilling and bottling. A more novel element, reflecting the new management philosophy, 'Think global – act local', was the creation of profit responsible regions, each with a manager handling the full brand portfolio. Two advantages were perceived: it moved key personnel into the market-place, closer to customers, and the brand portfolio could be segmented to the needs of each market and the position occupied by competitors. Segmentation too would have been familiar to managers in the 1930s. To service the regional profit centres a Central Strategic Unit had been created. This concentrated on global issues leaving regional managers to tailor strategies for local markets. Volume sales, described by one commentator during the bid as 'the way to a quiet life and zero profits', were not the aim, rather it was to enhance the value of brands and 'restore Scotch to its rightful position as the leading and most respected spirit product in the world'. Regaining control of global distribution was a key element in the strategy, to be achieved either through purchases, for example, of Schenley, Dewar's distributor in the United States since the 1930s or joint ventures, for example with LVMH (Moët Hennessy). The aims were to retrieve the distributor's profit margin and to control marketing. By 1988 United Distillers controlled 75 per cent of distribution compared to only 25 per cent in 1987. Independent distributors were pruned: from 244 in Europe to 30, from 211 in Asia-Pacific to 80, from 30 in North America to 7. Here there was a contrast with the interwar years when geography, the difficulty of communications, and the need for local knowledge in markets characterized by tariffs and anti-drink controls dictated a multiplicity of distributors.

Presentational idiom too was very different. Scotch was now 'a luxury, premium-priced product, relevant to the lifestyle and aspirations of successful people'. Luxury was a dangerous word in the interwar period, for it invited taxes and tariffs, and the language of marketing referred to a moderately priced stimulant which should be used in moderation. Blends in the late 1980s were to combine 'traditional heritage with contemporary imagery' and if this sounded a bit like *Hymns Ancient and Modern* the marketing people had discovered 'the art of brand repositioning'; brands could be moulded and shaped to suit whatever niche market research had discovered. Such flexibility would have puzzled managers between the wars, when DCL saw its role as setting standards for the Scotch whisky industry. It defined a 'fair average standard blend' in 1919 as 50 per cent malt, 50 per cent grain and of at least five years of age. By 1935 a standard blend was ten years old and a de luxe fifteen years, though the average percentage of malt and grain in Group blends was 58.4 per cent grain and 41.6 per cent malt.

Scotch whisky, in Tennant's view, was 'all about high value-added brands and margins. It has nothing to do with volume'. Application of this could be found in the regrading and repricing of Royal Lochnagar, once a rather anonymous malt, into a selected reserve whisky selling at £95 rather than £15 a bottle, or the upgrading of Haig's Dimple, or the 'six classic malts'. Nothing perhaps contrasts the whisky market of the 1930s and the 1980s more than the ability to sell single malts. DCL graded and planned to market five 'first-class makes' of malt in 1935 but abandoned the venture as unprofitable at prevailing income levels. (Those who think they know their malts might like to guess which they were; the answer appears at the end of this chapter.)

By 1990 company observers were convinced that United Distillers was reversing the bad habits of the early 1980s when Scotch was sold at a low price in the quest for volume. Quality paid: consumers were drinking less but spending more and, with production under control, there was less need for cheap brands to reduce stocks. Premium brands were no longer undermined. Pricing strategy could be 'confident'. By 1992 United Distillers was contributing 60 per cent to Guinness's sales and 80 per cent to its profits while the parent company with 38 per cent of the spirits market was the second most profitable beverage company in the world. Marketing was predicated on the belief that 'as people become more affluent, they don't buy more holidays, motorcars or clothes, but *better* holidays, motorcars and clothes' (*Sunday Times*, 23 December 1991). If true, premier brands were indeed a valuable asset in a global market which looked increasingly weak in the 1990s. Yet how much of United Distillers' success came from marketing and how much from long overdue rationalization? The problem with rationalization, as was clear between the wars, is that like some radioactive substances it has a short half-life. Squeezing added value from brands may have been relatively easy in the inflationary 1980s; in the price-sensitive, low-inflation 1990s 'confident' pricing may be less viable. When a further round of plant closures, as in January 1993, returns the focus of cost-saving to production and persuades financial journalists to turn an old advertisement against its owners by suggesting that 'the slogan that Guinness is good for you is wearing thin' it is perhaps time to question the marketing strategies pursued since 1986 (*Independent*, 13 January 1993). Will United Distillers organization prove as adaptable to new market conditions as DCL's did in the 1930s?

160   *Adding Value: brands and marketing*

REFERENCES

Published texts

Alford, B. W. E. (1977) 'Penny cigarettes, oligopoly, and entrepreneurship in the U.K. tobacco industry in the late nineteenth century', in B. Supple (ed.) *Essays in British Business History*, Oxford: Clarendon.

Booth, M. and Weir, R. B. (1990) 'Prevention policy and the Scotch whisky industry', in A. Maynard and P. Tether (eds) *Preventing Alcohol and Tobacco Problems*, vol. 1, Aldershot: Avebury.

Bowbrick, P. (1992) *The Economics of Quality, Grades and Brands*, London: Routledge.

Chandler, A. D. (1990) *Scale and Scope: The Dynamics of Industrial Capitalism*, Cambridge, Mass: Harvard University Press.

Devine, P. J., Lee, N., Jones, R. M. and Tyson, W. J. (1985) *An Introduction to Industrial Economics*, London: Allen & Unwin.

Morgan, N. and Moss, M. (1993), 'The marketing of Scotch whisky: an historical perspective', in R. S. Tedlow and G. Jones (eds) *The Rise and Fall of Mass Marketing*, London: Routledge.

Penrose, E. (1963) *The Theory of the Growth of the Firm*, Oxford: Basil Blackwell.

Ross, W. H. (1926) 'History of the company', *DCL Gazette*, October: 187.

Simms, C. (1993) 'Marketing before and after market research', unpublished paper, United Distillers.

Weir, R. B. (1984) 'Alcohol controls and Scotch whisky exports 1870–1939', *British Journal of Addiction* 83: 1,289–97.

—— (1990) 'The export marketing of Scotch whisky (1870–1939)', in E. Aerts and L. M. Cullen (eds) *Production, Marketing and Consumption of Alcoholic Beverages*, Leuven: Leuven University Press.

Manuscript sources

DCL/1   John Dewar & Sons Ltd, Original Amalgamation Papers, Meeting of James Buchanan, Sir Thomas Dewar and G. P. Walker (hereafter cited as JD&S, OAP), 19/10/1910.

DCL/2   John Dewar & Sons Ltd, Cameron Papers, James Buchanan and Sir Thomas Dewar (hereafter cited as JD&S, CP), 19/10/1910.

DCL/3   JD&S, OAP, J. King-Stewart to A. J. Cameron, 31/5/1910.

DCL/4   JD&S, OAP, J. King-Stewart to A. J. Cameron, 2/6/1910.

DCL/5   JD&S, CP, John Dewar to James Buchanan, 19/3/1915.

DCL/6   JD&S, CP, A. J. Cameron to J. F. Johnstone, 8/5/1915.

DCL/7   JD&S, CP, James Buchanan to Sir John Dewar, 12/5/1915.

DCL/8   JD&S, CP, A. J. Cameron to W. Harrison, 16/11/1915.

DCL/9   JD&S, CP, A. J. Cameron to J. F. Johnstone, 31/3/1916.

DCL/10   JD&S, CP. A. J. Cameron to J. F. Johnstone, 15/1/1916.

DCL/11   JD&S, Yoker Purchase, W. H. Ross to A. J. Cameron, 25/4/1918.

DCL/12   Works & Management Committee Minute Book No. 3, 11/5/1923 and 22/6/1923.

DCL/13   JD&S, Mackie Papers, Sir P. J. Mackie to the Lord Dewar, 22/5/1923.

DCL/14 JD&S, Mackie Papers, Sir P. J. Mackie to the Lord Forteviot, 23/7/1923.
DCL/15 JD&S, Haig & Haig Papers, W. H. Ross to A. J. Cameron, 29/10/1924.
DCL/16 JD&S, Haig & Haig Papers.
DCL/17 JD&S, Memorandum re—Haig & Haig.
DCL/18 JD&S, CP, P. M. Dewar to A. J. Cameron, 27/11/1924.
DCL/19 JD&S, Merger Papers, Memorandum from Sir Gilbert Garnsey, 22/12/1924.
DCL/20 JD&S, Correspondence, Lord Forteviot to Lord Woolavington, 19/11/1924.
DCL/21 John Walker & Sons Ltd, AGM, July 1925.
DCL/22 Board Minute Book no. 15, 14/7/1927.
DCL/23 Board Minute Book no. 17, 12/1/1933.
DCL/24 Circular to Shareholders 2/12/1985.
Argyll Group/1 Bid Document 2/12/1985.
Guinness/1 Bid Document 22/1/1986.
Guinness/2 The Guinness/DCL Merger 25/2/1986.
Guinness/3 Report and Accounts 1988.

Malts

The five first-class makes were Aultmore, Benrinnes, Glenlossie, Linkwood and Mortlach. United Distillers Classic Six are Cragganmore, Dalwhinnie, Glenkinchie, Lagavulin, Oban and Talisker.

9   The empire strikes back

Marketing Australian beer and wine in the United Kingdom

David Merrett and Greg Whitwell

The most striking aspect of the world beer and wine industries since the late 1960s has been its globalization. International trade in these products has grown rapidly. Production of beer in export markets under licence and then by direct investment in brewing capacity has become commonplace. The world beer market has become increasingly homogenized as lager has come to replace ale as the overwhelmingly favoured style of beverage in all major markets. Wine from the 'new world' has increasingly found favour in Europe which remains the major centre of both production and consumption. Both industries have come to be dominated by large multinational enterprises, some of which are diversified food, tobacco and beverage producers, although this process of concentration has taken hold more for beer than wine. Marketing has come to play a critical role in capturing sales (for a review of recent trends in the global industries, see Cavanagh and Clairmonte 1985; Unwin 1991; for a study of the European brewing industry, see Steele 1993). The success of Australian brands in both beer and wine in the United Kingdom market since the early 1980s reflects these broader trends in the global markets for alcoholic beverages. Sales of Australian beer and wine have expanded from a low base in 1985 to the point where both occupy an important place in the market.

This dramatic flowering raises a number of important questions. What led Australian brewers and wine makers to tackle the UK market already well supplied with known brands? What factors were responsible for the success of Australian firms? The problem facing Australian firms was to convince UK consumers to try and then to keep buying new products in preference to their usual brew or wine.

It will be argued in this chapter that the export drive can be properly understood only in the context of radical changes in the structure of the Australian brewing and wine industry. In brief, both underwent a period of greatly increased concentration to the point where two brewers hold some 90 per cent of the national market and three wineries hold roughly 60 per cent of national production. The changed industrial structure has been associated with improved technology in all phases of production, product innovation and a much more professional approach to marketing. Larger and well-managed companies were instrumental in the assault on export markets.

However, the marketing campaigns for beer and wine differed in many important respects. What was appropriate for selling beer would not have worked for Australia's wineries. The nature of the product, the nature of the distribution chain between the wine producer and the customer was different from that facing brewers, who ultimately purchased brewing assets and estates. The only significant similarity in the marketing campaigns of the two alcoholic beverages was the development of an image of Australia – warm, clean, friendly – as an integral attribute of the products. But beyond that the modus operandi of the Australian invasion and the reasons for their respective successes were markedly dissimilar. These contrasts will be explored in this chapter.

BEER

Developments in the Australian brewing industry

While Australian breweries registered the trade marks of their various draught and packaged beers from the late nineteenth century, marketing of those brands played a minor role until the late 1960s compared to the demands of increasing production facilities to satisfy increasing per capita consumption. From around the 1920s a dozen breweries were unchallenged in secure regional markets. Several Australian states had a brewing monopoly while others had two or three at most. The threat of entry seemed minimal owing to the high fixed costs of operating at volumes necessary to enjoy scale economies in brewing and packaging. The control of breweries over distribution channels was another important consideration. Hotels, the most important outlet for draught and packaged beer, were 'tied' to brewers while temperance-inspired licensing authorities severely limited the number of hotel and other types of licences (Merrett 1992).

The entry in 1967 of a new brewery, Courage, whose major shareholders were the UK brewery of the same name, and British Tobacco, into the Victorian market that was monopolized by Carlton & United

Breweries (CUB), was the catalyst for change in the Australian brewing industry. While domestic brewers had focused on advances in brewing technologies and cost minimization they were largely innocent of marketing their brands. The introduction of a range of beers by Courage forced the staid CUB to react. Carlton did not attempt to meet its new rival by cutting price. Rather, its first line of defence was to reinforce its control over the distribution channels by increasing the number of managed and tied houses. However, more importantly in the longer term CUB paid unparalleled attention to marketing its range of brands of draught and particularly packaged beers. There was a heightened attention to the amenities and decor of the hotels in its estate, and to the quality of draught beer at the point of sale (Dunstan 1987: ch. 12).

Courage's entry into the market coincided with a change in senior management and strategic direction at CUB. The brewery had been held in thrall by Reginald Fogarty, its chief executive and later chairman from 1949 until his death in 1967. During his long reign Fogarty had focused almost exclusively on production issues seeking to make the highest quality beer at minimum cost. Advertising expenditures had been held to a minimum as had undoubtedly been the case in previous decades. It is highly likely that beer advertising in Australia in the 1930s was similar to that in the UK where brewers spent less on advertising in relation to sales than other alcoholic beverages and most advertising was done on billboards rather than through the press or radio (Kaldor and Silverman 1948: T.69, 123–7; T.72, 130; T.75, 145). Advertisements for beers, wines and spirits in the Australian press took up a smaller percentage of advertising space than their share of advertising expenditure in the UK press at about the same date (Kaldor and Silverman 1948: T.69, 123–7; McNair 1937: 30). What advertising had been done was generic to the product rather than to the brand: billboards bore signs 'Good beer is good for you'. Fogarty's successors, Brian Breheny and Lou Mangan, recognized the need to market CUB's beers, especially packaged beer, in competition with Courage. This intuitive response was enlightened in so far as heavy advertising, particularly by the Philip Morris owned Miller's, had resulted in significant shifts in brand allegiance and market share in the US industry (Greer 1981: 101–3; Kelton and Kelton 1982: 300–1; Tremblay 1987: 73, 76).

CUB's marketing strategy was to push its range of beers to crowd the smaller set of Courage's off the bottleshop and supermarket shelves and to reinforce brand loyalty to its draught beers. A highly successful advertising campaign was designed and implemented by a local agency, George Patterson, following the first professional market research into the Australian beer market. The brands to be marketed dated back to the formation of the company in 1907 and comprised a range of draught and packaged beers bearing the names of the various breweries that formed the combine – Foster's, Melbourne, Abbotsford and Victoria. While each brand was parochial in that is was identified with the city of Melbourne or the state of Victoria, the advertising campaign put in place sought to promote a universally Australian image and a unique set of attributes associated with each of the brands. As Dunstan (1987) notes:

> Carlton Draught was presented as a reward for hard work. Foster's Lager was the beer with a distinctive taste. Victoria Bitter was the man's beer. Melbourne Bitter was depicted with rural settings and Abbots was the beer for the fellow with the discriminating taste.
>
> (Dunstan 1987: 133–360)

This image building was reinforced by the redesign of labels of all packaged beers with particular attention being paid to their colour and shape. The Carlton trade mark of its team of Clydesdale horses pulling the brewery cart was heavily promoted, recalling an earlier age when fewer divisions existed between city and country. The advertisements appealed to nationalistic images through their use of location shots, and drawing on core values of loyalty, mateship and the promotion of beer as reward for a fair day's work. Well-known actors were used in the voice-overs and actors in the television commercials were cast as representatives of stereotypes of the various target consumer groups for each brand (Dunstan 1987: ch. 12).

Responding to the threat of Courage in its core market honed CUB's marketing skills in ways that were essential prerequisites for the brewery's later attempts to 'Fosterise the world' (Dunstan 1987: ch. 18; Hewat 1988: ch. 7). There was unprecedented product innovation in Australia, following trends in the United States, with the release of a premium beer, Crown Lager, and a range of light alcohol beers. Advertising expenditures soared. Old-style point-of-sale advertising was extended to raise brand awareness as even the taps dispensing draught beer in tied houses were marked with the company's logo. Point of sale advertising was swamped by expenditure on product and brand exposure in the print media and particularly television. By the mid-1970s both Courage and CUB had entered the realms of sponsorship by giving financial support to football teams in the Victorian Australian rules competition which paid off in terms of a vast television audience (Dunstan 1987: 153). Perhaps the most important innovation in the longer term was the promotion of Foster's as an international beer with a series of television advertisements which ran from around 1976 until about 1983 showing Foster's being consumed in the cosmopolitan capitals of the world (Bruce Siney, personal communication, 1992). Foster's was to become Australia's first truly national brand (Langfield-Smith 1991b: 87).

The battle between Courage and CUB in Victoria, won decisively by Carlton, was little more than a sideshow for what was to follow. The sale of Courage's plant to a Sydney brewer, Tooth's, in 1978, signalled the death knell of the old order of market sharing. Regional markets disappeared in a wave of mergers in the late 1970s and early 1980s which resulted in the emergence of two national brewers, CUB, now owned by John Elliott's Elders IXL, and Bond Brewing, part of Alan Bond's empire. The new owners, whose corporations were heavily in debt, looked to their breweries to generate large cash flows from the sale of beer and to strengthen their balance sheets from the revaluation of brewery and hotel real estate. A national market for beer generated fierce competition with marketing strategies playing a major role. CUB and Bond were estimated to be spending $40 million each on advertising and promotion in 1985 or nearly 7 per cent of local sales (Australian Bureau of Statistics, ABS 1987; Dunstan 1987: 196 and 208–10). Much of this increased expenditure reflected the launch of new products, particularly the introduction of low alcohol beers. Stagnating per capita sales from the 1970s, a result of increases in excise duties, tough penalties for drunken driving and changing tastes, meant that increased revenues could come only from taking market share from the rivals. CUB won the battle by lifting its share from around 45 per cent of domestic sales in 1987 to nearly 50 per cent in 1989–90 (Shoebridge 1990: 34–6). It had more experience in managing production across a number of regional breweries, its new plants were highly efficient, and it had a better known set of brands, including Foster's. The earlier promotion of Foster's as a national brand paid handsome dividends.

The export drive

Both CUB and Bond breweries displayed a commitment to selling their brands overseas from the mid-1980s that was entirely new. The incentive for this strategy was essentially that driving the battle for market share in Australia, increased revenues. The undoubted ability of Australian brewers to produce consistently high-quality beers and the newly developed skills to command brand loyalties that were forged in the battle for domestic sales gave the new owners confidence to lift their ambitions about what might be achieved in the UK market.

It is important to recognize that the UK market for beer had been shifting from the 1970s in ways which greatly facilitated the acceptance of Australian beers. In particular, there was a marked shift in preference to lager rather than ale, the share of lager in total consumption rising from 4 per cent in 1967 to more than 45 per cent in 1987 while total sales stagnated. Lager consumption was concentrated in the more affluent and rapidly growing southern and eastern regions of the UK (Monopolies and Mergers Commission 1989). In many respects the UK market was undergoing a similar transition to that experienced in Australia decades before. The shift from ale to lager was driven by a variety of factors. Not the least important was the increased experience of mass travel by UK residents to other predominantly lager-consuming parts of the world. Rising incomes, improved housing standards, ownership of household appliances such as refrigerators and the ownership of motor cars, all conspired to change drinking habits. Sales of packaged beer rose relatively to draught, although draught still dominated the market.

Seeding a niche market: Foster's Lager

In these circumstances Australian brands, especially Foster's Lager, were particularly well placed to take advantage of the market opportunities that were presenting themselves. Foster's Lager had an established presence in the UK market from the late 1950s or early 1960s when Reginald Fogarty, the chief executive officer of Carlton, sent Foster's Lager in anticipation of his business trips to London so he could entertain with his own product (Bruce Siney, personal communication, 1992). Large numbers of expatriate young Australians came to Britain via P&O liners and more recently by QANTAS flights to study or to escape what was seen as the crushing conformity of Australian life under the conservative government of Robert Menzies. A disproportionate number of them lived in London. One young émigré, Barry Humphries, lampooned his gauche, homesick and, above all, intemperate countrymen who 'huddled in the Anglo-phobic ghetto of Earl's Court [where] they burnt gum leaves, frequented the few pubs which sold Australian beer and complained about the Poms'. The hugely popular adventures of one archetypal ocker, 'Barry McKenzie', began as a cartoon strip in *Private Eye* in 1963. Foster's Lager made the first of its many appearances in the ninth panel (Humphries 1988: x).

This combination of Australian-born residents and growing numbers of in-bound tourists together with free advertising in a cult magazine through the 1960s gave Foster's a niche market. A new and unexpected group of consumers, the next generation of Earl's Court residents, West Indians, developed a tremendous thirst for Foster's during the 1975 test series (Dunstan 1987: 151). Without any conscious marketing effort on the part of Australian breweries, exports of beer to the UK rose from 165,000 litres in 1960–1 to 759,000 a decade later (*Australian Trade Bulletins*, various dates). Consumption of Australian beer, 80 per cent of which was Foster's in 26 fluid ounce cans (Dunstan 1987: 152), grew at a compound rate of nearly 16 per cent per year. The next decade saw a continuation of these growth rates as exports leapt to 5,005,000 litres in 1980–1 (ABS, *Australian Exports*, various dates) or a compound rate of growth of nearly 21 per cent per year. By 1983 and 1984 the figure had surged to about 12.5 million litres. Australian brands made up nearly 10 per cent of total imports or about a half of 1 per cent of total consumption (Monopolies and Mergers Commission 1989: Fig. 2.11 and para. 2.16).

Selling packaged beer to an import agent who found retail outlets allowed Australian brewers to escape high barriers to entry which existed in the markets for draught ale and lagers arising from the structure of the brewing industry in the UK. Six national brewers supplied three-quarters of all production and exercised considerable control over the distribution of their brands, having integrated forward into wholesale and retail outlets (Monopolies and Mergers Commission 1989). However, the market power available to the brewers through vertical integration was being eroded (Hawkins 1979: 292). While draught beer had 70–80 per cent of the national market from the late 1960s to the late 1980s, that still left a very large market, some 7 million barrels, for packaged beers, particularly lager. Australian beers could find outlets via wholsesalers through 'free' houses whose sales were growing at twice the rate of tied houses in the late 1970s (*The Economist*, 16 June 1979: 78) and through clubs and off-licences who had 20 and 10 per cent respectively of the beer market (*The Economist*, 16 December 1978: 118) of whose prices were lower than in pubs (*The Economist*, 6 May 1978: 118). Changes in licensing laws in 1961 stimulated the growth of off-licences (G. Johnson and Thomas 1987: 345), the numbers of which increased from 30,000 to 50,000 from 1967 to 1987 (Monopolies and Mergers Commission 1989: 1). Additional outlets came from supermarket chains.

Foster's Lager, the principal export product, competed in the UK premium market with other imported lagers such as Carlsberg,

Tuborg, Kronenbourg, Budweiser and Miller's Lite. However, it was still targeted almost exclusively at young Australian expatriates. Despite the high price, which was determined by adding the commission of the importer, Austral Development, and the wholesale and retail margins to the landed price, the gross margins were lower than for most of the other lagers. For instance, in 1983 the average landed price of Australian beer was 43p per litre compared to 25p for West German and 14p for Irish imports (Kilgore and Alchin 1990: 7).

Niche market to mass market: old brands, new brands

The sales of Australian brands in the UK market were transformed from the early 1980s by the production of those brands under licence by British brewers and the direct investment in brewing capacity and distribution networks by Elders IXL. Imports of Australian beers peaked in 1984 at 12.8 million litres before falling to 5.4 million the next year (ABS Cty *Exports*, various years). At the same time total supplies placed on the market rose as both CUB (which was absorbed by Elders IXL in 1983) and Bond Brewing followed the example of many other foreign breweries in having their beers produced in the UK under licence.

CUB was attracted to a licence agreement as its export sales into the UK market were threatened by increased import duties following Britain's full membership of the European Community (Bruce Siney, personal communication, 1992). CUB was involved in discussions with a number of potential partners in 1980 when they were approached by Watney, Mann & Truman. Watney's interest sprang from the recent termination of their long-standing arrangement with Carlsberg to produce that company's draught lager under licence as Carlsberg began production in its own facilities (Monopolies and Mergers Commission 1989: para. 2.29). A CUB executive recalled the origins of the 1981 agreement: 'Watney's came to us. We didn't approach them and at first we were a bit sceptical. They wanted a product which wouldn't be confused with all the other European lagers on the UK market' (Dunstan 1987: 164).

The carefully negotiated arrangement with Watney's had important consequences for CUB's marketing strategies. First, Watney's was to share the distribution of Foster's Lager with the existing importer, Austral Developments, from the middle of 1981 until receiving exclusive rights to do so from October 1983 (Carlton and United Brewery 1981: internal documents). Watney's 4,500 tenanted and 1,700 managed hotels provided a far wider distribution channel than

Austral Development could match (Dunstan 1987: 163; Langfield-Smith 1991a: Fig. 5.4, 72). The volumes envisaged necessitated formulating a marketing campaign to promote Foster's. CUB marketing executives vetoed the campaign plan proposed by Watney's and insisted on the use of the Australian comedian Paul Hogan to sell Foster's. The fifty television commercials made by Hogan in the 1980s were widely successful in appealing to the British public and Australian expatriates and tourists. His laconic sense of humour and innate warmth personified Australian values. His charismatic persona imbued Foster's products with the same personality. Foster's and to a lesser extent other Australian brands rose to success on the back of the propagation of an extraordinarily positive view of Australia and things Australian among young middle-class people living in southern England (Bruce Siney, personal communication, 1992).

The success of Foster's Lager in the UK market led to its being brewed under licence. The original licence agreement with Watney's was that they would brew a new brand, Foster's Draught, designed specifically for the UK market. This product was sold primarily through the Watney's estate. By 1984, after even more difficult negotiations, CUB made its yeasts and brewing specifications available to Watney's to enable Foster's Lager to be produced in Britain. The marketing campaign now promoted both Foster's brands, Draught and the famous Lager. These were so successful that by 1985 Foster's brands, imported and locally produced, had captured 6 per cent of the UK lager market and 12 per cent of the London trade (Dunstan 1987: 163–4).

Bond Brewing was quick to follow suit having Castlemaine XXXX manufactured under licence by Allied Lyons and later by Courage and distributed through their pubs. As a result of this arrangement, which began in 1985, and heavy promotional expenditure Castlemaine XXXX had become the sixth largest selling draught beer by 1988 with nearly 5 per cent of the market. This brand briefly eclipsed Foster's share before slipping behind (Bond Corporation Holdings Ltd 1987: 15, 26; Langfield-Smith 1991a: Fig, 5.6, 73). Bond Brewing's other leading brands, Swan Premium and Swan Special Light, were also produced by Allied Lyons from 1987 and 1988 respectively (Bond Corporation Holdings Ltd 1988).

Having generated a powerful brand image of an Australian association, both CUB and Bond Brewing used the full gamut of domestic marketing strategies abroad to promote awareness of their products. Sponsorship of sporting events in the UK attracted a huge audience through TV coverage of cricket, rugby union, snooker, athletics, soccer, horse racing and Formula 1 motor racing (Elders IXL, *Annual Reports*, various years). Foster's was the 'official' beer for the Australian team at the 1984 Los Angeles Olympic games (Dunstan 1987: 191, 208). Bond's campaigns in the America's Cup 12 metre yacht races in 1983 and 1987 brought his Swan brand into international prominence (Barry 1990: ch. 12). By the mid-1980s these promotional campaigns had captured about 10 per cent of the UK lager market for Australian brands.

Joint ventures were a halfway house between exporting and direct investment in production facilities and their associated distribution channels. These arrangements were an invaluable learning experience. First, working with a brewer rather than through wholesale and retail distributors gave both companies a better insight into the technical capabilities and cost structures of UK brewers. Considerable opportunities existed to achieve a cost advantage over rivals who had not made the necessary investment in new plant and work practices (Cox 1990: 58–61). Second, CUB and Bond Brewing were much closer to the market that they were committed to serve. The success of the Hogan advertising campaign gave CUB insights into the communication engineering necessary to trigger the emotive responses that led consumers to buy their products (Bruce Siney, personal communication, 1992). The later decision to enter the market as a stand-alone brewer was conditional in large measure on the confidence that had been developed by the success of the joint ventures. Third, the successful launch of new brands such as Foster's Draught and Bond's brands had given important insights into marketing strategies, particularly market segmentation (*The Economist*, 2 September 1989: 57–8), brand positioning and package variation (Greer 1981: 101–2).

The final assault on the UK market took the form of acquisition of domestic brewers and their distribution networks. Direct foreign investment in UK brewing was made possible by the change of ownership of CUB. Although Elders IXL purchased CUB in 1983 it ran the brewery at arm's length until Lou Mangan retired as chief executive in February 1985. The appointmnent of a senior Elders' executive, Peter Bartels, signalled the dawn of an new era. Elders had ambitious plans for its brewing arm which included generating much of its revenues overseas. Europe and North America were recognized as the world's largest markets (Karrenbrock 1990; Kilgore and Alchin 1990; Langfield-Smith 1991a). Building up production capacity in the UK, a market where CUB brands were well established, would provide a beach-head for entry to the unified Europe market from 1992.

Elders, and John Elliott in particular, moved with characteristic speed by making a bid for Allied Lyons in October 1985 only eight months after Bartel's took command at CUB. Elders IXL had become a large conglomerate whose growth resulted to a large degree from debt-financed acquisitions. Elliott and his associates were experienced in financing large take-overs. The strength of the conglomerate's balance sheet and credit rating was employed in its bid of A$4 billion for Allied Lyons. No stand-alone Australian brewer could have mounted a bid for the much larger British company. Although Elders let its bid for Allied lapse after the matter was referred to the Monopolies and Mergers Commission it acquired Courage Breweries in September 1986 for £1.3 billion (Kilgore and Alchin 1990: 9–11). This purchase gave CUB control of brands that already held 9 per cent of the market (Monopolies and Mergers Commission 1989: Fig. 2.5, 16), together with 3,671 tenanted pubs, 1,334 managed pubs, a wine and spirit wholesaler and a chain of 386 off-licences (Denton 1987: 264–68; Dunstan 1987: 214; Kilgore and Alchin 1990: 8–13).

Having made its acquisition, Elders was no longer constrained by a complex contract with another party. Control was more complete and swifter in its execution. As the owner of brewing, packaging and distribution capacity Elders moved quickly to reduce costs (for an example of the potential savings and productivity gains see Cox 1990) and to improve quality. The world-class technical standards achieved in their Australian brewing operations were impressed on Courage's three plants. Heavy investments were made to increase capacity and to upgrade facilities, with £15.5 million being spent on the Bristol brewery (Elders IXL, *Annual Reports*, various years). By 1988 Courage's Berkshire brewery was the lowest cost producer in the country (Elders IXL, *Annual Reports*, various years). Economies in brewing were matched by the attention paid to the handling and presentation of the draught beers at point of sale in the tied and managed pubs. In the words of Elders' Brewing: 'To ensure that the high quality of product leaving the breweries is reflected in the presentation at point of sale, new dispense [*sic*] methods and standards have been adopted and a programme commenced to modify all pubs so that these standards are met throughout the estate' (Elders IXL, *Annual Report* 1989: 16).

Elders continued to expand its brewing capacity and share of distribution outlets in the late 1980s and early 1990s. The Irish brewer Beamish & Cornford, that was producing Foster's under licence, came under direct managerial control (Elders IXL, *Annual Report* 1987: 15) following Elders' acquisition of its parent, the Canadian brewer Carling O'Keefe, in April 1987 (Kilgore and Alchin 1990: 24–5). A strategic shareholding in the East Anglian-based brewer, Greene King, in late 1987 enabled Foster's to be distributed throughout another 770 pubs (Kilgore and Alchin 1990: 13–14). Not all the bids were successful. Elders failed to acquire Scottish and Newcastle (Kilgore and Alchin 1990: 14–17). However, that disappointment was compensated for by a complex pubs-for-breweries swap between Courage, Elders' brewing arm in the UK, and Grand Metropolitan, which was already producing Foster's under licence (Monopolies and Mergers Commission 1988: 461). The deal, which involved Courage exchanging some of its 5,000 hotels for Grand Met's four breweries, aroused the concerns of the regulatory authorities. Consent to the deal was finally forthcoming on 19 November 1990 (Kilgore and Alchin 1990: 17–24).

Strong marketing programmes, increased production in the UK by owned breweries or joint ventures, plus a still not inconsiderable import of Australian brewed beers, and greater access to distribution channels dramatically lifted the share of Australian brands. By 1986 Foster's and Bond Brewing's XXXX held more than 8 per cent of the UK draught lager market (Langfield-Smith 1991a: Fig. 5.7, 72–3). Foster's Draught, brewed locally, enjoyed great success displacing Carlsberg in 1988 to become the third largest selling draught lager before achieving second place in the next year (Elders IXL, *Annual Reports*, 1988; 1989). Bond products were not far behind. Castlemaine XXXX brewed under licence by Allied Lyons had become the sixth largest selling draught lager by 1988 while its new 400 ml can enjoyed 'the most successful lager beer introduction in the past 10 years' (Bond Corporation Holdings Ltd 1988). Elders held the whip hand through its greater production capacity. Its acquisition of Courage in late 1986 had brought nearly 10 per cent of the market for ale and lager, draught and packaged (First Boston Australia Ltd 1989: Appendix 11.1.1., 100). The Grand Met arrangement gave Elders, whose brewing arm was spun off as Foster's Brewing in March 1990, nearly one-fifth of the brewing capacity in the UK.

WINE

The global wine and beer industries: some comparisons

Whereas the global beer industry is highly concentrated, the global wine industry has been characterized by a long history of fragmentation and the dominance of family-owned enterprises. In the 1970s and 1980s, however, the structure of the industry was markedly altered by the entry of transnational beverage corporations. A process of rationalization and increased concentration began. Even so, and again in contrast to the beer industry, vertical integration remains limited. It is the exception to the rule for a single company to undertake each of the three main tasks of cultivating grapes, making the wine and distributing it. Commonly, contracts between wineries and growers and between wineries and distributors/importers are used to link the players in the three stages. Wine differs from beer too in that it is one of those rare commodities which is branded on the basis of its geographical origin. One consequence is that the ability of wine producers to influence consumer choice is much more limited than that of beer producers. The latter are able to promote specific brands for different market segments. A further consequence of the wine industry's geographical specificity, and another contrast with the beer industry, is that it is virtually impossible to use licensing agreements and to set up subsidiaries as part of a global marketing strategy. Exports have been and will continue to be the main route by which the globalization of the wine industry occurs (Cavanagh and Clairmonte 1985: 82–3).

Australian wine exports to Britain

Australia has been exporting wine to Britain for a long time. A rapid expansion in domestic production and in exports to Britain occurred during the interwar period (Windett 1933: 126–30). A Wine Export Bounty Act was passed by the federal government in 1924. The following year the British government granted to Australia and other imperial wine producing countries a 50 per cent preferential margin over foreign wine. As Evans (1990) explains, price was the key to the increased sales to Britain during this period:

> The wine was sold at a lower price than the European product, partly because it was regarded as inferior to the wines of Europe. The cheap fortified sweet red 'port style' wines sold well compared to more expensive Port from Portugal. Heavy, fruity Australian reds were sold as 'Australian Burgundy', which was advertised as being good for the health. This burgundy was alleged to contain lots of iron and thus be good for anaemia and invalids . . . Australian 'boarding-house burgundy' had a lowly reputation in Britain, and obviously the main reason it was bought was because it was a cheap form of alcohol.
>
> (Evans 1900: 47)

It was a mark of the success of Australian wine exports to Britain that a Wine Overseas Marketing Act was passed in 1929, which established a Wine Overseas Marketing Board whose primary purpose was to co-ordinate the export trade. This was renamed the Australian Wine Board in 1963 (Department of National Development 1952: 370).

Exports of Australian wine were severely hampered during the Second World War. In 1941 the British government imposed an embargo on imports of wines and spirits. Although the embargo was eventually removed, tariffs on all wines entering Britain were increased and the margin of preference on Empire wines was greatly reduced. Exports to Britain continued during the 1950s, 1960s and 1970s but at levels way below those achieved during the interwar years. In 1960 the Australian Wine Board took the initiative of estab-lishing the Australian Wine Centre in Soho, London. This was financed by the Board and by seventeen leading Australian wine com-panies. The Wine Centre was eventually closed in March 1982, shortly before the great boom in exports began (Evans 1990: 47). Part of the problem facing Australian exporters was the generally poor image of their product among British consumers, encapsulated in terms such as 'Kangarouge' and 'Chateau Chunder'. A major expansion in exports would require, among other things, the eradication of this image.

Against this unpromising background, a dramatic change occurred in the mid-1980s. The Australian wine industry became increasingly export conscious and export drives began to be launched in Britain, North America and, more recently, North-East Asia. The success of these drives has been remarkable, especially in Britain. Exports to Britain grew from 800,000 litres in 1985, at the start of the export drive, to 18.2 million litres in 1991 (Whitwell 1992). They have continued to rise since then.

Wine consumers versus beer consumers

In one sense, then, Australian wine companies are similar to Aus-tralian brewers in that they have enjoyed considerable success in selling their product in the UK in recent years. The challenges facing beer and wine industries, however, were noteworthy more for their differences than for their similarities. Out of necessity, quite different marketing strategies were adopted. The explanation for the increased market share of Australian beer in the UK cannot also be applied to wine. One difference in the challenge facing those who were marketing Australian beer and those marketing Australian wine was that they were selling to quite different sorts of consumers. Furthermore, while the promotion of beer involved a product with relatively few brands, the promotion of wine involved a great multiplicity of brands.

It is important to understand that decisions about which wine to buy are altogether more complex than choices about beer. The choice for the table wine consumer begins with having to make a decision on things such as whether to buy sparkling or still wine and then to choose between red, white and rosé. Consider the British consumer who has decided to buy a bottle of white wine. There is an excellent chance that the consumer will be a woman: wine is drunk more often by women, although fewer men never drink it. Our consumer is also likely to be in either the 25–34 year old or 35–44 year old age group. Visiting the local supermarket or off-licence shop, she is faced with a bewildering array of wines. It may be of course that our consumer remains unaffected by the choices available: she has that thing wine companies are so anxious to acquire, brand loyalty. Assume that she does not or that she has decided that she might like to try something new. What does she do? She narrows the selection by deciding on the maximum price she is willing to pay. For some consumers price is everything: anything will do provided it is cheap. For other consumers, setting a maximum price is merely the first step in making the selection of wine more manageable. What other factors might be involved? Perhaps our consumer is attracted to a particular label: she finds something appealing about the design. Perhaps she reads the winemaker's description or a quotation from a wine writer placed strategically above the bottle. Perhaps, in the off-licence shop, she seeks advice from a sales assistant. For those consumers whose knowledge of wine is more than rudimentary, their decisions will involve a consideration of the grape variety to be chosen: will it be Chardonnay, Muscat, Semillon, Riesling, Fumé Blanc . . . ? Another consideration, another way of narrowing the selection, is to consider the country in which the wine has been produced. Again, the variety can be bewildering: French, German, Austrian, Italian, Spanish, Chilean, New Zealand, Californian, Bulgarian, Australian. . . . Assume that our consumer has been attracted to two bottles of white wine, one from Spain at £3.85 and one from Australia at £3.95. Which will she choose? The decision will depend partly, if not largely, on the image she has of Australian and Spanish wines in general. For the more sophisticated wine drinker the decision will also be affected by knowledge of the different winemakers, the particular region in which the wine has been produced and the particular vintage. There are still other reasons why the choice of wine is a complex one. It may be that the consumer has to decide on what her guests are likely to enjoy and what will impress them. She might also have to decide on whether the wine will suit the particular meal she has in mind.

In summary, the marketing of wine must of necessity aim to educate consumers. Consumers have to be educated in the enjoyment of wine, in understanding the characteristics of wine produced in different countries and in different regions by different winemakers. They also have to learn about the great varieties of winegrapes. Even more importantly, the marketing of wine must aim to make consumer choice a less perplexing task.

Generic promotion: the role of the Australian Wine and Brandy Corporation

The decision as to who would market Australian beers was obvious enough: the breweries would take responsibility. Things were not as straightforward with wine. Certainly the task could have been left to individual wine producers. In the 'pioneering' days of the early 1980s this was in fact the case: companies such as Brown Brothers and Orlando attempted, with some success, to market their own products. Austrade, a division of the federal Department of Trade, provided valuable but limited assistance. From the mid-1980s, however, a radical change occurred. The efforts of individual companies were complemented, and to an extent superseded, by the promotional activities of the Australian Wine and Brandy Corporation (AWBC) which was the successor to the Australian Wine Board.

The AWBC is a federal government statutory marketing authority. It is funded by contributions from industry members. Voting power is determined by the size of the contribution. Among the corporation's various responsibilities is that of promoting and controlling the export of grape products from Australia. In 1991 the AWBC adopted a new mission statement and objectives. Its mission was 'to enhance the global demand for Australian wine by creating a marketing environment in which wine producers, individually and collectively, are able, through their own initiatives, to achieve maximum long-term demand for their products' (AWBC 1992: 1). The new set of objectives included trying to achieve for the Australian wine industry 'an international reputation for assurance of product quality', to improve 'the knowledge and image of Australian wine within the industry's target export markets', to facilitate 'the promotion of wine from Australia by producers in major export markets', and to achieve a corporate image which enhanced confidence in the corporation and in the Australian wine industry (AWBC 1992: 1).

The new mission statement and objectives were in effect a formal affirmation of what AWBC had been attempting to do for several years. An initiative of great importance was that of establishing in London a two-person committee called the Australian Wine Bureau, with funding provided by the AWBC and 39 contributing members. This was done in 1986. Hazel Murphy, a former Austrade representative, was appointed marketing and promotions director. She was to play a critical role.

The Australian Wine Bureau's task, in effect, was to encourage those consumers trying to decide which wine to buy, to choose an Australian wine. This also meant, necessarily, trying to convince wine distributors and wine writers to take an interest in Australian wine, indeed to be enthusiastic supporters of it. The initial campaign was a generic one: the aim was not to promote regions or individual brands but rather to generate interest in Australian wines generally. This involved trying to ensure that Australian wine was associated with a particular image. The image, as Hazel Murphy describes it, was that of 'the honest bottle'. To buy a bottle of Australian wine meant buying something that was very competitively priced and excellent quality. Consumers could and should feel that when they bought an Australian wine they were getting something which was undeniably 'value for money'.

Ensuring high quality

There is a contrast here with the way Australian beer was marketed. The AWBC could not itself ensure that the image accorded with reality: it had no direct control over prices and as for quality it could only really ensure that certain minimum standards were met. It was also true that the efforts of successful exporters could have been spoiled by the self-defeating tactics of other Australian companies. There are frequent examples in industry journals and in press reports of representatives from companies such as Orlando, Penfolds and Brown Brothers warning of the need for would-be exporters to ensure that they allowed only premium quality wines to enter the British market. Just as often there were warnings about the importance of avoiding price discounting. That these warnings were nearly always heeded can be ascribed only to the existence of what leading wine companies like to call 'industry willpower'. An example of the exercise of this willpower was the introduction in 1989 of a labelling integrity programme which sought to ensure the accuracy of information on labels regarding nomenclature, vintage and the region from which grapes were harvested. Together with the use of random sampling of wines at the time of shipment, and the AWBC's control over the granting of approval to export, the industry has attempted to ensure that the 'Wine of Australia' theme – 'Consistently good every year' – has been met.

The fact that Australian wines were, as a rule, of very high quality was no accident. We come back to a point mentioned at the start of this chapter: success in selling both beer and wine abroad was dependent on the prior achievement of certain domestic developments. Of considerable importance was a radical change in consumer preferences away from fortified wines to table wines. Walter James complained in 1952 that

> Port joins sweet sherry and muscat to form the terrible trinity of the Australian wine trade and reflects everything that is bad about it, not because these wines are disagreeable when well made but because the enormous demand of undiscriminating wine-saloon drinkers whose simple urge is for something sweet and strong has given rise to a yearly saccharine deluge pressed out of grapes of the first variety that comes to hand and bottled and put on the market almost as soon as the last fermentation bubble has risen.
>
> (James 1952: 91)

It would have been much more difficult to make this complaint twenty years later. By then, for reasons to do with the rising affluence of Australians and the greater incidence of travel to Europe as well as the impact of an ambitious post-war migration programme, the popularity of fortified wines had fallen markedly. By contrast, table wines emerged triumphant. Table wine was purchased either in bottles or, during the 1960s, in half-gallon flagons or, during the 1970s, in the much-loved one-gallon wine cask (an Australian invention). Furthermore, the palate of an increasing number of Australian wine drinkers had begun to appreciate the flavour of somewhat drier varieties. This transition in drinking habits and preferences has sometimes been described as the demise of the colonial influence and the rise of the continental influence.

One of the consequences of this shift in consumer preferences and, arguably, one of the reasons for it, was the fact that some of the major Australian wine companies became more sensitive from the late 1960s to the need to mount an effective marketing campaign. Some companies, notably Penfolds, anticipated the change but they were the exception to the rule (Layton 1969: 160–9). The aim of the domestic marketing campaigns was to promote the consumption of wine and to educate Australian consumers about wine (for examples, see Layton 1968: 117–24; 1974: 106–20). Those who took the lead here were later able to apply some of the lessons acquired in their domestic marketing ventures to the task of export marketing. Indeed success abroad was dependent on success in domestic marketing.

There were many other consequences of the shift in consumer preferences which, collectively, produced an upheaval in the Australian wine industry during the 1960s and 1970s. Vineyards began to be planted in areas of 'cool climate' suited to the production of premium quality wines. New varieties of wine grapes were planted in the 'cool climate' vineyards. In the older ones, Grenache, Mataro and Crouchen vines were uprooted: sherry and junk-wine vineyards were progressively eliminated and replaced by varieties such as Chardonnay, Sauvignon Blanc and Riesling. Accompanying the shift to table wines was a technological revolution (for a comparison of Australian developments with what was happening in other New World countries, see H. Johnson 1989: ch. 42). By the 1980s there had emerged a new breed of winemakers, technically sophisticated, innovative, willing to break with tradition, and who turned for assistance to scientists and a variety of other tertiary graduates (notably ones with computing skills) to improve the quality and consistency of their wines.

Another domestic development of great importance was the rationalization which occurred in the 1980s. The background to the rationalization was the emergence in the first half of the 1980s of chronic overproduction. Domestic sales slowed and, near the end of the decade, actually fell. Profits declined and margins, already slender, were reduced. A number of federal taxation initiatives served only to make the situation worse. It was in the midst of these difficulties that the export drive began – a panacea, so some believed, for their domestic ills.

Mergers, acquisitions and take-overs occurred with remarkable regularity, with the result that over time a smaller number of companies enjoyed a larger share of domestic sales. By 1990 just three companies – Penfolds, Orlando and Hardy's – held almost 60 per cent of domestic wine sales. One of the major benefits of this rationalization was that, with the major players reduced to a handful, it became that much easier to achieve what was referred to earlier as 'industry willpower'. There were other consequences of the rationalization. The 1980s saw the end of a long era of domination by family-owned firms which, as a rule, were product-oriented rather than market-oriented, were inward-looking, were unaware of the concept of long-term planning, and took no interest in mass marketing.

Unlike the achievement of high-quality standards, the competitive prices of Australian wines were due much less to conscious decision.

They resulted in part from the simple fact that the cost of producing wine in Australia was considerably less than in a great many other countries, which in turn was due largely to the fact that land was relatively cheap and to the industry's technological sophistication. There was also an important element of chance: the start of the export drive in the mid-1980s coincided with the collapse of the Australian dollar. The Australian currency has remained in a parlous state ever since.

Being seen as good value for money did not necessarily mean being seen as cheap. Almost invariably, Australian wine companies avoided the lower-end price threshold. Tim Atkin (1992) observed that

> The crucial fact as far as Australia is concerned is that the price of Australian wine is considerably higher than the general price of wines from other countries. As Michael Paul, director of Penfolds Europe, points out: 'For Australia, the growth has come in the £3–5 range, which is well above the average price of £2.78.' Further encouragement is provided by a second statistic – 80 per cent of wine retails at under £2.99. Australia, in other words, has a 15 per cent share of sales above £2.99.

> (Atkin 1992: 25)

The Australians were aware that if they pushed the majority of their wines into the upper-end price threshold – say from £10 upwards – they would run into what is known as the label problem: at £10 a bottle of wine with a French label would almost invariably be chosen over one with an Australian label, irrespective of the quality.

Creating an image

The 'honest bottle' image had another dimension. Amidst the adulteration scandals plaguing the Italian and Austrian wine industries and amidst the Chernobyl disaster of early 1986, Australia could be promoted as an isolated country of vast open spaces and pure air, far removed from the evils of pollution, and enjoying perennial sunshine. The idea took hold that Australia produced 'clean' and full-flavoured wines, perfect for the British palate. Some British wine writers began to describe Australian wine as 'bottled sunshine'.

In promoting this sort of image of Australia there was some similarity with the promotional campaigns of the Australian brewers. The wine industry, however, had no intention of associating its product with a character such as Paul Hogan. More importantly, whereas beer relied heavily on television and on advertising, the

Australian Wine Bureau concentrated on the strategy of getting glasses directly into people's hands, principally by organizing as many wine tastings as possible for trade and press, exhibiting at all the major trade fairs and any other wine and food shows that might yield results, and arranging for press visits by British wine writers to Australian wineries and wine districts. Hazel Murphy's conviction was that once consumers had tasted the wines they would find out for themselves just how good the product was and would thereby become its most effective advocates.

As part of its strategy of generic promotion, the AWBC introduced a distinctive corporate identity logo for the Australian wine industry. The logo was and continues to be displayed at all promotional events arranged through the corporation. It is reproduced on all official correspondence and publications and, so the corporation argued in 1992, 'is being progressively incorporated into export label design and packaging by an increasing number of Australian wine exporters'.

> In order to capture attention in the competitive international market place dominated by long-established and internationally famous brands [the AWBC announced] the simple uncomplicated statement 'WINE OF AUSTRALIA' has been combined with an explicit graphic symbol which communicates a similar visual message of 'wine' – the leaf of the grapevine, with the message 'of Australia' – symbolised by the image of the unique Australian kangaroo.
>
> (AWBC 1992: 7)

Peter Lewis of the Wine and Spirit Association argues that 'fundamental marketing principles' suggest that

> The most effective way to market a product is to differentiate completely by branding it, the second most effective way is to differentiate first the type of product, to promote it generically then develop a brand that is market leader in that field. In either case the larger the market the greater the need for product identity followed closely by good distribution; all that then has to be done is to so organize production of those products which offer genuine consumer benefits and distribute them to segments of the market that have been targetted.
>
> (Lewis 1989: 124)

The Australian wine industry chose a blend of these two strategies. While the AWBC was concentrating on promoting Australian wine, individual companies were simultaneously promoting particular labels. Unlike the AWBC, the latter made much use of advertising. The nature of this advertising could and did vary, though all companies shunned the use of television. At one extreme there was Rosemount's bold and brash 'Big Australian Red' posters plastered on London buses. At the other was Brown Brothers' elegant photographs of a bottle of wine set amidst appetising foodstuffs; accompanying the photograph was a text which did nothing to promote the fact that this was Australian wine and which stressed instead its qualities and the courses the wine best suited.

In the quotation above, Lewis refers to the importance of 'good distribution'. Another way in which the Australian wine companies faced a different set of challenges to the Australian brewers was that the former faced serious difficulties in establishing firm links with recognized, reliable and strongly supported distribution networks. Some companies sought to overcome the problem by buying British distribution companies. Others took a different tack. Since 1983 the main overseas investors in Australian wine companies and vineyards have been French. In the main, Australian companies actively sought French equity because of the access to distribution facilities that it was believed would come with the investment (Dwyer 1990: 116–18).

Labels and brand names

One of the keys to the success of Australian and other New World wines has been the use of varietal labelling, 'easily remembered and understood, and correlating strongly with colour and flavour' (Croser 1992: 126). Consumers know which sort of wine they are getting. The Wine and Spirit Association of Great Britain and Northern Ireland argues that the labelling of wines with the variety of grape has contributed to the increasingly catholic tastes of the British consumer. This is one of several ways in which labels can provide an important means of reducing consumer uncertainty. Philip Rawstorne (1992) observes that 'Just decoding a German wine label, cluttered with Gothic script, or identifying yet another French chateau inhibits many potential consumers'. This is not the case with varietal labelling: 'There are enough similarities between a Cabernet Sauvignon from California and one from Australia to reassure the drinker that if he has enjoyed one, he will enjoy the other' (Rawstorne 1992: 11).

There has been much debate in Australia about the use of French place names in the labelling of Australian wines: Chablis, Sauternes, Burgundy, White Bordeaux, not to mention Champagne. Some insist that they should be avoided whenever possible and be replaced by distinctively Australian names: Coonawarra, for example, could be used as a generic name for dry red wine (Smith 1991: 11). It has also been suggested that the commercial viability of certain Australian wines has been much weakened by the fact that they are not judged on their own intrinsic quality but rather according to whether they meet French standards. Ross Sheppard (1988) argues, for example, that

> Our best Cabernets . . . are *always* going to go up against the classi-fied growths of Bordeaux, and after all, Cabernet *is* Bordeaux. The English have been dealing with Bordeaux for five hundred years, and so Cabernet is not just a wine, it is expected to be 'Bordeaux', to fit a particular style and consumer perception. We will do much better to stay with the varieties that allow us to do what we are best at, and that is to be creative. We make unsurpassed wines at a given price level – the full-bodied Shiraz is an excellent example – and should make the most of the English love of that style.
>
> (Sheppard 1988: 63)

Familiar and recognizable labels can make the choice of wine less per-plexing. Brown Brothers, for example, have a great number of differ-ent wines but the labels are unique and instantly recognizable. The company developed a logo in the early 1980s and all the labels are built around that logo (Greg Quinn, personal communication, 1992). Pro-vided that experience has taught the consumer that Brown Brothers' wines are of exceptional quality – and the aim of all winemakers should be to build respect for the company brand name – then the choice to be made is simply between the various Brown Brothers' wines on offer. The colour and texture of labels are used to create an expectation of what is in the bottle. This is a complex field. Greg Quinn, export marketing manager at Brown Brothers, explains that the growing sophistication of the Australian market is such that when people see a soft lemony green label they will be expecting something without any wood treatment and probably something with a citrus character, fresh, young and aromatic, but if it is a deep yellow, almost orange-coloured label that looks perhaps a bit old, it is likely to be wood-aged white wine, a Chardonnay or Semillon; anything that is bright brick red is likely to be a Shiraz. Such colour associations, he believes, are not yet relevant in the British market (Greg Quinn, personal communication, 1992). Wine consumption in Britain is so much lower than in Australia: at the end of the 1980s the average level of consumption of wine in Britain was just half a bottle a head per week (Lewis 1989: 121).

Of importance in guiding consumer choice is an indication on the label of whether a wine has won a medal or trophy. On this point, Australian wine companies have been well aware of the importance of international recognition. A silver medal at the Hobart Show may mean nothing to a British consumer. Accompanying the export drive was a decision to enter Australian wines in a host of international competitions, a practice previously shunned. The phenomenal success enjoyed by Australian companies has reinforced consumer confidence, as well as providing copy for wine writers. It is also true, however, that wine companies have not been able to take as much advantage from winning international prizes as one might expect. The labelling of wine bottles in the UK is subject to European Community laws. Until 1989 the EC rules on awards and medals were very stringent. The award could be referred to only on bottles which contained wine from the same container that won the award. The rules were subsequently liberalized somewhat. As Lewis (1989) points out,

> the authorities have now realized (and of course the American pressure behind the scenes has had something to do with it) that it is another way to promote interest in wine. They still say you cannot mention an award unless the wine in question came from the same container as the prize-winning entry, but now they are talking about vat-sized containers: you must have at least 1,000 litres in bottle ready to market.
>
> (Lewis 1989: 122)

CONCLUSION

Marketing played an incredibly important role in the success of Australian beer and wine in the UK. A common feature to both beer and wine was the notion that the products had Australian attributes. With beer the image of 'Australianness' was focused on the personality of Paul Hogan, whereas with wine the 'Australianness' was the timeless environment: the latter was a more disembodied and a geographically physical notion. The relevance of 'Australianness' is likely to continue to be important for the winemakers and less important for the brewers, in part because the latter have their own portfolio of British brands and in part because of marketing campaign could not be linked indefinitely with one personality. In any case, Foster's now presents itself as an international rather than Australian beer. One thing that stands out is that the marketing campaign for beer was conceived in, and directed from, Australia. The same is true for wine, for although the Australian Wine Bureau provided much of the input into how the campaign should be conducted, the Australian industry remained in control. What the beer and wine industries had in common, in other words, was that they did not seek the assistance of British marketing firms to create the marketing campaigns.

ACKNOWLEDGEMENTS

The authors would like to acknowledge the assistance of Wendy Smith and comments by Alan Gunther, University of Melbourne. Greg Quinn, export marketing manager, Brown Brothers Milawa Vineyard Pty Ltd (interviewed 25 August 1992), and Bruce Siney, group director marketing and external relations, Foster's Brewing (interviewed 30 September 1992) provided invaluable insights from an industry perspective.

REFERENCES

Atkin, T. (1992) 'The Oz wine sale of the century', *Age*, 22 June: 21, 25.
Australian Bureau of Statistics (ABS) (1904–92) *Overseas Trade*, catalogue s5409.0, Canberra: ABS.
——— (1957/58–1984/85) *Australian Exports*, catalogue s54090.0, Canberra: ABS.
——— (1987) *Manufacturing Commodities*, catalogue 83030, Canberra: ABS.
——— (1987–92) *Exports*, catalogue 5434.0, Canberra: ABS.
Australian Wine and Brandy Corporation (AWBC) (1992) *News Information*, Adelaide: AWBC.
Barry, P. (1990) *The Rise and Fall of Alan Bond*, Sydney: Bantam.
Bond Corporation Holdings Ltd (various years) *Reports*, Perth: Bond.
Carlton and United Brewery (CUB) (1981; 1984) Internal documents relating to licence agreements with Watney, Mann & Truman, Foster's Brewing Group Ltd, Corporate Office, 1 Garden Street, South Yarra, Victoria, Australia, 3141.
Cavanagh, J. and Clairmonte, F. F. (1985) *Alcoholic Beverages: Dimensions of Corporate Power*, New York: St Martin's Press.
Cox, D. L. (1990) 'Doubling productivity at a major brewery', *Long Range Planning* 24(4): 58–64.
Croser, B. (1992) 'The Australian wine industry: taking a leadership role', *Australian & New Zealand Wine Industry Journal* 7(3): 126–7, 130.
Denton, P. (1987) *Elliott: A Biography of John D. Elliott*, London: Little Hills.
Department of National Development (1952) *The Structure and Capacity of Australian Manufacturing Industries*, Canberra: Commonwealth Government Publishing Service.
Dunstan, K. (1987) *The Amber Nectar: A Celebration of Beer and Brewing in Australia*, Ringwood: Viking O'Neil.
Dwyer, C. (1990) 'The new French connection', *Bulletin* 26 June: 116–18.
Elders IXL (various years) *Reports*, Melbourne: Elders IXL.
Evans, L. (1990) *Len Evans' Complete Book of Australian Wine* (rev. edn), Sydney: Weldon.

First Boston Australia Ltd (1989) *Elders IXL Limited Report on the Value of Fully Paid Ordinary Shares and Opinion Concerning Proposed Takeover Offers*, Melbourne.

Greer, D. F. (1981) 'The causes of concentration in the US brewing industry', *Applied Economics* **11**: 21–34.

Hawkins, K. (1979) 'The Price Commission and the brewing industry: a critical note', *Journal of Industrial Economics* **27**(3): 287–94.

Hewat, T. (1988) *The Elders Explosion*, Sydney: Bay.

Humphries, B. (1988) *The Complete Barry McKenzie*, Sydney: Sun.

James, W. (1952) *Wine in Australia: A Handbook*, Melbourne: Georgian House.

Johnson, G. and Thomas, H. (1987) 'The industry context of strategy, structure and performance: the UK brewing industry', *Strategic Management Journal* **8**: 343–61.

Johnson, H. (1989) *The Story of Wine*, London: Mitchell Beazley.

Kaldor, N. and Silverman, R. (1948) *A Statistical Analysis of Advertising Expenditure and of the Revenue of the Press*, Cambridge: Cambridge University Press.

Karrenbrock, J. D. (1990) 'The internationalisation of the beer brewing industry', *Federal Reserve Bank of St. Louis* November/December: 3–19.

Kelton, C. M. L. and Kelton, W. D. (1982) 'Advertising and interindustry brand shift in the U.S. brewing industry', *Journal of Industrial Economics* **30**(3): 293–303.

Kilgore, A. and Alchin, T. (1990) 'The globalisation of Foster's: a case study of Elders IXL', Working Paper no. 76, Department of Accounting and Finance, University of Western Sydney, Nepean.

Langfield-Smith, K. (1991a) 'Carlton and United Breweries Ltd (B): the internationalisation of the brewing industry' in G. Lewis, A. Morkel and G. Hubbard (eds) *Cases in Australian Strategic Management*, New York: Prentice-Hall.

—— (1991b) 'Carlton and United Breweries (C): the management of organisational change', in G. Lewis, A. Morkel and G. Hubbard (eds) *Cases in Australian Strategic Management*, New York: Prentice-Hall.

Layton, R. A. (1968) 'Penfolds Wine Pty Limited: the introduction to Australia of Penfolds Sparkling Mardi Gras – penetration of an established market', in R. A. Layton (ed.) *Australian Marketing Projects*, Sydney: Hoover Awards for Marketing.

——(1969) 'Penfold Wines Pty Ltd: twenty years to mature', in R. A. Layton (ed.) *Australian Marketing Projects*, Sydney: Hoover Awards for Marketing.

—— (1974) 'Wynn Winegrowers Ltd', in R. A. Layton (ed.) *Australian Marketing Projects*, Sydney: Hoover Awards for Marketing.

Lewis, G., Morkel, A. and Hubbard, G. (eds) (1991) *Cases in Australian Strategic Management*, New York: Prentice-Hall.

Lewis, P. (1989) 'The UK/EEC wine market: implications for Australia', *Australian & New Zealand Wine Industry Journal* **4**(2): 121–4.

McNair, W. A. (1937) *Radio Advertising in Australia*, Sydney: Angus & Robertson.

Merrett, D. T. (1992) 'Changes in the Australian brewery industry 1920–1990', unpublished paper, University of Melbourne.

Monopolies and Mergers Commission (1989) *The Supply of Beer*, London: HMSO.

Rawstorne, P. (1992) 'Follow your nose to the new world', *Financial Times* 22 October: 11

Sheppard, R. (1988) 'UK report', *Australian & New Zealand Wine Industry Journal* 2(2): 63.

Shoebridge, N. (1990) 'CUB shapes up to a revived competitor', *Business Review Weekly* 23 November: 34–6.

Smith, R. L. (1991) 'The Australian wine industry: its achievements and prospects', *National Economic Review* January: 1–13.

Steele, M. (1993) 'The European brewing industry 1992', in G. Johnson and K. Scholes (eds) *Exploring Corporate Strategy: Text and Cases* (3rd edn), New York: Prentice-Hall.

Tremblay, V. J. (1987) 'Scale economies, technological change, and firm-cost asymmetries in the US brewing industry', *Quarterly Review of Economics and Business* 27(2): 71–86.

Unwin, T. (1991) *Wine and the Vine: An Historical Geography of Viticulture and the Wine Trade*, London: Routledge.

Whitwell, G. (1992) 'Bottled sunshine for pasty Poms': an analysis of the Australian wine industry's export success', unpublished paper, University of Melbourne.

Windett, N. (1933) *Australia as Producer and Trader 1920–1932*, Oxford: Oxford University Press.

Part III

Food and non-alcoholic drinks

10 The pause that refreshed the world

The evolution of Coca-Cola's global marketing strategy

August W. Giebelhaus

When one thinks of readily identifiable brand names, the American soft drink giant, Coca-Cola, immediately comes to mind. The firm's distinctive script logo and its pervasive circular red sign testify to the phenomenal marketing success that has made the company perhaps the world's best recognized symbol of global US enterprise. Prior to the Second World War, however, Coca-Cola's presence abroad was limited and the company's profits largely derived from the huge domestic US market. One of the firm's most popular advertising slogans, 'The pause that refreshes', had since the 1920s captured the essence of the company's marketing strategy. As Richard Tedlow (1990) has argued in his study of mass marketing in the United States, the company's genius in advertising and marketing lay as much in its ability to sell the 'concept' of Coca-Cola as well as a beverage:

> Not only was Coke your friend; when you drank it, you became friends with other Coke drinkers. And they were the right kind of people – well-dressed, well-off, happy. There was also a luxurious aspect to Coca-Cola. It was a mystical, dark compound of magical ingredients with indeterminate powers.
>
> (Tedlow 1990: 62)

In the mid-1980s the Coca-Cola Company undertook a high-stakes gamble by tinkering with the mystique that had surrounded the beverage for one hundred years, its supposed secret formula known internally as 'merchandise 7X'. Increasingly frustrated by a relative decline of its dominant US market share and the success of arch-rival Pepsi-Cola's campaign to appeal to a younger generation of soft drink consumers with its sweeter-tasting cola drink, the company opted for a dramatic strategy. On 23 April 1985, the Chief Executive Officer (CEO) Roberto Goizueta announced that Coca-Cola was changing the formula of its flagship beverage. This soft drink, christened 'New

Coke', clearly represented a response to Pepsi. Indeed, Pepsico CEO Roger Enrico boasted prematurely that Coca-Cola's action had signified that Pepsi had won the 'cola wars'. Over the next few months the story of 'New Coke' would establish itself as one of the most spectacular events in the modern history of brands and marketing (Enrico and Kornbluth 1986: 1–14; Oliver 1986: 1–12).

To this day there remains debate as to whether one should interpret the 'New Coke' strategy as one of the biggest blunders or one of the most spectacular achievements in the history of food branding. What quickly became apparent was that brand loyalty to the original product, the drink that had created the firm's reputation, remained much stronger than any of Coke's management team could have envisioned. Thousands of angry telephone calls a day, negative media publicity, and organized resistance and boycotting by ad hoc organizations like 'The Old Cola Drinkers of America' led to the return of the old formula in less than three months. Now marketing the old brand as 'Coca-Cola Classic' alongside 'New Coke', the company tried to capitalize on a bad situation by citing its responsiveness to loyal customers. Increased shelf space to accommodate both products in the crucial supermarket sales category, coupled with the millions of dollars of publicity garnered by the entire incident, have led some cynics to suggest that Coke's management team had cleverly planned the entire episode. The evidence suggests that despite the serendipitous results (Coca-Cola's combined sales of 'New' and 'Classic' Coke would open further space between it and Pepsi), the company could not have predicted what would occur (Oliver 1986: 140–91; Pendergrast 1993: 355–71).

In addition to the tremendous success of Coca-Cola Classic, the firm in other ways now seemed to revert to its traditional pattern of business. There had been relatively recent experiments with diversification strategies in foods (Minute Maid and Hi-C juices, Butternut coffee) and entertainment (Columbia Pictures and Television, Merv Griffin Enterprises). But at the time of the firm's 1986 centennial celebration in Atlanta, 74 per cent of its total operating income came from soft drink activities. Equally as significant, more than 60 per cent of Coca-Cola's total soft drink sales volume originated in international markets where it enjoyed a clear three to one sales advantage over Pepsi-Cola (Coca-Cola Company 1986: 5). As the company moves into the 1990s, it has refocused even more on its traditional business, spinning off most of its non-food divisions. The Coca-Cola brand name, used for so long to describe only one product – the original cola beverage – now appears on a host of related products from 'Diet

Coke' to decaffeinated and fruit-blended versions (e.g. 'Cherry Coke'). How has this American marketing giant come to be such a recognizable force in the world food and beverage industry?

EARLY BEGINNINGS

Coca-Cola originated in 1886 when Jacobs' pharmacy in Atlanta sold its first glass of Joseph Pemberton's concoction, a product advertised for its 'invigorating' as well as refreshing characteristics. During Pemberton's tenure as owner and the first years of control by his successor, Asa G. Candler, who took over the business in 1889, one could obtain the beverage only at the soda fountain. When Candler organized the Coca-Cola Company of Georgia as a chartered corporation in 1892, no bottling of the drink had yet occurred. In 1894 Joseph Biedenharn of Vicksburg, Mississippi, inaugurated the unauthorized distribution of Coca-Cola in bottles along with a line of fruit-flavoured drinks that he had been marketing (Coca-Cola Company 1974: 3–20; Watters 1978: 54–72).

Although a formal arrangement with Biedenharn later emerged, there is no indication that Candler cared very much one way or the other; bottling apparently never captured his interest to any great degree, although it would become a path to riches in the Coca-Cola business. Tedlow (1990) speculates that the surrender of bottling operations to others may have had an overall positive effect; certainly it fostered extensive growth as well as providing markets for the home company's syrup. Yet it is also undeniable that Candler could have profited by vertically integrating into bottling (Tedlow 1990: 45).

Soda fountain sales dominated the early business and have remained important up to the present (as exemplified in the high stakes bidding in the early 1990s between Coke and Pepsi for exclusive fast-food franchise agreements), but franchised bottling operations have created the Coca-Cola empire at home and abroad. In 1899 Candler agreed to enter into a contract with two legendary Coca-Cola entrepreneurs from Chattanooga, Tennessee – Benjamin Franklin Thomas and Joseph Brown Whitehead. The two men obtained exclusive rights to bottle and distribute Coca-Cola in all parts of the United States with the exception of six New England States, Texas, and Mississippi, a domain that they quickly divided between them. This historic agreement became the model for all future franchise agreements. It soon became obvious that the market for bottled Coca-Cola was far greater than what Thomas and Whitehead could supply, and they undertook to grant exclusive rights to other bottlers. Thus was born into the Coca-Cola lexicon the term 'parent bottler' to designate Thomas, Whitehead, and other larger regional bottlers given such designation in perpetuity by the parent firm (Watters 1978: 67–72).

The parent firm in Atlanta took responsibility for the crucial task of trade mark protection. With the US Federal Trademark Law of 1905 as its basis, the legal staff inaugurated an aggressive policy of litigation against 'imitators' that still remains central to maintaining brand identity. Key to this strategy is the concept that the trademarked names 'Coca-Cola' and 'Coke' are unique to the beverage and distinguish it from all other cola drinks. A landmark event in the history of this struggle domestically occurred in 1920, when the US Supreme Court upheld the firm's claims and recognized once and for all the legal status of the brand. In order to continually safeguard the trade mark, however, the company still maintains an army of employees who will go into an establishment selling Pepsi-Cola (or another brand) and ask for a 'Coke'. Unless the seller states that he or she is selling Pepsi and not Coke, there is a technical violation of the law. The legal department initiates suits periodically in order to maintain a high profile for its trade mark policy and to discourage violators (Pendergrast 1993: 103–4, 185–6; Tedlow 1990: 53–5).

From its earliest beginnings, foreign operations have mirrored the development of the domestic Coca-Cola business. In this model the parent company manufactures and supplies the syrup or concentrate (all ingredients except sugar) ultimately to be mixed with carbonated water at the soda fountain or by the franchised bottler to make the beverage. In an address to the gala centennial meeting held in Atlanta in the spring of 1986, Claus M. Halle, the then head of Coca-Cola's International Soft Drink Sector, referred to the inherent advantages accrued from franchised networking: 'This fantastic, world-wide Coca-Cola system is unequaled. We possess the unique advantage of independent local management, keyed to each local market, but bound together in an interdependent and cooperative network' (Halle 1986: 8).

Franchising represents an inherently decentralized strategy, but the parent firm must still be in a position to manufacture and distribute syrup or concentrate efficiently, provide advertising and organizational assistance, and often undertake direct investment when initially penetrating foreign markets. Even more importantly, the success of the company depended on its ability to protect its trademarked brands and zealously safeguard its image. It would become essential to provide a modicum of direct assistance to its franchisees in fighting off the efforts of competitive firms to infringe on the Coca-Cola brand name. Since the 1920s there has been a designated home office in the United States, variously termed the Foreign Department, the Export Corporation, or the International Soft Drink Business Sector, that has assumed primary responsibility for administering the international business. Tensions have existed over the degree of home office control versus increasing decentralized autonomy for branch offices or subsidiary companies. Furthermore, there have been disagreements over whether wholly owned foreign subsidiaries or branch offices of the parent firm represent the better strategy to open up markets and manage them effectively.

Just as the development of Coca-Cola's domestic franchised bottling network proceeded somewhat cautiously under Candler leadership, so did efforts to spread the business abroad. Evidence suggests that Candler envisioned potential foreign sales for his syrup, but primarily for soda fountains and not bottling. In the company's 1897 *Annual Report* Candler noted that some business had already occurred in Canada and Hawaii, and that plans were afoot to ship syrup to Mexico. He added that 'We are firmly convinced that wherever there are people and soda fountains, Coca-Cola will, by its now universally acknowledged merit, win its way quickly to the front ranks of popularity' (Coca-Cola Company 1897: 2).

The first recorded manifest of a foreign sale was that to José M. Parejo, a Cuban wine merchant, in 1899. Parejo distributed the syrup to cafés and bars in one litre bottles where it found its way to customers as a soda fountain drink. The archives record similar limited sales of syrup to Canada, Jamaica and Germany (1900), Hawaii (1902), Bermuda, Mexico and Puerto Rico (1903) and the Philippines (1904). Fountain sales had become sufficiently large in Canada that in 1905 the firm registered its trade mark there and acquired property in Toronto for the opening of a branch office. The following year a company-owned bottling plant and syrup-manufacturing facility opened ('Brief History' 1958: 1–2; 'History and Organization' 1967: 1–5).

In 1906 Coca-Cola also established a small bottling plant in Havana which it operated from a branch office. Some have suggested that the Candlers' particular interest in Cuba directly related to the efforts of Methodist Bishop Warren Candler, Asa's brother, who had established a missionary movement on the island after the Spanish American War. This soft drink represented the perfect beverage to the abstemious clergyman as well as markets for the family business (Hall 1986: 98–101; Louis and Yazijian 1980: 29).

The Hawaiian Soda Works in Honolulu, granted a franchise in 1907, has the distinction of being the first overseas Coca-Cola bottler other than the one in Cuba. Independently financed franchises later appeared in Puerto Rico (1991), Panama and Manilla (1912), Nicaragua (1914), Guatemala (1915), Guam (1917) and Paris (1919) ('Brief History' 1958: 1–2). These experimental efforts in foreign bottling during the Candler era represented examples of both direct franchising (e.g. an agreement with the San Miguel Brewery in Manilla) and company-owned bottlers (e.g. Canada). All of these activities combined, however, represented a limited business only incidental to the main operation of the Coca-Cola Company – the manufacture and sale of syrup to bottlers and fountain owners within the continental United States.

THE WOODRUFF TRANSITION: GROWTH OF A FOREIGN VISION

Lessons learned through the ad hoc growth of Coca-Cola's limited foreign business would prove of value in later years, but the real expansion of the export business coincided with the change in ownership and control of the company that occurred in 1919. A consortium headed by wealthy Atlantan Ernest Woodruff acquired the firm from Asa Candler for $25 million, and in 1923 Woodruff's son Robert W. Woodruff became president. The younger Woodruff would become the architect of the world-wide expansion of Coca-Cola, a phenomenon not readily evidenced in sales until after the Second World War, but that had important roots in the 1920s and 1930s (Coca-Cola Company 1974: 71–5; Tedlow 1990: 55–8).

Robert W. Woodruff wasted very little time. In 1924 he created Coca-Cola's first wholly owned foreign subsidiary, Coca-Cola Canada Ltd. Based in Toronto and managed by Woodruff's close friend and a vice-president of the parent firm, Eugene Kelly, this subsidiary would provide efficient management of the burgeoning Canadian business as well as obtain certain tax advantages. A Canadian corporation importing sugar, syrup, molasses or sugar extracts enjoyed preferential duties not extended to the branch operations of a US firm (Horsey correspondence 1924; Nicholson interview 1984).

In the autumn of 1924 Woodruff sent Coca-Cola vice-president Hamilton R. Horsey on an exploratory trip to assess the British market. Recorded sales of small amounts of syrup in London date back to 1909, and soda fountains at Selfridges' department store and the London Coliseum were dispensing the beverage in 1920, but there had been no previous co-ordinated effort to open the British market.

Horsey registered the trade mark in 1924, and travelled widely in the UK, meeting with business people, bankers, mineral water industry spokesmen, potential investors, and public officials. His report, filed in December 1924, recommended the creation of a subsidiary company to sell fountain syrup in Britain and then quickly move toward the opening of a company-owned bottling operation, similar to the Canadian model. In order to take full advantage of Imperial Preference quotas on sugar, Horsey recommended that all syrup be imported from the new Canadian subsidiary, and suggested an initial direct investment of $500,000 over three years. The Coca-Cola Company Ltd, a wholly owned British subsidiary registered in 1929, managed fountain sales and began bottling operations in 1934, contracting actual bottling out to R. Fry and Co. Ltd of Brighton. In 1935 a company-owned bottling plant commenced operations in Chiswick (Horsey correspondence 1924; Williams 1961: 1–5).

Meanwhile, the irregular pattern of direct foreign franchising begun during the Candler years had continued. Coca-Cola filled orders for syrup from all over the world, but the firm had little control over what was actually happening in a given foreign market. The irony was that the company had developed an iron hand over domestic advertising, sanitary standards for bottlers, and trade mark protection – keys to its successful franchise operations at home. Woodruff had introduced a programme of standardization in the domestic business designed to achieve the goal that every bottle or fountain drink of Coca-Cola should taste the same, wherever it was sold across the United States (Pendergrast 1993: 169). Abroad, the business was in many areas in a state of disorganization. The parent company had no full-time sales agents, no one monitoring syrup shipments, and inadequate advertising and trade mark protection programmes. It generally followed the practice of hiring local attorneys to register the trade mark and follow up with appropriate legal protection. The parent firm exported syrup, frequently in large quantities, but didn't know for sure whether it was being sold in fountains or being bottled. Woodruff addressed these concerns with the creation of a new Foreign Department of the parent company located in New York in 1926 ('History and organization' 1967: 7–8; Jernigan interview 1966).

The Foreign Department, under Robert Woodruff's personal supervision, sought to bring greater control to the small but growing international business. To strengthen the trade mark as well as provide a mechanism for penetrating new markets, it introduced a new export bottle in September 1926 that was marketed until 1932. The Foreign Department also opted to export concentrate rather than syrup to its overseas customers. Concentrate, all flavour ingredients except sugar, reduced bulk shipping costs considerably. More importantly as a long-range strategy, sugar, the major ingredient in the beverage, fluctuated considerably in price around the world. The company had the flexibility to pass off higher sugar costs to its bottlers, a problem that would frequently pose problems in the domestic business (Brief History' 1958: 3–4; Jernigan interview 1966).

The major target for expansion abroad in the 1920s remained western Europe, but by 1929 the Foreign Department listed sixty-four authorized bottlers operating in twenty-eight different countries. In addition to a growing business in Latin America, European bottlers from Belgium, France, the Netherlands, Italy and Spain, as well as South Africa had joined on. In 1927 Coca-Cola extended the 1912 San Miguel Brewery agreement to all of the Philippines, and made its first appearance in China ('Coca-Cola as Sold' 1929: 4; Jernigan interview 1966; Nicholson interview 1984).

THE COCA-COLA EXPORT CORPORATION

The success of the Foreign Department led Woodruff to establish greater autonomy for the international business of the company. On 13 March 1930 he incorporated the Coca-Cola Export Corporation (Delaware), a wholly owned subsidiary, to administer the promotion and sale of Coca-Cola outside of the continental United States, Canada and Cuba. The growing Cuban business remained under the corporate umbrella of Coca-Cola Canada Ltd. Woodruff transfered all personnel of the former Foreign Department to the Export Corporation, also located in New York, and he served personally as president for four years. By this time the Export Corporation was supplying concentrate to franchisees and company-owned bottlers in seventy-six different countries (Coca-Cola Company 1974: 75–7; Stephens interview 1983).

The longer list of 'concessionaires' or franchised bottlers in Europe required the presence of Coca-Cola's expertise in legal, financial and marketing matters, but it was difficult to find efficient administrative mechanisms to do so. Export sought a solution by forming national subsidiaries in France, Belgium, Spain, Italy and Germany. Staff members of these companies managed company-owned concentrate plants, the occasional company-owned bottling plant, the licensing and franchising of local bottlers, and the crucially important advertising and promotional programmes. Two holding companies formed in 1930 – the Société de Placements Alimentation SA (a

Luxembourg corporation) and N. V. Nederlandsche Coca-Cola Matt-schappij (a Dutch corporation) – in turn controlled the national subsidiaries ('Report on Subsidiary Companies' 1930).

German operations prior to the Second World War represented by far the most successful of the European subsidiaries on a per capita consumption basis. The business began in 1929 when Woodruff awarded a parent bottling franchise to fellow Georgian Ray Rivington Powers. Powers had previously obtained a local bottling franchise for Essen and formed a company, Essener Vertriebs GmbH fuer Natur-getranke (Esverna). He now convinced Woodruff to extend him a loan with which he could launch his parent bottler sub-franchising efforts. Meanwhile, the Export Corporation in 1930 formed the separate subsidiary in Cologne, Coca-Cola GmbH, as a 'trade mark' company in Germany (Horsey 'German Subsidiary Companies' 1935: Keith interview 1966).

Friction between Ray Powers and the Coca-Cola Export Corpora-tion over management and financial matters led to a merging of the two German companies into Coca-Cola GmbH in 1937, now located in Essen. In exchange for Powers's surrender of his parent bottlers' rights, he received a negotiated settlement of a royalty fee to be paid on each gallon of Coca-Cola syrup delivered, sold, or bottled in Germany. Although Powers died in a 1938 automobile accident, royalty payments continued to his wife (Jones correspondence 1936; Powers correspondence 1929–30).

Coca-Cola GmbH management in Essen now resided in the capable hands of Max Keith, a German national who had briefly trained with a US bottling company. An imaginative businessman, Keith had enjoyed great success in promoting the soft drink during the 1936 Berlin Olympic games, a strategy that the firm would employ success-fully with subsequent Olympic pageants. On the eve of the war in 1939, GmbH sold 4.5 million cases of bottled product, an impressive figure when compared with the 151,000 cases sold in Britain that same year. An advantage of the German market was that the Germans drank their beer cold, and most establishments possessed either cooling equipment or ice. An article of faith within the Coca-Cola family was that the product had to be drunk cold. The British market, on the other hand, was always handicapped because pubs served beer at room temperature and rarely had cooling facilities (Keith interview 1966; Ward interview 1983).

The strategy of establishing foreign subsidiaries continued through-out the late 1930s. The Coca-Cola Company of South Africa made its appearance in 1938 and Aktieselkabet Coca-Cola, a Danish subsidiary appeared in 1939. These companies functioned as did the German subsidiary – as analogues of the domestic US strategy of a manufacturer– wholesaler franchise relationship. In the case of Australia, however, the Export Corporation reverted to an earlier strategy, the creation of branch offices rather than subsidiaries, and company-owned bottlers rather than franchised networks (Ladas 'Memorandum on Export' 1944).

Export conducted a study of potential markets in Australia and New Zealand in 1937 which concluded that there was insufficient capital and interest to attract local investors. A direct investment of $900,000 in 1938 funded a company-owned bottling plant in Sydney and a major advertising programme. The effort achieved only limited success, but the war and presence of US service personnel saved the day. The bottling operation was turned over to the military programme (discussed later in the chapter) and the presence of the product in Australia slowly won over some civilian converts. The resumption of a civilian marketing programme in 1946 generated a decided upturn in business, and Export sold 75 per cent of its bottling operation to Australian investors, thus converting to a franchised structure ('Coca-Cola in Australia' 1973).

Coca-Cola continued to aggressively protect its branded trade mark at home and around the world. A serious challenge emerged in the 1930s when the company was forced to take seriously for the first time a reborn Pepsi-Cola Company. Pepsi traces its roots back to a North Carolina pharmacy in 1893, sharing a similar early history with Coca-Cola – both beverages beginning life as health drinks in the American 'New South' of the late nineteenth century. Pepsi-Cola had remained only a marginally successful regional company, however, and had gone into bankruptcy twice, in 1922 and again in 1932. After the firm's acquisition by the New York based Loft Candy Company in 1932, however, its fortunes rebounded. Adopting a competitive pricing strategy of offering a twelve-ounce bottle for five cents, twice as much as the six and one-half ounce standard Coca-Cola bottle for the same price, Pepsi gained success as a bargain cola drink during the Depression-ridden years of the 1930s (Louis and Yazijian 1980: 49–51).

Concerned by the challenge at home and abroad, Coca-Cola initiated a series of trade mark suits against Pepsi-Cola in 1938, all essentially focusing on the use of the term 'cola'. Personal negotiations between Woodruff and the dynamic new president of Pepsi, Walter Mack, resulted in Coca-Cola agreeing to drop its suit in New York and to thereafter recognize the Pepsi-Cola trade mark in the United States.

According to Walter Mack, the key to this settlement was evidence obtained by Pepsi lawyers that Coke had made a potentially embarrassing pay-off in a similar case. The truce lasted only briefly. Coca-Cola now filed suit in twelve foreign countries, the first one in Canada, charging Pepsi-Cola with trade mark infringement. After intense litigation, the Canadian Privy Council ultimately declared in Pepsi-Cola's favour in 1942, urging the two companies to adopt a policy of coexistence. The competitors did declare an armistice of sorts, dropping a series of suits and countersuits, and agreeing to recognize each other's trade mark throughout the world. This would prove to be a major victory for Walter Mack and the Pepsi-Cola Company. The company survived a war and increasingly become a troublesome rival in the post-war era (Louis and Yazijian 1980: 49–55; Pendergrast 1993: 194–7).

WARTIME CHALLENGES TO FOREIGN OPERATIONS

US enterprise rationally turned its attention from foreign to domestic operations as war loomed closer after 1939. In the period after Pearl Harbor this trend became even more apparent as the national goal of increasing output for military needs increasingly dominated business decisions. Mira Wilkins's (1974) survey of US multinational corporations during the war demonstrates that foreign subsidiaries and affiliates soon assumed more functional autonomy. With return of profits to US corporations impossible for those units operating in occupied or enemy territory, many subsidiaries followed a strategy of reinvesting profits. This was precisely the approach of the successful German subsidiary, Coca-Cola GmbH (Wilkins 1974: 267–8).

Anticipating war in Europe, Max Keith followed the parent firm's urging to invest whatever funds he could in German real estate. Keith continued to market Coca-Cola until his supplies of concentrate ran out in 1940, and then trademarked a substitute beverage which he named 'Fanta' for 'fantastich (phantastich)'. Caramel-coloured and sweetened with saccharin when sugar became severely rationed, this speciality drink became a successful substitute for Coca-Cola in Germany and the occupied territories during the period of the conflict. The company retained the Fanta trade mark in the post-war years and it is now associated with a line of fruit-flavoured beverages marketed in many sectors of the world. Keith used his influence to become appointed official administrator of all Coca-Cola property in Germany and the occupied territories by the Nazi Office of Enemy Property. This designation allowed him to travel freely in order to oversee company business. Coca-Cola personnel, arriving in Essen soon after the German surrender in May 1945, found Keith's still-functioning operations ready to be turned over to the bottling of Coca-Cola for US and Canadian occupying troops (Curtis, 'Coca-Cola in W.W. II' 1946; Ladas, 'Memorandum on Export' 1944; Bacon interview 1966; Keith interview 1966).

A similar survival story emerged in Belgium as Brussels manager Carl West faced numerous hardships under German occupation. Although able to bottle small amounts of Coca-Cola from pre-war stores of concentrate up to the time of liberation in 1944, West had converted most of the Belgian business to a fruit-flavoured line termed 'Cappy'. When the Germans sequestered the Belgian company in June 1942, the Enemy Property Administration in Berlin appointed Max Keith 'Verhalter' and responsible for the maintenance of its assets. Keith visited Brussels every three or four months and was able to use his influence to assist West. Coca-Cola personnel discovered a viable bottling operation when they entered Belgium in December 1944 with the US military (West 1946).

COCA-COLA GOES TO WAR: THE TECHNICAL OBSERVER STORY

Coca-Cola's wartime experience represented a departure from the general view that US multinational companies retrenched for the duration and concentrated on their domestic businesses. During the conflict, the Coca-Cola Company provided approximately 95 per cent of all soft drinks sold to military personnel through the post exchange (PX) system. Whereas acute sugar rationing at home would handcuff Coca-Cola and the rest of the carbonated soft drink industry, the Atlanta company was able to place facilities and personnel in place throughout Europe, Asia, Latin America, and Africa ready to implement the massive expansion of the post-war period.

Robert W. Woodruff undertook two direct actions early in the war that would contribute greatly to achieving his vision of a world-wide market for Coca-Cola. In September 1940 he enlisted James A. Farley, one of the best-known and popular of Franklin D. Roosevelt's New Deal entourage, as chairman of the Board of the Coca-Cola Export Corporation. Farley had served as Roosevelt's campaign manager during his 1932 and 1936 presidential campaigns, as chairman of the Democratic Party National Committee, and as Postmaster-General of the United States. The 'General', as he was frequently called, split with Roosevelt over the third presidential term issue and had just resigned from the Cabinet. Farley provided instant public relations value and represented implied if not real political clout for Coca-Cola. During his long reign as chairman, Farley travelled extensively on behalf of Export, almost always gaining access to Cabinet-level ministers rather than having to deal with underlings ('James A. Farley Heads up' 1940; Farley interview 1975).

Woodruff's post-Pearl Harbor pledge to make Coca-Cola available at five cents a drink to every American in the armed forces, wherever he or she might be stationed, constituted a second shrewd decision. Cloaked in patriotism, this announcement was a stroke of business genius. It was apparent that sugar rationing would severely curtail domestic sales (E. J. Kahn Jr 1960: 15–16; J. Kahn 1946: 1–5). Indeed, the company noted a decline of $5 million in net income for 1942, but could report that

> While the major portion of our investment in countries held by the enemy has been charged off, the volume of our business in other countries continued to expand and facilities in friendly overseas territories have contributed to making Coca-Cola widely available to our fighting forces.
>
> (Coca-Cola 1942: 1)

A group of 164 paid employees, who served as technical observers (TOs) in uniform, became the assault troops for Coca-Cola's wartime offensive. Although civilians, these 'Coca-Cola Colonels' received privileges as commissioned officers with regard to accommodation, transportation and mess facilities, and were under the orders of the military theatre commanders in the sector where they served. In addition to the TOs themselves, who were generally in charge of establishing bottling or syrup plants, hundreds of other enlisted men, many of whom had some soft drink industry experience in civilian life, became attached to Coca-Cola operations (Coca-Cola 1941, 1942, 1943, 1944; 1974: 80; J. Kahn 1946: 1–15; Bacon interview 1966).

Although a trial run in establishing a bottling plant for the military occurred in Reykjavik, Iceland, in early 1942, the first major effort in a war theatre was in North Africa. US Vice-Consul in Algiers, John Boyd himself a pre-war Coca-Cola concessionaire in Marseilles, played a key role in these efforts. Concerned with GI consumption of Algerian wine and believing 'Coke' would provide an invaluable morale boost, Boyd also recognized the vast market that the military represented. His negotiations with General Mark Clark beginning in July 1943 subsequently led to the summoning of Export's James C. Curtis to Washington where he arranged for the shipment of eight bottling plants to North Africa (Boyd correspondence 1943; Bacon interview 1966; Boyd interview 1966; Davis interview 1966).

From the North Africa landings in November 1942 up to the surrender of Japan in Tokyo Bay in September 1945, the Coca-Cola Company supplied approximately 3 billion drinks to US armed forces overseas. Technical observers served in the Alaskan Defense Command, the African Middle East, China–Burma–India, European, Mediterranean, and Pacific Theatres, and in South America. These men established bottling plants, and syrup and concentrate facilities in battle zones from Oran, Algiers and Casablanca in North Africa to Saipan, Guam and New Guinea in the Pacific. At the end of the war there were 155 Coca-Cola bottling plants turning out drinks around the world. Of this number 64 self-contained plants had been shipped from the US by the Export Corporation at government expense from 1943 to 1946. The TOs and their support staffs were in a position to provide the 'pause that refreshes' to US occupation forces as well as a new civilian market that was in many instances getting its first taste of Coca-Cola. For example, the Japanese business, currently a major profit sector for the firm, had its beginnings with the plants established to supply US occupation troops (Coca-Cola Company 1974: 80; Moss 1972: 1–4). In comparison to the great success enjoyed by Coca-Cola in these wartime operations, there is evidence of only one Pepsi-Cola bottling plant established under the military programme. This was a small facility in Paris, and Coca-Cola TOs performed the bottling operation (Bacon interview 1966).

POST-WAR STRATEGIES

The great potential market for Coca-Cola's 'foreign business' had clearly been an underlying motivation for its co-operative work with the US military. In a memo on 18 September 1944 to Woodruff, vice-president and sales genius Harrison Jones had thrown his support behind the boss's prophetic view:

> You have stated, and all agree with you, that twenty-five years from today the export business will be the largest business of this company —two billion mouths against one hundred thirty million. . . . This export thing is hot! When the war is over in Europe, which might be tomorrow, who is going to Europe? What is going to be done? The sooner we can bring order out of chaos, the sooner we can get going, and while thousands and thousands of Americans are occupying these countries will be the time to 'hit the rock'.
>
> (H. Jones 1944)

With the TO operations still in place with the occupying troops in Europe and Japan, and with the pre-war subsidiaries and franchised concessionaires being revived and brought back into the fold, the company was poised on the brink of major international expansion.

In their study of the management of international business, Raymond Vernon and Louis T. Wells, Jr, suggest that Coca-Cola has been relaxed about franchising local bottlers in foreign lands because the parent company still controlled such vital marketing functions as the trade name, advertising programme, and the flavour (through the manufacture and sale of concentrate which contains the 'secret formula') (Wells and Vernon 1976: 29). Yet, despite such strong central control of key stages in the franchising and marketing system, there have been disagreements over the optimal degree of de-centralization.

The pre-war experience of the firm abroad had been mixed. There had been both company-owned bottlers and franchises, branch offices and wholly owned subsidiary companies. The Export Company's New York legal staff in 1944 developed a blueprint for much of the strategy the firm undertook in the immediate post-war era. Citing the success of branch offices in Australia, New Zealand, Hawaii and the Philippines before the war, and more recent similar experiences in Mexico, Brazil and Argentina, the report argued for this approach over the establishment of subsidiary companies as a base of operations. Meanwhile, Export had liquidated the two holding companies organized before the war to manage the Dutch, Belgian, French and Italian businesses in 1943, and dissolved its British subsidiary, Coca-Cola Ltd, in 1948 (Ladas 'Memorandum on Export' 1944).

With the exception of Germany and Spain, where strong sub-sidiaries remained at the heart of operations, branch offices of the Export Corporation administered all franchising, advertising and trade mark operations in Europe. In addition to the arguments that the branch offices were in a better position to maintain centralized control over administrative policy, finance, technical information, and the all-important trade mark, there also existed perceived United States tax advantages. The Export Company could write off market development expenses incurred by a branch in entering new territories. The firm could also deduct certain tax exemptions on profits derived from the branch since they represented income on active trade as con-trasted with investment (Ladas 'Memorandum on Export' 1944; 'Presentation to Coca-Cola Board' 1947).

With the branch strategy now dominating the firm's international operations, it adopted a more fully developed pattern of regional decentralization in 1946 that would become modified in subsequent years, but retain its essential form in the 1990s. The initial structure featured seventeen separate geographic divisions, each represented by a branch of the Export Corporation, and directed by a division manager in the field. Reporting to each division manager were country managers. The division managers in return reported to one of four area vice-presidents stationed in New York. As operations expanded into new areas, the New York office would create additional divisions. By 1948 branch offices or permanent headquarters functioning in forty-six countries reported to twenty overseas division managers. Export boasted that it employed over 6,000 individuals outside of the United States and that 99 per cent of them were foreign nationals ('Head Office Memorandum' 1946; Nicholson interview 1984; Stephens interview 1983).

As business grew, however, greater decentralization became necessary. In 1954, Lee Talley replaced long-time Export operating head James F. Curtis as president. Very much a line manager rather than a staff man, Curtis's long tenure was testimony that Bob Woodruff had remained the brains behind the Export business. Talley, a personal favourite of Woodruff's and a veteran of many years in the business in Canada and abroad, introduced a modified structure abolishing the old division managers. They were replaced by region managers who reported to area vice-presidents located not in New York, but in the field. Initially, four area vice-presidents now represented Europe, the Pacific, Latin America and Africa. Talley had become convinced that an increasing amount of autonomy had to be delegated to the field (Talley 1957).

By 1960, area designations and resident vice-presidents existed for Africa, the Caribbean, Central Europe, the Mediterranean and Middle East, North Pacific, South America, the South Pacific and Far East, the United Kingdom and western Europe. At the next level were regional managers, and under them country managers. During the 1960s Coca-Cola tinkered with this structure in an attempt to achieve a better blend of central office control and regional autonomy. In 1967 the firm adopted a system of 'zone' offices located in key areas that oversaw area and region subdivisions ('Home Office Memorandum' 1960; Nicholson interview 1984; Stephens interview 1983).

In 1972 further administrative changes resulted from the merging of the Coca-Cola Export Corporation into the parent company and the moving of all central office personnel from New York to Atlanta. Movement for even greater integration of the foreign business into the home office occurred in the 1980s with the absorption of the Export

Corporation into what is still termed the International Soft Drink Business Sector of the parent Coca-Cola Company. Effective from 1 January 1989 this sector was reorganized into four operating groups, replacing what had been only three previously. A new Coca-Cola EC Group housing the Common Market countries under a single management structure anticipated the new changes within the economic community. A second North-east Europe/Africa (NEA) group includes all countries in the previous Europe and Africa Group that were not in the EC. The remaining two groups are a reorganized Pacific Group and a Latin America Group. Within the overall structure, however, a great deal of decentralized autonomy still exists. In general, the firm has succeeded in striking a balance between the conflicting needs for centralized control of advertising, trade mark and formula, and the market flexibility associated with decentralized local management ('Regrouping the World' 1988; Stephens interview 1983).

PROBLEMS ASSOCIATED WITH 'COCA-COLONIZATION'

The expansive growth of Coca-Cola abroad after the Second World War was not without its political difficulties. As the Cold War in Europe heated up in the late 1940s and early 1950s, the firm became the target of attacks in Italy, Germany and especially France. In Europe and Latin America problems arose over charges of health law violations in specific countries, many of which were rooted in political and economic opposition to the company. Many of these cases related to the presence in the beverage of what the company has termed internally 'merchandise #3' (caffeine) and 'merchandise #4' (phosphoric acid) (Ladas correspondence 1947).

One of the more publicized episodes occurred in France in the early 1950s. Initial opposition focused on caffeine and phosphoric acid, additives already banned by existing regulation, but that had been successfully circumvented in the pre-war period and under Vichy. Soon, however, more direct attacks emanated from competing wine and mineral water interests who perceived the aggressive US marketer as a serious competitor, and from more radical and broad-based attacks against the Marshall Plan and Coca-Cola as a symbol of US economic imperialism.

Legislators introduced three separate draft laws into the National Assembly in 1949 threatening Coca-Cola. Two of them were generic in their wording and sought to ban all beverages in which 'toxic vegetable or chemical substances are part of their composition'. The third Bill, introduced by the Communist Party, specifically banned the importation, manufacture and sale of Coca-Cola, mentioning the product by name. The left-wing press took up the cry against the 'Coca-Colonization' of France, comparing US-style advertising and mass marketing with totalitarian propaganda by which 'whole peoples have become intoxicated'. The French lower house passed a more moderated version of this Bill in February 1950, sponsored by Paul Boulet, a Popular Republican Deputy from the wine-growing district of Montpelier ('Memorandum Concerning France' 1950).

The colourful story of how the Coca-Cola Company overcame this challenge involved massive public relations and lobbying at home, an organized boycott of French wines by Jim Farley's New York restaurateur friends, behind-the-scenes negotiations in Paris, and pressure from the US ambassador David Bruce and the US State Department. The pressure paid off as the advisory Second House of the French Parliament unanimously rejected the Boulet Bill in June 1950. The US media had played the story to the hilt, portraying the threatened ban of Coca-Cola as an attack on American pride as well as its generosity exhibited through the Marshall Plan. Problems would still crop up periodically in France, but Farley succeeded in enlisting US State Department help when others made similar attempts to attack Coca-Cola through existing health laws (Farley correspondence 1950–2; Ladas correspondence 1950; Makinsky correspondence 1950–2).

In Switzerland, US Embassy intervention smoothed over health law difficulties in 1949, and similar problems were overcome in Belgium in 1951 with the aid of the US ambassador. Italian wine interests became involved in a mid-1950s attempt to ban caffeine and phosphoric acid. Even in Germany, where the firm's subsidiary enjoyed particular success, a coalition of German wine interests, competing mineral water and soft drink bottlers, and left-wing political groups organized an attack in the press (Makinsky correspondence 1952).

Other subsequent well-publicized political problems included the boycotting of Coca-Cola by the Arab League in 1966 and the firm's expulsion from India in 1977. When Coca-Cola granted a franchise to an Israeli investor in response to growing political pressure at home, the Arabs acted against it, but not rival Pepsi-Cola, which did not do business in Israel. It was not until skilful negotiations and investment strategies undertaken by Coke executives J. Paul Austin and Sam Ayoub in the mid-1970s led to the opening up of the Egyptian market, that the Arab blacklist was penetrated for the first time. There had been opposition to the company in India for many years, based mainly on the tremendous profits that it seemed to be making in the less developed country. The firm had managed to avert trouble under the Congress Party of Indira Ghandi, but the election of Morarji Desai's Janata Party in 1977 led to the break. Ostensibly because it had refused to divulge its secret formula, '7X', in conformance with Indian law, the government banned Coca-Cola from India, only to see it return in 1992 ('Coke Going Back' 1992; Louis and Yazijian 1980: 159–62; Stephens interview 1983).

Political attacks against Coca-Cola and other US firms operating abroad have not completely abated with the waning of the Cold War. Coca-Cola has re-entered India, made a significant rebound in the Middle East, opened joint ventures in China, and penetrated Russian markets once thought under the thumb of 'the imitator' (Pepsi-Cola). But foreign critics still complain about the company's high-pressure marketing, particularly in the less developed world, and scholars largely remain divided on their overall assessment of the role played by US multinational firms in the post-1945 epoch.

CONCLUSION

Coca-Cola management both defends its role in the world, and claims as the secret of its world-wide success, its longstanding franchising strategy. There has been a legitimate and historical difference that has distinguished Coca-Cola from other US multinational companies abroad. Aside from the issue of adopting appropriate structural organizations to balance the forces of centralization and decentralization, Coca-Cola's inherent decentralized relationship with local bottlers has fostered a positive working relationship that has benefited both partners. Ironically, a dominant strategy of very recent years has been to eliminate the franchising system in the United States through a policy of expanding company-owned bottling operations. To a great extent, this development represents a response to the changing nature of distribution through supermarkets and large central warehouse arrangements; the role of the local bottler in small town America has waned. By 1988 for example, the ten largest bottlers in the US accounted for 78 per cent of the brand's volume sold, and the parent firm had a large equity share of all of them (Pendergrast 1993: 382).

The history of the Coca-Cola Company's international operations has exhibited experimental and limited attempts to replicate the domestic franchising strategy prior to the Second World War, and a story of dramatic expansion abroad in the post-war era. The strategy of operation would vary with the local circumstances in each country. In Germany, where the business had become very well established over many years, the company moved in the mid-1980s to consolidate its bottling operations, a strategy similar to what it followed in the United States. In large part this reflected the evolution of strong supermarket sales and other modes of modern merchandising in western Europe. In Indonesia and China, on the other hand, initial efforts had to focus on the building of an appropriate infrastructure, including concentrate factories, glass manufacturers, bottling plants, trucks, and point-of-sale signs (Pendergrast 1993: 377). It is precisely this positive influence in building local industry more widely in the less developed world of which Coca-Cola frequently boasts.

In the 1990s the largest share of the company's centrally important soft drink business takes place abroad, and foreign-born executives sit at the highest levels of every division, domestic and international. The Cuban-born Roberto Goizueta, who has been at the helm of the company since 1981, dramatically signifies this change. Goizueta and chief operating officer Donald Keough have framed their world strategy with the phrase 'think globally – act locally'. This most typically US firm, still rooted in the red clay hills of Atlanta, Georgia, has truly become an international giant.

One key to Coca-Cola's strategy of brand identification and marketing has been its consistent association with popular music and sports. In Brazil the firm has sponsored 'Rock in Rio', a mammoth nine-day rock concert attended by over 1 million fans, and in the Philippines, the company has long recruited and sponsored local pop artist and groups. Young people in Thailand began wearing Coca-Cola clothing to rock concerts because of the beverage's close identification with sponsorship, and in France there is a popular radio and television show entitled the 'Coca-Cola Top 50' (Pendergrast 1993: 389).

Ever since 1936 the company has shown a strong presence at the Olympics, and in 1988 invested over $80 million in promotions at Calgary and Seoul. It is equally as present in a wide array of sports sponsorship all over the globe, including the Tour de France bicycle race and World Cup Soccer, where it sent its message to an estimated 25 billion viewers. Coke supports almost every type of sporting event all over the world, including field hockey, basketball, volleyball, gymnastics, Sumo wrestling, motorcycle races, and American football games in Europe and Japan.

Special events, such as 'Georgia Week' in France in the late 1980s, featured American football, a showing of the motion picture, *Gone with the Wind*, and imported grits (an American Southern delicacy whose charm eludes me still after living for seventeen years in the

American South). By 1987 soft drink profits in Japan were greater than even in the United States, with a coffee-based product trade named 'Georgia' accompanied by a *Gone with the Wind* advertising motif leading the way. An 84 per cent market share signified this great success, but warning signs began to develop. Japanese companies had begun to have relative success marketing healthier non-carbonated and vitamin-laced drinks, and the American image so successfully leveraged since the war was no longer so positive. Things American were associated with a declining economy, poverty, crime and AIDS. Concerns for these issues have engendered serious efforts to undertake new advertising and marketing strategies (Pendergrast 1993: 392–3).

The stakes are now much higher than ever before in both the firm's domestic and international business. Prior to the Second World War, for example, Coca-Cola maintained a virtual monopoly with no real competition to speak of; in the 1990s Pepsi-Cola is continually barking at its heels at home and abroad, and one might more accurately describe the global cola business as a duopoly. In the 1950s Pepsi-Cola International, the foreign marketing arm of 'the imitator', adopted a decentralized organizational structure very similar to the model that had evolved within the Coca-Cola Export Corporation. Pepsi-Cola has competed very effectively in several world markets, capitalizing early on its leads in the Soviet Union and the Middle East. Although a new team of professional managers, largely individuals who have arisen from the international ranks, now determine the world-wide marketing strategies of the Coca-Cola Company, one may see the roots of many of the current challenges and the organizational responses that have emerged through a study of the earlier history of the firm's operations abroad.

The firm's phenomenal record in selling what amounts to flavoured sugar water around the world is a tribute to one of the most successful marketing stories in business history. The loyalty demonstrated in the controversy over 'New Coke' in 1985 simply represented the most dramatic example of the strong consumer identification with the brand. Each can, bottle or soda fountain drink of Coca-Cola contains the collective lore and mystique of one hundred plus years of history and legend. There are numerous stories told within the firm of German, Brazilian or Japanese visitors to the United States remarking that 'you have Coca-Cola too; I feel right at home!' The familiar red and white advertising of the Coca-Cola Company is to be found in all corners of the globe, truly 'the pause that has refreshed the world'.

REFERENCES

Published texts

Coca-Cola Company (1897, 1941, 1942, 1943, 1944, 1986) *Annual Report of the Coca-Cola Company*, Atlanta, Ga: Coca-Cola Company.
—— (1929) 'Coca-Cola as sold throughout the world', *The Red Barrel* (magazine of the Coca-Cola Company) **8**: 1–30.
—— (1974) *The Coca-Cola Company: An Illustrated Profile*, Atlanta, Ga: Coca-Cola company.
'Coke going back to India' (1992) *New York Times* 10 March: C7.
Enrico, R. and Kornbluth, J. (1986) *The Other Guy Blinked: How Pepsi Won the Cola Wars*, New York: Bantam.
Hall, B. (1986) 'Coca-Cola and Methodism', *Southern Exposure* Fall: 98–101.
'James A. Farley heads up export corporation' (1940) *The Coca-Cola Bottler* **32**(6): 14, 39, 44.
Kahn, E. J., Jr (1960) *The Big Drink: The Story of Coca-Cola*, New York: Random House.
Louis, J. C. and Yazijian, H. Z. (1980) *The Cola Wars*, New York: Everest House.
Oliver, T. (1986) *The Real Coke, The Real Story*, New York: Random House.
Pendergrast, M. (1993) *For God, Country, and Coca-Cola*, New York: Charles Scribner's Sons.
'Regrouping the World' (1988) *Journey* (magazine of the Coca-Cola Company) **2**(3): 2–13.
Tedlow, R. S. (1990) *New and Improved: The Story of Mass Marketing in America*, New York: Basic Books.
Watters, P. (1978) *Coca-Cola: An Illustrated History*, Garden City, NY: Doubleday.
Wells, L. T. and Vernon, R. (1976) *Manager in the International Economy*, Englewood Cliffs, NJ: Prentice-Hall.
Wilkins, M. (1974) *The Maturing of Multinational Enterprise*, Cambridge, Mass: Harvard University Press.

Manuscript sources

Bacon, P. B. (1966) 'A history pertaining to the bottling and distribution of Coca-Cola for the United States and Canadian Armed Forces in the E.T.O. (European Theater of Operations) and the M.T.O. (Mediterranean Theater of Operations), Jan. 1944 to Dec. 1946', unpublished manuscript, Coca-Cola Archives, Atlanta, Georgia (hereafter cited as CCA): file, W.W. II.
Boyd, John H. to F. F. Curtis (25 September 1943) CCA: file, W.W. II Records.
'Brief History of the Coca-Cola Export Corporation' (1958) unpublished manuscript, CCA: file, Export History.
'Coca-Cola in Australia, 1938–1973' (1973) CCA: file, Export, Australia.
Curtis, J. F. (1946) 'Coca-Cola in W.W. II', CCA: file, W.W. II Records.
Farley, James A. (1950–2) correspondence with Henri Bonnet, Gen. Charles de Gaulle, and James E. Webb, CCA: file, Legal, Health Laws (France).

Halle, Claus J. (1986) 'The International Sector: Centennial Celebration, Our World', CCA: file, 1986 Centennial Celebration.

'Head Office Memorandum, General No. 11' (1 Augest 1946) CCA: file, Export Administration, Box 1.

'History and Organization of the Coca-Cola Export Corporation' (1967) unpublished manuscript, CCA: file, Export History.

'Home Office Memorandum, Executive No. 12' (25 July 1960) CCA: file, Export Co. History, Box 2.

Horsey, Hamilton R., to R. W. Woodruff (16 December 1924) CCA: file, Export, England Market Analysis.

—— (1935) 'The German Subsidiary Companies', CCA: file, Legal Agreements, R. R. Powers.

Jones, Harrison, to R. W. Woodruff (18 September 1944) CCA: file, Jones Collection, Box 3 (Woodruff, R. W.).

Jones, Turner, to R. W. Woodruff (27 January 1936) CCA: file, Legal Agreements, R. R. Powers.

Kahn, James M. (1946) 'Coca-Cola in World War II', unpublished manuscript, CCA: file, W.W. II.

Ladas, Stephen P. (1944) 'Memorandum on the Coca-Cola Export Corporation', Atlanta: CCA; file, Legal, Box 1.

—— (1947–50), correspondence with Pierre Gide, Pope Brock and Alexander Makinsky, CCA: file, Legal, Health Laws (France).

Makinsky, Alexander (1950–2) correspondence with Lee Talley, Carl West and C. A. Shillinglaw, CCA: file, Legal, Health Laws (France, Italy).

'Memorandum Concerning the 'Coca-Cola' Product in France' (1950) CCA: file, Legal, Health Laws (France).

Moss, Frank H. (1972) 'The History of Coca-Cola in the Japanese Market', CCA: file, John Talley Collection, Box 1.

Powers, Ray Rivington (1929–30) correspondence with H. R. Horsey and Harrison Jones, CCA: file, Legal Agreements.

'Presentation to the Coca-Cola Board of Directors' (1947) CCA: file, Export III, 1.3.

'Report on Formation of Subsidiary Companies in Europe' (1930) CCA: file, Legal, Box 1 (European Liquidated Subsidiaries).

Talley, Lee (1957) 'Present Organization of the Export Corporation; Theory and Effect of Decentralization', CCA: file, Legal, 1957 Homecoming.

West, Carl (1946) 'Report on A. A. Belge Coca-Cola', CCA, file, History, Box 2.

Williams, A. S. (1961) 'The Story of Coca-Cola', paper presented to the London School of Economics, CCA: file, Public Relations.

Interviews

Bacon, Paul B. (1966) by Hunter Bell, Atlanta: 16 March 1966, CCA: file, Oral History Tapes.

Boyd, John H. (1966) by Hunter Bell, Atlanta: 15 March 1966, CCA: file, Oral History Tapes.

Davis, Albert 'Red' (1966) by Hunter Bell, Atlanta: 5 October 1966, CCA: file, Oral History Tapes.

Farley, James A. (1975) by Hunter Bell, New York: 18 October 1975, CCA: file, Farley biographical (transcript).

Jernigan, Carl (1966) by Hunter Bell, Atlanta: 25 January 1966, CCA: file, Oral History Tapes.

Keith, Max (1966) by Hunter Bell, Atlanta: 29–30 June 1966, CCA: file, Export Files II (transcript).

Nicholson, H. Burke, Jr (1984) by August W. Giebelhaus and Philip F. Mooney, Atlanta: 22 October 1984, CCA: file, Nicholson, H. Burke, Jr (transcript).

Stephens, C. Preston (1983) by August W. Giebelhaus and Philip E. Mooney, Atlanta: 14 June 1983, CCA: file, Export History (transcript).

Ward, A. H. (1983) by August W. Giebelhaus, London: 15 August 1983, CCA: file, Export History, England (transcript).

11 Best-practice marketing of food and health drinks in Britain 1930–70

T. A. B. Corley

Given the plentiful evidence on Britain's relative economic decline in the twentieth century, it is not surprising that British firms should have been criticized for their generally poor marketing efforts. Top management pressures appeared to be all too often absent for the development of positive and dynamic marketing programmes. By contrast, US giant managerially run enterprises in this period evolved a three-pronged investment strategy, for production, management and marketing. Hence the manager of a US subsidiary in Britain declared in the mid-1950s that 'the average (indigenous) British firm treats the function of selling as did America thirty years ago', just when the multidivisional corporate form was beginning to emerge in the United States (Dunning 1958: 264).

Such criticisms can be supplemented from a variety of sources. In 1960 *The Economist* blamed Britain's lack of effective salesmanship abroad on two significant groups in British political life – the extreme wings of both main parties – to whom advertising was a 'dirty word'. Consequently, it believed, the Britain of the 1960s faced the real peril of a 'desire to luxuriate in the attributes of an affluent society before we have achieved it' (*The Economist* 1960: 246). Two years later, the British companies which 'accept, apply and promote' marketing principles were said to be 'few and far between', despite their having adopted most of the other necessary managerial techniques (Wells 1962: 23ff).

In 1970 a British Institute of Management survey of current marketing practices in over 500 of the largest British companies – with annual turnover above £750,000 – found that the majority of their chief executives fully appreciated the importance of marketing and had shaped their strategies accordingly. However, this encouraging conclusion was blunted by the rider that there were 1,900 companies in this size category which had not been surveyed (British Institute of

Management 1970: 139). More forthrightly, a National Economic Development Office report of 1981, when discussing the UK's industrial record, concluded that, in the previous two decades, the single most important reason for the disappointing performance of British companies by international standards was the lack of marketing expertise (Pickering and Cockerill 1984: 132).

Although the weight of this evidence invites respect, it remains too impressionistic to be fully accepted as it stands. The charge against British industry apparently runs as follows. Nowadays marketing lies at the heart of business policy because it covers a far broader field than just sales, distribution or even advertising. Since final consumers provide all or most of any firm's revenue, that firm best serves its interests by standing ready to meet consumers' reasonable wants. Thus both current production and publicity decisions, and future planning – of new products, markets and so on – should properly be undertaken in such a way as to achieve these marketing objectives (Corley 1993: 99–104). Hence, it seems to follow, that Britain's corporate failures in the second and third quarters of the twentieth century can be attributed to weaknesses in marketing.

However, even if the average standard were low, examples of high-quality marketing companies in the 1930–70 period readily come to mind, such as Beecham, Castrol, Rowntree, Schweppes and Unilever. Did some consistent pattern therefore exist in the goodness or badness of British marketing, or was there merely a random process? The hypothesis discussed here is that industry-specific variations existed, so that better-quality marketing was broadly found in the industrial sectors where Britain enjoyed a relative advantage, and vice versa.

This hypothesis can first be tested by an examination of marketing standards in US industries which had a comparative international disadvantage. Doubtless the marketing by US corporations of high-technology goods in Britain – from mass-produced cars to typewriters and sewing machines – was very effective; yet there was the opposite tendency with less advanced products. Most US patent medicine manufacturers, who were active in the UK, had little understanding of the British market. Only two brands sold consistently well, Carter's Little Liver Pills and Dr Williams' Pink Pills for Pale People: the agent of both was an American expatriate of many years' residence. Curiously enough, the remarkable success of Beecham's pills in the United States was partly due to the general manager, in charge of publicity, being an Anglo-American (Corley 1987b: 118–26). In foodstuffs, US product leaders such as Nabisco in biscuits and Hershey in chocolates, and General Mills and Ralston Purina in breakfast cereals, as well as the major flour millers, failed to sell their products in Britain, or elsewhere abroad, at this time (Horst 1974: 40–6; see also Collins, Chapter 12 in this volume). As Giebelhaus has explained (see Chapter 10), before the 1920s Coca-Cola made little headway in Britain against the competition of warm beer and plentiful variations of enticingly flavoured indigenous soft drinks (cf. Dunning 1958: 265).

It seems as if the industrial sectors, in which US corporations performed least well in Britain, were precisely those where British firms were able to market most effectively. One such sector, that of making food and health drink products, is considered in the next section.

THE FOOD AND HEALTH DRINK MARKET IN BRITAIN

The areas in which the UK has done best by international standards are clearly documented. As Alfred Chandler (1990) has pointed out, many of the largest and most successful firms in Britain have been engaged in producing consumer rather than industrial goods, most notably branded and packaged products making or processing 'sugar, flour, chocolates, biscuits, and other confectionery', as well as 'jams and sauces, condiments, meat extracts, and certain other foodstuffs' (Chandler 1990: 262). Michael Porter (1990) has confirmed that 'the largest concentration of British competitive advantage is in consumer packaged goods, including alcoholic beverages [and] food such as confectionery products and biscuits'. Among the internationally competitive UK industries in 1985, he noted breakfast cereals, nonchocolate sugar candy, chocolate and products, pastry, biscuits, cakes, jams and marmalades (Porter 1990: 484, 490).

The British food and drink industry therefore provides an ideal case study for this chapter. Alcoholic drinks are not dealt with here as they are discussed in several chapters of this volume and in a recent book on marketing history (Tedlow and Jones 1993). Non-alcoholic 'health' drinks include carbonated or still (plain or flavoured) waters and cocoa and malted drinks. Thus defined, the industry forms a reasonably self-contained group, which has historically made up an influential sector of the economy. For example, it supplied nearly 37 per cent of all consumer goods in 1935 (Kaldor and Silverman 1948: 144–7).

Britain's comparative advantage in this industrial group sprang in part from being able to obtain cheap basic foods, such as grain, sugar and meats, from overseas. Low unskilled wages and relatively simple manufacturing techniques allowed the ingredients to be processed at moderate cost. The consequent high gross profits permitted substantial advertising outlays where required. Customers on the whole responded positively to the industry's marketing efforts, thanks to a combination of social trends in this area of rising average disposable incomes – trends which have not hitherto been adequately explored in social histories of Britain. Two such trends were a growing concern with personal health, and an underlying demand for convenience foods.

Until the end of the nineteenth century, few sections of the British population understood the relation between diet and health. Patent medicines had to treat two sorts of unwise eating. In the 1830s Dr James Cockle of London claimed to be selling his anti-bilious pills to half the Cabinet, from the prime minister Lord Melbourne down, as well as to no fewer than fifty-three peers and fifteen archbishops and bishops. Since the pills were said to counteract effectively the derangement of the stomach's functions, 'connected with a torpid state of the liver and bowels', the ruling classes were plainly eating and drinking to excess (*Satirist* 1838; 1839). Poorer people, too, endured a whole range of ailments, brought on by deficiencies in diet, as well as inadequate housing and environmental conditions, and exacerbated by widespread adulteration. The people as a whole so desired good, or at least improved, health that when real wages in Britain began to rise sharply from the early 1860s onwards, patent medicines were among the first products which they demanded. Between 1865 and 1914, while real wages increased on average by 40 per cent, sales of patent medicines rose over sixfold (Corley 1987b: 113).

The way in which Beecham, of pill fame, exploited this demand, and marketed no fewer than 10,000 million pills in the 1865–1914 period, provides a standard of comparison for later marketing policies (Corley 1993: 109–11). In the year 1900, consumer expenditure on its pills, net of tax, was £340,000, of which 38 per cent represented an advertising bill of £100,000. The latter sum was by no means a record in Britain, with some food and drink companies spending even more. Market segmentation was crude by present-day standards, based on entrepreneurial hunch: the two principal groups targeted by the firm were those with lower incomes, and women.

In the 1890s, the founder Thomas Beecham maintained that he expected a 20 per cent profit from advertising in newspapers and magazines, and could tell within three years whether or not he was securing such a return. To appeal to the less well-off, he advertised mainly in periodicals costing less than 2*d.* (1p) (Beecham's Archives 1893). In 1913, when giving evidence to a parliamentary committee, his son Sir Joseph Beecham admitted that he did not know how his pill sales were divided between men and women. However – with the experiences of one (estranged) wife, six surviving daughters and numerous mistresses – he declared that 'women are more habitually constipated than men' (*British Parliamentary Papers* 1914: Qs. 9186, 9204). Some medical evidence in the 1980s supports this assertion, since food takes twice as long to pass through the gut in women than in men (Day 1982). Hence the firm advertised intensively in women's magazines, where it sometimes obtained editorial recommendations for its pills, such as 'a certain cure for most of the ills of childhood'. It thus effectively built up a cycle of dependency on laxative pills from one generation to the next. As late as 1945, its annual turnover on pills still exceeded £230,000.

Turning now from 'cure' to prevention, even towards the end of the nineteenth century some food companies were obtaining testimonials from doctors that their products were both wholesome and health-giving. However, it was the First World War which proved to be a watershed in the development of 'healthy' food products, for two reasons. First, on the health side, wartime food shortages and subsequent rationing schemes led to what Derek Oddy has called 'a reduction in ostentatious eating which had characterised some sections of fashionable society before the [First World] war' (Oddy 1990: 267). Among middle-class people, vitamins and calories had been widely known since the early years of the century, and by the 1920s attracted considerable public interest, as did slimming diets, milk bars, breakfast cereals – as substitutes for heavy cooked breakfasts – and health drinks.

Second, a sharp fall in the supply of competent domestic servants precipitated demands both for household appliances such as gas and electric cookers (rather than inefficient kitchen ranges) and refrigerators (which did away with the need for daily shopping) and for convenience foods of all kinds. If unemployed and other poor people had to subsist on tinned milk and bread and dripping, a benign dispensation ordained that what was healthy was also convenient, as breakfast cereals, packet soups and milky desserts and all-the-year-round tinned fruit regularly graced middle-class tables.

The foregoing introductory remarks form a prelude to a discussion of trends in the period 1930–9, and the marketing responses to such trends; this is pursued in the following section.

MARKETING 1930–9

The year 1930 is an appropriate one at which to begin the present study for two reasons. First, as explained earlier in this chapter, plenty of moneyed people – at least away from the distressed areas of Britain – and much of the younger generation by then appreciated the advantages of sensible eating. Second, the 'servant problem' in so many parts of the country led to a search for easy-to-prepare menus. Although the term 'convenience foods' did not enter into common use in Britain until the early 1960s (Burchfield 1972: I, 626), the underlying concept, of a food that helped to save time in preparing or providing a meal, had been familiar for nearly a century. Bird's custard was first marketed, as a cold pudding, in 1839, and the earliest machine-made biscuits appeared in 1846. The forerunner of Oxo dates from 1865, Bovril from 1886 and the unappealing Camp Coffee essence from the 1890s; the more palatable Nescafé was not made or marketed in Britain until 1938.

A second reason for choosing 1930 as a starting-date is that by then, many large British manufacturing firms were taking advantage of technical progress on both the management and the distribution sides. Communications and control systems, such as telephones and office machinery, became standard equipment, while the physical distribution of goods was speeded up by, for example, the use of road transport along the new trunk roads, being more flexible and efficient than using the pre-1914 railway network. As in the United States, although on a more modest scale, these developments were paralleled by the evolution of certain specialist skills in marketing. As Leslie Hannah has put it, 'the foremost exemplars of corporate growth based on marketing were . . . in the food industry' (Hannah 1983: 77 ff, 114).

A yardstick of good marketing is the amount of market research being carried out. Incidentally, *marketing* research, which investigates all problems entailed in delivering a good or service to the customer, was a later phenomenon (Chisnall 1986: 5). It is now becoming clear that market research among British firms was more widespread before 1939 than had been previously realized. A knowledge of the structure of the market allows it to be effectively segmented, thus yielding economies in advertising costs. Two separate aspects are involved. Existing data needed to be systematically processed, and new relevant data acquired.

As to processing available data, for too long even top managers relied on travellers' necessarily impressionistic verbal or written reports, for instance at McVitie & Price until the late 1930s (Adam

1974: 23). Cadbury claimed to be one of the pioneers of market research in Britain. In 1917 it installed a punch card system for collating sales information, although it later found calculating machines to be more effective (Cadbury 1945: 32; 1964: 28). For acquiring fresh data, since the first decade of the century firms ranging from Peek Frean to Rowntree gained geographical and other information from coupons or applications for special offers submitted by consumers. A further underlying requirement was the existence of reliable social survey techniques: these had already been pioneered in Britain. Early examples are Charles Booth's inquiry of 1889 into poverty in London and that of Seebohm Rowntree in York ten years later. The first sampling techniques for this purpose, by (Sir) Arthur Bowley in his investigations into working-class conditions in Reading and four other English towns in 1911−14, allowed the sample survey to claim to 'occupy a similar place in social science to that occupied by the laboratory experiment in the natural sciences' (British Market Research Bureau 1956: xiv).

For food companies the value of such techiques was demonstrated in a study of *The People's Food* of 1938, by the advertising magnate Sir William Crawford. To obtain really trustworthy information on, for example, the relation between income and food expenditure and the nutritional value of food consumption, careful survey methods were used, as fully explained in Appendix I of the book (Crawford and Broadley 1938: 308−20). By that time, food companies could draw on much general information by which to judge their own sales performance: official censuses of production were held in 1924 − the year in which the *Daily Sketch*'s *Survey of the British Market* appeared − 1930 and 1935. There were also important household budget surveys (Massey 1942; Ministry of Labour 1940−1). How far did individual companies make use of such data and techniques for marketing purposes?

In the United States market research dates back to 1879; at least in the food sector, the diffusion of its techniques to Britain seems to have occurred in the 1920s. The US-owned advertising agency of J. Walter Thompson established its London branch in 1899, but did not launch a campaign in Britain to publicize market research until 1924, when it issued a *Population Handbook of Great Britain*. Two years later it acquired the account of Horlicks (West 1987: 200) and in 1930 that of Rowntrees, which was specifically attracted by the agency's expertise in market research (Fitzgerald 1989: 57).

In 1933 J. Walter Thompson established what was claimed to be Britain's first market research agency, the British Market Research

Bureau. One of its two main rivals was Lintas, the agency of Lever Brothers first set up in 1929, when that company was centralizing the publicity of its many British units as part of the Unilever merger (Wilson 1968: 92). Another rival was the London Press Exchange, mainly concerned with readership surveys for the English press. These three firms were carrying out probably two-thirds of all market research in Britain by 1939 (Abrams 1951: 55n). However, other firms are recorded, such as Sales Research Services, which undertook the fieldwork for *The People's Food* in association with Crawfords' own research department, and which from 1938 onwards conducted a quarterly 'brand barometer' series of consumer surveys (British Market Research Bureau 1956: 123).

Advertising-sales ratios 1935

To investigate, as systematically as possible, the question of which food and health drink firms in the 1930s employed good marketing practices, and which the opposite, advertising data for 1935 are presented in Table 11.1. These were compiled, for a range of product groups, from that year's Census of Production and from an associated industry-wide inquiry into advertising expenditure. The table specifies the thirteen products which were most intensively advertised in relation to net sales, as well as the five at the bottom of the list.

Such data, informative as they are, do have their limitations, for two reasons. First, advertising expenditure forms only part of the total cost of marketing. It omits the difficult-to-quantify 'below the line' items such as money spent on exhibitions, free samples and window displays (Critchley 1972). Second, while a high advertising/sales ratio may indicate an appreciation of the importance of widespread publicity, it may also represent an extravagant waste of resources if the market is not being segmented in the interests of economy. The amount of competition, too, may cause the ratio to vary from one product to another. Even so, the data provide a valuable framework for structured survey of the industry before 1939.

Advertising in these industry groups as a whole was not unduly heavy by British standards. Food and health drinks accounted for just under 37 per cent of manufacturer's net sales of consumer goods nationally, but for less than 23 per cent of aggregate consumer-good advertising expenditure. Among more intensively advertised products in other industries were bottled cider, tonic wines, tobacco, some household equipment, toiletries, health salts, sparking plugs and fountain pens.

Table 11.1 Advertising expenditure on food products and health drinks in the UK, 1935

	Manufacturers' net sales (£000)	Manufacturers' total advertising in UK (£000)	Advertising as % of net sales
Malted health drinks	2,300	950	41
Custard powder and blancmanges	1,200	450	38
Gravy mixtures	480	160	33
Beef extracts and essences	2,600	570	22
Canned and packet soup	730	160	22
Cocoa and chocolate powder	1,400	290	21
Proprietary breakfast cereals	3,900	700	18
Dog biscuits and food	1,400	190	14
Baking powder	380	40	11
Mustard	1,000	100	10
Table jellies	1,450	140	9.7
Sauces, pickles and salad cream	2,500	230	9.2
Coffee extracts and essences	1,100	100	9.1
Meat and fish paste	1,600	60	3.8
Chocolate confectionery	16,800	630	3.8
Soft drinks	9,400	340	3.6
Sweets and toffee	13,800	460	3.3
Biscuits, rusks and crispbread	17,200	390	2.3
Total food and health drinks	302,940	8,840	2.9
Total consumer goods	827,640	38,712	4.7
Food and health drinks as % of total consumer goods	36.6%	22.8%	

Source: Kaldor and Silverman 1948: 144–5

At the top of the list in Table 11.1 are malted health drinks, with an astonishing 41 per cent of net sales devoted to advertising. The brand leader, Ovaltine, was then buying much time on the pirate radio station, Radio Luxembourg. That promotion, and the effort of building up a children's club – the Ovaltineys – to 5 million members by 1938, while onerous, maintained the firm's leadership. Vernon Ward (see Chapter 13 in this volume) has discussed Horlicks' strategy in this period, which involved much market research from 1927 onwards. While the early inquiries were apparently to discover (for instance) the times of day when milky drinks were consumed, during the 1930s J. Walter Thompson carried out sample surveys to discover the demand by the various income groups. Interestingly enough, in 1930 Horlicks gained information from a competition which attracted more than 6,000 entries. As to the next four categories in the table, the makers of Bird's custard, Bisto, Bovril and Oxo skilfully, but clearly at great cost, used posters and press displays to stamp their products indelibly on the public mind (Hadley 1970: Scarborough 1965: 9).

The breakfast cereal market is a significant one. It was the largest group, in terms of sales, apart from confectionery, biscuits and soft drinks. Moreover, as E. J. T. Collins has shown (see Chapter 12 in this volume), it was dominated by US firms, which might have been expected to advertise lavishly in a highly competitive market. The relatively moderate advertising/sales ratio of 18 per cent therefore seems surprising. The ratio of the brand leader Kelloggs was about 28 per cent that year, but the marketing war must have intensified later in the decade. Indeed, by 1938 cereal firms' publicity expenditure had risen from one-twelfth to one-tenth of total food advertising, more than 80 per cent promoting Kellogg, Quaker Oats, Shredded Wheat and Postum Cereals (Collins 1976: 36–8). It is not known what kinds of market research these firms carried out, but they targeted their advertising principally at children among consumers and grocers' chains among distributors. While proprietary dog foods were already of importance, not until after the Second World War did the US confectionery firm Mars successfully launch Kit-e-Kat for feline consumption.

In any attempt to assess advertising quality, the categories at the lower end of Table 11.1 are of much interest. Whereas in 1935, cocoa and chocolate powder were number six on the list, chocolate bars and confectionery were well down. The brand leader, Cadbury, consistently pushed its 'house name' as synonymous with both quality and value. It therefore relied heavily on price reductions in the depressed 1930s to stimulate and then maintain demand. It advertised only 4 of its 237 varieties; because of the considerable number of outlets nationally, it found regular contact by sales staff an acceptable substitute for advertising. On a 2 oz. Cadbury's bar, selling and advertising costs, no doubt including below-the-line items, came to 8 per cent of the retail price (Cadbury 1945: 41; 1964: 13–28).

The smaller and less profitable Rowntree by 1930 was quite unable to challenge the national leadership of Cadbury, and sought niches in the market. That year it set up a marketing department; as a client of J. Walter Thompson, it used the agency's test marketing facilities, said to be the most advanced in Britain at that date. The astute George Harris, having personally acquired marketing expertise in the United States, from 1933 onwards promoted a succession of novelties, including the seductively advertised Black Magic and Dairy Box assortments and less expensive products such as Kit Kat, Aero and Smarties. All these initiatives increased Rowntree's turnover by 1939 to two and a half times that of 1931, so that its advertising/sales ratio probably altered very little (Fitzgerald 1989: 52–4).

Coincidentally, the toffee makers Mackintosh, already aggressive in the marketing field, diversified into chocolate through acquiring Caleys, and in the late 1930s launched Quality Street, Rolo and Milk Tray Assorted. No information is available about its market research activities. In 1932 Mars Ltd, the subsidiary of a US confectionery firm, started up in Britain, after an intensive survey of the demand for candy throughout Europe. It soon introduced Mars Bars, Milky Way and other brands to compete against the Rowntree's and Mackintosh's novelties.

Schweppes resembled Cadbury in relying on its name. Although before 1939 it spent £100,000 a year on advertising, it employed no agent and concentrated on notices in sporting and glossy magazines, theatre programmes and on luxury liners; it also undertook some sponsorship. Like Bovril, it had an illuminated sign in Piccadilly Circus (Simmons 1938: 125–9). As to biscuits, few if any of the quality producers could boast a coherent marketing policy. Huntley & Palmers until 1939 was largely production-orientated, with 400 varieties; Macfarlane Lang's board minutes disdainfully referred to advertising as 'propaganda'. When two firms, the British Meredith & Drew (Betta biscuits) in 1931 and the Canadian Westons in 1934, began mass-producing ultra-cheap biscuits, by 1939 they had scooped over one-third of the market. As their biscuits sold at less than half the price of the high-class brands, they did not trouble to advertise, and granted no discounts or credit. The high-class makers responded with outrage rather than any direct counter-measures, apart from reluctantly introducing automatic plants (Corley 1972: 219–31).

Summing-up 1930–9

The data in Table 11.1, and associated information from other sources, provide evidence of much marketing vigour in this industry during the 1930s. Where advertising/sales ratios appeared to be unexpectedly low, good reasons could usually be found. Doubtless the quality of the advertising, and the amount of market research, were below those of equivalents in the United States. As to the quantity, some instructive findings can be cited. Total advertising formed a higher proportion of the US national income than in Britain. Yet the advertising/sales ratio in both countries for canned and bottled foods, coffee, tea, cocoa, and beef and other extracts were almost identical. However, for cereals, biscuits, preserves, sweets and toffee, the US ratio was about half as high again. The 3.6 per cent ratio for soft drinks in Britain compares with a remarkable 15 per cent in the United States, for which no doubt the cola manufacturers were largely responsible. Thus the greater relative outlay on publicity in the United States was apparently due to advertising having been used more extensively than intensively in US industry (Kaldor and Silverman 1948: 18, 30–1).

It is worth noting that foods and health drinks were beginning to take on some of the functions earlier performed by patent medicines, at least as tonics. Bovril, which claimed to have independent scientific evidence of its product's body-building powers, from 1920 onwards exploited the slogan 'prevents that sinking feeling'. Horlicks stressed the vital need to sleep well, and in 1933 invented the affliction of 'night starvation'. Huntley & Palmers feebly imitated this with its own ailment of 'afternoon fatigue', cured by consuming Osborne biscuits. In 1935 the Milk Marketing Board spent £59,000 on advertising; to some extent its message had been anticipated by Cadbury, which since 1928 had proclaimed that a glass and a half of 'fresh full-cream milk' went into every half-pound block of milk chocolate. Breakfast cereals, when combined with milk, were advertised as providing a balanced and sustaining meal. Even so, until the environmentally conscious 1970s, manufacturers in this industry emphasized the enjoyment to be gained from their products rather than the latter's health-giving properties.

MARKETING 1945–70

During the Second World War, both the production and the marketing of foodstuffs and health drinks were severely restricted by government controls. There were both direct and points rationing, the latter permitting some choice between a range of scarce foods such as biscuits and breakfast cereals. Individual brands were replaced by anonymous standardized lines, such as non-alcoholic drinks sold under the soft drinks industry (SDI) label, while distribution was subject to zoning. These restrictions were eased only gradually after 1945; food rationing was not fully wound up until 1954. Moreover, in the early years of austerity until 1950, the post-war government secured a voluntary limitation on advertising, so as to discourage demand as long as product shortages continued.

The 1950s then became the decade of the 'domestic revolution', in which the pre-1939 demand for household appliances was intensified by the recruitment of over 1 million married women to the labour force. An equally buoyant demand arose for convenience foods, in which ease of cooking and/or serving outweighed cheapness. Concurrently, revolutionary changes were taking place in the distribution and marketing of food. Large self-service stores, or supermarkets, sprang up, while collective and later individual resale price maintenance was outlawed; these events transformed the pattern of shopping. The food makers, who grasped the need to step up their marketing efforts accordingly, were offered an entirely new, if costly, advertising medium when commercial television transmissions started up in Britain from 1955 onwards. When the sellers' market eroded from the later 1950s onwards, even more persuasive methods were needed to induce the public to buy.

To assess the 1945–70 period, it would have been very helpful to have data of sales and advertising that were comparable with those given in Table 11.1 for 1935. Unfortunately, post-war advertising figures have to be estimated from the space (for press notices) or time (for television commercials), multiplied by the known rates charged by publishers or television companies. The estimates in Tables 11.2 and 11.3 should therefore be regarded as providing no more than orders of magnitude. Indeed, most firms have been extremely coy about revealing their own advertising expenditure. Some rare figures by Beecham show advertising costs as more than doubling from £2.5 million in 1950 to £5.5 million in 1960 (Houchen 1966: 73). This is below the £6.3 million estimated in Table 11.2, perhaps because of the discounts offered. With this reservation, the top spenders on press and television advertising, in 1960 and 1970, are cited in Table 11.2.

By far the largest advertiser was Unilever. In 1960, advertising represented about three-fifths of its total marketing expenditure, the remainder going on 'promotions' (Wilson 1968: 99). Ten years later, about one third of its outlay on advertising proper was used on pushing soaps and detergents, over which it had fought costly brand wars with rivals since the late 1940s. Many innovations in its general marketing strategy originated in the United States, most notably in the US armed services, which refined certain market research techniques to assess

Table 11.2 Top spenders on TV and press advertising in the UK, 1960 and 1970[a]

	1960			1970		
	Order[b]	Estimated outlay (£million)	TV share of whole (%)	Order[b]	Estimated outlay (£million)	TV share of whole (%)
Unilever	1	13.1	69	1	16.7	74
Beecham	2	6.3	78	4	6.3	70
Cadbury	5	3.2	65	2[c]	7.0	89
Mars	6	2.9	93	7	5.0	97
Nestlé	7	2.2	43	20	2.3	78
Rowntree	9	2.1	99	8[d]	4.5	99
Rank Hovis McDougall	—	—	—	11	3.6	89
Heinz	—	—	—	19	2.3	85

Sources: For 1960 Harris and Seldon 1962: 48
        For 1970 Critchley 1972: 20

Notes: [a] Food and soft drink firms only; Unilever and Beecham have considerable non-food output
        [b] Non-food companies omitted
        [c] Cadbury Schweppes 1969
        [d] Rowntree Mackintosh 1969

wartime military and civilian morale. The group maintained Lintas as an agency open to all clients, but internalized its own market research in a separate division, later extended into a fully-fledged research bureau to co-ordinate all group market research activities.

A spin-off from the American experience was a realization – previously, it seems, confined to firms such as Rowntree – that a crucial feature of marketing was product development. As the Unilever chairman reported to shareholders, in 1957 no less than 22 per cent of sales of its food products (and 20 and 25 per cent of detergent and toiletry sales respectively) comprised those which had not been on the market six years previously. As to the group's total range of food product groups in 1968, almost half were new since 1955 (Rodger 1974: 115–16). Some of the pre-1955 specialities, such as frozen foods, had become very popular, with national sales to households rising fifty-fold between 1950 and 1970; by the latter date Unilever (through Birds Eye) enjoyed one-third of the market. Birds Eye was then spending 2.5 per cent of net sales on advertising and about 2.1 per cent on other forms of sales promotion (Monopolies and Mergers Commission 1976: 223).

Table 11.3 Sales of and advertising expenditure on food products and health drinks in the UK, 1970[a]

	Retail sales (£million)	Manufacturers' total advertising in UK (£million)	Advertising as % of retail sales
Crispbreads	7	1.5	21.4
Malted and cocoa drinks	15	1.7	11.3
Meat and vegetable extracts	20	2.1	10.5
Desserts	33	3.4	10.3
Breakfast cereals	45–50	4.4	9.2
Milk products	32	2.5	7.8
Margarine	50	3.1	6.2
Infant foods	25	1.5	6.0
Instant coffee	45	2.3	5.1
Canned cat food	28	1.4	5.0
Suet, cooking fats and oils	15–20	0.8	4.7
Dog biscuits and food	63	2.7	4.3
Food mixes	6	0.2	3.3
Canned and packet soups	50	1.4	2.8
Chocolate confectionery ⎱ Sugar confectionery ⎰	414	8.8 ⎱ 2.3 ⎰	2.6
Tea	145	3.6	2.5
Ice cream	56	1.2	2.1
Jams and preserves	50	1.0	2.0
Soft drinks	120	2.3	1.9
Biscuits	150	2.5	1.7

Source: Critchley 1971: Section B

Note: [a]Twenty most advertised items: advertising outlay estimated; includes only advertisers spending more than £100,000 in 1970

Unilever's US-inspired marketing approach can fruitfully be compared with that of Beecham, 30 per cent of whose sales world-wide in 1970 were of food and health drink products; however, they contributed only 13 per cent of trading profit. Leslie Lazell, in charge as managing director and then chairman from 1951 to 1968, described Beecham as 'one of the first British companies to practise marketing in the American style'. He claimed to have 'improved on American practice by requiring the chief executive [i.e. himself] to lead the marketing team'. Without such direction, he maintained, none of the company's principal brands would have made the progress that they did (Lazell 1975: 199). He was able to take rapid decisions, whether to exploit success or to withdraw in the event of failure; he could also stamp out national or departmental rivalries, bully advertising agencies into doing what he wanted, and press for continual improvements to products, packaging and formulae.

Thus under Lazell, Beecham displayed a marketing aggression then not all that common in British consumer enterprises. Among its drinks advertised as health products was Lucozade, acquired via Maclean in 1938 and for a time after 1945 contributing over one-third of the Beecham group's profits. Lucozade and Ribena (acquired in 1955) were used as the core of Beecham Foods Ltd, 'the soft drink business of [Lazell's] dreams' which he hoped to market as vigorously and effectively as the soap giants pushed their products (Lazell 1975: 100, 113). The unimportant canned vegetable and food products had been mistakenly bought by Lazell's predecessor to counter the expected fall (which did not take place) in home remedies once the National Health Service was introduced. Horlicks joined Beecham in 1969; by the following year its advertising outlay was one-third greater than that of Ovaltine, which enjoyed half the malted drink market to Horlicks' one-third.

Since consumption of confectionery in Britain, at 7.6 ounces a head per week, was by 1970 the highest of any country in the world, it is not surprising that the four top advertising spenders, after Unilever and Beecham, listed in Table 11.2 were all in the chocolate and cocoa business. Cadbury remained the brand leader in block chocolate up to 1970 and beyond, but the contribution of this range in tonnage terms had fallen since the Second World War from 60 to 43 per cent. While the 'value for money' concept was no longer so valid in post-war boom conditions, the firm consistently stressed the Cadbury name in all its publicity, as synonymous with quality. To keep down costs, it pared its varieties from 240 to 60, of which 20 were now regularly advertised; it also improved manufacturing efficiency and reduced distributors' margins (Cadbury 1964; Foster 1970: 64). However, by the 1960s low product growth and intense competition from rivals compelled it to diversify, into sugar confectionery, cakes and convenience foods prepared with American technology. In 1969 it merged with Schweppes, so as to achieve economies in distribution and in product development. This was shortly after the Registrar of Restrictive Practices had refused an application by the chocolate and sugar confectionery industry for resale price maintenance to be upheld for its products (*British Parliamentary Papers* 1969/70: 27–30).

Rowntree had less need to stress a company name, since the marketing reputation it had built up in the 1930s had rested on specific brands such as Black Magic and Kit Kat. After 1945 it therefore went in for concentrated single-line marketing to push these brands, and also post-war novelties such as the chocolate mints After Eights and Matchmakers. It also introduced costly production plant that was difficult to copy. Of its thirty branded products, nineteen were intensively advertised. It employed no fewer than six advertising agencies, which it reckoned to call in far earlier at the development stage than before 1939. To some extent, it did diversify into dessert and snack foods but in 1969 merged with Mackintosh, wholly a confectionery firm and still a brand leader in certain specialities. Like Cadbury Schweppes, the combine looked forward to economies in marketing, distribution and product planning (Thomas 1970: 102).

As to Mars, while its range of products continued to sell briskly, including Mars Bars, Maltesers, Milky Way and Galaxy, none of them was a brand leader in 1970, despite intensive advertising, mainly on television. Although it had a divisional structure, specific financial targets and an incentive system to encourage the meeting of targets, its role in the market was far from outstanding. To be sure, there had been disagreements within the family, only just resolved by the late 1960s. Its subsidiary (Pedigree) Petfoods did relatively better, by then holding over half the British petfood market (Meyers 1967: 157). While Nestlé had a marketing function in its central office, there was no structure to control and co-ordinate production (Channon 1973: 171). Perhaps, therefore, Nescafé and other convenience foods were being developed and pushed at the expense of the confectionery side.

Schweppes, whose pre-war advertising had been exclusively for affluent people, continued to rely heavily on its rather unusual name. After 1945 it did aim its publicity at a wider public, rapidly expanded the appeal of its mixer drinks, and between 1951 and 1970 doubled advertising expenditure to £600,000 a year. However, the embarrassingly fanciful publicity at home was less effective overall than the more direct targeting of the United States, which in those years took that country by storm. In 1959, it began to diversify into other foods, such as Chivers' and Hartley's jams, but until 1962 did not have a marketing department (Simmons 1983: 133ff). A year later, three marketing-orientated divisions were set up, but when the merger with Cadbury took place in 1969, much still needed to be done on the marketing side.

As to biscuits, a consequence of the post-1945 prosperity was to halt the demand for ultra-cheap kinds. All manufacturers automated production and packing, thus cutting costs; for many years standard biscuits were cheaper in real terms than before 1939. Huntley & Palmers and Peek Frean, as part of Associated Biscuits, kept their two sales teams separate and competed against one another. Not until

Jacobs joined in 1960 did the top management begin to reorganize Associated Biscuits into divisions, with a unified marketing function along American lines. Even so, the group held only 20 per cent of the UK biscuit market in 1970.

Leadership had in fact passed to the Scottish manufacturers, two – McVitie & Price and Macfarlane Lang – merging as United Biscuits in 1948. Initially, this was simply a holding company until they were joined by Crawfords and Macdonalds in the early 1960s. Yet even by 1970, the three operating units still had their own boards and other functions. The group later acquired some smaller companies and also diversified into snack foods, pre-packed cakes and retail outlets. However, these organizational weaknesses were offset by McVitie & Price's decision to put virtually the whole of its allocation of ingredients into the four best-selling brands, notably the Digestive biscuit; there had been 387 varieties before the war. This bold step was masterminded by (Sir) Hector Laing, backed by able sales and works managers. Laing also sought the maximum cost savings from automation. He kept discounts low, to 2.5 per cent for large customers. The resulting high gross profits permitted twice as much advertising as the low-earning Associated Biscuits could spare, over £1 million, and gave United Biscuits about 40 per cent of the British biscuit market, or twice that of its main rival (Pugh 1991: 45ff).

Malted health drinks were at the top of both the 1935 and the 1970 lines. If chocolate beverages are omitted from the 1970 category of 'food drinks', the advertising/sales ratio for Ovaltine and Horlicks remains at a high 10 per cent. The rather basic custard and cold shape (blancmange) of the 1930s had by 1970 given way to heavily advertised desserts, notably that unfailing stand-by creamed rice, and enticingly named concoctions such as Sweet Magic and Angel Delight. In Table 11.3, gravy mixtures and beef extracts are combined in 'meat and vegetable extracts'. Bisto and Oxo jointly had advertising budgets five times as large as Bovril and Marmite combined; the irrepressible Bisto kids had by then become boringly middle class, while affluent housewives were being wooed with Golden Oxo. As to breakfast cereals, if the hot varieties are excluded, the advertising ratio rises to over 12 per cent, and thus almost at the top of the league; this was despite heavy own-brand, by definition unadvertised, sales.

Near the bottom of the 1970 list in Table 11.3 are dog biscuits and food, with a 4.3 per cent advertising/sales ratio, chocolate and sugar confectionery at 2.6 per cent, jams at 2.0 per cent and biscuits at 1.7 per cent. These low ratios are as yet unexplained. Frozen cooked meats had a ratio of only 0.7 per cent; no data are available for frozen fish. Perhaps the particular methods of selling frozen foods encouraged below-the-line techniques such as merchandising. Among the basically new products was the potato crisp, a convenience food par excellence. Introduced into Britain in the 1920s, it did not come into its own until after 1945. By 1960, Smiths enjoyed 80 per cent of the market, and clearly got by with much inefficient production and unimpressive marketing. Then Imperial Group's Golden Wonder Crisps entered the market in the early 1960s, with improved production techniques and a very able market-by-market promotion strategy; they soon captured half of Smiths' market and forced that company into becoming marketing-orientated (Simmonds and Leighton 1973: 103–8).

Summing-up 1945–70

In a period when many commentators discerned a lack of marketing skills throughout British industry, the number of food and health drinks manufacturers that demonstrably exhibited high standards of marketing is impressive. Above all, there has been a willingness to benefit from American know-how; sometimes entrepreneurs obtained this know-how directly, and sometimes through advertising agencies. Without this absorption of good marketing techniques, companies in the industries under review would have been less able to contend with the twin problems of market saturation in so many products and with growing overseas competition.

CONCLUSION

This chapter has investigated marketing practices in Britain's food and health drinks firms between 1930 and 1970. For this important segment of the British economy, its finding has been to cast doubt on the apparently widespread view that the country's marketing efforts were of indifferent quality.

While this chapter has recited such cases of good marketing as the author has happened to come across, it also seeks to point the way towards a more structured future programme of research, which in the current state of business history studies is so badly needed. All too many national, and overseas, business historians strive to portray Britain's marketing strategy, in common with its industrial performance generally, as having been incompetent, amateurish, ill thought out and narrow. This poses a serious danger that the signal achievements of many British entrepreneurs will be crowded out altogether.

To be sure, it would be foolish to attempt to defend the indefensible. Yet the framework of advertising and sales data, presented in Table 11.1, is both valuable and undeservedly neglected. With its aid, researchers should be able to go back to the archives of individual manufacturers and of advertising agencies (as Collins and Ward have done – see Chapters 12 and 13 in this volume), to trade journals and similar sources, in order to gain as complete a picture as possible of pre-1939 marketing policies in each product group.

For the period since 1945, the absence of comprehensive and reliable data on advertising expenditure is a serious handicap, which will persist until companies are legally obliged to disclose annual figures. Even so, the estimates of television and the press advertising, and of market shares obtained from sample surveys, should yield a reasonable proxy of the actual data. All in all, some systematic research along these lines, to supersede the earlier intuitive speculation, would be highly welcome.

REFERENCES

Abrams, M. (1951) *Social Surveys and Social Action*, London: Heinemann.
Adam, J. S. (1974) *A Fell Fine Baker: The Story of United Biscuits*, London: Hutchinson Benham.
Beecham's Archives (1893) Unidentified New York newspaper, August 1893, now held by the Local History and Archives Library, St Helens, Lancashire.
British Institute of Management (BIM) (1970) 'Marketing organization in British industry', BIM Information Survey no. 148, *Management Today*, July.
British Market Research Bureau (1956) *Readings in Market Research*, London: British Market Research Bureau.
British Parliamentary Papers (1914) 'Report from the Select Committee on patent medicines', House of Commons Papers 1914 (414), 9. Evidence of Sir J. Beecham, 23 January 1913: 495–517.
—— (1969/70) 'Restrictive trading agreements; report of the Registrar 1966–9: chocolate and sugar confectionery', 18 Cmnd 4303: 27–30.
Burchfield, R. W. (ed.) (1972) *A Supplement to the Oxford English Dictionary I*, Oxford: Clarendon.
Cadbury (1945) *Industrial Record 1919–39*, Bournville: Cadbury Brothers Ltd.
—— (1964) *Industrial Challenge*, Bournville: Cadbury Brothers Ltd.
Chandler, A. D. (1990) *Scale and Scope: The Dynamics of Industrial Capitalism*, Cambridge, Mass: Harvard University Press.
Channon, D. F. *The Strategy and Structure of British Enterprise*, London: Macmillan.
Chisnall, P. H. (1986) *Marketing Research*, 3rd ed. London: McGraw-Hill.
Collins, E. J. T. (1976) 'The "consumer revolution" and the growth of factory foods: changing patterns of bread and cereal-eating in Britain in the

twentieth century', in D. Oddy and D. Miller (eds) *The Making of the Modern British Diet*, London: Croom Helm.

Corley, T. A. B. (1972) *Quaker Enterprise in Biscuits: Huntley & Palmers of Reading 1822–1972*, London: Hutchinson.

—— (1983) 'From national to multinational enterprise: the Beecham business 1848–1945', *University of Reading Discussion Papers in International Investment and Business Studies* no. 76, November.

—— (1987a) 'Consumer marketing in Britain 1914–60', *Business History* 29(4): 65–83.

—— (1987b) 'Interactions between the British and American patent medicine industries 1708–1914', *Business and Economic History* 2nd series **16**: 111–29.

—— (1993) 'Marketing and business history, in theory and practice', in R. S. Tedlow and G. Jones (eds) *The Rise and Fall of Mass Marketing*, London: Routledge.

Crawford, W. and Broadley, H. (1938) *The People's Food*, London: Heinemann.

Critchley, R. A. (ed.) (1971) *IPC Marketing Manual of the United Kingdom*, London: International Publishing Corporation.

—— (1972) *UK Advertising Statistics*, London: Advertising Association.

Day, J. (1982) 'Regular dose of salts?', *Observer* 12 September.

Dunning, J. H. (1958) *American Investment in British Manufacturing Industry*, London: Allen & Unwin.

Economist (1960) 'Reviving Poffenheimer', *The Economist* **196**, 16 July.

Edwards, R. S. and Townsend, H. (eds) (1966) *Business Growth*, London: Macmillan.

Fitzgerald, R. (1989) 'Rowntree and market strategy 1897–1939', *Business and Economic History* 2nd series **18**: 45–58.

Foster, G. (1970) 'The Cadbury Schweppes mix', *Management Today* April: 64–73.

Hadley, P. (1970) *The History of Bovril Advertising*, London: Bovril Ltd.

Hannah, L. (1983) *The Rise of the Corporate Economy*, 2nd ed., London: Methuen.

Harris, R. and Seldon, A. (1962) *Advertising and the Public*, London: André Deutsch.

Horst, T. (1974) *At Home Abroad*, Cambridge, Mass: Ballinger.

Houchen, A. E. V. (1966) 'The marketing of branded consumer goods', in R. S. Edwards and H. Townsend (eds) *Business Growth*, London: Macmillan.

Kaldor, N. and Silverman, R. (1948) *A Statistical Analysis of Advertising Expenditure and of the Revenue of the Press*, Cambridge: Cambridge University Press.

Lazell, H. G. (1975) *From Pills to Penicillin: The Beecham Story*, London: Heinemann.

Massey, P. (1942) 'The expenditure of 1360 British middle-class households in 1938–39', *Journal of Royal Statistical Society* **105** Part III.

Meyers, H. B. (1967) 'The sweet, secret world of Forrest Mars', *Fortune* **75** May: 154–212.

Ministry of Labour (1940–1) 'Weekly expenditure of working-class households in the United Kingdom in 1937–38', *Ministry of Labour Gazette* December and January.

Monopolies and Mergers Commission (1976) *Report on the Supply in the United Kingdom of Frozen Foodstuffs for Human Consumption*, HC 674, London: HMSO.

Oddy, D. J. (1990) 'Food, drink and nutrition', in F. M. L. Thompson (ed.) *The Cambridge Social History of Britain 1750–1950*, vol. 2, Cambridge: Cambridge University Press.

Pickering, J. F. and Cockerill, T. A. J. (eds) (1984) *The Economic Management of the Firm*, Oxford: Philip Allan, quoting National Economic Development Office (1981) *Industrial Performance: Trade Performance and Marketing*, London: HMSO.

Porter, M. E. (1990) *The Competitive Advantage of Nations*, London: Macmillan.

Pugh, P. (1991) *A Clear and Simple Vision* (biography of Hector, now Lord Laing), Cambridge: Cambridge Business Publishing.

Rodger, L. W. (1974) *Marketing in a Competitive Economy*, 4th ed., London: Associated Business Programmes.

Satirist, The London (1838; 1839) Advertisements of Mr. Cockle's antibilious pills, 7 January 1838 p. 8; 28 April 1839 p. 130.

Scarborough, C. (1965) . . . *about Oxo*, London: Spectator Publications.

Simmonds, K. and Leighton, D. (1973) *Case Problems in Marketing, 14, Smith's Potato Crisps Ltd*, London: Nelson.

Simmons, D. A. (1983) *Schweppes: The First 200 Years*, London: Springwood.

Tedlow, R. S. and Jones, G. (eds) (1993) *The Rise and Fall of Mass Marketing*, London: Routledge.

Thomas, D. (1970) 'How Rowntree matched Macintosh', *Management Today* September: 102–56.

Wells, H. S. H. (1962) 'Putting marketing in its place', *The Manager* August.

West, D. C. (1987) 'From T-square to T-plan: the London office of the J. Walter Thompson advertising agency 1919–70', *Business History* 29: 199–217.

Wilson, C. (1968) *Unilever 1945–1965*, London: Cassell.

12 Brands and breakfast cereals in Britain

E. J. T. Collins

The early history of breakfast cereals is part of the folklore of the modern food industry and well enough known to require here only a brief restatement (Collins 1976; *International Directory of Company Histories* 1990: II; Marquette 1967; Powell 1956). They originated out of an interest in health foods that can be traced back to the 1830s, and specifically to the experiments carried out from the 1860s by John Harvey Kellogg, the pioneer nutritionist, at the sanitorium at Battle Creek, Michigan. His search for 'Food in a condensed form excellently suited to the wants of the human system', designed for use by vegetarian religious sects such as the Seventh Day Adventists and gastric sufferers generally, produced first Granula, a mixture of wheat and oats, then Granola, a mixture of wheat, oats and maizemeal. The 1890s saw in quick succession the development of all the main types of ready-cooked breakfast cereal. In 1892 Shredded Wheat was formulated by Henry D. Perky, a Denver lawyer. Two years later Kellogg created the first flaked cereal, Granose, and in 1898, the corn flake. Around the turn of the century, oat flakes were pioneered by the Beck Cereal Co. of Detroit, and Grape Nuts, a dextrinized cereal similar to Granola, by the inimitable Charles Post. Soon after, the Quaker Co. launched Puffed Wheat and Puffed Rice, based on the Anderson patent of 1902, and the Battle Creek Pure Food Co., malted wheat flakes.

By the time of the First World War, the basic manufacturing processes – dextrinizing, flaking, shredding and puffing – had been perfected, and formulations – maize, wheat and oat flakes, puffed and shredded wheat, and dextrinized grain mixtures – were being produced on a factory scale. Out of the myriad of individual products and manufacturers – up to 1912 an estimated 107 different brands of corn flakes had been produced in the United States – there had emerged the hierarchy that was to dominate the industry, at home and abroad, for the remainder of the century. Kellogg, Quaker, Shredded Wheat (later part of Nabisco), the Postum Cereal Co. (later the Post Division of General Foods), the Force Food Co. of Buffalo, and Armour Grain Co. of Chicago (later part of the Ralston Purina Co.), were the already established market leaders.

In Britain, there had existed a small niche market for cereal health foods since the 1830s when a Grahamite school, based on the American prototype, was established in Surrey, dedicated to simple living and a diet based on vegetables and Graham bread (Griggs 1988: 54–61). In 1880, *Zwieback*, a German cereal food consisting of slices of bread thoroughly baked a second time till crisp throughout, was popular among dieticians as a readily digestible alternative to ordinary bread at breakfast and other meals (Olsen and Olsen 1912: 284). At least sixty-four different proprietary brands of cereal-based foods and drinks suitable for infants, invalids and food reformists were in production in 1912 (Tibbles 1912: 438–50). Most of the leading brands of US breakfast cereal were obtainable in Britain before the First World War. Tibbles (1912) mentions Grape Nuts, Malta-vita, Shredded Wheat, Vigor, Granose, Vitos, Quaker Rolled Oats, plus formulations by Pettjohns, Ralston and Eustace Miles. At this stage there is no direct evidence for the importation of Kellogg products, but Kellogg himself was a powerful influence among health reformers such as the Olsens, managers of the Surrey Hills Hydropathic and Leicester Sanitarium, who prescribed Toasted Wheat Flakes and Granose for invalids and 'persons of weak digestion' (Olsen and Olsen 1912: 169–70).

The most successful product by far, prior to the First World War, was the hot cereal, Quaker Oats. The Quaker Co. began shipping to Britain in 1877, selling initially through a local distributor; it established its own importing agency in 1893 and, in 1899, a wholly owned marketing subsidiary, Quaker Oats Ltd, with branches in London, Liverpool, Newcastle and Glasgow (Bound 1966: 1; Marquette 1967: 213ff). By 1914, oatmeal porridge had become almost a mass consumption food, whereas ready-to-eat cereals had only a very limited distribution, being sold mainly through high-class grocers such as Fortnum and Mason in London, and specialist health food shops. Force Wheat Flakes were first imported in 1902, Post Toasties in 1907 (originally under the name of Elijah's Manna) and Shredded Wheat in 1908. Advertising in society magazines, such as *Strand* and *Black and White*, they ranked as food curiosities but, as Quaker had already demonstrated, with skilful merchandising there existed a clear potential for dramatic growth.

The appeal of the British market for US companies was not only one of language and culture, but also the UK's relatively high average income per head, and clear evidence that by 1914, in the United States' footsteps, Britain was about to enter the stage of high mass consumption, with all that implied for patterns of food consumption and expenditure (Horst 1974: chs 2, 3). Higher standards of material welfare and a revolution in lifestyle created a demand for novelty and convenience, and so provided a niche for modern consumer-orientated products such as ready-cooked breakfast cereals (Ward 1989: pt 1.2). Scientifically formulated, socially engineered, and mass-produced, ready-cooked breakfast cereals are, in every respect, the exemplary twentieth-century branded foodstuff. This chapter is concerned primarily with cold cereal brands and in particular the firm of Kellogg, market leaders in Britain and the United States; it will begin with a general review of trends in production and consumption in the inter-war and post-war periods.

THE INTERWAR PERIOD

It was between the two world wars that ready-to-eat cereals became an established part of the British diet, being transformed inside a single decade from a specialized into a mass consumption food. The 1923 edition of Mrs Beeton's cookery book lists only a small handful of cereal breakfast foods, and only two ready-cooked cereals – shredded wheat and toasted wheat biscuits. By 1936, ready-cooked cereals had become accepted fare on middle-class tables on both sides of the Atlantic; on American Independence Day in that year all leading brands (barring Kellogg) were served at breakfast on the transatlantic liner, MV *Britannic* (Cunard White Star Line). In 1937, according to the John Bull Survey, about two-thirds of families in Britain then purchased breakfast cereals, including oatmeal, and over half the ready-cooked varieties (J. Walter Thompson Archive).

Trade estimates give the average consumption per head of ready-to-eat cereals in 1939 as 29 ounces, which is consistent with the Ministry of Food estimates of 40 ounces in 1943–5, and 62 ounces in 1949, the year in which, for the first time, sales by weight of ready-cooked cereals exceeded those of oatmeal (National Food Survey Committee 1952). Production statistics, though, are patchy. Up to 1939, a large percentage, probably over 70 per cent of oatmeal porridge and, prior to 1937, most ready-cooked cereals were imported. Breakfast foods are not separately enumerated in the annual Trade and Navigation Accounts, corn flakes being lumped with maizemeal, and wheat products subsumed under 'farinaceous preparations'. Groats and rolled oats are distinguished from 1938 when net exports from Canada, the principal source of the Quaker supply, were about 25,000 tons, that is 19 ounces per head, or 40 per cent of estimated total oatmeal consumption. Output data in the Censuses of Production do not always accord with manufacturers' or consumption estimates. The 1924 Census does not list breakfast cereals, while the 1935 Census in its original published form includes them under the general head of 'farinaceous preparations', with a factory value of £2.276 million (Board of Trade 1936). Retrospective figures for 1935 and 1937 (see Table 12.1), recorded in the 1948 Census, are highly questionable. The stated maize output of over 700,000 tons is a gross error, being ten times the consumption in 1970. Indeed there was no significant production of maize-based breakfast cereals in the UK until the opening of the Kellogg factory in 1938. It is suggested that the Census of Production maize figures should read not thousands of tons but tons, and that total output in 1935 was 10,700 tons, rising to 12,700 tons in 1937 (Board of Trade 1952; Collins 1976: 38).

Table 12.1 Census of production estimates of ready-to-eat breakfast cereal outputs and values in the UK, 1935 and 1937

	Wheat products		Maize products		Total	
	Output (tons)	Value (£)	Output (tons)	Value (£)	Output (tons)	Value (£)
1935[a]	10,000	707,000	718[c]	3,897	10,718	710,897
1937[b]	12,000	825,000	733[c]	5,612	12,733	830,612

Source: Board of Trade 1952

Notes: [a] Production
 [b] Packeted for retail sale
 [c] Adjusted figure

The breakfast revolution between the wars was the outcome of the vigorous targeting of the British market by US manufacturers who, encouraged by the rising sales of direct imports of brands already popular in the United States and Canada, began manufacturing in Britain (Horst 1974: chs 2, 3; Monopolies Commission 1973: 3–4). The Shredded Wheat Co. erected a factory at Welwyn Garden City, Hertfordshire, in 1926, and Quaker Oats Ltd a small plant at Ware in the same county in 1920 for the manufacture of Puffed Wheat and Puffed Rice, and a much larger plant at Southall, Middlesex, in 1936.

Kellogg, which began exporting Corn Flakes and All Bran to Britain in 1922 and Rice Krispies in 1928, opened its Trafford Park factory in Manchester, the largest of its kind outside the United States, in 1938. General Foods intensified its sales efforts after 1932, as did the Force Food Co. of Buffalo, makers of Force Wheat Flakes. Of the leading North American companies, only General Mills and Ralston Purina, neither a specialist cereal company and each with extensive other grain and milling interests, declined the challenge. In the Second World War and after, General Foods and Force paid the penalty for their failure to establish a local manufacturing base in the crucial pre-war expansionist decades.

Rapid sales growth and, after 1932, the imposition of tariffs on imported breakfast foods, induced a number of British companies to enter the market, and a number of older-established companies manufacturing mainly hot cereals and health foods, to expand production. The most successful British company, Weetabix, founded in 1932 in a run-down corn mill at Burton Latimer in Northamptonshire, had South African and Battle Creek connections. Most of the 189 different brands mentioned in the 1937 John Bull Survey were indigenous, but only 2, Weetabix and Scotts Oats, had a market share greater than 1 per cent (J. Walter Thompson Archive). Typical British products were Tribrek, introduced by the biscuit-makers, Huntley and Palmers, in 1934, and Zesto corn flakes and wheat flakes launched by Brown and Polson, the cornflour and cereal manufacturer, in 1934–6 (Corley 1972: 228; Ward 1989: 322–3). One bizarre entrant was 'Farmers Glory', a brand of wheat flakes first manufactured in 1933 by the Alley Brothers, the motorized farming pioneers, at Bluestone Farm, South Creake, near Fakenham in Norfolk, at the suggestion it was claimed of the then General Manager of Woolworths, who promised to stock the product in his stores. After a promising start and the opening of a second factory at Huntingdon, it lost ground and was eventually disposed of in 1938 to Reckitt and Colman of Norwich (Barbara Allen, personal communication, 1993).

The crucial turning-point was the decision by Kellogg in 1931 to launch an all-out assault (J. Walter Thompson Archive). Aggressive and perfectly timed, it achieved a fivefold increase in Kellogg sales by weight by the end of the decade, and a rise in the Kellogg share of ready-cooked sales from less than 5 per cent to over 50 per cent and of total cereal sales from 3 to 30 per cent. Kellogg increased its own market share but, equally important, also the total market for ready-to-eat cereals to the point where, by 1939, they were purchased by the majority of households. The growth of Kellogg sales is described in Table 12.2.

Table 12.2 Kellogg sales in the UK, 1931–9

	Sales (million cases)			Value of sales ($million)		
	All Bran	*Corn Flakes*	*Rice Krispies*	*All Bran*	*Corn Flakes*	*Rice Krispies*
1931	0.391	0.241	0.043	0.107	1.000	0.119
1932	—	0.305	0.064	—	1.253	0.174
1933	—	0.406	0.107	—	1.669	0.276
1934	—	0.523	0.113	—	1.934	0.305
1935	—	0.659	0.131	—	2.217	0.357
1936	—	0.804	0.174	—	2.431	0.469
1937	—	0.901	0.224	—	2.704	0.604
1938	—	1.092	0.327	—	3.300	0.880
1939	0.597	1.311	0.523	1.300	3.960	1.410
1931–9 av. pa %	+ 5.7	+ 49.3	+ 125.0	+ 123.9	+ 32.9	+ 120.5

Source: J. Walter Thompson Archive

Information about other company sales is scanty. In 1939 sales of Quaker Puffed Rice were in the region of 3,500 and of Puffed Wheat 7,000 cwt. Sales of Brown and Polson wheat flakes rose from 1,835 cwt in 1934–5 to 6,619 cwt in 1937–8, while Farmers Glory is claimed to have produced 3 million packets in 1935 and Tribrek half a million in 1939 (Bound 1966: 1; Corley 1972: 228; Ward 1989: 322). Consumption estimates suggest that the total volume of all breakfast cereals in 1939 was 1.9 million cwt, and of ready-cooked about 0.8 million cwt. Total values are even more problematical, but in 1937 were probably of the order of the £9 million–10 million estimated by A. V. Ward from the John Bull Survey. Kellogg sales figures suggest on the basis of a 30 per cent market share and a store value of $8 million–9 million, a total value for all ready-cooked sales of $25 million (about £5 million at the then current rate of exchange). On the assumption that ready-cooked cereals represented 55 per cent of total sales, this gives an industry value of about £9 million in the later 1930s.

THE POST-WAR PERIOD

By the late 1930s the per capita consumption of breakfast cereals in Britain, though substantially larger than at the start of the decade, was much smaller than in the other main consuming countries. Of the Kellogg brands, for example, the consumption of corn flakes was only 40 per cent that of Canada and 55 per cent that of Australia. The gap narrowed over the Second World War when, in spite of government restrictions, average consumption per head of all cereals increased until in 1950 it stood at 140 ounces per annum, compared with 74 ounces in 1938, while that of ready-cooked rose from 29 to 73 ounces (National Food Survey Committee 1952). By 1950, too, ready-cooked had overtaken hot cereals in terms of both value and weight. Porridge reached its historic peak in 1947–8 following the failure of the potato harvest. Between 1934–8 and 1954, whereas total sales of ready-cooked cereal rose by an estimated 120 per cent, those of oatmeal fell by 24 per cent. From an estimated 69 ounces per year in 1950, consumption per head of porridge fell to less than 20 ounces in 1986, and its market share by value from about 40 per cent to just 10 per cent. By the mid-1980s, volume sales had levelled off at about 37,000 tons per year, compared with 330,000 tons of ready-to-eat cereals (Breakfast Cereals 1987; National Food Survey Committee 1991).

Table 12.3 Consumption of breakfast cereals in the UK, 1932–90[a]

	1932	1939	1945	1950	1960	1970	1975	1980	1985	1990
Oat and oatmeal cereals	0.60	0.80	1.00	1.32	0.94	0.50	0.50	0.42	0.60	0.46
Ready-to-eat breakfast cereals	0.20	0.60	0.90	1.40	1.80	2.74	3.05	3.50	4.04	4.47
Total breakfast cereals	0.80	1.40	1.90	2.72	2.74	3.24	3.55	4.02	4.64	4.93

Sources: *National Food Survey*; J. Walter Thompson Archive

Note: [a]Consumption in ounces per head per week

Table 12.4 Sales of breakfast cereals in the UK, 1939–90

	Ready-to-eat cereals (tons)	*Hot cereals (tons)*
1939	39,000	60,000
1950	69,500	66,000
1960	92,000	48,000
1970	133,000	28,000
1980	196,000	37,000
1985	254,000	40,000
1990	360,000	46,000

Sources: A. C. Nielsen; J. Walter Thompson Archive

Tables 12.3 and 12.4 show a more or less continuous growth in the consumption of ready-cooked cereals from the early 1930s and, after a hiatus in the 1950s, a continuing advance to the point where, at the present day, consumption per head exceeds 13 lb per year, more than seven times larger than pre-war and, but for Ireland, the largest in the world, ahead even of the United States and Canada.

BRANDS AND BRAND SHARES

Central features of the history of the breakfast cereals industry have been, first, the continuing popularity of the five leading pre-war brands which, in 1980, still accounted for 76 per cent of ready-cooked sales. Second, high levels of sales concentration, and at the same time a remarkable stability in manufacturing shares, the same four companies – Kellogg, Quaker, Weetabix and Shredded Wheat – controlling over 70 per cent of sales in 1939, 87 per cent in 1980 and 78 per cent in 1990.

The readership surveys conducted in 1932 and 1937 by the publishers of the popular weekly magazine, *John Bull*, and trade estimates for 1939, summarized in Tables 12.5 and 12.6, provide a measure of changing consumer preferences and brand shares over the 1930s. Of the 189 different brands of hot and cold breakfast foods specified, only 13 were purchased by more than 1 per cent of the 8,048 households sampled (J. Walter Thompson Archive).

Unquestionably the most striking development between the two world wars was the dramatic advance of the Kellogg brands, from third position behind Shredded Wheat and Force to market leader with an estimated 56 per cent of ready-cooked sales. Total sales of hot cereals increased while their overall share declined. The major brands gained at the expense of the minor, but in so rapidly an expanding market some of the latter were able to achieve, at any rate temporarily, a measure of success, especially in the regions. In 1937, for instance, the majority of sales of Farmers Glory was in the eastern, home and east Midlands counties, and of Tribrek and Clark's Creamed Barley in London and the home counties (J. Walter Thompson Archive). Kellogg and Shredded Wheat were the principal gainers. Quaker sales advanced substantially only after 1936 following the opening of its Southall factory, whence its share of the ready-cooked market rose from 7 per cent to 15 per cent within two years. The Post Division of General Foods (Grape Nuts and Post Toasties), achieved modest growth, while Force Wheat Flakes lost relative ground. At this stage Weetabix was still a third-rank, very much a regional company.

Table 12.5 Leading brand share of breakfast cereals in the UK, 1932 and 1937[a]

Manufacturer	Product	Percentage share	
		1932	1937
Kellogg Co.	Corn Flakes	4.67	17.71
	All Bran	29	2.29
	Rice Krispies	—	1.13
		4.96	21.13
Quaker	Quaker Oats	26.64 } 28.60	18.01 } 19.42
	Quick Quaker	1.96	1.41
	Corn Flakes	—	1.02 } 2.63
	Puffed Wheat	—	0.88
	Puffed Rice	—	0.73
		28.60	22.05
Shredded Wheat Co. (Nabisco)	Shredded Wheat	14.22	17.05
Force Food Co. of Buffalo	Wheat Flakes	10.19	8.23
Post Division of General Foods	Post Toasties	1.26	3.87
	Grape Nuts	1.35	1.62
		2.61	5.59
Scotts Oats	Scotts Oats	4.78	2.05
Weetabix Co.	Weetabix	—	1.99

Sources: John Bull Survey; J. Walter Thompson Archive

Note: [a]Percentage of homes using cereals

Table 12.6 Market shares of leading ready-to-eat and hot cereal brands in the UK, 1939[a]

Ready-to-eat cereals	%	Hot cereals	%
Kellogg brands	56	Quaker	62
Shredded Wheat	23	Scotts	9
Quaker (Corn Flakes 9, Puffed Wheat 4, Puffed Rice 2)	15	Unpacketed	15
Force	10		
Weetabix	2		

Source: Bound 1966: 1

Note: [a]Percentage of homes using cereals in 1939

In the Second World War the geographical rationalization of sales and shortages of maize dampened competition and led to a realignment of market shares. Kellogg declined from about 56 to 46 per cent, while the cessation of imports of Quaker Oats and the discontinuance of Puffed Rice and Quaker Corn Flakes in 1942 reduced the Quaker share in both markets. Weetabix, though, moved into third position, displacing Force, its market share rising from 2 per cent to 14 per cent between 1939 and 1950. Shredded Wheat edged up to 17 per cent and Quaker Puffed Wheat to 6 per cent.

From the 1950s the regular audits by A. C. Nielsen of sales through retail grocers permit brand and manufacturers' shares to be determined with fair accuracy (A. C. Nielsen; Monopolies Commission 1973: 6–9, 35). Manufacturers' brand shares plotted in Table 12.7 show a steady rise in the Kellogg share to a peak of 58.5 per cent in 1969, followed by a decline to just under 50 per cent in the 1980s. Nabisco, meanwhile, peaked in the late 1950s and Quaker in the early 1950s, while Weetabix, the success story of the early and middle postwar years, began to sink after 1979 in which year, taking advantage of strikes at the Kellogg and Nabisco factories, it achieved a heady 26 per cent. Perhaps the most significant development has been the advance of retailers' own brands, from next to nothing in the mid-1960s, to over 20 per cent by 1985. However, against the decline in manufacturers' brands, should be set the fact that a significant proportion of retailers' own brands was produced by those self-same companies.

From the 1930s the breakfast cereals market in Britain has been dominated by a tiny handful of manufacturers with limited competition between them in the supply of like products. Concern as to the extent to which this oligopoly operated against the public interest, led in 1970 to an anti-monopoly investigation into breakfast cereals in the United States where, in 1964, 90 per cent of sales of ready-cooked cereals were controlled by the largest four companies. There followed, in 1971, a similar investigation by the Monopolies Commission in Britain, where, much more even than across the Atlantic, the industry was dominated by Kellogg (Monopolies Commission 1973). The Commission report is a valuable statement about brands and oligopolistic competition in a modern consumer goods industry. Immediately clear is that neither prices nor patents were competitively important. Apart from the 1930s, when Kellogg used price reductions to stimulate sales in a young expanding market, and to a limited extent the marking down of retailers' own brands from the 1960s, there was little price competition. The logic is that in a highly concentrated industry the pricing tactics of any one oligopolist must affect the market shares of

Table 12.7 Manufacturers' brand shares of ready-to-eat cereals in the UK, 1939–88

	1939a	1950	1955	1960	1965	1970	1975	1980	1985	1988
Kellogg Corn Flakes	39	N/A	36.8	37.7	36.7	32.5	27.7	22	17	14
All other Kellogg	11	N/A	17.0	19.3	20.6	24.4	25.9	26	32	35
Total Kellogg	50	51.2	53.8	56.9	57.3	57.9	53.6	48	49	49
Weetabix	2	14.4	15.3	13.9	18.6	20.5	21.9	22	17	15
Nabisco	16	16.8	18.0	17.5	14.2	11.9	10.3	10	8	9
Quaker	11	10.4	9.6	7.0	7.2	5.7	4.2	4	5	4
Force	7									
Corn Flakes own label					6	3.1	4.6	7	5	4
Total own label					N/A	N/A	N/A	16	21	20

Sources: A. C. Nielson; Retail Business; Monopolies Commission Report 1973: 35; Quaker Oats Ltd

Note: a Based on percentage of homes using each product and total combined market share of 70 per cent, in 1939 only

others but, where there is significant product differentiation between brands and a strong brand loyalty, individual manufacturers enjoy a degree of insulation from the price competition of rivals. In short, price cutting was unlikely to lead to a significant increase in sales. Manufacturing patents, most of which had anyway expired by 1950s, were not a serious obstacle and could in most cases be circumvented. Production techniques were, anyway, basically simple. Trade marks and brand names, on the other hand, were more jealously guarded.

The much more effective barrier to entry was the high, often seemingly prohibitive cost of developing and marketing competitive products. The view of the industry was that money spent on promotion was of more lasting benefit than price reductions, special offers or in-packet promotions. Reputation made for increased sales and larger price premiums. Supporting evidence is scanty, but the report on the breakfast cereal industry in the United States compiled for the National Commission on Food Marketing (1966) provides possible useful pointers to business behaviour in Britain. Significantly, the four largest 'grain mill product' firms in the United States – Kellogg, General Mills, Pillsbury, and Quaker – ranked in the top eight of food manufacturing corporations in terms of advertising to sales ratios. Sales and administrative expenses as a share of the value of shipments of the leading breakfast cereal companies in 1963 were nearly 30 per cent, advertising alone accounting for 55 per cent of all marketing and development expenditure compared with less than 20 per cent for distribution and 8.5 per cent for Research and Development (National Commission on Food Marketing 1966: chs 9, 10). US data illustrate both the risks as well as the costs of new product development. According to Buzzell and Nourse (1966), the average time elapsing between first activity and full distribution was 55 months, compared with 29 months for cake mixes and 41 months for frozen dinners, with the average new breakfast cereal product not breaking even until the fourth year after its first introduction (Buzzell and Nourse 1966: 89–108). These hazards were reflected in the fact that relatively few new products – just 21 – were introduced by the 6 leading manufacturers between 1947 and 1961. In 1964 only 393 breakfast cereal items were on offer in retail grocery shops compared with 5,132 cookie and cracker items (National Commission on Food Marketing 1966: 189–91).

ADVERTISING
Break
Beakfast cereals in Britain were likewise aggressively promoted. The two classic advertising campaigns, in the best Charles Post and W. K. Kellogg tradition, were the Quaker in the early 1900s, when Frederick A. Seymour erected a large signboard advertising Quaker Oats across the face of the cliffs of Dover, provoking questions in the House of Commons; and the Kellogg in the 1930s (Marquette 1967: 213–18). Breakfast cereals ranked high in national food advertising expenditure, in 1938 totalling £400,000, third after malted beverages and confectionery, and in 1948 comprising 18 per cent of net sales compared with under 3 per cent for all food (Bishop 1944: 86–7; Kaldor and Silverman 1948: 144). Kellogg claimed that in the thirty-four-year period up to 1940, about $100 million had been spent on advertising (Powell 1956: 142). W. K. Kellogg's response to the Great Depression was to increase advertising budgets, with the aim for further consolidation at home, and establishing Kellogg as the brand leader in Britain and Australia. Table 12.8 demonstrates the relationship between sales and advertising expenditure in Britain between 1931 and 1939.

Table 12.8 Sales of and advertising expenditure on Corn Flakes by Kellogg in the UK, 1931–9

	Sales (cases)	Sales in ($million)	Advertising and promotion ($million)	Advertising as % of sales
1931	241,233	1.000	0.180	18.0
1932	305,368	1.253	0.278	22.2
1933	406,024	1.669	0.295	17.7
1934	523,401	1.934	0.376	19.4
1935	659,321	2.217	0.493	22.2
1936	804,484	2.431	0.470	19.3
1937	901,369	2.704	0.541	20.0
1938	1,092,067	3.300	0.619	18.8
1939	1,311,381	3.960	0.689	17.4

Source: J. Walter Thompson Archive

Kellogg's advertising appropriation increased from 12 per cent of sales in 1930 to a peak of 27.7 per cent in 1935. Expenditure by the other manufacturers, with the qualified exception of Shredded Wheat and, prior to 1936, Quaker Oats, were by comparison small. Small companies at any rate took the view that in a rapidly expanding market they could enjoy windfall gains at little direct cost to themselves. At Brown and Polson, for example, advertising expenditure between 1935 and 1937 was less than £500, compared to annual sales of £23,000 (J. Walter Thompson Archive). With the easing of restrictions on newspaper advertisements and the advent of commercial television advertising expenditures rose quickly from 1955. According to data supplied to the Monopolies Commission, Kellogg expenditure on advertising and promotion peaked at over 15 per cent of sales in 1959 and averaged 12.1 per cent between 1966 and 1971 (Monopolies Commission 1973: 5–6). As regards the other major companies, the ratios were in two cases well below and in one about the same as Kellogg. Expenditure stabilized in the 1970s, but then advanced sharply from £5.4 million in 1975–9 to £65 million in 1987–8. Of this, 70 per cent was expended by Kellogg in defence of a brand share of 50 per cent, and 17 per cent by Weetabix possessing 15 per cent. With 65 per cent of the market the two were responsible for over 85 per cent of the industry's total advertising and promotional expenditure. In 1992, Kellogg brands ranked 3rd, 7th, 11th, 19th and 21st; Weetabix 8th; Shredded Wheat 30th; and Nestlé and General Foods 32nd, in the national food advertising register (Register MEAL 1993). In general there existed a direct correlation between market and advertising shares but with a tendency for the largest relative expenditures to be reserved for new products.

PRODUCT INNOVATION

'It is by no means clear', opined a leading market researcher, 'why companies need new brands at all, or if yes, how many they need'. After all, contrary to the maxim that new products are the lifeblood of a company, was it not the case that most new branded products failed, while staple products generated the overwhelming majority of profits (King 1973: v)?

In the 1930s the five leading manufacturers of ready-cooked cereals produced between them just eleven products. The overriding imperative was to widen the appeal of the new-style breakfast foods, and to achieve the maximum possible volume of sales, irrespective of social class or type of consumer. Post-war strategy, on the other hand, in a now more fully developed market, was more concerned with inter-firm competition and market share. Here product innovation played a key role. It afforded a broader base for profits in the longer run as the old brand staples, incapable of significant further modification, entered the mature phase of their product cycle. Successful new products helped reinforce brand image and intimidate rivals.

The three major changes in the product composition of breakfast cereal foods in the post-war period were broadly as follows. First, there was a shift from staple to health and children's brands. Between 1957 and 1990 the market share of corn flakes, shredded wheat, puffed rice, puffed wheat, and rice krispies, the pre-war favourites, fell from 85–90 per cent to 45 per cent, while that of health and children's cereals rose from 10–15 per cent to over 50 per cent (J. Walter Thompson Archives).

Second, there was a relative and absolute decline in hot cereals, and in ready-cooked cereals a shift from maize- and rice- to wheat- and oat-based products.

Third, there was an increase in the total number of products produced by the four leading manufacturers from ten in 1937 to twenty in 1972 and fifty-four in 1992 (A. C. Nielsen). The emphasis shifted from pre-sweetened products in the 1950s to mueslis and related products in the 1970s, to bran and fibre products in the 1980s.

Market research surveys in 1937 and 1956 (see Table 12.9) indicated that homes with children eat more cereals than those without, and that children preferred ready-cooked to hot cereals and some brands more than others. Thus in 1954, following the end of sugar rationing, Kellogg launched Sugar Frosted Flakes, the first pre-sweetened cereal, which had proved very popular in the United States, followed soon after by the Quaker products, Sugar Puffs and Honey Snaps. In the 1960s Kellogg brought out a new range of child and nursery cereals – All Stars, Frosties and Koddles, and General Mills its matching trio, Cheerios, Lucky Charms and Frosty Os. Nabisco launched a miniature shredded wheat, Cubs, in 1958. The 1970s and 1980s saw further additions, mostly modifications to existing lines, the emphasis now less on sweetness for dental reasons, and more on flavour and texture. By 1969 all three major hot cereal producers – Quaker, Lyons and Scott-Energen – had introduced flavoured porridges. Sales of pre-sweetened cereals were estimated to be growing at 11 per cent per annum in 1969–70, with Kellogg's Ricicles rising 30 per cent in just one year (*Grocer* 28 March 1970). The value of children's cereals, put at about 15 per cent of total cereal sales in 1973, had risen to over 20 per cent by the mid-1980s (*Grocer* 14 April 1973).

The other major area of opportunity for successful diversification was nutritional cereals. In the 1930s in the United States, milk and breakfast cereals had been promoted as the complete food, the American Dairy Association and the Cereal Institute joining together in April each year in a Spring Cereal and Milk Festival (J. Walter

Table 12.9 Market research survey of brand sales in the UK, 1956

	To homes with children (%)	To homes without children (%)
All ready-to-eat cereals	57	43
Kellogg Corn Flakes	46	54
Sugar Frosted Flakes	62	38
Rice Krispies	51	49
Quaker Puffed Rice	82	18
Sugar Puffs	76	24
Shredded Wheat	64	36
Weetabix	76	24

Source: J. Walter Thompson Archive

Thompson Archive). In Britain, on the other hand, according to a J. Walter Thompson inquiry in 1937, flavour and texture much more than nourishment and digestibility were the reasons most commonly stated for purchasing ready-cooked cereals. All Bran, the most popular of the early health cereals, had only a small following, while the first protein-cereal, Special K, was introduced by Kellogg in 1959 in the foreknowledge that housewives in general did not regard cereals as a major source of protein. The high protein content claimed for Shredded Wheat did little for its market share. Although originally promoted as health foods, the nutritional value of breakfast cereals was questioned in the late 1930s by a group of doctors who claimed that the use of superheated steam in their manufacture destroyed Vitamin B, thus rendering them 'worse than useless' (Grant 1954: 101). In the early 1970s allegations by the American Dental Association, that cereals seriously damaged the nation's health, led to the first fall in sales of sugar-coated cereals. This, together with adverse press comment, that 'corn flakes were made from the stuff the French fed their chickens on', and which likened shredded wheat to a 'soapless Brillo pad', led to frantic efforts to develop new and different types of cereals with a positive health image. The breakthrough was achieved, almost accidentally, by Weetabix in 1971, with Alpen, a simple formulation on the lines of muesli, the traditional Swiss breakfast food made of wholewheat and rolled cereals mixed with nuts and dried fruit, whose possibilities as a utilitarian breakfast food had been suggested by the marketing director's Swiss au pair girl (R. Richards, personal communication, 1973). The most successful non-American cereal product research by J. Walter Thompson confirmed its appeal among housewives, many of whom came to regard it as more of a dietary staple than a food. It was instantly perceived as a novel and exciting product, natural and intrinsically good (J. Walter Thompson Archive). Thus encouraged, the Weetabix brand share rose to a peak of 26 per cent in 1979, when strikes cut back the output of its two main rivals, but falling subsequently in the face of mounting competition from own-label brands.

Medical discoveries leading to the conclusion that lack of fibre was partly responsible for a wide range of diseases from gallstones and diabetes to heart disease, provided yet another opportunity for concept innovation. Biochemical research suggested that bran, especially oat bran, reduced blood cholesterol and atherone levels, and favourably altered blood-fat composition. Also, there was a pre-sumed connection between roughage in diet, constipation and various forms of cancer. Opinion surveys suggest that the public is more con-cerned about dietary fibre in the United States than in Britain, where surfeits of unhealthy elements, such as fat and sugar, are reckoned more consequential. None the less, medical endorsement of oat and bran foods helped spawn a new generation of products, such as Bran Fare and Farmhouse Bran (Weetabix), and Common Sense Bran Flakes, and Fruit 'n' Fibre (Kellogg), and temporarily revive the flagging fortunes of ageing products like All Bran, Oat Krunchies and even traditional stoneground porridge. Other beneficiaries included specialist manufacturers of oat products such as Jordon, Mornflake, Whitworth and Mapleton. Since 1980 'lifestyle products' have been the most dynamic sector, propelling total cereal sales to new heights. Bran and muesli now account for nearly 30 per cent of sales of ready-cooked cereals compared with 5 per cent in the 1950s, whereas maize-based cereals have declined from 50 to less than 30 per cent.

THE KELLOGG ACHIEVEMENT

Persistent features of the breakfast cereals industry in Britain have been first, its domination by US companies, and second, the regnant position, its market share ranging between 48 and 59 per cent, of the Kellogg Company, notwithstanding the dramatic advance since the early 1970s of retailers' own-label brands, which have taken a heavy toll of its competitors. The Kellogg achievement is the more remark-able, given that it beat off not just the UK-based American rivals, Quaker and Shredded Wheat, but other US companies such as General Foods and General Mills, each with a large share of the United States' market, some of whose products, it might be thought, could have done well in Britain. Market research and its own experience taught Kellogg that there existed important differences between the British and American markets. In the 1950s it had forecast that sales of children's cereals, and of breakfast cereals generally, would grow far less strongly in Britain than in the United States (J. Walter Thompson Archive). The Quaker Oats Co., on the other hand, was under intense pressure from its parent to promote US products (Bound 1966). A basic problem was that corn meal, hominy grits and other dry-milled products, large sellers in the United States, had little appeal in Britain. The difficulties of adaptation are illustrated by American-style porridge which, because it was designed to be made with water rather than milk, had to be reformulated several times before it achieved a form suitable for the British market. Problems of quite another kind were encountered with the brown bear associated in the United States with Sugar Puffs. The European brown bear was different from the North American in that its cubs, which were to feature in a TV commercial, proved up to the age of 4 months too stupid to take part in children's picnics, but after six months too dangerous and, in the words of one marketing executive, much more liable to eat the children than the Sugar Puffs. Several imported Quaker products – a protein-fortified cereal, plain and pre-sweetened puffed rice, and wheat flakes – had to be withdrawn after test-marketing. One well-publicized failure was the attempt by General Mills in the early 1960s to introduce Betty Crocker cakes and Big G cereals, market leaders in the United States (*Marketing* 1970). Of the seven products supplied by the firm in 1973 only two were really successful, the remainder achieving only a very limited distribution. General Foods, too, made little headway, its US brand-leader, Grape Nuts, never capturing more than a modest share of the British market. Much more disappointing was the much-trumpeted campaign to reintroduce Force Wheat Flakes, the popular pre-war brand (*Grocer* 4 July 1970; 29 April 1992).

In the 1930s Kellogg established a commanding lead over its rivals with just three products. To preserve its market share in the post-war period required not only high levels of advertising, but also a continuous flow of new products to replace the old staples, the decline of which had been foreseen by analysis of the age distribution and social class of regular users in the 1950s. The Kellogg strategy was to segment the market, identify and occupy the obvious niches, and command the largest possible selling space on supermarket shelves. By virtue of its dominant market share it was often in a position to set prices at an optimum level, high enough to generate satisfactory profits, low enough to deter would-be competitors. Though caught off balance by the meteoric rise of muesli and the 'natural' cereals in the early 1970s, Kellogg led the field in product innovation, launching the first pre-sweetened cereal in 1954 and, following a loss of share in the 1970s, fighting back with its range of skilfully tailored health and children's cereals. According to the *Grocer* Price List of 5 September 1992, Kellogg was offering twenty-four different pre-cooked breakfast cereals compared with Weetabix's thirteen and Quaker's and Cereal Partners' nine. The increase in own-label brands, from 0.6 per cent of ready-cooked sales in 1966 when the first retailers' own-label corn flakes, manufactured by Viota, came to market, to 20 per cent in 1990, reflects the growing strength of the multiple retailers who, during the 1980s, were able to induce most major manufacturers, excepting Kellogg, to produce for them.

The Kellogg files in the London office of the American market research firm, J. Walter Thompson, dating from the 1930s, evidence the closeness of the relationship between market research, product development and promotion strategy. The fact that up to 1980 consumption per head of breakfast cereals in Britain was much lower than in the United States meant that much effort was directed at those who eat only small quantities of ready-cooked cereals, eat other kinds of breakfast food, or did not eat breakfast at all. In the late 1930s, according to the John Bull Survey (J. Walter Thompson Archive), just over half the population purchased ready-cooked cereals. The W. S. Crawford survey (Table 12.10) suggests, however, a much lower figure, the overwhelming majority of those questioned preferring a cooked breakfast of bacon and eggs or just bread (Crawford and Broadley 1938: 39), and in the high and middle-income groups only 17 per cent consuming ready-cooked cereals. The second Rowntree and Carnegie surveys show widely differing consumption between social classes, and an income elasticity of demand of breakfast cereals of at least 1.5 (Rowntree 1941: 188ff).

By the 1950s, class differences had been largely erased but, according to the second W. S. Crawford survey in 1955–6, still only 20 per cent of adults ate ready-cooked cereals, compared with 55 per cent bread or toast and 35 per cent bacon and eggs. Yet, by 1967, the proportion had risen to an estimated 25 per cent (*Grocer* 8 July 1967), by 1976 to 40 per cent (J. Walter Thompson Archive), and by 1990, 92 per cent (Breakfast Cereals 1991: 22). In the late 1950s Kellogg began to target the growing number of non-breakfast eaters, estimated in 1976 at 17 per cent of the population. Another trend, successfully exploited, was that of 'snacking' or 'grazing'. Where, in 1956, ready-cooked cereals were just a breakfast food, by 1990 some 45 per cent of

Table 12.10 Foods consumed at breakfast by social class in the UK, 1938

	Class AA 422[a] (%)	Class A 466[a] (%)	Class B 971[a] (%)	Class C 2,124[a] (%)	Class D 1,006[a] (%)
Bread, rolls or toast	79.9	85.8	83.1	82.8	91.7
Butter	36.7	41.8	54.0	60.5	56.6
Margarine	—	—	—	3.2	17.5
Dripping	—	—	0.1	0.1	2.7
Marmalade	58.5	50.6	36.6	13.1	5.2
Jam, honey and syrup	4.3	2.6	2.9	8.0	7.3
Porridge	28.9	24.7	26.6	25.8	18.3
Other cereals	18.0	21.9	21.4	14.5	7.0
Eggs	70.4	67.4	64.9	52.8	31.6
Bacon or ham	62.3	59.9	58.3	53.0	31.7
Fish	12.3	6.4	5.3	2.4	2.7
Sausages	6.6	5.8	3.1	2.2	3.0
Fruit or fruit juice	31.0	22.3	15.9	4.6	1.3
Tomatoes	4.3	4.5	4.5	3.5	2.2

Source: Crawford and Broadley 1938: 39

Note: [a]Number of families surveyed in each class

housewives claimed to eat them at other times of the day as a light meal, mainly in the late evening (Breakfast Cereals 1991: 22).

The Kellogg objective since the Second World War has been to defend its market share. In fact, it rose from 53 per cent in 1950 to 58.5 per cent in 1969, and held at a steady 48–50 per cent during the 1980s while the position of its rivals, Weetabix, Quaker and Nabisco, steadily deteriorated, their combined share falling to 28 per cent where in the mid-1950s it had stood at over 40 per cent. Whether in the future, Kellogg will hold its ground is a nice question. Success, declares Porter (1985), lies in product differentiation and creating special niches within a market that distinguishes the product from their rivals. Though true of competition between manufacturers, it may not answer the threat posed by retailers' own brands. The multiples which now dominate food distribution are much larger than any food manufacturer barring Unilever and General Foods, enjoy an established reputation for quality and value for money, and in the case of own-brand basic cereals, such as corn flakes, puffed wheat, wheat biscuit and muesli, are able increasingly to set prices. Kellogg's advantage lies in its dynamic product range and the relatively small proportion of sales now derived from the old staples. Recent blind tastings of selected grocery products suggest that the majority of customers actually prefer retailers' to manufacturers' brands, with the exception of corn flakes, where Kellogg's is preferred. Retailers' own brand are the most obvious threat, but threatening too are recent changes in the industrial structure, specifically the formation of Cereal Partners UK, a joint venture between two multinational companies, Nestlé, with its extensive European sales and distribution network, and the US cereal firm of General Mills. The new company comprises Shredded Wheat (acquired from Nabisco in 1988), Viota Foods (makers of own-label cornflakes) and A. A. Fincken (distributors of Force Wheat Flakes), as well as General Mills own brands. This unification of global brands may have already set the stage for a battle to be waged, this time in mainland Europe, where breakfast cereals, so long the dietary and cultural preserve of the Anglo-Saxon nations, are just beginning to take hold.

ACKNOWLEDGEMENTS

The author wishes to thank the Kellogg Company of Great Britain for its consent in allowing him to consult its market research files, 1933–75 (Fiches 1–140), and Patricia Oliver of J. Walter Thompson, Berkeley Square, London, for making these available (hereafter referred to as J. Walter Thompson Archive). He is also grateful to Dr Vernon Ward for his advice on breakfast cereals in the 1930s; to Pam Scopes of A. C. Nielsen, Abingdon, for information on brand shares 1959–75; Quaker Oats Ltd, Cereal Partners UK Ltd, and Weetabix Ltd, for information about the history of their firms; and Mrs Barbara Allen of Morley's Farm, South Creake, near Fakenham, Norfolk, for sharing with me the results of her research into the firm of Alley Brothers, manufacturers of 'Farmers Glory' wheat flakes.

REFERENCES

Bishop, F. P. (1944) *The Economics of Advertising*, London: Robert Hale.
Board of Trade (1936) *Final Report on the Census of Production and the Import Duties Inquiry, 1935*, London: HMSO.
—— (1952) *Final Report on the Census of Production for 1948*, vol. 8A, London: HMSO.
Bound, J. A. (1966) *A Brief Marketing History of Quaker Oats Limited* (2nd edn), Southall: Quaker Oats Ltd.
Breakfast Cereals (1987) *Retail Business* **349** March: 15–21.
—— (1990) *Retail Business* **386** April: 32–52.
—— (1991) *Market Intelligence* April: 1–29.
Buzzell, R. D. and Nourse, R. E. M. (1966) *Product Innovation, the Product*

258 *Adding Value: brands and marketing*

Life Cycle and Competitive Behaviour in Selected Food Processing Industries, 1947–64, Cambridge, Mass: Arthur D. Little.

Collins, E. J. T. (1976) 'The "consumer revolution" and the growth of factory foods: changing patterns of bread and cereal-eating in Britain in the twentieth century', in D. Oddy and D. Miller (eds) *The Making of the Modern British Diet*, London: Croom Helm.

Corley, T. A. B. (1972) *Quaker Enterprise in Biscuits: Huntley & Palmers of Reading 1822–1972*, London: Hutchinson.

Crawford, W. S. and Broadley, H. (1938) *The People's Food*, London: Heinemann.

Cunard White Star Line (1936) Menu, MV *Britannic*, 4 July. In the possession of the author.

Grant, D. (1954) *Dear Housewives*, London: Faber.

Griggs, B. (1988) *The Food Factor: An Account of the Nutrition Revolution*, Harmondsworth: Penguin.

Horst, T. (1974) *At Home Abroad*, Cambridge, Mass: Ballinger.

International Directory of Company Histories (1990) Volume II, Chicago and London: St James.

Kaldor, N. and Silverman, R. (1948) *A Statistical Analysis of Advertising Expenditure and of the Revenue of the Press*, Cambridge: Cambridge University Press.

King, S. (1973) *Developing New Brands*, London: Pitman.

Marketing (1970) 'When US products fail', *Marketing* May: 26–9.

Marquette, A. F. (1967) *Brands, Trademarks and Good Will: The Story of the Quaker Oats Company*, New York: McGraw Hill.

Monopolies Commission (1973) *Report on the Supply of Ready Cooked Breakfast Cereal Foods*, London: HMSO.

National Commission on Food Marketing (1966) *Studies of Organization and Competition in Grocery Manufacturing*, Washington, DC: US Government Printing Office, Part II, pp. 55–240.

National Food Survey Committee (1952) *Domestic Food Consumption and Expenditure (1950)*, London: HMSO.

—— (1991) *Household Food Consumption and Expenditure (1990)*, London: HMSO.

Olsen, A. B. and Olsen, M. E. (1912) *The School of Health*, Watford: International Tract Society.

Porter, M. E. (1985) *Competitive Advantage*, New York: Free Press.

Powell, H. B. (1956) *The Original has this Signature*, Englewood Cliffs, NJ: Prentice-Hall.

Register MEAL 1992 (1993) London: Media Expenditure Analysis Ltd.

Rowntree, B. S. (1941) *Poverty and Progress*, London: Longmans, Green.

Tibbles, W. (1912) *Foods*, London: Ballière, Tindal & Cox.

Ward, A. V. (1990) 'Economic change in the UK food manufacturing industry 1919–39: with special reference to convenience foods', unpublished PhD thesis, University of Reading.

13 Marketing convenience foods between the wars

Vernon Ward

In Tedlow's three-phase development model of consumer marketing in the United States, the interwar years are located within phase II (1880s–1950s) during which national markets were created and national brands established (Tedlow 1990). In this schema marketing in the UK is generally perceived to lag behind developments in the United States particularly before 1950. Corley (1987) found few studies of marketing operations before 1939, although one (Davenport-Hines 1986) does contain case studies from this period. In the Unilever history, Wilson (1968) treats marketing as a post-1945 development, and Nevett (1982), although informed about advertising and the agencies, says little about their market research work. There is a view that no market research work was conducted in the UK before 1930 (BMRB 1956, Abrams 1951). Consumer marketing is closely linked with the coming of commercial TV which – unlike the United States where, by 1945, there were six commercial TV stations (Tedlow 1993: 16) – did not arrive in the UK until 1955 (Henry 1986). In short, UK marketing operations are seen to be located firmly in the post-war world.

This view is being modified as new research emerges. Fry's Cocoa was marketed before the First World War (Davenport-Hines 1986); Cadbury practised and published on marketing distribution (Cadbury Ltd 1945); Wagner (1988) has examined the Cadbury v Rowntree product development battles of the 1930s; and Church (1993) has examined how far the Tedlow model is applicable to UK car production and marketing between the wars. This chapter provides further evidence that UK operations were well developed in the 1930s. It examines the planning, research and marketing campaigns which established the Horlicks brand within the food and drink markets of that decade.

This chapter first provides the necessary background to the prevailing economic and competitive conditions, and second, reviews what might be meant by convenience foods. The third section is the substance of the chapter, and sets out in some detail a case study of the formation and establishment of the Horlicks brand within the milk food-drink market. The final section pulls the main points together.

THE COMPETITIVE BACKGROUND TO MARKETING OPERATIONS WITHIN THE UK FOOD INDUSTRIES

It is well-known that although the interwar British economy experienced high unemployment levels, there were gainers as well as losers among consumers. There was an observed growth in real income which is variously put at 20–30 per cent (Matthews et al. 1982; Stone 1954). The average household wage found in many of the social surveys of the period was double the unemployment benefit paid; the social changes observed in entertainment, leisure, transport and meals and clothing were very extensive indeed (Glynn and Oxborrow 1976; Jones 1984; Stevenson 1984). It was in particular the period of the 'servant problem' – the move of young women away from domestic service into more attractive employment in the growing retail trades. With more new but generally smaller houses resulting from the housing boom of the 1930s (Saunders 1990) and the difficulty in attracting even daily help the convenience of the new foods becomes clearer. The success of marketing campaigns (discussed later in the chapter) must be due in large part to the growth in real income and the related social and economic changes observed between the wars.

The food industries in the UK between the wars

The UK food industries between the wars were large. If they are defined to 'cover that part of the food production system from the farm gate to consumer, encompassing the manufacturing and distributive stages, with some mention of catering where information allows' (Burns et al. 1983: 4) then the food industries were almost certainly the largest of UK industries between the wars (Ward 1990). They were also diverse. The Census of Production of 1907 records only seven food and drink industries, including flour milling and distilling. By the time of the 1930 Census, separate figures are available for bread, biscuits, margarine, milk and milk products, bacon and meat products. The 1948 Census has the full set of twelve food industries and four drinks industries used until the Standard Industrial Classification (SIC) was revised in 1980 (Business Statistical Office, BSO 1978).

Given these differences in diversity it is not surprising that different strategies were adopted by firms within industries to escape the effects of the recession. Some chose new technologies either to lower costs or to improve product quality. The Solvent extraction technology for oil seed refining was developed; quick freezing became an innovation ready for market; Nescafé instant coffee was launched in 1938; high speed canning came to Britain with the licensing of American technology by Metal Box (Reader 1976). It was not simply the 'new industries' that used technology to extract themselves from recession.

By contrast, the flour milling industry among others chose concentration and 'rationalization' as a solution. Between 1924 and 1934 many mills were brought within the control of the Flour Millers Mutual Organization dominated by Rank and Spillers (Burnett 1945; Edwards 1948). Other industries such as sugar and liquid milk/dairying relied directly or indirectly on government action. The beet sugar industry was reorganized by government support for the British Sugar Corporation in 1935 and Tate and Lyle were excluded (Hugill 1978); the Milk Marketing Board was established in 1933 (S. Baker 1973; Jenkins 1970).

Other firms and industries chose marketing and product differentiation as a strategy for survival and growth in difficult trading conditions. Some, like Cadbury and Bovril, were already engaged in such activities; others, like Horlicks, came to recognize the benefits of such a strategy. They were strengthened in this view by the competitive behaviour of foreign multinationals which located in the UK in this period. CPC (Corn Products Company) acquired Brown and Polson in 1935; Heinz, Kraft and Kellogg established plants in the UK; Mars arrived in 1932. Competition based on brand marketing became particularly intense as domestic firms fought both each other and the newcomers in these industries. Marketing was a key feature in the competitive strategy adopted by most of these firms. This chapter will demonstrate how these marketing operations were conducted.

CONVENIENCE AND CONVENIENCE FOODS

It is not obvious what convenience foods might be but the point is important for two reasons. First, much marketing activity involved making the products more convenient to prepare and serve. The 'unique selling point' often had much to do with convenience. Second, the range of foods which came to be called 'convenient' turn out to be mostly branded food products, many of which were established in this period. It is recognized that 'convenience foods' are conceptually different from branded foods but given the close relationship it will be useful to briefly indicate the dimensions of convenience which foods – especially branded foods – sought to establish and exploit.

'Convenience foods' is a relatively recent phrase. Driver (1983) places it in the mid-1960s as frozen foods, snack foods and ready-prepared dishes began to make an impact upon our meal habits. Wilson notes that 'From 1951 onwards Birds Eye had conducted a planned campaign of advertisement to educate retailers and house-wives in the possibilities of the new frozen foods' (Wilson 1968: 104). The most common meaning of convenience is that used by the National Food Survey (NFS) when it first classified such foods in 1959: 'those processed foods for which the degree of preparation has been carried out to an advanced stage by the manufacturer and which may be used as labour saving alternatives to less highly processed products' (MAFF 1959). This view implies that there is a spectrum of convenience which moves along a single dimension – convenience in preparation. At some point in the spectrum a food may be regarded as not being convenient, while at the other end a food may be like corn flakes or quick-frozen, ready-to-eat meals.

A serious weakness in this unidimensional view of convenience is that many formulated, branded convenience foods have no less con-venient alternative. There seems no less convenient version of Kit Kat, Heinz ketchup or Kellogg's Corn Flakes. So, two points follow: first, there is a discontinuity or quantum leap in the gradual scale of 'con-venience'. Such formulated branded foods seem to have no realistic less convenient form. Second, what distinguishes branded foods is that consistency of taste and performance is guaranteed in purchase after purchase. The brand must have a pleasant distinctive taste and also be consistent and reliable.

This must be a major explanation for the success of brands. Although it may be possible to make chocolate or malted milk drinks in batch after batch in domestic production, it must be almost impossible to produce the taste and consistency of Cadbury's Dairy Milk chocolate or Horlicks drink. Few would attempt domestic production because consumer requirements are met at a price and quality which make alternative forms (if available) much less convenient. Value added is great, and the product is deemed convenient. Consumers buy jams, marmalade, soups and other convenience foods for the same reasons. The convenience resides not only in preparation but also in a taste which is pleasant and where each purchase gives consistent, reliable performance. It is good to know that the product is the same. As Sir Dennis Robertson remarked 'there is a real convenience . . . and a real spiritual comfort in buying a packet of a known and trusted brand of cocoa rather than a shovelful of brown powder of uncertain origin' (Robertson 1963: 169).

Thus convenience has more than one dimension. Firms marketing branded foods make special efforts to differentiate their products by reference to certain aspects of 'convenience' – and it is not simply convenience in preparation that is the distinguishing attribute of some convenience foods.

ESTABLISHING BRANDED FOODS IN THE UK BETWEEN THE WARS

This section sets out in some detail a case study developed from research work reported elsewhere (Ward 1990). The material relates to Horlicks, the well-known malted milk food drink.

Background

The partnership J. & W. Horlick was formed in 1873 in Wisconsin, USA, by James Horlick, who emigrated from Britain in 1867 with a new product for infants and invalids, and his brother William, who had emigrated earlier to found a leather and saddlery business. The development which became 'Horlicks' arose from the suggestion that if the product could be ready-made with water rather than fresh milk it would be more convenient. Further trials and development work led to the malted milk powder 'Horlicks' being marketed in 1883. It was successful and the Horlick Food Co. was incorporated in 1885. Exports to the UK began almost immediately and production facilities were established in the UK in 1906. This was largely through the influence of James Horlick, and against the wishes of his brother William. These facilities were completed by Wisconsin-trained staff in 1908. The firm expanded steadily until 1914.

After the war Horlicks drifted. Sir James Horlick, as he then was, died in 1921 and family disputes between his sons, James and Ernest, and his brother William concerning the business did nothing to give direction and control to the company. In the event the business was divided into two separate companies. William kept the production and marketing rights for the United States and South America, while Ernest and James Horlick bought out the UK company with marketing rights to the rest of the world with a cash adjustment. The finances of the UK company were restructured in 1927 when it was capitalized at £0.5 million. It may be noted that the main rival Ovaltine (the Swiss company Wander) was capitalized at £1 million in 1923. What was needed was a strategic view of the market: that is where J. Walter Thompson enters the picture.

Marketing Horlicks between the wars

The central point of interest is how a single product company grew so rapidly in what was generally regarded as a hostile trading environment. The explanation has something to do with product development but more to do with marketing innovation led jointly by a British family owned and managed firm and a US advertising agency. The explanation provides an excellent case study of positioning within a market – what Porter (Caves and Porter 1977; Porter 1985) calls barriers within markets – and it also reveals the successful development of a planned campaign run over several years which was so very different from the one-shot stunts so favoured by Lipton, Lever and the other pioneers of marketing and advertising (Nevett 1982). We consider first the position in 1927–8, then trace the growth of the company over the 1930s and examine the competitive behaviour of rival firms in this market to the end of the period.

The Horlicks works in 1927 is recorded as employing about 350 people, of whom about 70 were office and 100 were 'outdoor staff', presumably sales and/or drivers (Luff 1927). The factory produced about 50 tons per week of powder using some 15,000 gallons of milk mostly from its own farms in the West Country where Sir James Horlick had acquired his estate. Malt was brought in from the Horlick maltings at Thetford. By the end of the 1930s the firm employed about 1,500 according to the company magazine. At the time of the merger with Beecham in 1969 the company employed about 1,000. The firm thus grew fourfold in little more than a decade. Sales also grew fourfold as shown in Table 13.1

Sales fluctuated as might be expected in the recession years: the trough of 1932–3 is clearly marked as is the sharp recovery of 1934–5. Profits also grew but these are readily available only after 1937 when the company went public. The prospectus and other data suggest growth as shown in Table 13.2.

Profits trebled over four years, a remarkable performance in what was a sluggish market with stable or falling prices in the period 1930–4. The total size of the market in which Horlicks competed is not easily calculated. Figures for 1938 suggest a market between £2.5 million and £5 million. The lower figure is based on the retail market calculations for health drinks from Jefferys (1954); the higher figure

Table 13.1 Index of sales of Horlicks in the UK, 1928–37

1928	1929	1930	1931	1932	1933	1934	1935	1936	1937
88.2	124.9	120.7	127.1	113.4	110.9	145.7	230.0	283.3	320.0

Source: J. Walter Thompson Archive
Note: January 1929 = 100, by interpolation as no base year is given

Table 13.2 Trading profits of Horlick Co. Ltd, 1933–7[a]

1933 (£000)	1934 (£000)	1935 (£000)	1936[b] (£000)	1937 (£000)
76.2	125.7	185.9	246.8	243.1

Source: Stock Exchange Yearbook
Notes: [a] Net profits before tax
[b] 1936 figures cover 15 months

is based on J. Walter Thompson calculations in a 1937 report on annual sales of Horlicks (£1.26 million), Ovaltine (£1.95 million) and estimates of the third force (Bournvita, £0.7 million) and the long tail which might have amounted to a further £0.5 million. Neither figure is inconsistent with a high advertising/sales ratio of over a third estimated by the National Institute for Economic and Social Research (NIESR) which, when applied to estimated advertising expenditure in 1938 of around £1 million, suggests sales close to £3.5 million (Kaldor and Silverman 1948). The Census of Production data for 1935 are not very helpful in identifying a health food or milk/drink market but can be construed to support a figure of about £4 million. There are no data on the size of the market in the 1920s (no reliable figure can be computed from Census data of 1924).

The range of market competitors over the period grew as dramatically as sales. In the 1920s the competitors were the invalid foods such as Benger's, the infant foods supplied by Glaxo and of course the market leader Ovaltine. The distinctive chocolate taste to the malted milk made Ovaltine a rival of Fry's cocoa and Cadbury's drinking chocolate but neither of these products claimed the properties of the health food drinks. In this sense Horlicks and Ovaltine were establishing a niche in the milk food drinks market. However, by the end of the 1930s Bournvita had been launched by Cadbury in 1930 as an important third force; as the advertising data available from Legion (an organization which collated and published media expenditure:

see Harrison and Mitchell 1936) make clear there were a dozen other contenders in the market-place. It was a standard case of a growing profitable market with apparently few barriers to entry. Success in such markets according to Porter (1985) lies in product differentiation and/or creating some special niche within a market which distinguishes the product from rivals. Horlicks did just that, as this chapter will show.

Product range, product development and pricing policy

The product range inherited from the First World War period did not alter very much at all during the interwar years. Tablets for use in the armed forces had been developed in 1915 and this line was retained during the 1920s; a deal with Sharp's toffee allowed Horlicks flavoured toffee to be marketed by both companies; and Horlicks flavoured rusks made by Huntley and Palmers were launched in the early 1920s. There was some expansion of the range of sizes offered with the launch of a catering tin in 1922: a 5lb and 10lb tin for the institutional and café trade. But with one other exception, the price lists of the period offer no indication that product development was active. The exception was chocolate-flavoured Horlicks – an obvious counter to Ovaltine – launched in February 1929. It was used in all four sizes and sold for the same price as plain Horlicks. The full product range was exhibited at the British Industries Fair in February 1930. Price lists of 1937 suggest no other product innovation.

Sales of Horlicks were dominated by the no. 1 bottle. This accounted for over half of sales in the 1920s and became even more important in the 1930s (see Table 13.3).

No distinction is made between plain and chocolate-flavoured Horlicks, which is unfortunate because there seems to be no other document with quantitative data on the product range. Other documents make it fairly clear that chocolate-flavoured Horlicks was never a success, and while there are no definitive data on the point, the strong impression remains that neither rusks (made at Huntley and Palmers) nor the toffee (made by Fry at Bristol) were major contributors to sales. Horlicks remained throughout the period a one-product company.

To a modern reader this seems disastrous: the importance of product innovation to food companies is almost impossible to over-estimate. Whether the concern is to prolong the product life cycle, or reposition the product, or to constantly generate new products, the focus of modern marketing is to anticipate the replacement market for

Table 13.3 Sales of Horlicks malted milk, 1933–7[a]

	1933 (%)	1934 (%)	1935 (%)	1936 (%)	1937 (%)
No 1 pack	55.9	58.2	61.2	59.9	62.1
No 2 pack	40.7	38.5	36.1	37.0	34.8
No 3 pack	2.0	2.0	1.7	2.0	1.9
No 4 pack	1.4	1.3	1.0	1.1	1.2

Source: J. Walter Thompson Archive

Note: [a]Percentage of annual consumer sales

current products. The evidence from the 1930s is that such matters were discussed but that in the case of Horlicks the advice was largely ignored.

J. Walter Thompson wrote in September 1931 reminding Horlicks that new products were essential, 'In view of the fact that you have only one basic product and have all your eggs in one basket'. It then pointed out the dangers of such a position and noted that competitors could come from several directions. Observation of food manufacturing and distribution suggested that 'the trend is towards both vertical and horizontal combination' (J. Walter Thompson Archive). This is evidence of the recognition of improved security for companies. The letter continued with the remark that 'within your own experience you have seen the gradual elimination of Horlicks Malted Milk from the infant food market which was one of its primary markets' and urged Horlick to 'protect your business investment by the development of additional related products by a policy of product development and research and experimentation'.

The letter suggested some ideas. It was recognized that the existing product did not appeal to the child market and 'its high price excludes it from the C and D class markets' (see pp. 273–4 for discussion of social class C and D). But the letter went on to suggest that this market is where future growth must take place unless the export market is pursued more vigorously. Export markets are not thereafter considered. The suggestions were new products designed to attract the C and D groups. The name suggested was Maltova and (although the letter does not say so) it was clearly designed to fight back against Ovaltine because some emphasis was given both to the chocolate taste and the price which was to be much lower than Horlicks so that the two brands would be quite separately positioned in the market. Other new products included 'Dutine', a slimming product, and 'Fillip', a new name for the café trade Horlicks. It was also suggested that the café trade Horlicks be clearly separated from the 'proper' Horlicks – perhaps even a new formula. It would prevent any possible confusion with the branded product in the event that the café trade became a generic commodity milk drink.

Another obvious line to develop was to recapture the infant food market. Horlicks had a good name in the segment; distribution contacts existed through pharmacies; the hospital and institutional markets were regular customers. There was every reason to suppose that a sound, newly devised product would do well. There had been apparently some product development but J. Walter Thompson urged swift action. This was because there was some suspicion that the US companies were about to enter the UK malted milk market because the US market had become dominated by generic products based on the milk bar trade. Such drinks were purchased because of the setting and just 'upon acceptance as a pleasurable drink'. J. Walter Thompson urged the paramount importance of taste and price in such a market and commented ruefully 'as you know prior to the introduction of the present chocolate flavoured Horlicks we conducted a prolonged series of tasting experiments. Unfortunately the chocolate malted milk as finally developed was not one which could appeal on the ground of taste. We feel that the resultant general lack of consumer acceptance of the chocolate malted milk is an experience by which we should profit'. The letter concluded by advising that this cheaper, reformulated product should be developed and 'held ready until such time as the anticipated American competition forces us to further action' (J. Walter Thompson Archive). It turned out that the US competition did not materialize – but neither did the new products.

The threat of competition particularly from the United States was not new. In an earlier letter dated October 1930, J. Walter Thompson had sent to Horlicks samples of 'Vitamalt', 'Vitamalt' toffee and 'Vitamin' chocolate. These were products developed and marketed by Boots the Chemists. The suspicion was that the new product development had been completed by their US owners and that although no immediate threat to Horlicks was expected because the products were to be limited to the Boots shops (more than 1,000 across the UK by 1933) nevertheless some contingency development work by Horlicks would be wise. As Horlicks was being distributed mostly through grocery stores rather than pharmacies, this advice was ignored.

It is, however, a compliment to the power and profit of Horlicks that a multiple retailer/manufacturer would wish to develop an own-label imitation and a warning to a branded product about how easily such multiples could create rival, generic products. It is also an interesting case of international or multinational transfer of brands. Jesse Boot, who was aged 70 in 1920, was disabled by rheumatoid arthritis and unable to control his business, and with no obvious successor (because of estrangement from his son), decided to sell out. His choice fell on Louis K. Liggett, whose United Drug Co. dominated US pharmacy operations. He sold out for £2.3 million in 1920 (Chapman 1974: 146). Liggett immediately began to integrate the Boots operations with the 1,000 or more Rexall stores already owned by Liggetts in Britain and Ireland. A Retail Executive Committee organized the retailing side and a parallel manufacturing executive committee organized the production side of the business. A system of inter-company transfers took place so that the British managers learned something of US production and retailing methods, while Americans came to understand the UK market and its overseas connections with the Empire. Thereafter the British end of Liggetts/Boots became more soundly based. Boots was introduced into the London Stock Exchange in 1923 after 25 per cent of the stock was released by Liggetts back into British hands. John Boot, the son of Jesse, was given a post in the new arrangements and worked well, despite never accepting the necessity for the sale to the US company. Later 'in 1933 the financial difficulties of United Drug in the United States permitted John Boot . . . to regain control of the family firm, Boots Pure Drug, which had come to be administered through an extensive managerial hierarchy' (Chandler 1990: 368). It was little wonder that Horlicks took note of such developments.

It is even more surprising that so few resources seem to have been devoted to new product development, given the potential for competition from rivals such as Boots. Perhaps there was such development which has not been recorded, but in an otherwise full set of records held by J. Walter Thompson there seems to be no data on such activity. The price lists of the period – for the grocery trade – indicate no change between 1929 when chocolate Horlicks was introduced and 1939. It seems remarkable that Horlicks should have allowed its old infants' market to be eroded without some effort to recapture a slice of what was still a substantial market. A new infant food might require another name and/or repositioning in the market if the same product was to appeal to both infants and adults. That is not impossible – Johnson's baby soap and shampoo appeals to both infants and adults – but it does require quite explicit positioning. Horlicks came to mean bedtime drinks for adults and the company made little effort to develop either differently named products for adjacent segments or to position the brand to encompass a class of malted milk drinks for all purposes. The reason for this, one suspects – there is no documentation – is that staff were struggling to meet the challenge of a fourfold increase in sales; to establish a system of national distribution; to establish plants overseas in Australia and South Africa; and to protect the margins of a premium product from vigorous attack by competitor manufacturers and the emerging power of multiple retailers. It may have been shortsighted but with a successful product in place it is tempting to devote resources to protect it rather than to develop alternatives. How it became successful and how it resisted the issues noted above is the subject of the next section.

Pricing policy, consumer research, advertising and promotion

That Horlicks was a premium product may be readily seen from the price lists in Table 13.4 taken from a list of the Proprietary Articles Trade Association (PATA) which acted as a co-ordinating body for many manufacturers of branded grocery and household products and had some role to play in the regulation of what became a policy of resale price maintenance. In total there were twenty-four competitors in this 1938 price list. If the various sizes are regarded as competitive there are over sixty products in competition. Horlicks as can be seen is the most expensive product. J. Walter Thompson examined the point by undertaking combined taste and value for money sessions, in effect creating unit price comparisons. The main competitors and their value for money position are set out in Table 13.5.

The conclusion is quite clear. Horlicks was a premium product selling at twice the price of its competitors. This relative position had not changed throughout the interwar years although some increase in absolute price is apparent after the war. Price lists at the end of the First World War indicate prices of 1s. 3d. and 2s. 6d. for the bottles; these had risen to 1s. 10d. and 3s. by 1925. A further increase had clearly occurred by 1938. Premium prices were the result of effective marketing innovations and it is to these that we now turn.

Consumer research

To establish a marketing campaign it is usual to know something about the market. The question was posed: who uses Horlicks and why? No one knew for certain. It was agreed that it was important to find out and consumer research work was conducted.

In November 1928 some 150 in-depth interviews were held in

Table 13.4 Product lines and prices of milk food drinks in the UK, 1938[a]

Product	Retail price s. d.		Wholesale price[b] s. d.		Discount (%)
Allenbury's Malted Food	1	3	12	0	20.0
Almata (J & J Colman)	2	6	32	2	22.8
Ambrosia	1	8	15	0	25.0
Barlova		6	4	9	20.8
Bemax	1	3	11	3	25.0
Bordens Malted Milk	1	3	11	6	23.3
Bengers Malted Milk	2	3	21	9	19.4
Bournvita	1	5	13	0	23.5
Cow and Gate Malted Food	2	0	18	0	25.0
Frys Malted Milk Cocoa	1	2	11	0	20.0
Horlicks	2	0	19	2	20.0
Marshalls Malted Milk	1	0	9	0	25.0
Masons Malted Milk	1	6	–	–	–
Ovaltine	1	1	10	4	20.5
Queens Malted Milk	1	0	9	0	25.0
Robinsons Barley	1	3	12	9	27.8
Instant Postum	1	6	25	6	20.0
Virol	1	3	12	10	14.6
Vitacup (Colman)		11	9	6	13.6

Source: J. Walter Thompson Archive

Notes: [a] In the 1930s £1 = $4.86; in pre-decimal currency 12 pence = 1 shilling and 20 shillings = £1
[b] Wholesale price is per dozen, thus 20% discount on 12 times 1s. 3d.

Table 13.5 Unit prices of Horlicks and main competitors, 1938

	Price per pack d.	No. of spoons	Spoons per drink[a]	No. of drinks	Price per drink d.
Horlicks	24	39	3	13	1.84
Ovaltine	13	36	2	18	0.72
Bournvita	9	32	2	16	0.56
Vitacup	6	36	2	19	0.34
Marshalls	15	38	2	19	0.79

Source: J. Walter Thompson Archive

Note: [a] According to instructions on pack (powder only)

London and the Midlands. The main conclusions were that proprietary milk food drinks were chiefly consumed at bedtime to promote sound sleep; that women were the major users of such drinks; and that children took (or were given them) as a general builder of sound nourishment. These first findings shaped the launch of chocolate-flavoured Horlicks in 1929. The advertising copy stressed that the flavour was distinctive, pleasant and appetizing; it also stressed that the drink was nourishing. The results of the launch, and the winter advertising expenditure, were to boost sales of plain Horlicks, but to leave chocolate-flavoured Horlicks a disappointing second to Ovaltine, which remained an overall market leader and dominated the child market.

A reconsideration of the position of Horlicks was, therefore, undertaken in 1930 before the start of the autumn advertising spend. It was based on research carried out in August 1929. This found that while 34 per cent suffered from insomnia, a further 38 per cent were conscious that they were restless sleepers and 48 per cent (mostly women) complained of waking tired. The work was replicated in summer 1930 but this time based around a competition for which there were over 6,000 entries. The results again showed about 43 per cent of respondents – including many men – took Horlicks to help them sleep and for building up energy the next day. The main plank in the advertisements was the notion that it is quality of sleep that is important, not the length of sleep. It was stressed that many people suffered from such a condition and that the solution to such a problem was to drink Horlicks at bedtime. The advertisements were addressed to women and the captions – like many such ads in the late 1920s and early 1930s – showed testimonials from both medical authorities and satisfied customers. The 1930 ads season continued the story line but extended it to men showing how their work performance was enhanced after a good night's sleep.

The advertisements were based on the growing body of consumer research conducted by J. Walter Thompson. A list survives of some twenty-seven studies carried out between September 1927 and July 1935. These range from small pilot studies of 40 men and women on patterns of use of Horlicks to a major 3,000-plus survey across A, B, C and D classes covering all milk-food drinks. They also include some media studies – the Ovaltineys radio campaign had an impact after 1934 – and several studies of promotional aids such as free beakers and competitions. Most of these studies have been lost but the findings are frequently noted in surviving documents.

A study of the size and share of the products in the market was carried out in April 1936. It covered 1,240 men and 1,345 women across A, B, C and D households in England and Scotland. Overall some 39 per cent took proprietary milk food drinks. Of the brands available, Ovaltine was the market leader (21 per cent), with Horlicks second (13 per cent) and Bournvita third (8 per cent). There was a long tail of other products. It is worth noting the market implications of such a finding. In 1931 there were 44.8 million people in England and Wales and Scotland. If the J. Walter Thompson results are broadly right then a 39 per cent penetration rate implies that some 17.5 million people purchased a milk food on a regular or occasional basis; that is a huge national market to reach. It is of course a characteristic of food products that they are low-price items aimed at regular and frequent purchase, but it was a major achievement of the food industries to create such a huge following for branded products.

It is also interesting to note that the research identified the social class background of consumers. This analysis is explored in more detail later so it is important to grasp quite what social class A, B, C and D represent. It is also useful to note the sources for market research between the wars. The Census of Population did not produce tables of numbers by social class until the post-war period so researchers devised their own measures. They were all similar, being some compromise between annual income of head of household, total household income, occupation (a status measure as well as income measure), size of house, and number of servants (a wealth and social position measure). There were several such measures available between the wars. Boyd-Orr (1935) in his study of income and diet established six categories (I–VI); Crawford and Broadley (1938) in their more comprehensive survey of food consumption preferred to distinguish an AA as well as A–D groups. Another source of consumer data was the survey conducted by the weekly magazine John Bull (around 1 million households read it in the mid-1930s) which used four social class categories (J. Walter Thompson Archive). The more systematic National Readership Survey carried out in pilot form in 1937–8 by the Institute of Practitioners in Advertising to guide advertising rates and media placements and formally conducted and published in 1947 by the Hulton organization established the now familiar A, B, C1, C2, D categories (Harrison and Mitchell 1936). These categories varied slightly but were broadly as follows:

AA   £1,000+ per year, based on income per week per head of household

A   £500–1,000 per year

274   *Adding Value: brands and marketing*

B   £250–499 per year
C   £125–249 per year; C1 = £2 10s–£4; C2 = under £2 10s per week
D   less than £125

Average earnings of working-class employed persons (CD) was less than £3. Social security payment was 19 shillings for a single person and 32 shillings for a married couple. Classification, although based mainly on income per head, was adjusted for social status. Thus young bank employees might earn barely £250 per year but were category B, while some train drivers or print workers might earn over £250 per year but would be classified to C or C1. Crawford and Broadley (of William Crawford advertising agency) described their category A household as £500–1,000 income per year, having a large house, detached or semi-detached of eight to ten rooms, with one servant, with the head of household a successful professional person or proprietor of middle-sized business. The B class would not normally employ a live-in servant but would have a daily domestic assistant. The estimated proportions of population taken by these social class categories varied slightly but were about 1, 4, 20, 40 and 35 per cent respectively. J. Walter Thompson and Horlick's used these data for further analysis of the market.

In a study of the social class characteristics of milk-drink users, it was found that a high proportion were from social class D, which was important because of the potential size of this market. A follow-up study in 1937 explored the social class characteristics of the drink in more detail. The precise classification used is not made clear but from the data in Tables 13.6 and 13.7 it may be that J. Walter Thompson categorized their findings using weights closer to 30 per cent and 45 per cent for social class D compared with social class C. These figures seem to suggest that Horlicks was very well represented among working-class households. Although primarily an upmarket premium product directed at AB homes it turned out that around 13 per cent of class D used Horlicks and that this represented some 60 per cent of Horlicks sales. This must be true of any mass consumption product because the numbers in the AB categories were unlikely to support a nationally marketed product, but it does indicate a surprising level of penetration of a premium product into working-class homes and it is also clearly the growth area for the product during the 1930s. The penetration of social class D market was facilitated by the distribution arrangements. During the 1930s Horlicks was promoted through co-operative multiples, which sold heavily to social classes C and D.

Research on the reasons for taking Horlicks and other proprietary

Table 13.6 British homes consuming Horlicks by social class, 1928–37

	1928 (%)	1934 (%)	1935 (%)	1936 (%)	1937 (%)
AB	14	14	15	18	21
C	6	7	9	13	20
D	3	3	5	7	13

Source: J. Walter Thompson Archive
Note: Percentages are of all homes in each social class

Table 13.7 Distribution of Horlicks sales by social class, 1928–37

	1928 (%)	1934 (%)	1935 (%)	1936 (%)	1937 (%)
AB	30	29	22	19	14
C	26	29	26	28	26
D	44	42	52	53	60

Source: J. Walter Thompson Archive
Note: Percentages are of all homes using Horlicks

milk food drinks continued to find that 'just a drink' and sleep-inducing properties were the main reasons, although Horlicks by the mid-1930s was bought more frequently than other brands for health reasons – 'nourishment/body-building'. Children were less convinced (see Table 13.8). The results show how successful Horlicks' campaign was during the mid-1930s. Clearly adults had been convinced and were now buying the products for the claimed benefits. Children – never a major market for Horlicks – mostly consumed it for other reasons.

A year later in 1937 a replication study found no great change in the total market but some shifts in brand characteristics. Some 17 per cent of adults were regular users while 21 per cent were occasional users – about the same as in 1936. But Horlicks closed the gap on Ovaltine slightly among regular users (31 to 52 per cent) and among occasional users (46 to 51 per cent). Horlicks again scored well as 'just a drink' as well as a sleep-inducing, nourishing drink. The household-based research found that Ovaltine dominated the child market (65 per cent of regulars) while Horlicks came a weak second (21 per cent).

It might be expected that these drinks were consumed at bedtime. This is not so (see Table 13.9). Although the drinks were mostly consumed at bedtime, for Horlicks there was a substantial group consuming during the morning – especially by 1937; this was because of

Table 13.8 Trends in reasons for taking Horlicks, 1928–36

	1928	1934	1935	1936
Adults using for medicinal reasons (%)	29	40	47	48
Children using for medicinal reasons (%)	25	24	30	25

Source: J. Walter Thompson Archive

Table 13.9 Time of day Horlicks and Ovaltine taken, 1934 and 1937

	Horlicks		Ovaltine
	1934	1937	1937
All who take	100	100	100
During morning	5	27	16
Lunch/tea	4	7	1
Evening/bedtime	84	64	89

Source: J. Walter Thompson Archive

Table 13.10 Mid-morning and evening drinks in the UK, 1937

	All adults drinking at mid-morning and bedtime	
	Mid-morning (%)	*Night (%)*
Total drinking	38	71
Tea	23	26
Coffee	5	5
Milk	2	7
Cocoa	2	9
Beer	2	6
Ovaltine	0.6	7
Horlicks	1.4	3.3
Bournvita	—	2.6

Source: J. Walter Thompson Archive

the café trade. J. Walter Thompson therefore studied the general drinking habits of adults (see Table 13.10).

Tea was confirmed as the great British drink for all occasions, but Horlicks seemed to have both an opportunity and a threat in developing a café-based mid-morning drink: it was an obvious opportunity to expand sales and introduce people to the drink. Indeed other questions suggest that some 28 per cent of all Horlicks users first tried Horlicks in a café as a mid-morning drink, so this was a real advantage. The threat lay in the US experience – that competition between suppliers would create a generic or commodity image for the drink, so that the Horlicks brand name and image would be lost in the general request for a low-cost milk drink. As noted earlier no action was taken on this point.

The sleep campaign

This was devised by J. Walter Thompson in the summer of 1933 ready for the autumn campaign season. It built on earlier efforts, but was carefully crafted as a coherent, well integrated campaign of complementary messages. It was designed to establish Horlicks Malted Milk as 'Horlicks' – not as a milk drink – by investing the product with special characteristics. It was also hoped that the message would convince social class D that despite the price premium the product still represented good value. The strategy was based on the research work undertaken in the early 1930s, which built on the findings that many people reported that they were poor sleepers and that milk drinks at bedtime promoted health. The strategy was to establish poor sleep as a common problem and to promote Horlicks as the answer to this problem. It was an early example of what is now an exercise in cognitive dissonance. To achieve the goal J. Walter Thompson developed what is still remembered as the 'sleep campaign'.

The autumn 1933 season began with a focused appeal on the importance of a good night's sleep for effective work the following day. Two innovations were made. First, photographs were used rather than line/wash drawings for the stand-alone block advertisements. Second, a story-board was based on the comic strip then becoming popular in the daily press. Line drawings showed people sleeping well and then performing successfully at work. Both men and women featured in these stories, which typically credited good work and success to the sound sleep promoted by Horlicks. The usual ABC1 occupations were used, including engineers and architects, army officers and nurses; C2 occupations such as bus drivers, postmen and secretaries were also used. The appeal to children (or rather their parents) was continued based on replaced lost energy which helped them at school.

Fear was also used to establish the problem; strips showed people being warned about poor performance or worry that they were too tired to cope. Horlicks then came to the rescue recommended by medical men, scientists or other figures of authority. In 1932 the results of some experiments by Sir E. Charles Dodds, an eminent consultant to several companies, were used in the advertisements to support claims about energy losses and the replacement value of Horlicks. These proved successful and the decision to work this story line was taken for the 1933 season. Based on these 'scientific' results the campaign introduced the famous concept of 'night starvation' and in straight photograph-based advertisements, story-line comic strip advertisements and in radio jingles the same point was made in many different ways for many different groups: poor sleep led to poor work or social performance but by taking Horlicks, the problem was solved and hence all turned out well, both at work and in one's social life. This was directed at men, women and children. For men the concern was often fear of losing jobs, which applied to B and C1 groups as well as C2s. The social occupations were the subject of several discussions: J. Walter Thompson was careful to keep them in groups earning about £5−6 per week, such as engine drivers and draughtsmen; they were rarely placed in up-market occupations earning over £10 per week for fear of upsetting the AB market.

Test marketing of a women's campaign in Hull and Portsmouth in 1933 focused attention on 'asking your mirror' − contrasting the tired, listless woman with the bright, radiant woman who had clearly taken her Horlicks and thus never known the dire effects of night starvation. The campaign proved quite successful and it was extended into the 1936−7 season with story-lines indicating fear of losing looks and hence household happiness. The social position of the woman was again important: although facial lines were to be shown (in order to be erased by Horlicks) the occupations used should not be associated with 'drudgery because then tiredness would be a natural result', as J. Walter Thompson nicely put it. So, a busy AB mum or a secretary or nurse would be used.

The deliberate targeting of social class D did not go unchallenged; it clearly caused some disagreement. Horlicks' management presumably liked their up-market image and sought to limit the appeal to social class D. J. Walter Thompson, however, argued that it was too huge a market to ignore and that while recovery (after 1934) was in progress it was foolish to deny the evidence of such sales:

> It has been suggested that by building up this market we should lay ourselves open to a very rapid sales decline in the event of another economic crisis. While it is true that price resistance increases as the income scale declines we do not think that the weight of evidence can be held to support the suggestion that the market for Horlicks

at its present price amongst working class people is likely to be affected seriously by any normal fall in general prosperity.

(J. Walter Thompson Archive)

That shows a sound perception of income elasticities and price elasticities and the power and comfort of a brand. It is also an important plank in the marketing strategy: a strong product, well differentiated by careful advertising organized around a sustained campaign which offers a clear health reason for buying a pleasant drink. The marketing of the product was supported by a sound distribution policy through co-operatives, as is shown later.

Both the scale of expenditure and the range of advertising media were extended as the campaign stretched on through 1933–7. Horlicks in 1928 had used mainly national newspapers and a few provincial papers with a total spend of £5,840. By 1935–6 total spend was nearly £100,000 and covered national dailies, Sunday papers, provincial daily and evening papers, magazines, religious papers, medical and nursing papers. There was a separate budget for the child campaign featuring national dailies and the comics/hobby magazines. By this time Horlicks had prepared radio advertisements and seriously thought of film-based work. Hoardings, buses and railway stations were targeted as was a range of promotion activities. Horlicks sponsored Arctic expeditions and other prestigious activities such as sports including the Olympic Games. By 1936 the range of such work had expanded both in scale and in precision. A range of persons and organizations was associated with Horlicks' promotion – the Ideal Home Exhibition was supported, some well-known sports personalities were shown using the product – and various merchandise such as beakers, long spoons and measures were available free or later for sale. Unlike Kellogg's, and some other J. Walter Thompson clients, there is no record of free gifts for children, such as toys, models or books, perhaps because the pack did not lend itself to such enclosures.

Pressure from retailers and wholesalers was endemic in the severe competition of the 1930s. Horlicks, like most manufacturers, managed to hold out against distributors. It held a strong position in independent grocers and had a supporting trade in pharmacies, but the pressure from multiples was strong. It was directly approached by Woolworth in 1929 for a special low-price pack but after much thought it rejected the deal because

> we could not offer them a package which is not also available to the trade and, if we could put up a package we should lay ourselves open to reproach from our chemists customers. Though we might

do a considerable business through such channels our sales in other directions might be prejudiced. Owing to the high costs of packing, the profits would be almost negligible and buyers who take our products in sizes which show us a satisfactory margin might purchase the small Woolworth package with disastrous results to our main interest.

(J. Walter Thompson Archive)

Woolworth continued to take the standard pack and also sold Horlicks in the cafeteria area of the stores from the catering sized tin. Clearly advertising had contributed to sales. In a 1936 report (J. Walter Thompson Archive) the relationship is charted: the index of sales used is not explained but must have been supplied by the Horlicks' management (see Table 13.11) This strong relationship is confirmed by graphical analysis and regression calculation ($r = 0.99$ and t-test significant at .001 level).

Table 13.11 Indices of annual sales and advertising expenditure of Horlicks, 1928–38

	Sales	*Advertising*
1928	88.2	75.5
1929	124.9	124.0
1930	120.7	121.0
1931	127.1	129.0
1932	113.4	120.1
1933	110.9	106.8
1934	145.7	128.7
1935	230.0	221.5
1936	283.3	310.9
1937	320.0	336.1
1938	336.1	383.0

Source: J. Walter Thompson Archive

One area in which Horlicks (like Kellogg) was not very successful was in altering the pattern of seasonal sales. There were several efforts to persuade consumers to drink Horlicks with cold milk as a summer beverage, but throughout the period Horlicks remained essentially a winter drink: 65 per cent of advertising expenditure was made during September–March and some 68 per cent of sales were in the same period.

Distribution

No account of the marketing of a food product can be complete without some note of distribution channels, although information on retailing between the wars is far from complete (Braithwaite and Dobbs 1932; Jefferys 1954). Horlicks distributed through four channels: grocers, pharmacies, co-operatives and 'other' – the institutional sales to schools, hospitals and cafés. Horlicks held nearly 16,000 accounts with retailers in 1928, of which 2,000-plus were pharmacies and grocers, 700 schools and hospitals, and 13,000 cafés. Although trends in distribution can be examined through the 1930s, there seems to be no further data on the actual number of accounts. The volume of sales reflected by these channels is nowhere clearly stated. It is likely that the café trade accounted for about one-third of volume sales while the main bulk of sales was through grocers and pharmacies; the pattern between pharmacies and grocers changed over the period (see Tables 13.12 and 13.13).

The picture is clear enough: as Horlicks established itself as a widely purchased brand, so retailers stocked and sold more of the product. It became more a beverage with health-giving properties and less an invalids' and infants' health drink. While grocers sold more than pharmacies, what is interesting is the share of the co-operatives in this market – another indication of the appeal of the product to working-class groups.

It was pointed out by J. Walter Thompson that management time involved in handling 15,000 accounts was excessive, and that to focus sales through fewer channels might be beneficial. The details of such actions have not survived but something like this must have occurred: Table 13.14 shows the results of developments through the 1930s.

Sales clearly more than doubled while outlets rose by something over half. A large part of the explanation for this development is the growth of the co-operative trade which grew from 15 per cent of sales in 1930 to over 22 per cent by 1936. Other multiples maintained their share at the expense of the multiple pharmacies trade which declined in line with the total trade with pharmacies reflecting the repositioning of Horlicks in the beverage market. There was also some increased trade through wholesalers, which is a little unusual during this period as many branded foods turned to direct sales as a means of enforcing resale prices. The move towards wholesalers may have been necessary because Horlicks was a nationally distributed product (see Table 13.14).

It comes as no surprise to find that sales grew fastest in the more

Table 13.12 Changing patterns of Horlicks distribution, 1930–6

	% sales through retail channels			
	1930	*1932*	*1934*	*1936*
Grocers	53	58	61	67
Pharmacies	47	42	39	33
Of grocers co-operatives	15	18	21	22
Others	85	82	80	78

Source: J. Walter Thompson Archive

Table 13.13 Index of Horlicks sales and distribution outlets, 1933–6

	1933	*1934*	*1936*
Total sales (1933 = 100)	100	132	246
Total outlets (1933 = 100)	100	109	175

Source: J. Walter Thompson Archive

Table 13.14 Sales of Horlicks by region, 1930–6

	% growth on 1930 sales value			
	1930	*1932*	*1934*	*1936*
Southern area	47.1	48.2	65.7	139.2
Northern area	45.0	40.3	50.1	93.0
Scotland	7.9	7.1	8.9	13.2

Source: J. Walter Thompson Archive

prosperous south of England; indeed the surprise is that the product was marketed as a national brand from the outset and developed sales throughout the north of England and Scotland even through the recession. National distribution was an expensive and management-intensive operation. As Cadbury have shown, the operations involved in delivering high-volume products into many retail units was a complex business (Cadbury Ltd 1945). Train, lorry, combined operations between own transport and contracted transport absorbed large resources. It was not surprising that trade through wholesalers increased. It is a tribute to the power of the brand that there seems little correspondence concerning pricing and price maintenance.

The success of Horlicks during the 1930s is not in doubt. Sales grew fourfold, employment trebled: it became a national brand. The explanation of that success has been given in terms of marketing: the conscious shaping of the brand image, differentiation from competitors, the positioning of the product as a premium-priced but value-laden product supported by a carefully contrived campaign based on research into the consumer behaviour associated with buyers. J. Walter Thompson, writing to Horlicks in 1937, argued 'it is our belief that the policy of the last few years has so far differentiated Horlicks from the competition which existed in the 1920's that there is today no direct competitor'. That may be an overstatement from advertising agency to client, but it carries some conviction. The consumer purchased sleep and health as well as a pleasant drink and seemed to think it good value to pay twice as much for the product as for rivals such as Ovaltine and Bournvita.

CONCLUSION

This chapter adds to the small number of studies which offer evidence of consumer brand marketing in the UK between the two world wars. It has demonstrated that companies – and not just US companies – were well aware of how to establish and promote brands. The study shows that Horlicks and J. Walter Thompson had strategic acumen in assessing the competitive situation in 1928. In deliberately choosing to maintain a premium product (twice the price of rival brands) and seeking some means of giving added value to customers so that the brand might achieve a protected position within the market, they represent an early example of what Porter has called a strategy of 'product differentiation' (Porter 1985: 119). The specific condition for which Horlicks came to be the best solution was the need for a sound sleep or the problem of 'night starvation': a marketing message sufficiently precise to be meaningful to many people, while permitting the product to be sold as a more general health food and still lose nothing of its claim to be a pleasant drink. It was a very successful campaign waged over three or four years which was in sharp contrast with most one-shot advertising efforts of the period, although, as the Guinness advertising suggests, it was not unique (Nevett 1982).

The marketing mix used to implement this strategy encompassed all the techniques used in the 1990s except commercial TV. An early decision was made to protect the price premium attached to the product. Given this policy only carefully controlled special promotions were permitted; no special prices or packaging deals were made with multiple retailers. Every effort was made to protect the resale price arrangement. It was a premium product and was protected to maintain its premium position. The main component of the mix was promotion through carefully researched advertising campaigns. A sound sleep was identified as the distinctive attribute of the product and the message was developed through a sustained, coherent campaign over almost a decade. Sound sleep is a universal need and the condition of night starvation for which Horlicks was the solution was carefully fostered through all forms of media.

To support the campaign J. Walter Thompson engaged in consumer research to discover how consumers perceived Horlicks in relation to rival brands; how, when and where the product was consumed; and how important sleep and other health issues were as 'problems' afflicting consumers. Market research in the sense of measurement of the size and composition of the market was also important: it quickly revealed the potential importance of the social class D market segment and sparked a debate about how best to develop this segment. Distribution policy with some emphasis on sales through the co-operative stores and a judicious choice of marketing messages seemed to be an effective means of developing this segment. The marketing mix was therefore based on price and promotion with a supporting role for distribution. The lack of product development is noted below.

The marketing communications mix was critical to the success of the campaign. The messages were based solidly on consumer research and the media used were extensive and innovatory. National press and magazine advertising was quickly adopted making Horlicks a nationally distributed product from 1929. Horlicks were among the first to use film (UK films shown in the 1930s had advertisements between films) and radio, although it should be remembered that commercial radio in the UK during the 1930s was based in France and Luxembourg, and did not cover the whole of the UK. Although useful, Horlicks never quite matched the huge success achieved by Ovaltine with their 'Ovaltiney's' radio club for children, and given their market strength Horlicks were right to make press advertising their main media channel.

Two weaknesses may be noted. First, there was almost no product development over the interwar period. Apart from the introduction of chocolate-flavoured Horlicks (which was not a success) there is no evidence that Horlicks devoted any effort to the various suggestions made by J. Walter Thompson. The failure to develop a new baby product seems very odd, given the continuing good name of Horlicks among the pharmacy retailers and the institutional market, which included hospitals and nursing homes. The second weakness was the failure to tackle the problem of the café trade. There was always a tension between the generic milk drink – a commodity – available in a café and the premium position established in retail grocers. On several occasions it was suggested that a new product – and a new name – be developed for the café trade. Nothing came of these suggestions.

It was these two weaknesses that in large part account for the slow decline in the post-war position of Horlicks. The market – or rather the consumers of Horlicks – grew older and no attempt was made to capture the younger, post-war generation. Unlike Ovaltine, Horlicks had no great strength in the child market and therefore had to rely on converting adult users to Horlicks. This proved difficult in the post-war period: the image of Horlicks as a comfortable, middle-aged, pleasing nightcap did not lend itself to the new generations. Sales declined until the firm was sold to the Beecham group in 1969. The attempts to reposition Horlicks – just as other Beecham brands such as Lucozade and Ribena have been repositioned – are beyond the scope of this chapter.

An important theme has been the relationship between Horlicks and its advertising agency in the development of marketing strategy: J. Walter Thompson were instrumental in the success of Horlicks. Although the British management took ultimate responsibility, they were ably advised on most aspects of the campaign by their US agency. It could be seen as a case of technology transfer: a US agency transferring standard US marketing techniques to a backward British company. That may be so, but the files do not support that interpretation, nor does the presence in the UK of so much market research data suggest that the British were so laggard. The J. Walter Thompson files suggest similar work for firms such as Rowntree, Kellogg's and Brown and Polson (after they had been taken over by CPC the new US owners switched to 'their' agency). The same kind of research-based service was given to these clients. The agency was clearly an important influence on UK marketing between the wars; it adds further details and another gloss to reported accounts of J. Walter Thompson (West 1987). This chapter has shown how one convenience food product was established in the UK diet between the wars. It is to be hoped that more such studies will gradually fill out our picture of marketing before 1945.

286 *Adding Value: brands and marketing*

REFERENCES

Abrams, M. (1951) *Social Surveys and Social Action*, London: Heinemann.

Aldcroft, D. H. (1986) *The British Economy 1920–57*, Brighton: Harvester.

Baker, M. J. (1979) *Marketing: An Introduction* (3rd edn), London: Macmillan.

Baker, S. (1973) *Milk to Market: Forty Years of the Milk Marketing Board*, London: Heinemann.

Barna, T. (1945) *Income Redistribution Through Taxation*, National Institute for Economic and Social Research (NIESR), Cambridge: Cambridge University Press.

Bourdieu, P. (1984) *Distinction: A Social Critique of the Judgement of Taste*, London: Routledge.

Boyd-Orr, J. (1935) *Food, Health and Income*, London: Macmillan.

Braithwaite, B., Walsh, N. and Davies, G. (1986) *Ragtime to Wartime: The Best of Good Housekeeping*, London: Ebury.

Braithwaite, D. C. and Dobbs, S. P. (1932) *The Distribution of Consumable Goods*, London: Routledge & Kegan Paul.

British Market Research Bureau (BMRB) (1956) *Readings in Market Research*, London: BMRB.

Broadberry, S. N. and Crafts, N. F. R. (1992) 'Britain's productivity gap in the 1930s: some neglected factors', *Journal of Economic History* 53(3): 531–58.

Burnett, R. G. (1945) *Through the Mill: The Life of Joseph Rank*, London: Epworth.

Burns, J., McInerny, M. and Swinbank, A. (eds) (1983) *The Food Industry: Economics and Policy*, London: Heinemann.

Business Statistical Office (BSO) (1978) *Historical Record of the Census of Production 1907–1970*, London: HMSO.

Cadbury Ltd (1945) *Industrial Record 1919–39*, Birmingham: Cadbury Ltd.

Campbell, C. (1987) *The Romantic Ethic and the Spirit of Modern Consumerism*, Oxford: Basil Blackwell.

Caves, R. and Porter, M. E. (1977) 'From entry barriers to mobility barriers: conjectural decisions and contrived deterrence to new competition', *Quarterly Journal of Economics* 91, May: 241–61.

Chandler, A. D. (1990) *Scale and Scope: The Dynamics of Industrial Capitalism*, Cambridge, Mass: Harvard University Press.

Chapman, S. (1974) *Jesse Boot of Boots the Chemist*, London: Hodder & Stoughton.

Church, R. (1993) 'Mass marketing motor cars in Britain before 1950: the missing dimension', in R. S. Tedlow and G. Jones (eds) *The Rise and Fall of Mass Marketing*, London: Routledge.

Collins, E. J. T. (1976) 'The "consumer revolution" and the growth of factory foods: changing patterns of bread and cereal-eating in Britain in the twentieth century', in D. Oddy and D. Miller (eds) *The Making of the Modern British Diet*, London: Croom Helm.

Corley, T. A. B. (1972) *Quaker Enterprise in Biscuits: Huntley and Palmer of Reading 1822–1972*, London: Hutchinson.

—— (1987) 'Consumer marketing in Britain 1914–60', *Business History* 29 October: 65–83.

Crawford, W. S. and Broadley, H. (1938) *The People's Food*, London: Heinemann.

Davenport-Hines, R. P. T. (ed.) (1986) *Markets and Bagmen*, Aldershot: Gower.

Douglas, M. and Isherwood, B. (1973) *The World of Goods*, Harmondsworth: Pelican.

Driver, C. (1983) *The British at Table*, London: Chatto.

Edwards, H. V. (1948) 'Flour milling', in M. Fogarty (ed.) *Further Studies in Industrial Organisation*, London: Methuen.

Featherstone, M. (1991) *Postmodernism and Consumer Culture*, London: Sage.

Floud, R. and McCloskey, D. (1981) *The Economic History of Britain since 1700*, Cambridge: Cambridge University Press.

Fraser, W. H. (1982) *The Coming of the Mass Market 1850–1914*, London: Macmillan.

Glynn, D. and Oxborrow, J. (1976) *Interwar Britain: A Social and Economic History*, London: Allen & Unwin.

Harrison, G. and Mitchell, F. (1936) *The Home Market*, London: London Press Exchange.

Henry, B. (1986) *TV Advertising: The First 30 Years*, London: Century Benham.

Hirst, I. C. R. and Reekie, W. D. (eds) (1976) *The Consumer Society*, London: Tavistock.

Horst, T. (1974) *At Home Abroad: A Study of the Domestic and Foreign Operations of the American Food Processing Industry*, Cambridge, Mass: Ballinger.

Hugill, A. (1978) *Sugar and All That*, London: Gentry.

Jefferys, J. B. (1954) *Retail Trading in Britain 1850–1950*, Cambridge: Cambridge University Press.

Jenkins, A. (1970) *Drinka Pinta*, London: Heinemann.

Johnston, J. P. (1976) 'The development of the food-canning industry in Britain during the inter war period', in D. Oddy and D. Miller (eds) *The Making of the Modern British Diet*, London: Croom Helm.

Jones, G. (1984) 'Multinational chocolate: Cadbury overseas 1918–39', *Business History* **26** June: 59–76.

Jones, S. G. (1985) 'The leisure industry in Britain 1918–39', *Service Industries Journal* **13**(4): 90–106.

Kaldor, N. and Silverman, R. (1948) *A Statistical Analysis of Advertising Expenditure and of the Revenue of the Press*, Cambridge: Cambridge University Press.

Kotler, P. (1978) *The Principles of Marketing*, Englewood Cliffs, NJ: Prentice-Hall.

Levitt, T. (1985) *The Marketing Imagination*, Glencoe: Free Press.

Luff, E. A. (1927) *Our Local Companies: no 5 J & W Horlick*, Slough: E. A. Luff.

McKendrick, N., Brewer, J. and Plumb, J. H. (1982) *The Birth of a Consumer Society*, London: Europa.

MAFF (Ministry of Agriculture, Fisheries and Food) (1951) *The Urban Working Class Household Diet 1941–49*, London: HMSO.

—— (1959) *Domestic Food Consumption and Expenditure in Britain*, Annual Report of the National Food Survey Committee, London: HMSO.

Mathias, P. (1967) *Retailing Revolution*, London: Longman.

Matthews, R. C. O., Feinstein, C. H. and Odling-Smee, J. (1982) *British Economic Growth 1856–1973*, Oxford: Clarendon.

Nevett, T. (1982) *Advertising in Britain: A History*, London: Heinemann.

Porter, M. E. (1980) *Competitive Strategy*, New York: Free Press.

—— (1985) *Competitive Advantage*, New York: Free Press.

Reader, W. J. (1976) *Metal Box*, London: Heinemann.

Richardson, D. J. (1970) 'The history of catering with special reference to J Lyons and Co Ltd to 1939', unpublished PhD thesis, University of Kent.

Ritson, C., Gofton, L. and Murcott, A. (eds) *The Food Consumer*, Chichester: Wiley.

Robertson, D. H. (1963) *Lectures on Economic Principles*, London: Fontana.

Saunders, P. (1990) *A Nation of Homeowners*, London: Unwin Hyman.

Silverman, R. and Reddaway, W. B. (1951) *Advertising Expenditure in 1948*, London: Advertising Association.

Stevenson, J. (1984) *English Society 1914–45*, Harmondsworth: Pelican.

Stone, R. (1954) *The Measurement of Consumers' Expenditure and Behaviour in the UK 1920–1938* vol 1, Cambridge: Cambridge University Press.

Tedlow, R. S. (1990) *New and Improved: The Story of Mass Marketing in America*, Oxford: Heinemann.

—— (1993) 'The fourth phase of marketing: marketing history and the business world today', in R. S. Tedlow and G. Jones (eds) *The Rise and Fall of Mass Marketing*, London: Routledge.

Wagner, G. (1987) *Chocolate Conscience*, London: Chatto.

Ward, A. V. (1990) 'Economic change in the UK food manufacturing industry 1919–39', unpublished PhD thesis, University of Reading.

West, D. C. (1987) 'From T-square to T-plan: the London office of the J. Walter Thompson Advertising Agency 1919–70', *Business History* 29(2): 199–217.

Wilkins, M. (1974) *The Maturing of Multinational Enterprise: American Business Abroad from 1914 to 1970*, Cambridge, Mass: Harvard University Press.

Wilson, C. (1954) *The History of Unilever* 2 vols, London: Cassell.

—— (1968) *Unilever 1945–65*, London: Cassell.

Manuscript sources

The Horlicks material, including the Guard book, is kept in box 4 at the J. Walter Thompson Library and Archive, Berkeley Square, London. Fiche material is listed under Beecham.

Part IV
Retailing

14 Multiple retailing and brand image

An Anglo-American comparison 1860–1994

Bridget Williams

The most important difference between multiple food retailing in Britain and the United States is the relative significance in each country of the own brand. In 1992 British retailer brands accounted for 33 per cent of the market by value for packaged groceries, whereas US private brands had a market share of 18 per cent (O C & C Strategy Consultants 1992). These figures understate the importance of the most successful British supermarkets' brands: in 1992 the two largest companies – Sainsbury's and Tesco's – own brand groceries had 55 per cent and 42 per cent of company market share respectively (figures from Audits of Great Britain, AGB 1992). This chapter examines the historical reasons for this discrepancy, while also analysing the social, political and structural factors which have influenced own brand development in Britain and the United States.

It is surprising that the contrast is so marked: so heavily did British retailers draw in the post-war years on US experience in importing retailing methods, technology and merchandise that one might expect a degree of similarity in their trading patterns. The post-war Anglo-American Council on Productivity was specifically set up to promote such links. The tendency has been to ascribe the predominance of manufacturers' brands in the United States jointly to their advertising power and to the relative post-war prosperity of US consumers (Cooke 1970; Productivity Team Report 1951: 38; 1952: 36–7). This view is limited in its historical perspective. While it is true that round-the-clock advertising was influential in the United States, the importance of the relative prosperity of US consumers over their British counterpart has been exaggerated. In Britain the sale of Tesco's own brand products as a proportion of total sales more than doubled between 1978 and 1992 during a period of unprecedented consumer prosperity (Powell 1992: 198).

At the outset it is important to clarify the terms used to describe own-brand products. The term 'own brand' is used to describe goods bearing the retailer's name or those specifically identifiable as the retailer's products. 'Private label', on the other hand, is a US term used to identify products which are not sold under the manufacturer's (or proprietary) brand. It includes own brands, bearing the name of a packet, warehouse or co-operative, generics ('no-name' brands) and sub-brands which may or may not be identifiable as retailer brands. Because of the broad nature of the term 'private label' it is used here only in its umbrella meaning.

In examining the contrasting legal and political contexts of British and US retailing, this chapter takes as case studies the experience of J Sainsbury plc in the UK and Shaw's in the United States. Both companies established own brand identities early in their histories (Sainsbury's was founded in 1869 and Shaw's in 1860). The essential difference between the two companies was that Sainsbury's enjoyed an uninterrupted tradition of own branding which helped to determine the company's corporate image, while Shaw's private label was discontinued in 1944. In 1992 Sainsbury's UK supermarket profits were £628 million, making it the UK's most profitable retailer. The company – including its hypermarket subsidiary Savacentre – has a share of 10.4 per cent of the markets in which it operates (J Sainsbury plc 1992a). Shaw's too is the market leader in the four states in which it operates (Maine, New Hampshire, Massachusetts and Rhode Island) with a market share of 16 per cent (figures from IRI Inc. 1992). In 1992 its sales were $1.8 billion.

In addition to their significance as leaders in their respective markets, Shaw's and Sainsbury's share a remarkable number of historical characteristics. Each has retained a corporate culture that reflects a long history of family ownership and both enjoy a high degree of customer loyalty. As companies they have been regional rather than national in character and expanded less rapidly than competitors such as Lipton or Home and Colonial in Britain or the Great Atlantic and Pacific Tea Company (A & P) and Kroger in the United States. One reason for this has been that Sainsbury's and Brockton Public Market (BPM) – the former name of Shaw's southern region – specialized in fresh foods which were difficult to distribute effectively over long distances.

This chapter begins with an analysis of the comparative retailing structures of Britain and the United States, followed by case studies of the introduction of own brands at Sainsbury's and Shaw's in the late nineteenth and early twentieth centuries. The permissive nature of British Resale Price Maintenance is contrasted with the compulsion of the US Robinson Patman Act to assess the respective fortunes of pack-aged own brand groceries. The reintroduction of Shaw's own brand, following the company's acquisition by Sainsbury's in 1987, is then used to challenge the view of branding as a simple marketing device.

RETAILING STRUCTURE

The complex structure of mid-nineteenth-century British retailing resulted in the development of several different own brand traditions. Producer-retailers, such as butchers who made pies and sausages on the premises, took personal responsibility for their own product development and quality control. In doing so they exploited the advantage of exclusivity and incorporated the image of their 'own brand' into that of the business as a whole. Buyer-retailers, on the other hand, did not take an active part in the production or manufac-ture of the goods they sold. Their general and specialist stores relied on purchasing through the wholesaler network. This could be either passive buying, taking goods recommended by commercial travellers or manufacturers' agents, or active buying in which they dictated the quality of the products they purchased. Active buying enabled buyer-retailers to claim the same exclusivity as that enjoyed by the producer-retailers. Own brands of this type relied on the product knowledge and handling skills of the retailers rather than their manufacturing expertise.

The distinction between these two types of brands depended on the products involved. While producer-retailers sold fresh home-produced foodstuffs, buyer-retailing was associated with grocers who relied on non-perishable imported goods sold through factors and shipping merchants. The less integrated nature of the buyer-retailer's supply chain made it more vulnerable to competition from proprietary products.

A sub-category of buyer-retailing was the packer-retailer. As pro-prietary goods gained market share, such people established copy-cat brands by repacking goods bought at a discount from wholesalers. Inevitably these brands were associated with the bottom end of the market. In Britain a notable example of this type of branding occurred in the 1920s when Jack Cohen began to buy tea from T. E. Stockwell, partner in the firm of Torring and Stockwell, importers and blenders of Mincing Lane, London:

I negotiated a deal for an initial order, based on a price equal to 9d per lb . . . I reckoned to have this packed in half-pound packets to sell at 6d. We had then and there to think of a name for the market brand I would sell. We scratched our heads and came up with the name TESCO.

(Corina 1971: 53–4)

Commentators such as Alexander and Jefferys (Alexander 1970: 234–5; Jefferys 1954: 130) have noted how the traditional boundaries between retailers were eroded during the late nineteenth century by the rise of multiple retailers. Among the largest of these were Lipton, Home and Colonial, and Maypole Dairies. Although these companies drew on the existing traditions of brand identification they sold only a handful of products (Mathias 1967: 166). This distinguished them from the smaller regional companies such as Sainsbury's and David Greig's, which had far fewer branches yet sold a much wider range of products. However, it was these companies, rather than the national multiples, that inherited the producer-retailer and buyer-retailer traditions.

In the United States there was a less complex pattern of retailing. According to H. S. Peak and E. F. Peak there were only two principal types of retailer – the general store and the specialty store (Peak and Peak 1977: 4–5). Both types fall into the category of buyer-retailer. The general store stocked every conceivable item from molasses to gunpowder and occupied a position of central importance in many small communities. A number of commentators have noted the sentimental affection many post-civil war Americans had for the 'traditional' general store (Greer 1986: 51; Tedlow 1990: 184–6). Daniel E. Sutherland has suggested that this was due to the overwhelmingly 'rural' nature of mid-nineteenth-century America and the central importance of the local store to social survival (Sutherland 1989: 158). The vital importance of the shopkeeper's role in the local community and economy enabled him or her to exercise considerable political influence both locally and nationally.

The importance of the buyer-retailing general store in post-civil-war America strengthened the already well-established manufacturer–broker–retailer network (Porter and Livesay 1989: 5–10). While this network was not immune from attack from manufacturers' integration forward into marketing it was rarely threatened by retailers' integration backwards into distribution and manufacturing as in Britain. However, in the latter part of the nineteenth century this network was challenged by the rise in specialty stores. Specialty stores were urban rather than rural in location and appealed to shoppers of all social classes. Although they sold a wider range of products than the British multiples they had nothing like the multifarious stock of the average general store. Instead their aim was to provide their customers with variety and choice over most of the basic food items. As they developed, many specialty stores began to offer a mail order business to complement their downtown trade, thus placing them in direct competition with rural general stores. As their trade increased many specialty stores opened further branches – often in expanding towns in rural areas – and developed into chains. The economies of scale that this produced enabled them to offer goods at a discount, thus threatening the proprietary brands. Some such as A & P, Kroger and Safeway, even developed own brands of considerable strength.

At first these developments aroused little opposition. In the case of A & P, for example, its growth went virtually unchallenged until 1913 when it began to open its chain of discount stores and threaten the livelihood of general shopkeepers. A powerful lobby immediately arose to defend traditional interests and encourage anti-chain sentiment. Its success in this is illustrated by the popularity of the film *Forward America*, which was reviewed by *Business Week* in 1934:

> 'Forward America' hits hard and fast . . . the story tells of John Adams of Adamsville, an independent retailer who is ruined when chain stores invade his town. Arguments are presented to support claims that the chains drain capital from communities, hurt the local markets of farmers, oppress manufacturers, lower living standards by depressing wages, add to unemployment by substitution of machines for men.
>
> (Greer 1986: 47)

The rise of the chain stores also threatened manufacturers' proprietary brands not only by breaking the traditional link with the general store but also through discounting and own brands. The result was that the chains came under a sustained attack from a powerful coalition of manufacturing and farming interests. A succession of legal cases heightened opposition to the retail chains on anti-trust grounds and led ultimately to the passing of the Robinson Patman Act 1936. This effectively denied buying advantages to multiple retailers and slowed the development of own brands.

All this contrasts sharply with the British experience where the initiative for retail change came directly from the multiples. In Britain there were no vested interests comparable to the farming and manufacturing lobbies in the United States so the multiples were free to develop their businesses into whatever part of the distribution chain they wished. They were greatly aided in this by the free trade policy of the British government, which opened up new sources of supply from overseas. Soon New Zealand lamb, Argentinian beef, Dutch butter, Danish bacon and American grain, cheese and bacon were essential elements of the British diet. All of these had in common mass production techniques ideally suited to the needs of the multiples.

Many national multiples ventured into production; for example Lipton with its tea plantations and meat packing; and Maypole with margarine production (Mathias 1967: 219). These activities played an important part in establishing brand identity. Thomas Lipton's production on his tea estates, while representing only a fraction of the tea sold by his international business, enabled him to establish his own brand with the slogan 'Direct from the tea garden to the tea pot'. Not only did this provide him with some useful publicity but also gave him a presence in production by which to judge costs and quality independently (Mathias 1976: 96).

However, it was the smaller regional multiples who were to become most clearly identifiable as producer-retailers. They often began in humble ways. David Greig, for example, decided to complement his retailing activities by manufacturing sausages at his shop at 58 Atlantic Road, Brixton, in London. These soon became so popular with the customers in his small chain of shops that in 1895 he converted the next-door premises into a small factory with a gas engine which powered the chopper and filler in full view of passers-by. Greig's manufacturing activities thus served as a simple but effective advertisement for his own brand products (David Greig Ltd 1970: 7).

THE DEVELOPMENT OF THE SAINSBURY BRAND

A similar integration back into production occurred at Sainsbury's. Like David Greig's, Sainsbury's also began by making sausages with in-store sausage machines. These were replaced in 1891 by a cooked meats factory at the firm's Blackfriars (London) headquarters. Here the company diversified into pies and sausages and other pork products. Integration was carried a step further backwards with the purchase of a farm at Haverhill, Suffolk, in 1902. This farm was managed by Frank Sainsbury, third son of the firm's founder. Like Lipton's tea plantations, the farm produced only part of the shops' needs, but it provided a useful means for promoting quality control. Frank Sainsbury began by buying and slaughtering pigs from local farmers but soon purchased several prize boars to enable them to improve their stock. In 1912 he set up an egg-collection business, grading and packing eggs from hundreds of small producers in East

Anglia. In return for a guaranteed market, Sainsbury's was able to make both quantitative and qualitative demands of its suppliers, while marketing these products as own brands.

Even when Sainsbury's continued to act in a buyer-retailer capacity it worked closely with its suppliers. In 1903 the firm acquired from Thomas Deacock a grocer's shop which sold tea. Up until this time none of the Sainsbury stores had stocked tea but it was decided to add the product to the firm's general range. The firm therefore enlisted the help of George Payne, a tea merchant based at Tower Bridge, to develop a range of quality own brand blends. These were marketed as exclusive to Sainsbury, with each blend taking its name from the colour of the seal on the packet.

Sainsbury's also served as a wholesaler for its own branches. A depot was set up at Blackfriars so that the company could buy in sufficient bulk to be competitive with the major multiples (J. B. Sainsbury 1947). However, the company did not support the various defensive pacts that were set up by the smaller retailers to combat the direct-buying activities of the multiples and co-operatives (Barty-King 1986: 59). Although the company was a member of the Home and Foreign Produce Exchange, it never became involved with the Wholesale Provision Merchants' Association or the Provision Agents' Association's attempts to combat the buying power of the multiples.

Wholesaling was the key to Sainsbury's competitiveness and its success in establishing a brand identity. By eliminating the middleman the company ensured that a greater proportion of the value added to a product was retained. It also had the secondary advantage that it enabled the company to exercise control over product development and quality control. This was of crucial importance in the successful marketing of own brands. As Tedlow has pointed out, the wholesaler-retailer had a significant advantage over the independent retailer in having reliable information about sales and customer preferences (Tedlow 1990: 210). This information, coupled with the economic advantages of bulk buying and multiple retail outlets, greatly aided the development of own brands.

SHAW'S BRAND

The George C. Shaw Company was founded in 1860 in Portland, Maine. Originally a specialty tea store, it soon extended its product range into general groceries. In 1875 a second shop was opened and the firm began a mail-order and rail-freight business. This provided free deliveries to railroad stations and steamer quays within 100 miles of Portland. In 1919 Shaw's was taken over by Brockton Public Markets (BPM), a chain of five stores in Southern Massachusetts which had been founded by Maynard Davis in 1891.

For many years Shaw's and BPM traded as separate companies. However, as they expanded their trading areas following the Second World War this made less and less strategic sense, particularly for BPM, whose name was locational in origin. It made it difficult to establish a corporate image while duplicating brands and dissipating advertising revenue. For this reason all BPM's branches were renamed Shaw's in 1978; the stock of the two companies was merged the following year.

A price list for the George C. Shaw Company dated 15 September 1882 lists an enormous product range, including twelve blends each of tea and coffee, sixteen types of cheese, nine varieties of mustard, eighteen brands of wheat flour and a full page of 'farinaceous goods'. The company also sold non-foods such as candles, stove powder, lamp oils and toilet soaps. A large proportion of the goods offered were proprietary brands and the price list contains full pages devoted to brand names such as Kennedy's biscuits and Thurber's canned goods. At a similar date Sainsbury's sold fewer than one hundred product lines, almost all of them fresh provisions.

However, the number of Shaw's own brand goods was limited; most of them were 'specialty' lines of tea, coffee and butter. The price lists describe each blend and reinforce the authority of the brand with information on the provenance of each line. The most important Shaw's brand was fresh mayonnaise which, by 1926, was available post free throughout most of New England, and in 'eighty-odd of the best food shops in as many towns and cities in Maine' (George C. Shaw Co Ltd 1926). It was only later that Shaw's introduced sub-brands such as 'Royal Lily' canned goods and 'Table d'Hôte' coffees.

Within the company emphasis was placed on its buying expertise for both proprietary and own brand goods. The business was consequently integrated backwards into jobbing and forwards into mail-order. In many respects the mail-order business hindered the development of own brand products by placing a greater emphasis on customer services and choice. It would have been totally impractical to have established own brand products over such a diverse product range.

BPM, with stores in Brockton and New Bedford, developed in much the same way as Shaw's. It too was an urban-based specialty store. Like other 'public markets' − a term applied to all undercover markets whether under single ownership (such as BPM) or genuine 'public' markets such as Faneuil Hall in Boston, where several traders gathered under one roof – it offered a full range of fresh foods and groceries as well as hardware and non-foods. It also had a limited range of own brand goods which included 'Our Roan' canned goods and 'Trustworthy' coffee. After the pattern identified by Porter and Livesay, BPM relied on local wholesalers and had no central warehouse until 1957 (Porter and Livesay 1989: 12, 215).

Apart from the individual retail circumstances of Shaw's and BPM a number of external factors made it very difficult to establish own brand credibility in the United States. The first of these was the introduction of self-service. The opening of new self-service stores in unfamiliar locations made it virtually impossible to market unknown private labels, especially as the assistants no longer had the opportunity to recommend them to customers. Instead, self-service favoured proprietary goods because of their manufacturers' national advertising power. The second was the Robinson Patman Act, which undermined the competitiveness of private labels by depriving retailers of any buying advantage. (This will be considered in more detail in the next section.) Shaw's and BPM finally abandoned their private label goods when they joined the Topco buying co-operative in 1944.

THE BATTLE OF THE GROCERY DEPARTMENT: RETAIL PRICE MAINTENANCE AND ROBINSON PATMAN

Both Retail Price Maintenance and the Robinson Patman Act were designed to curb the activities of multiple retail chains, yet they were to have widely differing consequences for the development of own brand goods in Britain and the United States. In Britain the introduction of manufacturers' proprietary brands paralleled the standardization of products and retail practices typified by the major multiples. Previously unbranded goods were offered ready-prepared and prepackaged to the retailer on the understanding that they would not be offered for resale below the manufacturer's predetermined price. The aim was to protect small independent retailers from price-cutting by multiples. Although such agreements were entirely voluntary the manufacturer could punish any breaking of the agreement by retailers by refusing to supply them in future.

Not all specialist retailers regarded these new proprietary goods with enthusiasm. Prior to Resale Price Maintenance they had been able to buy their supplies direct from the manufacturer and sell them as branded goods. This had enabled them not only to benefit from the value added normally to the product but also to gain an additional margin by endorsing it with their own name. Once these benefits had been removed grocers found themselves in a state of near-perfect competition (Yamey 1952: 522–5). Tate's decision in 1898 to brand and package their previously unbranded sugar in 2lb and 4lb packets met with a distinctly mixed reception from the grocers. In a letter to the *Grocer* dated 18 June 1989, John J. Wolstenholme, of Eastbank, Southport, complained of

> an attempt to capture a most important source of profit by making it a proprietary article . . . the magnificent profit of a farthing per pound will, I hope, meet with the acceptance it deserves. The list of proprietary articles is at the present time sadly too large. Many articles could be mentioned which have been exploited for the benefit of the wholesaler (not necessarily the manufacturer) to the injury of the retailer.

For medium-sized firms such as Sainsbury's, Resale Price Maintenance threatened to remove their competitive edge over small independent retailers. It also stimulated them to circumvent such restrictions by developing their own brands in direct opposition to proprietary products. In response to Resale Price Maintenance, Sainsbury's greatly extended the number of grocery lines bearing its name in the first half of the twentieth century. Sub-brands such as 'Gay Friar' pickles and 'Selsa' dry goods were also heavily advertised as own-label goods. In 1920 the firm set up grocery packing lines at its Blackfriars depot which greatly facilitated the growth of its own product range. By the 1930s Sainsbury's stocked over 100 own brand products.

In marketing these new lines Sainsbury's placed great emphasis on purity and fair dealing. One problem with unpacked generic groceries was that they could easily be contaminated or adulterated. 'Sainsbury's High Grade Groceries' were therefore advertised as 'Packed in sealed containers, thereby ensuring perfect freshness and freedom from dust'. Another problem with non-proprietary brands was that they allowed sharp practices by retailers. It was not uncommon for them to sell their products by gross weight, thus including the wrapping as part of the purchase. Sainsbury's 1911 price list assured its customers that the purchase of its own brand products avoided any danger of short-weight:

> Paper is so much cheaper than Tea, that most tradesmen find a huge profit in charging Tea prices for the paper wrapping. When you buy Tea of Sainsbury, you get 16ozs of Tea in each packet:– you do not pay for the packet, nor the paper about it.

Sainsbury's established a sufficiently strong reputation for value and quality to be able to use its own name to endorse its products. The following advertisement from 1939 for the Selsa own brand is built entirely on mutual trust between retailer and customer:

> Let us tell you about Selsa. Selsa sets a standard of quality. It means that each product has been made, not necessarily *by* Sainsbury's, but specially *for* Sainsbury's. Selsa goods are prepared, often to Sainsbury's own recipes, by manufacturers who have been singled out for their skill and integrity . . . on the single word – Selsa – Sainsbury's stake the reputation of seventy years. For Quality. For Value. For Freshness. For Purity.

However, the development of Sainsbury's own brand was not popular among those who supported Retail Price Maintenance. It was felt that unless the smaller retail chains such as Sainsbury's could be persuaded to support the scheme it would be impossible to challenge the multiples. On 28 November 1929, Arthur Giles, Secretary of the Federation of Grocers' Associations, wrote to John Benjamin Sainsbury requesting an urgent interview when he came across a company price list. Giles was dismayed to discover that of the 237 lines listed, only 80 were proprietary items, and a mere 10 on the current list of price maintained goods (Grocery and Proprietary Articles Association 1929). However, as Resale Price Maintenance was a purely voluntary measure, there was little that Giles could do to persuade John Benjamin Sainsbury to change his retail practices.

Whereas Resale Price Maintenance attempted to influence the price charged to consumers, the Robinson Patman Act regulated the wholesale price and was legally binding. This meant that it was far harder for retailers to challenge, especially as the responsibility for test cases lay with manufacturers. In many cases it took years to successfully challenge the Act. For example, the most important provision in the Act forbade manufacturers giving discounts on quantities over one railcar load of goods 'of like grade and quality'. This was interpreted in successive judgments as referring equally to proprietary goods and own label products packed specially for retailers. It was not until 1964 that Borden established that a price differential could be charged for its condensed milk on the basis that consumer preference for a branded product had a monetary value, and that identical products sold under different brands are not of 'like grade and quality' (*Borden Co* v *FTC*, US Court of Appeals, 5th circuit, 4 December 1964).

The most obvious way for retailers to circumvent the Robinson Patman Act was to integrate backwards into production in the same way as Sainsbury's had done in Britain. However, this was a far less attractive option in the United States for legal reasons. Multiple retailers had been relatively unsuccessful when invited to co-operate with wholesalers, producers and independents in drawing up codes of fair practice under a programme initiated by the National Recovery Administration (Greer 1986: 32–49). This was because successive Federal Trade Commission inquiries refused to accept that the chains' competitiveness was based on efficiency rather than the unfair use of buying muscle (Greer 1986: 62) despite evidence to the contrary (Tedlow 1990: 214). For this reason any movement into production was viewed with suspicion. Furthermore, the anti-trust proceedings against A & P, which effectively dismembered the firm's production and distribution capacity, prevented many other retailers following such a course.

The fear of anti-trust action greatly hindered the development of own brands in the United States. Some retailers actually disguised their own brands as packers' brands. During the 1930s and 1940s Safeway established a family of over 100 such names, a practice they later admitted 'got out of hand' (Fitzell 1982: 56). As these brands were not identified directly with the retailer the link between own brand products and a firm's corporate image was never made in the same way as in the UK.

One aspect of Robinson Patman did favour the smaller multiples. As the Act specified one railcar load as the maximum quantity on which a discount could be given it was possible to achieve this by a number of retail chains grouping together into a co-operative. One of these co-operatives was Topco, which was formed in 1944. John Mugar, President of Star Markets, stated:

> With Topco we were big enough to buy in carloads, then we could fight them on price. All we wanted was an even break. With or without Robinson Patman, we were going to get there. But the Act gave us a breather, and we grew faster because of it . . . the act showed us the peak – a carload. So we climbed to that peak and learned that we could do other things too, such as be more efficient.
>
> (Greer 1986: 86)

Despite this the Act still prevented the smaller retailers moving into distribution. Stanton Davis, President of BPM, complained that:

> The Robinson Patman Act . . . prevents BPM's own trucks from backhauling when making deliveries from its East Bridgewater

Warehouse to its chain of 32 stores. The consumer would be better off if [Brockton Public] Market trucks could pick up merchandise directly from the wholesaler, thereby cutting transportation costs. . . . Because this practice is against the law, industry can't get discounts.

(S. D. Davis 1975)

From its origins in the co-operative buying of dairy produce and paper bags, Topco expanded into the packaging of groceries for its members. These appeared under the Food Club and Elna labels. In 1950 Topco merged with Top Frost a co-operative supplier of frozen foods. Greengrocery was added to the range in 1960 and fresh meat in 1966. By 1990 Topco had a turnover of $2.4 billion. Although Topco has been extremely successful, its structure has prevented its members developing a brand identity comparable to that of Sainsbury's. To the customer there is no link between the various Topco labels and the stores in which they are sold. Moreover, as membership has grown, Topco labels have actually been sold in stores who are in active competition with each other.

SELF SERVICE

The most striking feature of the introduction of self-service in the United States was that it was initiated by the independents rather than the multiples. Although there had been earlier experiments, it was during the Depression of the 1930s that self-service became popular, stimulated by the desire to cut costs and prices. Independents were well placed to use the many empty warehouses and could open stores unhampered by the labour and capital costs incurred by the chains. The existence of the Robinson Patman Act also ensured that the multiples were unable to secure buying advantages over the proprietary products so that with their lower costs the independent supermarkets became very competitive. Fitzell has noted how, in an unfamiliar environment, customers invariable prefer a known product (Fitzell 1982: 52). Even Safeway's Pay 'N Takit stores only sold proprietary goods (Tedlow 1990: 243).

In Britain the stimulus for the introduction of self-service came not from a depressed economy but from the desire of the government and the major chains to relieve the problems of post-war scarcities. In 1949 John Strachey, Minister of Food, offered special building licences to retailers willing to experiment with self-service trading. Those who took up this offer had the advantage of being able to draw on the experience of the United States and utilize and refine an existing technology. The companies with the most efficient management and greatest financial resources were thus best fitted to introduce self-service.

The introduction of self-service came at a time of great shortages. During the war many products had become 'generic' or simply disappeared from sale altogether. The few proprietary brands that were still available were in short supply because the output of the manufacturers was still determined by wartime production quotas (Harrison 1977). Since neither retailers nor manufacturers could command any qualitative advantages the success of self-service depended to a large degree upon the consumers' trust in the reputation of the retailer with whom they were registered. Although there was some initial hostility to self-service it was not long before the prevailing food shortages had predisposed even the most unadventurous housewives to experiment with unusual products like snoek and whalemeat.

Self-service methods were well suited to the sale of packaged groceries. However, they were less suited to fresh meats and provisions, because the latter required complex packaging and needed to be stored in costly refrigerated cabinets. In Britain there was also a certain amount of consumer hostility as many people expected their meats to be served to them by a skilled butcher.

One effect of the growth in importance of self-service grocery departments after the war was that own brands came to be seen as 'copy-cats' of proprietary brands. The lack of any qualitative difference between own brands and proprietary goods encouraged customers to regard them merely as cheaper alternatives. By the early 1980s own brands were actually leading product innovation in many convenience foods. More recently the increased responsibilities of the retailer in setting standards of product description (for example nutritional labelling and wine coding) and in enforcing legal requirements such as those of the Fair Trading Act 1973 and the Food Safety Act 1991 have reinforced the consumer's reliance on the retailer, rather than the manufacturer, as the source of information and good practice.

REINTRODUCING THE SHAW'S BRAND

The reintroduction of the Shaw's brand has confirmed the lessons of both the US and British experience. In September 1990 Shaw's launched a three-year programme to introduce a range of 1,300 own brand products. This has drawn heavily on Sainsbury's experience and on customer confidence in Shaw's reputation. It has addressed the central problems of corporate identity with own brands and of vertical integration into product management.

> The concept of a supermarket assuming total repsonsibility for products manufactured for them, including factory vetting, product specifications, packaging design and labelling information, is new.
>
> (McEwan 1992: 4–5)

Shaw's label products conform to a consistent pattern of packaging design, including the 'Shaw's Quality Seal' which bears the words 'Quality since 1860'. The company also promises a money-back guarantee, prices at least 10 per cent below the regular level of the national proprietary brands and quality at least equal to, or better than the brand leader. Sainsbury's long-standing slogan 'Good Food Costs Less' has also been adopted by Shaw's.

The relaunch of Shaw's own brand has highlighted the central difference that exists between proprietary brands and the retailers' own brands. While the former depend for their success on customer recognition of their 'personality' (Arnold 1992: 14, 25) the latter are established by a firm's corporate identity. A number of factors are important in establishing such an identity. The most obvious is the 'shopping environment': the house style and the presentation of the goods in the store itself. But equally important is the need for the company to instil into its customers, employees and suppliers a belief that an own brand represents the highest standards in product development, quality control and design. If this is successful own brands can become more than a mere marketing tool. As Margaret McEwan has said of Shaw's:

> It is not so much what the customer perceives he or she is buying, as what the buyer knows he is selling. In other words, the product specification dictates the product and that it is different from a branded product. For example yesterday I was contacted by a customer who wanted to know who supplied our frozen peas. . . . In refusing to give the name of our suppliers it is necessary to explain that they are Shaw's peas, and that even if they are cropped from the same field as a national brand it is *our* product specification which determines the nature of the product. This is what the buyer is buying.
>
> (Margaret McEwan, personal communication, 1993)

This is important because traditionally US retailers have not regarded product development as their responsibility. As Jack Cohen has written: 'Retailers do not consider their role to be that of initiators of new products, they are seekers, finders and purveyors of new products initiated by others' (Cohen 1992: 28). Part of the reason for this has been the continuing existence of the Robinson Patman Act, which has required private labels to be readily distinguishable from proprietary goods; this has led customers to believe that this also means that they are inferior in quality. Shaw's development of high-quality own label products on the European model has sought to challenge this assumption. It is possible, as Guy de Jonquières (1993) has suggested, that European retailers such as Sainsbury's, Ahold of the Netherlands and Delhaize of Belgium – which have all acquired US supermarket groups – may soon be in a position to challenge such assumptions.

CONCLUSION

As Leigh Sparks demonstrates (Chapter 15 in this volume), while centralized control of distribution has proved important to the most successful modern retail chains, from the 1960s onwards this has tended to involve subcontracting rather than vertical integration. A similar story is true in the areas of product development and quality control. As Anthony Rees, Sainsbury's director of marketing, pointed out in a lecture on Corporate Branding (Rees 1992), centralized controls have allowed some retailers to assume brand status. The retailer's access to information about its market (and marketing) dynamics has both facilitated product innovation and reinforced the desirability of controlling the supply chain and the distribution chain. In doing so an own brand takes on many of the characteristics of a proprietary brand. Control over the whole distribution chain from the sources of supply through to the point of sale – and beyond, since consumer education programmes extend into the home – replicates the vertical integration of the late nineteenth and early twentieth centuries. The ability to dictate product specifications and ensure standards of quality control have been substituted for the production of goods.

US private labels have failed to achieve the status of British own brands. Whereas the concept of an own brand as equal to a manufacturer's is well established in Britain, the imprecision of the term 'private label' reflects its weak position. In the United States private labels of all kinds, including own brands, have been dogged by their 'cheap' image. The consumer's belief that the retailer's role in sourcing a product consists mainly of jobbing and of repackaging an existing product under another name suggests to him that the intention is to obscure its origin. This has conflicted with the concept of branding as a guarantee of quality and consistency. In Britain retailers have been able to establish their own brands as equal in quality to manufacturers' brands *and* lower in price. The most damaging effect of Robinson Patman has been in focusing competition primarily on price.

The roots of this are historical. In the US legal restrictions and the political hostility to retail chains during the interwar years damaged retailers' self-confidence at a time when proprietary brands were rapidly growing in strength and number. Economic depression fuelled public opinion against the chains and encouraged the introduction of cost-cutting self-service methods by independent retailers. This coincided with the early days of radio and television advertising.

We cannot ascribe the lack of success of US own brands merely to factors which impeded their effective marketing. Food products depend for their success not on a single purchase decision but upon regular shopping patterns. Manufacturers' advertising or retailers' point of sale promotions may influence the initial purchase of a product, but in a highly competitive environment subsequent sales depend on customer satisfaction and trust. The difference between Sainsbury's experience and Shaw's is that the former has never broken the ties which it established early in its history between its corporate image (manifested in a standardized house style and trading practices) and its own brand goods, whereas Shaw's has a well-established corporate image, but has needed to re-establish the link between this and the quality of its own brand goods. The vertical integration which was necessary to achieve this in the early twentieth century has been replaced by active participation in product development, product specifications and quality control.

NOTE

*The company name changed as follows:
1922 J. Sainsbury Ltd
1971 J Sainsbury Ltd
1982 J Sainsbury plc.

REFERENCES

Alexander, D. (1970) *Retailing in Britain during the Industrial Revolution*, London: Athlone.

Arnold, D. (1992) *Handbook of Brand Management*, London: Century Business/Economist.

Barty-King, H. (1986) *Making Provision: A Centenary History of the Provision Trade*, London: Quiller.

Cohen, J. (1992) 'Private labels, the real story', *Supermarket Business* February, 25–8.

Cooke, J. (1970) (President of Penn Fruit Co) Lecture to Topco Members, George Washington Motor Lodge, 7 October.

Corina, M. (1971) *Pile it High, Sell it Cheap*, London: Weidenfeld & Nicolson.

David Greig Ltd (1970) *1870–1970 David Greig: The Story of a Family Firm*, London: David Greig.

Davis, D. (1966) *A History of Shopping*, London: Routledge & Kegan Paul.

Davis, S. D. (1975) *Brockton Daily Evening Enterprise*, 14 July.

—— (1992) *And the Two Became One . . . An Informal History of Shaw's Supermarkets*, Bridgewater, Mass: Shaw's.

de Jonquières, G. (1993) 'A trolley full of troubles', *Financial Times* 6 May.

Diamond, S. A. (1965) 'Private brands and the Federal Trade Commission', *Advertising Age* 18 January: 85.

Fitzell, P. P. (1982) *Private Labels, Store Brands and Generic Products*, Westport, Conn: AVI.

Food Processing (1991) Diamond Jubilee issue, June.

George C Shaw Co Ltd (1882; 1926) *Price Lists*.

—— (1926) Advertisements in *Sun Up*, January.

Greer, W. (1986) *America the Bountiful*, Washington, DC: Food Marketing Institute.

Grocery and Proprietary Articles Association (1929) *48th Price Maintenance List*, London: Grocery and Proprietary Articles Association London, November.

Harrison, R. J. (1977) (Sainsbury's grocery buyer 1946–66) unpublished interview with H. Godfrey, 3 August.

J. Sainsbury Ltd (1903–54) *Price Lists*, Sainsbury's Archives, London (private collection).

J Sainsbury plc (1906–90) *Advertising Guard Books*, London: Sainsbury.

J Sainsbury plc* (1946–93) *JS Journal*, London: Sainsbury.

J Sainsbury plc* (1971–92) *Reports and Accounts*, London: Sainsbury.

J Sainsbury plc (1992) *Some Facts about Sainsbury's*, London: Sainsbury.

Jefferys, J. B. (1954) *Retailing Trading in Britain 1850–1950*, Cambridge: Cambridge University Press.

Kintner, E. W. (1979) *A Robinson Patman Primer* (2nd edn), New York and London: Macmillan.

Knopp, J. Jr (1966) 'Branding and the Robinson Patman Act', *Journal of Business*, January: 24–43.

Lebhar, G. (1963) *Chain Stores in America 1859–1962*, New York: Chain Store Publishing Corporation (first published 1952).

McEwan, M. (1992) (Vice-President, Consumer Relations, Shaw's Supermarkets Inc) 'A home economist in retailing', *Home Economics & Technology*, May.

Mathias, P. (1967) *Retailing Revolution*, London: Longman.

—— (1976) 'The British tea trade in the nineteenth century', in D. Oddy and D. Miller (eds) *The Making of the Modern British Diet*, London: Croom Helm.

O C & C Strategy Consultants (1992) *Private Label International*, quoted in *Eurofood*, May.

Peak, H. S. and Peak, E. F. (1977) *Supermarket Merchandising and Management*, Englewood Cliffs, NJ: Prentice-Hall.
Porter, G. and Livesay, H. C. (1989) *Merchants and Manufacturers: Studies in the Changing Structure of Nineteenth Century Marketing*, Chicago: Elephant Paperbacks (first published 1971, Johns Hopkins Press).
Powell, D. (1992) *Counter Revolution*, London: Grafton.
Productivity Team Report (1951) *Packet Foods*, London and New York: Anglo-American Council on Productivity.
—— (1952) *Retailing*, London and New York: Anglo-American Council on Productivity.
Rees, A. (1992) 'How Sainsbury as a retailer has become a successful brand', Paper given at a *Marketing Week* conference, London, 2 April.
Sainsbury, A. (1947) 'Mr Alan discusses', *JS Journal* April: 12–14.
Sainsbury, A. (Lord Sainsbury of Drury Lane) (1964) 'Problems in business administration', Lecture to London School of Economics, Paper 353, May.
Sainsbury, J. B. (1947) Handwritten notes for 'Mr John's Diary', *JS Journal*, May, London: J. Sainsbury Ltd.
Schneidau, R. E. and Knutson, R. D. (1969) 'Price discrimination in the food industry: a competitive stimulant or tranquillizer?', *American Journal of Agricultural Economics* December: 1,143–8.
Sutherland, D. E. (1989) *The Expansion of Everyday Life*, New York: Harper & Row.
Tedlow, R. S. (1990) 'Stocking America's pantries: the rise and fall of A & P', in R. S. Tedlow (ed.) *New and Improved: The Story of Mass Marketing in America*, London: Heinemann.
Weil, G. H. (1954) 'Legal trends: pricing of private brands vs National brands', *Printers' Ink* 21 May: 78–81.
Weiss, E. B. (1965) 'The sophisticated shopper and over-priced store brands', *Advertising Age* 18 January: 86.
Winstanley, M. J. (1983) *The Shopkeeper's World 1830–1914*, Manchester: Manchester University Press.
Yamey, B. S. (1952) 'The origins of resale price maintenance', *Economic Journal* 62: 522–45.
Zimmerman, M. M. (1959) *The Supermarket: A Revolution in Distribution*, New York, Mass Distribution Publications Inc.

15 Delivering quality

The role of logistics in the post-war transformation of British food retailing

Leigh Sparks

If you're smart enough to make it, aggressive enough to sell it – then any dummy can get it there.

(Lalonde quoted in Langley 1986: 13)

The many sided nature of the distributive processes tends to obscure the possibilities for improvements in productivity that stem from the physical movement, storage and handling of goods.

(Stacey and Wilson 1958: 278)

British food retailing has been transformed since the Second World War (Fulop 1964; Jefferys 1950; Levy 1948; Stacey and Wilson 1958). The nostalgic 'idyll' of small retail outlets, run mainly by independents and co-operatives, based on a corner shop model where counter service dominated, has been replaced by large-scale, off-centre, self-service-based food superstores operated by multiple retailers. Quality, value and choice have become the key words. The rationing and utility of the 1950s have been replaced by the choice and quality of the 1980s and the 1990s with an intermediate stage of pricing consciousness in the 1960s and 1970s (Dawson 1987; Sparks 1993). As this transformation has occurred, so too there have been changes to the supply system for retail stores. The retail revolution has had a supporting logistics (or distribution) revolution.

The distribution changes that have occurred have been, with notable exceptions (Fernie 1990; McKinnon 1985; 1986; 1989), ignored by academics. There are a number of reasons for this. First, the operations that comprise logistics are not deemed to be particularly interesting in themselves: distribution is often seen as lorries, and lorries are decidedly not worthy of academic study! Second, the logistics changes are often not visible to most consumers and academics. Third, the subject of retailing itself is only now being seen as a serious academic subject and thus distribution has had to wait its place in line. Finally, distribution represents the component of marketing that everyone forgets about or does not understand. The one conceptual element of marketing that everyone remembers is the 4Ps – product, price, promotion and yes, distribution (place). However, the awkwardness of this conception for distribution is clear, and most marketers concentrate on the rather more understood elements of price, product and promotion (see Chaston 1993; Nilson 1992 for recent examples of this). In short, distribution or logistics has often been ignored and neglected, despite its vital importance to most businesses.

This chapter attempts to remedy this neglect by providing an assessment of the role of logistics in the post-war transformation of British food retailing. This assessment is undertaken in five main sections. First, it is important to understand the components of change in post-war British food retailing itself. Second, a discussion of the role and concept of logistics and distribution is provided in order to understand the importance of the topic. Third, the development of a logistics approach in British food retailing is examined. Fourth, the changes that have occurred in British food retailing logistics are illustrated via a case study of Tesco Stores. Finally, conclusions are drawn and pointers are given for the direction of future changes and research.

THE TRANSFORMATION OF POST-WAR FOOD RETAILING

There have been a considerable number of commentaries on the changing food retailing sector in Britain (see Sparks 1993 for references). What all such commentaries show is that the food sector is one where change has been dramatic and concentration ratios have increased strongly. The food retailing sector is at the leading edge of change and its leading companies are among the largest in Britain. In essence the food retailing sector has been transformed from a production to a marketing-oriented sector and retailers have come to dominate the distribution process. Growing concentration (Akehurst 1983; Baden-Fuller 1986) has been associated with the increasing power of the multiple retailers through particularly economies of scale (McClelland 1990; Shaw et al. 1989) and replication. This has produced a situation where only a handful of retailers dominate food retailing. A review of the operational changes in food retailing undertaken by these multiples suggests that a number of common themes can be identified.

First, there has been a massive increase in the average size of a store, associated particularly with the growth of the food superstore (Davies and Sparks 1989; Thorpe 1991) and large supermarkets (Institute of Grocery Distribution 1991).

Second, there has been a move towards out-of-town or off-centre locations, again linked to the superstore and the need for a large site for both the store and the associated car parking (Dawson 1984; Davies and Sparks 1989). Food retailing by mainline food retailers has currently been withdrawn from the majority of high streets (Dawson 1988).

Third, there has been a steady increase in the percentage of own-brand food products (Davies et al. 1986; McGoldrick 1984). J Sainsbury has had a high level of such products for a number of years (see Williams, Chapter 14 in this volume) but Tesco (Leahy 1992) and the predecessors of Gateway and Safeway moved strongly into own brands in the 1970s. Asda followed suit in the mid-1980s. The retailer, to all intents and purposes, has become the brand (Burt 1992).

Fourth, there has been a range extension and quality improvement in many food stores based particularly on new demands from consumers. This extension has included frozen products in the past, but now involves chilled and microwaveable products as well as developments in organic and fresh produce.

Fifth, there has been financial availability to enable the expansion to take place. Superstores are costly, with high land and building costs. The expansion policies of the major food retailers has required them to raise substantial sums of money (Wrigley 1991).

Sixth, the major food retailers have become increasingly reliant on service and added value to sell to customers, rather than price competition.

Seventh, all the major food retailers have invested heavily in technology. The most visible manifestation of this is at the point-of-sale with laser scanning, but, in practice retailers have introduced computing, including data capture facilities and communications throughout their operations (Dawson and Sparks 1986; Lynch 1990).

Finally, the physical distribution systems of the major food retailers have undergone fundamental changes, partly in response to these other changes and partly in association with them. This process of change is not complete. In particular, physical distribution systems have become increasingly centralized with a high level of subcontracting. This process was started in the UK by J Sainsbury (Fernie 1990; Quarmby 1989), Marks & Spencer (Tse 1985) and Kwik Save (Sparks 1990), but the other major food retailers have all moved in the same direction (Christensen 1990; McClelland 1990; McKinnon 1986; 1986; 1989; Millar 1983; Sparks 1986; 1990; 1992).

THE EVOLUTION OF LOGISTICS

Retailing and distribution are concerned with product availability, which is often summed up as getting the right product to the right place at the right time. This implies that retailers must be concerned with the flows of product and information into their companies in order to make products available to consumers. In particular, the concern is with the structure and management of marketing and physical distribution channels (Bowersox and Cooper 1992; Cooper 1988; Cooper et al. 1991). The management task in physical distribution can therefore be summarized as

> the planning, co-ordinating and controlling of the physical move- ment of products to provide a level of timely and spatial physical availability for customers, appropriate to the needs of the market place and the resources of the company.
>
> (Christopher et al. 1983: 19)

It is thus concerned with a number of elements, that can be described as the distribution mix (storage facilities, inventory management, transportation, unitization and packaging, communications), which have to be integrated for successful retail distribution.

The distribution function has to manage the distribution mix to provide a balance for the selected market sector and the company between the lowest possible distribution costs and the highest possible customer satisfaction (Sparks 1992). Distribution is concerned explicitly with costs and customer service and the elements of decision- making that influence these. To a considerable extent it is the emergent awareness of the investment required to achieve the optimal balance and the potential service gains that are available that have caused the development of a new professionalism in physical distribu- tion (Bowersox 1969; Drucker 1962; Sharman 1984). It is also becoming clear that to be successful, physical distribution has to become integrated with the business strategy and the positioning of the retail business.

It is increasingly common to see the term 'physical distribution' replaced by the term 'logistics'. In many cases the terms are used inter- changeably (Langley 1986) although there are differences. Christopher (1986) defines logistics management as

> the process of strategically managing the movement and storage of materials, parts and finished inventory from suppliers, through the firm and on to customers . . . [logistics] is thus concerned with the

management of the physical flow which begins with sources of
supply and ends at the point of consumption.

(Christopher 1986: 1)

Physical distribution is thus somewhat narrower than logistics, being
concerned with finished products rather than the combination of
materials management of components and raw materials as well as
finished products as implied by logistics. The logistics extension to
physical distribution is also concerned with strategic management of
the supply chain (Christopher 1992). For retailers it would seem that
while companies are extending their influence back into logistics
management and concepts such as integrated distribution and just-in-
time distribution are becoming increasingly important, the narrower
concept of physical distribution management remains more common.
However, the term logistics is gaining widespread currency and
strategic management is more common (Dawson and Shaw 1989a).
Logistics is therefore the term used here, reflecting the current business
terminology.

Langley (1986) explores this changing terminology by examining the
evolution of the logistics concept; he subdivides the chronology into
past, present and future. In the period 1950–64, he sees the emergence
of marketing practices forcing a reconsideration of distribution, or in
most cases *transport*, costs. Drucker (1962), in a seminal piece,
focused attention on the need for integration of product movement
activities. Since the mid-1960s, this call has been answered by a commitment to distribution and logistics professionalism. The key
elements have been co-ordination, control and customer service. The
effect has been the raising of the status of the distribution or logistics
functions within companies. Langley's third phase, or the future, sees
a closer integration among the logistics elements and a concentration
on service quality. While there can be arguments about the timing and
to a degree the content of these phases, Langley is suggesting a progression from a transport operation through a distribution function to
a logistics orientation.

THE DEVELOPMENT OF A LOGISTICS APPROACH IN BRITISH FOOD RETAILING

The earlier sections of this chapter have suggested that the transformation of post-war British food retailing has been accompanied by
a transformation of the supply of products and information in the
supply chain. The supply chain has changed both as a consequence

of retail change and as a driving factor in retail competitive positioning. In the transformation of supply there have been large alterations
to distribution operations and their control. As these have progressed
it can be suggested that there has been a movement from a transport
function, first to a distribution operation and now towards a logistics
approach. It is this transformation that is examined below.

McKinnon (1989) argues that there have been three phases in the
evolution of manufacturers' distribution channels, and thus by extension in retailers' distribution channels as well. McKinnon sees an
expansion of the market area of manufacturing companies and a
dependence on direct channels before the First World War. By direct
channels McKinnon means for retailers the receipt of product direct at
the store level, whether from manufacturer or wholesaler. The
elements of the distribution mix are essentially uncoordinated and
fragmented. McKinnon's second phase is the emergence of market
consolidation through the development of echelon channels. For a
multiple retailer this means directing incoming products through a
warehouse under its control. This phase is seen as being primarily
interwar, with manufacturers setting up depots around the country
where stock could be held much closer to retail customers and from
which local delivery to shops could be more easily organized.

McKinnon's third phase is that of market rationalization or the
reversion to direct distribution, which he dates to the period since the
mid-1960s. He phrases this 'direct distribution' as he is examining the
process from the manufacturer's viewpoint. Manufacturers in this
period have reacted to the polarization of retailing and to their own
closer examination of distribution costs by focusing on larger customers. This concentration allows them to focus on deliveries to
multiple retailers' central warehouses or distribution centres and for
smaller retailers to channel their products through wholesale intermediaries. In this sense *for a manufacturer* direct delivery has
increased.

Ward (1973) indicates that the evidence suggests that considerations
of retail structure, the commodity group and the production structure
determine the prevailing method of distribution. He concurs with
Jefferys (1950) that for domestically produced products, 'the decision
of producers on how to distribute appeared to be scarcely of their
making' but was readily appreciable in terms of structures. Thus
multiples dealt directly with manufacturers due to the ability to undertake functions such as wholesaling or to purchase in bulk. Such
linkages do not imply direct to store delivery or through central
warehouse delivery exclusively, but rather the ability of retailers to

negotiate terms centrally. Ward (1973) concludes his discussion of the factors underlying the method of distribution of any commodity group by noting that

> any increase in the share of sales made by multiple . . . organizations is likely to cause a reduction in the proportion of trade distributed through wholesalers and, more generally, any change which results in an increase in the average size of order which retailers are able to place with individual manufacturers has a similar tendency.
>
> (Ward 1973: 139)

In other words, as retailers began to grow larger and as they operationally began to change their outlets as discussed earlier, so too their physical distribution demands altered. In particular retailers began to integrate the distribution mix elements by internalizing the wholesaling functions. As Hussey (1972) notes

> it is possible to argue that transfer of business from a traditional type of outlet to a supermarket is a matter for marketing people: but is it really of concern only to them? The sort of changes that are inevitable mean alteration in the location of customers, a decrease in customer numbers, an increase in customer size, and a new pattern of risks. All these are very much matters of concern for the physical distribution function.
>
> (Hussey 1972)

We must therefore also consider McKinnon's phases from a retailer's perspective. McKinnon has highlighted a movement from a purely transport orientation in his phase I to a transport and storage operation in phases II and III, that is essentially a distribution operation. From the retailers' viewpoint, there is a need to intervene in the channel operation in order to better serve their retail needs. In essence retailers have taken over the functions of wholesalers for commercial reasons. They have chosen to develop distribution centres of their own in order to control and organize their supplies to stores (Fernie 1990; Harris 1987; McKinnon 1989).

As food retailers have examined their operations they have recognized more closely the costs of distribution in terms of delivery timing, stock costs and customer service as well as 'straight' costs. For example the 'cost' of stock-outs is both real and also indirect in the form of reduced consumer loyalty. To combat such a problem therefore retailers have tightened delivery conditions, taken control via centralization and utilized information more widely (Dawson and

Shaw 1989b). In order to improve the situation they have attempted to exert control over the distribution channel. This control is helped by the changing size relationship between retailers and manufacturers. The first stage in this control is the imposition of centralized distribution and the channelling of products to such centres rather than direct to the store. This process gives retailers greater control of stock levels and quality of stock, better in-stock positions in store, quantity discounts for bulk purchasing, improved ratio of selling space to storage space at branch level, reduced shrinkage and better business data. Centralization aims at improving the control that retailers have over suppliers and the stores; however, it demands managerial and operational disciplines at the store and the distribution centre and enhanced communications. No longer do stores wait on deliveries from suppliers and hold stock just-in-case. Instead suppliers deliver full loads to distribution centres at predetermined times. Suppliers thus benefit as well, although at the cost of improving *their* managerial and operational disciplines. Price and supply negotiations reflect the new balances and operational opportunities (Mercer 1993), but the closer integration should provide channel-wide benefits.

Another reason for the greater control of distribution channels by retailers is that of product range extension and particularly the emergence of own brands, which are not a prerequisite for centralized distribution (see Kwik Save: Sparks 1990), but do encourage the movement to centralization and control. This is because of retailers' involvement in the production process and the concern that retailers have for products carrying their name (Leahy 1992). Own brands are in the control of retailers for longer than manufacturer brands and a very close control of the entire process, including the distribution channel, can be maintained. With a higher proportion of own brands in the stores, retailers have reduced the number of manufacturer brands that are stocked. One element of this assessment of which manufacturer brands to stock is their distribution performance. In essence therefore, the own brand strategy has a direct bearing on the distribution strategy (Burt 1992).

Fulop (1964) indicates that in the early 1960s, retailer brands were relatively few in number in food retailing, quoting figures of 300 for Tesco and 200 for J Sainsbury (although see Williams, Chapter 14 in this volume). Fulop (1964) comments that while such brands are unlikely to develop too extensively 'the marketing policies of manufacturers must . . . take account of potential competition from large scale retailers able to integrate backwards by producing or marketing home brands' (Fulop 1964: 195). The very close links

between retailer and its own-brand suppliers is exampled by J
Sainsbury:

> Even greater skill is required to organize our own lines than is
> needed to buy similar national branded lines. We have to ensure
> that our manufacturers have suitable facilities for producing the
> product we want from quality, quantity and costs point of view.
> That means factories that are up to date in standards of cleanliness
> and hygiene, and have built into the production system a degree of
> quality control that satisfies us that the chances of error or mistake
> affecting the product are reduced to an absolute minimum. There-
> fore, the task of organizing the purchase of 'own lines' is a complex
> one and demands a great deal of work and research by the buying
> departments concerned and very active participation by laboratory
> and technical staff.
>
> (Boswell 1969: 82).

With such technical involvement at production, involvement in distribution is also required to protect product quality and to ensure
supply. As own labels expand, such distribution involvement became
critical first in cost reduction to take advantage of Resale Price
Maintenance abolition and then in quality protection. As own
brands moved from generics to quality premier brands (Burt 1992;
McGoldrick 1984) so the quality aspects of their distribution became
more important. Thorpe et al. (1973) found a high level of distribution
by manufacturers involved in own brands to central retail facilities
suggesting that centralization and own brand involvement are closely
linked.

Walters (1976) points to a number of impacts of own brands on
physical distribution, including that the manufacturer can run production at a higher level of capacity, can enjoy sales without advertising
and promotion, distribute to a few depots, plan on long-term sales
and profits, maintain sales on brand leaders and, if co-operating with
retailers, can boost manufacturer brand sales. Walters (1976) indicates
these relationships diagrammatically (see Figure 15.1) and points to
larger consignments to fewer destinations, pack size rationalization
lowering total packaging costs, lower stockholding costs and order
processing costs, providing production scheduling works. Retailer
involvement in own brands thus involves operational consideration of
the linkages in the supply chain. As McKinnon concludes, 'a multiple's
policy on the development of its own label business can, therefore,
carry important implications for physical distribution' (McKinnon
1986: 57).

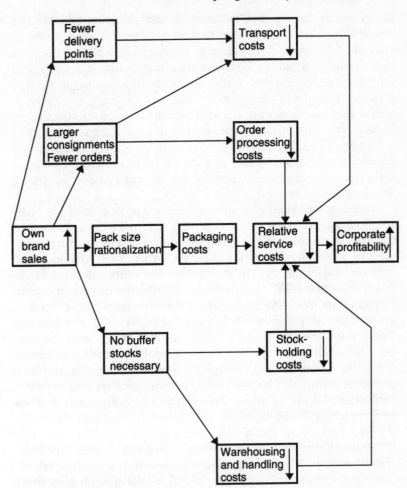

Figure 15.1 The effects of own brands on physical distribution systems
Source: Walters 1976: 63

The discussion above generally and in particular on own brands has pointed to a change in retailing. The initial indications were of manufacturers and retailers being linked by transport functions that were the prerogative of the manufacturer. The development of retail storage and distribution centre functions add a layer of complication to the situation. Distribution in the wider sense is therefore required and has to be managed. This management becomes a crucial issue as retailers grow larger and begin to have to compete, on price and then quality. With the abolition of Resale Price Maintenance in the 1960s, the emphasis for retailers switched to cost reduction and product availability. Distribution costs became a target for change. Better control of the channel allowed cost savings as well as other benefits (Lekashman and Stolle 1965). The expansion of own brands focused attention on distribution. With own labels, retailers began to have influence over the product composition, its packaging, and so on, as well as its physical supply. The approach is therefore for effectively a logistics one. This orientation is aided by the increasing importance of information in distribution to control activities. The information revolution at retailing outlets and the ability to use this information throughout the distribution channel has enhanced retailer control of the channel enormously.

It needs to be emphasized that in the changes outlined above, there has been a movement both of control and of operations. Table 15.1 attempts to encapsulate this. Control has migrated from the manufacturer to the retailer. Operations have similarly moved from the manufacturer, but in this case to distribution specialists employed by the retailers (Fernie 1989). Such contract distribution has become widespread in the food retailing industry. Retailers exert their control by information (McKinnon 1990) rather than by 'doing' (Quarmby 1989). For some specialized products this has always been the case, but contractors now run the latest composite distribution centres providing operations and managerial expertise. Cooper et al. (1991) provide a sequence of innovations by multiple retailers that has transformed the logistics process. The sequence is summarized in Table 15.2, which again highlights the transformation that has occurred.

One aspect of this transformation concerns the stability and types of relationship among retailers and their suppliers. Dawson and Shaw (1990) point to the varying relationships that can and do exist in physical distribution. They suggest combinations of integrative, transactional and administered relationships depending on the situation

Table 15.1 Logistics changes, 1950–90

	1950s	1960s–1970s	1980s–1990s
Orientation	Transport	Distribution	Logistics
Control	Manufacturer	Retailer/Manufacturer	Retailer
Operations	Manufacturer	Manufacturer/Retailer/Contractor	Contractor

Table 15.2 Major logistics innovations by multiple retailers in the UK

	Problem	Innovation	Consequences
1960s and 1970s	Disorderly delivery by suppliers to supermarkets; queues of vehicles led to both inefficiency and disruption	Introduction of regional distribution centres (RDCs) to channel goods from suppliers to supermarkets operated by retailers	Strict timing of supplier delivery to RDC imposed by retailer; retailer builds and operates RDC; retailer operates own delivery fleet between RDC and supermarkets within its catchment area
Early 1980s	Retailers becoming too committed to operating logistics services in support of retail activity	Operations of retailer-owned RDCs and vehicle fleets to specialist freight companies	Retailer can concentrate on 'core business' of retailing; retailer achieves better financial return from capital invested in supermarkets than in RDCs and vehicles
Mid-1980s	Available floorspace at retail outlets being underused; too much floorspace used for storage	Conversion of storage floorspace at supermarkets to sales floorspace	Better sales revenue potential at retail outlets; RDCs absorb products formerly kept in store at supermarkets; just-in-time (JIT) delivery used from RDC to replenish supermarket shelves

Source: Cooper et al. 1991: 109–10

of the retailer, supplier and the products to be transferred. While they accept that there are a variety of situations, they point to a general increase in the stability of relationships and a move towards vertically administered channels (Dawson and Shaw 1989a; 1989b; 1990). The reasons for this stability are contained in Table 15.3. To these factors in the table can be added recent legal environment changes which are making retailers more responsible for, and therefore concerned in, the production and packaging processes. For example food hygiene legislation in the UK and German packaging laws are placing a duty of care on the retailers for actions in the channel of distribution. From Table 15.3 it can be seen that distribution relationships are central to many of these factors and that the emerging logistics orientation is a reflection of this development of stable relationships.

Table 15.3 Factors enhancing stable relationships between retailers and suppliers

Factor	Distribution issues
High, consistent quality	Distribution quality; consistency
Flexible response	Just-in-time; technology; inventory
Joint product development	Own brands; unitization
Specific delivery systems	Distribution contractors; unitization
Frequent ordering	Technology; consistency
Wide product range	Distribution contractors; inventory
High product differentiation	Individuality; product handling
Strong manufacturer brands	Unitization; technology
Number of suppliers	Unitization; technology; inventory
Buying groups	Facility sharing; inventory
Buyer decision-making	Unitization; technology; consistency
Technological complexity	Technology
Co-ordinated product range	Unitization; technology
Export marketing	Just-in-time; inventory
Personalities	Technology
Deal structures	Unitization; inventory
Strategic management issues	Systems; technology; service

Source: Adapted from Dawson and Shaw 1990: 24–7

McClelland (1990) illustrates many of these changes in respect of Laws Stores, a medium-sized multiple food retailer in the north-east of England, which was bought by Wm Low in 1985. McClelland indicates that 'In the mid-1970s the Company was still depending on a three-storey warehouse and office building which had been erected in 1931, with 800 sq m on each floor' (McClelland 1990: 132). Despite some modernization and expansion, the warehouse was so congested as to force direct-to-store deliveries for products which were more economically delivered via a central depot. Acquisitions in the 1970s added a Scottish warehouse which complicated delivery procedures. By 1981 a new site and premises were located and built to consolidate operations. The company undertook the transport and distribution operation itself until a decision to contract out was made in the early 1980s. At this stage the Edinburgh depot was closed, with consequent savings in delivery volumes, security, stock levels, paperwork and staffing. As McClelland comments 'these various moves meant that services were brought in which Lows had formerly performed itself. However greater control was achieved over stocking and supply, instead of that control being exercised by suppliers' (McClelland 1990: 134). In short, distribution was now so important on cost and service levels that suppliers could not be expected to be acting in the interest of the retailers they served. Control over this situation became crucial.

What emerges from this discussion and the illustration above is something of a generally understood tendency, but an ill-understood set of actual circumstances. At any time there are many variations in operations among retailers and suppliers (Thorpe et al. 1973) and attempts to find an all-encompassing explanation have not been successful (McKinnon 1985; Thorpe et al. 1973). Instead, issues such as company history and development and product mix are shown to be important. The oligopolistic outcome in British food retailing in the 1980s has produced a more common distribution set-up among retailers. The examination of a particular case aids this understanding of both the general processes and the specific reasons for them.

RETAIL LOGISTICS: THE CASE OF TESCO STORES

The best documented retail logistics case is probably that of Tesco (see Smith and Sparks 1993 for full details). A summary of the key elements of this case are provided here. Tesco is an apposite case to use as it expanded considerably from the 1960s but from a direct-to-store delivery orientation rather than the more centralized operations of J Sainsbury and Kwik Save at this time. While involving a shorter historical period than other companies therefore, the Tesco example does provide an encapsulation of the transformation argued for earlier.

The transformation of Tesco (Corina 1971; Powell 1991) from the era of 'pile it high, sell it cheap' has seen the number of stores decline, while the average size of store has risen dramatically (Figure 15.2).

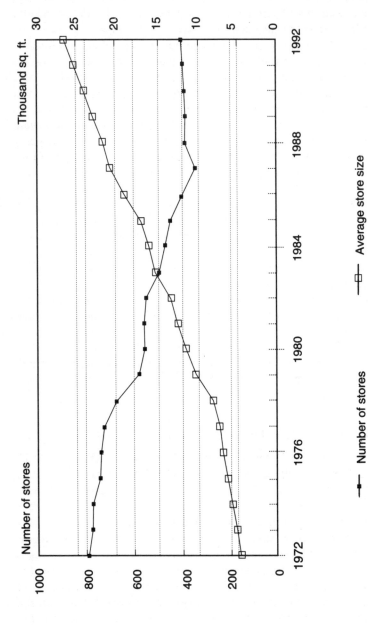

Figure 15.2 Tesco stores: number of stores and average store size
Source: Tesco Annual Reports

There have been large increases in turnover and pre-tax profit, and an enormous increase in the scale of the business between the 1960s and the late 1980s. The boost to turnover began in 1977 when the company through Operation Checkout (Akehurst 1984) stopped giving trading stamps, cut prices by 4 per cent, and also started to move up-market.

The changes that the customer sees are obviously focused at the store, but behind the store revolution and the changing store portfolio (location, scale, type, age) lies a distribution transformation without which the success of the 1980s could not have been achieved, and the base for the 1990s would be insufficient. The distribution policies and strategies of Tesco have been the subject of previous study (Smith and Sparks 1993; Sparks 1986; 1988). It can be suggested that there have been three main phases in distribution strategy and operations. First, there was a period of primarily delivery direct to store. Second, there was a move to centralization and the refinement of the process of centralized distribution. It is this phase that has received most of the attention. Third, there has been the development of composite distribution.

The Tesco distribution system in the late 1970s in the wake of Operation Checkout (Akehurst 1984) almost came to a halt. The volume of goods being moved by Tesco proved too large to handle in the time-scales required. As Powell (1991) comments, quoting Sir Ian Maclaurin:

> Ultimately our business is about getting our goods to our stores in sufficient quantities to meet our customers' demands. Without being able to do that efficiently, we aren't in business, and Check-out stretched our resources to the limit. Eighty per cent of all our supplies were coming direct from manufacturers, and unless we'd sorted out our distribution problems there was a very real danger that we would have become a laughing stock for promoting cuts on lines that we couldn't even deliver. It was a close-run thing.
>
> (Powell 1991: 184)

Powell continues:

> How close is now a matter of legend: of outside suppliers having to wait for up to twenty-four hours to deliver at Tesco's distribution centres; of stock checks being conducted in the open air; of Tesco's four obsolescent warehouses, and the company's transport fleet working to a round-the-clock, seven-day schedule. And as the problems lived off one another, and as customers waited for the emptied shelves to be refilled, so the tailback lengthened around the

stores, delays of five and six hours becoming commonplace. *Possibly for the first time in its history, the company recognised that it was as much in the business of distribution as of retailing.*
(Powell 1991: emphasis added)

Operation Checkout provided a short-term shock to the distribution system. There were major problems in handling the peak weeks and the increased volumes, but generally the company coped, albeit through running multi-shifts in the distribution centres. Having weathered the distribution effects of Operation Checkout it became clear that other changes to distribution would be needed as the 'new' business strategy took hold. In effect, by Operation Checkout and the move up-market that followed, Tesco were changing the mission, vision, strategy and culture of the company. This included distribution operations.

The decision was taken to move away from direct delivery to stores to centralization. The basis of this decision (in 1980) was the realization of the critical nature of range control on the operations. Tesco always had delivered some products centrally, but the majority had come direct from manufacturers to stores. At its peak this reached a direct to store to warehouse ratio of 83 to 17. In addition to being inefficient for the store operations and being unable to cope flexibly with increased volumes and quality, the system allowed almost no control or standardization of the retail outlets and of store managers. Powell (1991) uses the euphemism of 'private enterprise' (Powell 1991: 185) to describe the pricing and stocking behaviour of individual store managers. With direct-to-store delivery, managers were 'encouraged' to 'buy-in' extra products on secondary lines to cover stock losses. The realization of the effects that this was having on the business forced the decision to end buying-in and managers' deal books and allow the introduction of true stock results and range control. Centralization of control was established for the modern business. Tesco head office had to have this control if the company was to be transformed: centralized distribution was one plank in the control strategy.

Tesco adopted a centrally controlled distribution service (Kirkwood 1984a; 1984b) by delivering the vast majority of stores' needs, utilizing common handling systems, with deliveries within a lead time of a maximum of forty-eight hours (Sparks 1986). Seven key areas of this strategy can be identified. First, there was an extension and change to the existing fixed distribution facilities, including the building of new distribution centres. The location of these facilities was aimed at more closely matching distribution needs to the store location profile and to changes in this profile. Second, lead times improved. Improvements in technology allowed faster stock-turn, allied to which was the scheduling of vehicles at all points in the channel. Third, common handling systems were used at the distribution centre and stores to handle stock replenishment more easily. Fourth, the demands of modern retailing required multi-shift working. Fifth, computer software modelled company decisions, allowing the best use of all facilities. Sixth, dedicated (i.e. contract) distribution was used to meet high levels of performance. The standards required are set by Tesco and monitored by it. The contractors have to meet these specifications. Finally new technology was used to maintain a strict inventory control. Fuller details of these changes can be found in Sparks (1986; 1988).

In 1989 Tesco had forty-two depots, of which twenty-six were temperature controlled. This in itself was a massive reduction from the plethora of small stock locations (including back-ups) found in the 1960s and 1970s, but was still capable of improvement. Fresh foods were basically handled through single-temperature, single-product depots. These were small, inefficient and used for only part of the day. Tesco had reviewed the service that the network gave the stores and implemented improvements in all product areas in 1986 and 1987. This meant for example in the short life provisions network that stores received more frequent deliveries from a rationalized number of depots (from eleven to six). Investment was made in the Dallas computer system in the frozen depots; accounting and budget changes allowed a more accurate idea of the cost of distribution.

The tactics in the late 1980s were to make as many improvements as possible in order to give the stores a better service, but there were still some disadvantages of the network. First, each product group had different ordering systems. Some were designed by the distribution contractor for their general use and not sympathetic to Tesco needs. This complicated distribution. Second, with so many sites it was prohibitively expensive to have on site Tesco quality control inspection at each location. This meant that the standards of quality desired could not be vigorously controlled at the point of distribution. Third, because only single product groups were handled, each store's delivery volume was low. Hence, it was not economic to deliver some products to all stores daily, so that consumers were not receiving fresh produce daily. Fourth, to maintain the best quality, some goods require a temperature-controlled environment during delivery. As single products in warehouses they had to be carried on separate vehicles, which meant that five vehicles were needed to deliver the full range of products to each Tesco store. This added complication and congestion and was costly. Fifth, it was realized that the network would neither cope with the growth Tesco forecast in the 1990s, nor, as importantly, be ready to meet expected high legal standards on temperature control in the chill chain. These factors combined to revise the changes necessary to meet emerging operational requirements.

The major change to the centralization strategy as presented above is that the company is now concentrating its distribution further by focusing on the development of composite distribution, which enables ambient, chilled, fresh and frozen products to be distributed through one system of multi-temperature warehouses and vehicles. Composite distribution uses specially designed vehicles with temperature-controlled compartments to deliver any combination of these products. It aims to provide daily deliveries of products at the appropriate temperature so that the products reach the stores and customers at the peak of freshness. The insulated composite trailer can be sectioned into one, two or three chambers by means of moveable bulkheads. There is independent control for up to three temperature regimes. For example, frozen products at −20°C can be carried with fresh meat at 0°C and bread and bananas at +15°C without affecting product quality in any way. The size of each chamber can be varied to match the volume to be transported at each temperature. The composite distribution process is focused on eight distribution centres; seven of these are new purpose-built composite distribution centres with the other an extension at Livingston in Scotland. Centralizing distribution of these products in this way has reduced costs and improved sales and productivity through improved quality of product and service. These eight centres replace twenty-six centres in the previous system.

The eight distribution centres each service a region of Britain and approximately fifty stores. The sites are all close to key motorway intersections or junctions to allow rapid access. Of the eight composite distribution centres only two are run by Tesco. The remainder are operated by specialist distribution companies with Glass Glover running three, Exel Logistics two, and Hays Distribution one. Cross-comparisons of performance of these centres and the subcontractors enable 'league tables' to be drawn up of performance.

The composite centres are linked by computer to head office to allow the passing of data and the imposition of monitoring and control. For all products handled by the composite centres, forecasts of demand are produced and transmitted to suppliers. The aim of the system is to allow suppliers to have a basis for preparing products.

This is particularly important for short-life products where the aim is to operate a just-in-time system from the factory through the composite centre to the store. To meet such targets on delivery, each supplier needs information on predicted replenishment schedules.

This sharing of information is part of a wider introduction of electronic trading to Tesco. In particular Tesco have built a Tradanet community (Edwards and Gray 1990; INS 1991) involving direct-to-store and distribution centre suppliers. Tesco claim that this community of over 900 suppliers (as at April 1992) is the largest such in European food retailing. Improvements to scanning in stores and the introduction of sales-based ordering has enabled Tesco to better understand and manage ordering and replenishment. Sales-based ordering automatically calculates store replenishment requirements based on item sales and generates orders for delivery to stores within twenty-four to forty-eight hours. This information is used via Tradanet to help suppliers plan ahead both in production and distribution.

Composite distribution provides a number of benefits. Some derive from the process of centralization of which composite is an extension. Others are more directly attributable to the nature of composite. First, the movement to daily deliveries of composite product groups to all stores in 'waves' provides an opportunity to reduce the levels of stock held at the stores and indeed to reduce or obviate the need for storage facilities at store level. In aggregate terms the changes in distribution stock position in the company has improved continuously (Figure 15.3). Over the 1980s, the changes have succeeded in halving the stock days in the system.

The second benefit of composite is an improvement to quality with a consequent reduction in wastage. Products reach the stores in a more desirable condition. Better forecasting systems minimize lost sales due to out-of-stocks. The introduction of sales-based ordering produces more accurate store orders and the more rigorous application of code control results in longer shelf life on delivery, which in turn enables a reduction in wastage. This is of crucial importance to shoppers, who are requiring better quality and fresher products. In addition, however, the tight control over the chain enables Tesco to satisfy and exceed the new legislative requirements on food safety.

Third, the introduction of composite distribution provided an added benefit in productivity terms. The economies of scale and enhanced use of equipment provide greater efficiency and an improved distribution service. Composite distribution means that one vehicle can be used instead of the five needed in the old network. The result is reduced capital costs and less congestion at the store. Within composite

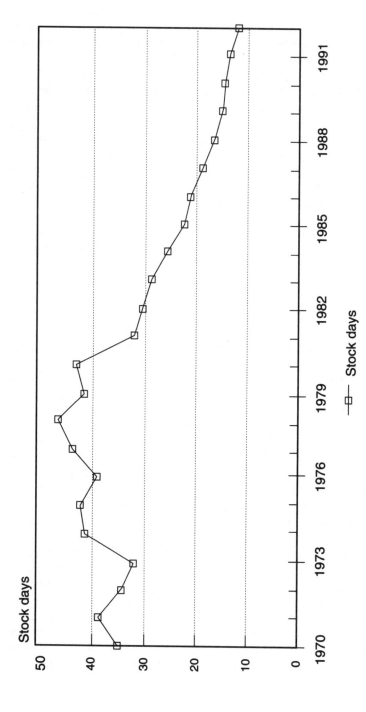

Stock days

Figure 15.3 Tesco stores: inventory 1970–92
Source: Tesco Annual Reports

changes such as in-bound scanning and radio-linked computers on fork-lift trucks further enhance productivity. In essence, throughout the system there is an emphasis on maximizing productivity and efficiency of the operations.

CONCLUSIONS

Retailing is a constantly changing industry. Components of retail distribution therefore are also subject to considerable stresses and strains, generally in the two competing directions of cost reduction and service improvment. The changing consumption patterns in Britain are interlinked with changing retail patterns. The inexorable rise of the food retailing multiple has therefore transformed the retail landscape. Underpinning this transformation, however, are a range of other changes, often less apparent and understood. The concomitant transformation of physical supply from a transport operation to a distribution function to a logistics orientation is one such change.

Multiple retailers have progressed from simply being the innocent recipients of manufacturers' transport and storage whims, to controlling and organizing the supply chain, almost in its entirety. The adoption of a logistics approach requires the intervention in wholesaling and manufacturing processes. Retailers began this intervention through the mechanics of own-brand production, but have extended it to encompass almost all product distribution. The expanding data and information capabilities have allowed retailers to exercise this control in an even greater fashion. However, this does not mean that retailers have to actively undertake the operations and indeed distribution specialists have been contracted for this purpose in many instances.

The transformation of transport, distribution and logistics is thus a major change that has had far-reaching effects. Without the changes, modern food retailing could not function as it does. Whether the retail orientation is price based or service based, effective and efficient distribution is a prerequisite of such operations and of success. Distribution is as necessary in a discount chain such as Shoprite as it is in Harrods food hall, although with a different emphasis. It can be argued that much of the enhanced British food retailing profitability in recent years stems from the major enhancements to distribution. The reduction of inventory, the improvement in consistency and quality, the emphasis on effectiveness all improve the selling process in terms of cost and service. Distribution is all about adding value, whether a price-based or service-based retailer is involved.

The major chains are again changing or considering change to their distribution operations. As the retail environment alters, so too is there a need for distribution responses. Equally, however, the logistics orientation is focusing attention on the opportunities at manufacturing and retailing levels. Change can be expected in the future as in the past.

There is a research need for there to be a greater understanding of the relationships and how they have changed. The pioneering work of McKinnon has helped our understanding enormously, but there could be many more studies of distribution in retailing. Detailed operational work is required to transform our understanding of the general tendencies presented here into a deeper knowledge of the operations involved. There are many opportunities in this direction to aid our understanding of the role of distribution in delivering quality and adding value.

REFERENCES

Akehurst, G. (1983) 'Concentration in retail distribution: measurement and significance', *Service Industries Journal* 3(2): 161–79.
—— (1984) 'Checkout: the analysis of oligopolistic behaviour in the UK grocery retail market', *Service Industries Journal* 4(2): 198–242.
Baden-Fuller, C. W. F. (1986) 'Rising concentration in the UK grocery trade 1970–80', in K. Tucker and C. W. F. Baden-Fuller (eds) *Firms and Markets*, London: Croom Helm.
Boswell, J. (1969) *JS100*, London: J Sainsbury.
Bowersox, D. J. (1969) 'Physical distribution, development, current status and potential', *Journal of Marketing* 33.
Bowersox, D. J. and Cooper, M. B. (1992) *Strategic Marketing Channel Management*, New York: McGraw Hill.
Burt, S. L. (1992) 'Retailer brands in British grocery retailing', *Institute for Retail Studies, Working Paper 9204*, University of Stirling.
Chaston, I. (1993) *Customer-Focused Marketing*, Maidenhead: McGraw-Hill.
Christensen, L. (1990) 'The impact of mergers and acquisitions upon retail distribution: the Safeway case', in J. Fernie (ed.) *Retail Distribution Management*, London: Kogan Page.
Christopher, M. (1986) *The Strategy of Distribution Management*, London: Heinemann.
—— (1992) *Logistics: The Strategic Issues*, London: Chapman and Hall.
Christopher, M., Mole, R., Rushton, A. and Wills, G. (1983) *Effective Distribution Management*, London: Pan.
Cooper, J. (ed.) (1988) *Logistics and Distribution Planning*, London: Kogan Page.
Cooper, J., Browne, M. and Peters, M. (1991) *European Logistics*, Oxford: Basil Blackwell.
Corina, M. (1971) *Pile it High, Sell it Cheap*, London: Weidenfeld & Nicolson.

Davies, B. K., Gilligan, C. and Sutton, C. (1986) 'The development of own label product strategies in grocery and DIY retailing in the UK', *International Journal of Retailing* **1**(1): 6–19.

Davies, B. K. and Sparks, L. (1989) 'The development of superstore retailing in Great Britain 1960–1986', *Transactions of the Institute of British Geographers* **14**(1): 74–89.

Dawson, J. A. (1984) 'Structural–spatial relationships in the spread of hypermarket retailing', in E. Kaynak and R. Savitt (eds) *Comparative Marketing Systems*, New York: Praeger.

—— (1987) 'The evolution of UK food retailing: inventory, prospect and research challenges', Paper presented at the Twelfth Annual Macromarketing Conference, Montreal, August.

—— (1988) 'Futures for the high street', *Geographical Journal* **154**(1): 1–12.

Dawson, J. A. and Shaw, S. A. (1989a) 'The move to administered vertical marketing systems by British retailing', *European Journal of Marketing* **23**(7): 42–52.

—— (1989b) 'Horizontal competition in retailing and the structure of manufacturer–retailer relationships', in L. Pellegrini and S. K. Reddy (eds) *Retail and Marketing Channels*, London: Routledge.

—— (1990) 'The changing character of retailer–supplier relationships', in J. Fernie (ed.) *Retail Distribution Management*, London: Kogan Page.

Dawson, J. A. and Sparks, L. (1986) 'New technology in UK retailing: issues and responses', *Journal of Marketing Management* **2**(1): 7–29.

Drucker, P. (1962) 'The economy's dark continent', *Fortune* April: 265–70.

Edwards, C. and Gray, M. (1990) 'Tesco case study', in Department of Trade and Industry', *Electronic Trading*, London: HMSO.

Fernie, J. (1989) 'Contract distribution in multiple retailing', *International Journal of Physical Distribution and Materials Management* **19**(7): 1–35.

—— (ed.) (1990) *Retail Distribution Management*, London: Kogan Page.

Fulop, C. (1964) *Competition for Consumers*, London: Audré Deutsch.

Harris, D. G. (1987) 'Central versus direct delivery for large retail food outlets', *Institute for Retail Studies, Working Paper 8703*, University of Stirling.

Hussey, D. (1972) 'Physical distribution: the environmental context', in M. Christopher and G. S. C. Wills (eds) *Marketing Logistics and Distribution Planning*, London: Allen & Unwin.

INS (1991) *Tesco: Breaking down the Barriers of Trade*, Sunbury-on-Thames: INS.

Institute of Grocery Distribution (IGD) (1991) *Food Retailing '91*, Watford: IDG.

Jefferys, J. B. (1950) *The Distribution of Consumer Goods*, Cambridge: Cambridge University Press.

Kirkwood, D. A. (1984a) 'The supermarket challenge', *Focus on DDM* **3**(4): 8–12.

—— (1984b) 'How Tesco manage the distribution function', *Retail and Distribution Management* **12**(5): 61–5.

Langley, J. R. (1986) 'The evolution of the logistics concept', *Journal of Business Logistics* **7**(2): 1–13.

Leahy, T. (1992) 'Branding – the retailer's viewpoint', in J. M. Murphy (ed.) *Branding: A Key Marketing Tool* (2nd edn), Basingstoke: Macmillan.

Lekashman, R. and Stolle, J. F. (1965) 'The total cost approach to distribution', *Business Horizons* **8**: 33–46.

Levy, H. (1948) *The Shops of Britain*, London: Routledge.

Lynch, J. (1990) 'The impact of electronic point of sale technology (EPOS) on marketing strategy and retailer–supplier relationships', *Journal of Marketing Management* **6**(2): 157–68.

McClelland, W. G. (1990) 'Economies of scale in British food retailing', C. Moir and J. A. Dawson (eds) *Competition and Markets*, Basingstoke: Macmillan.

McGoldrick, P. J. (1984) 'Grocery generics – an extension of the private label concept', *European Journal of Marketing* **18**(3): 63–76.

McKinnon, A. C. (1985) 'The distribution systems of supermarket chains', *Service Industries Journal* **5**(2): 226–38.

—— (1986) 'The physical distribution strategies of multiple retailers', *International Journal of Retailing* **1**(2): 49–63.

—— (1989) *Physical Distribution Systems*, London: Routledge.

—— (1990) 'Electronic data interchange in the retail supply chain', *International Journal of Retail and Distribution Management* **18**(2): 39–42.

Mercer, A. (1993) 'The consequences for manufacturers of changes in retail distribution', *European Journal of Operational Research* **64**: 457–61.

Millar, J. L. (1983) 'Distribution in multiples food retailing', in *The Changing distribution and Freight Transport System in Scotland*, Centre for Urban and Regional Research (CURR) Discussion Paper 8, University of Glasgow.

Nilson, T. H. (1992) *Value Added Marketing*, Maidenhead: McGraw-Hill.

Powell, D. (1991) *Counter Revolution: The Tesco Story*, London: Grafton.

Quarmby, D. A. (1989) 'Developments in the retail market and their effect on freight distribution', *Journal of Transport Economics and Policy* **23**(1): 75–87.

Sharman, G. (1984) 'The rediscovery of logistics', *Harvard Business Review* September/October: 71–9.

Shaw, S. A., Nisbet, D. J. and Dawson, J. A. (1989) 'Economies of scale in UK supermarkets: some preliminary findings', *International Journal of Retailing* **4**(5): 12–26.

Smith, D. L. G. and Sparks, L. (1993) 'The transformation of physical distribution in retailing: the example of Tesco plc', *International Review of Retail, Distribution and Consumer Research* **3**(1): 35–64.

Sparks, L. (1986) 'The changing structure of distribution in retail companies', *Transactions of the Institute of British Geographers* **11**(2): 147–54.

—— (1988) 'Technological change and spatial change in UK retail distribution', in R. S. Tolley (ed.) *Transport Technology and Spatial Change*, Institute of British Geographers, North Staffordshire Polytechnic.

—— (1990) 'Spatial–structural relationships in retail corporate growth: a case study of Kwik Save Group plc', *Service Industries Journal* **10**(1): 25–84.

—— (1992) 'Physical distribution management', in W. S. Howe (ed.) *Retailing Management*, Basingstoke: Macmillan.

—— (1993) 'The rise and fall of mass marketing? Food retailing in Great Britain since 1960', in R. Tedlow and G. Jones (eds) *The Rise and Fall of Mass Marketing*, London: Routledge.

Stacey, N. A. H. and Wilson, A. (1958) *The Changing Pattern of Distribution*, London: Business Publications.

Thorpe, D. (1991) 'The development of British superstore retailing: further comments on Davies and Sparks', *Transactions of the Institute of British Geographers* **16**(3): 354–67.

Thorpe, D., Kirby, D. A. and Thompson, P. (1973) *Channels and Costs of Grocery Distribution*, Manchester: Retail Outlets Research Unit.

Tse, K. K. (1985) *Marks and Spencer*, Oxford: Pergamon.

Walters, D. W. (1976) *Futures for Physical Distribution in the Food Industry*, Farnborough: Saxon House.

Ward, T. S. (1973) *The Distribution of Consumer Goods*, Cambridge: Cambridge University Press.

Wrigley, N. (1991) 'Commentary: is the 'golden age' of British grocery retailing at a watershed?', *Environment and Planning A* **23**: 1,537–44.

Index

patents 82
Peak, H. S. and E. F. 294
Pears (A. & F.) Ltd 83
Peasnell, K. V. 94
Pedigree pet foods 231
Peek Frean 231
Pendergrast, M. 192, 194, 197, 201, 209, 210, 211
Penrose, E. 154
Pepsi-Cola 191–2, 200–1, 204, 211
perishability of goods 23
Pernod Ricard 76
persuasion, advertising as 54, 60–1, 67
pet foods 231, 232
pharmacies and Horlicks 281
physical distribution 313–14
Pickering, J. F. 216
Pike, R. 93
pioneer brands 62
Pixley, F. W. 82
point of sale advertising 29–30, 224
political opposition to Coca-Cola 207–9
porridge 238, 243, 251, 254
Porter, G. 294, 299
Porter, M. E. 2, 20, 38, 217, 256, 264, 266, 283
Postum Cereals 224, 238
potato crisps 233
potential of brands, unexploited 155
Powell, D. 291, 323, 325–6
Powell, H. B. 237, 249
Power, M. 92, 93–4, 95
Pratt, E. A. 113
preferences of consumers 50
premium brands 68–9, 71, 73; beer 165; Horlicks as 270, 278, 283, 284; Scotch whisky 142–3, 149, 153, 154, 158–9
prices: Australian wines 174, 178, 180–1; beer 106–7, 131, 169; and brand names 25; breakfast foods 247, 248; cola drinks 200; and competition 62; confectionery 224; Horlicks 269, 270–1, 283; milk food drinks 270–1; and monopoly 46; in oligopolies 246; and producers' associations 48; retail price maintenance 227, 292,

299–303; Sainsbury's 300–1; Scotch whisky 159; spirits 144; wholesale 301–3; wine 176
Pripps Bryggerier AB 135–6
private consumption 41, 50
private label goods 292, 299, 306
producer-retailers 293
producers and distribution 315
producers' associations 45–6, 48
product characteristics 43
product development: Horlicks 284–5; and marketing 228; retailers 297
product differentiation 42, 43–4, 56; and entry to market 61–2, 73, 248; Horlicks 283; and niche markets 256; and price competition 248; and scale/scope economies 64
product evaluation 46–7
product proliferation: breakfast foods 251–3; food industry 35
product range 317
product specification of own brands 305–6
production costs and brand names 19
production efficiency: alcoholic drinks industry 70; and brand names 63
profit and loss accounts 77
profit maximization 143
proliferation 142; and entry 61–2; food industry 35
Proprietary Articles Trade Association 270
proprietary goods 299–300, 306
prosperity *see* affluence
protection of brand names 22, 29; Coca-Cola 194–5, 197, 200–1
protection of market, and producers' associations 48
psychology of advertising 42
public houses 107, 111, 121
publicity about defects 47
Pugh, P. 232

Quaker Co. 224, 237–56 *passim*
quality: and advertising 68, 134; audits of 49; cultural standards 48; and distribution 327–8; of